MW00979411

WATER PAPER STONE

WATER PAPER STONE

JUDY O'SHEA

LETTERS FROM A MILL IN FRANCE

MOSSY PRESS
INVERNESS, CALIFORNIA

Copyright © 2014 by Judy O'Shea

All rights reserved

Printed in the United States of America

Published by Mossy Press

P.O. Box 833

Inverness, CA 94937

www.water-paper-stone.com

ISBN: 978-1495957253

Library of Congress Control Number 2014930468

Designed by Josef Beery

Photographs by Judy and Michael O'Shea

For Linda, with whom all secrets were safe

CONTENTS

June 1991

"I've been fired." Even though I'd been expecting it, it was inconceivable. A dark, compressed pain went straight to my gut. I'd been told I didn't have the stomach to fire enough people, to stiff contractors and suppliers. I'd been working with investors on early-stage startups, and the latest was a cardiovascular company I helped start when my husband, Mike, came home with a serum cholesterol level of 340. The company had good diagnostic technology and a drug we were testing, which had failed in the initial clinical trials. We had to cut back staff and expenses, and I wasn't very good at it. Now I was moving in a fog in my office, pushing things into boxes, refusing to show my emotions, sweat beading on my forehead. People were huddling in their offices, afraid of the uncertainty; most of them I'd never see again. It would be too painful to return, after all we'd been through, from the startup to all those financing cycles to the heartache of a failed product and investor restrictions.

What to do? How would I explain this to my kids? My husband would get it; Mike had seen it all before. In fact, I knew he'd be pleased that we might actually have some time together. He'd seen how many hours I spent working, how exhausted I was. I had spent almost twenty-five years in the biomedical industry, starting in marketing, moving on to executive positions, and ending up in venture capital, starting small companies. I loved what I did, and I understood the inevitable hard knocks during the early stages. While being one of a handful of women CEOs was extremely stressful, I was determined to redo another company. "I'll show them," I said.

"Can't you take a year off? A sabbatical to decompress? You can always go back and show them later," Mike reasoned. I was exhausted, slightly pleased to sleep in. But to drop out for a year? That would be instant death for a career in full bloom. After not much thought, I agreed to one year off, but said that we would have to do something in that time. I didn't want to wake up in a year with nothing to show for it.

Mike and I had been married for ten years, years full of adjustment, us getting to know each other, him getting to know my three young children, me getting to know his three, and the kids all getting to know each other. But by 1991 they had all left home, and

Mike, who had been an executive in a financial company swallowed up by a much larger one, had decided at fifty-one years of age to fulfill his dream of becoming an artist. He'd pulled his parachute the year before and had gone back to art school at the San Francisco Art Institute to get his master's in fine arts: a license to play, guilt-free, in his studio. His engineering and MBA degrees from Stanford weren't enough to go directly into their program, so he was taking some required undergraduate classes at the time.

"Okay, but let's make a list. You know, all the things we want to do before we die, and go do them." We'd never heard of a bucket list then. "Not just travel destinations, but big ideas," I directed, fist slapping palm, with every intention of going back to venture capital when the year was up. I even had a job lined up with one of my previous investors. (I had made a lot of money for a lot of folks.) Mike was accustomed to my excess energy and drill sergeant demeanor, which came from working long days and organizing four children and an active social life. A lanky six foot five, he was always calm and tolerant of my misplaced enthusiasm. He had consciously left business plans, mission statements, and five-year goals behind when he went back to school, but he understood their value.

So in June 1991, we sat down at our limestone table in our house on Twin Peaks overlooking San Francisco and made our lists. Separately, quietly, we scrawled lines of fantasies. Easy things came quickly, but grander schemes began to emerge as well. We both sensed something important was happening. Mike started first, reading his list out loud.

"I've always wanted to sail around the world, but I'm sure you'd never stand for that," he said tentatively. Mike had raced sailboats in his youth and still crewed for others on San Francisco Bay and rallied our kids for family races on Tomales Bay, where we spent weekends at our beach house. My youth in Michigan had been spent on boats of all kinds (I'm particularly skilled at convincing old outboard motors to start), and I too loved pulling in the mainsheet, the water rushing over the gunwales. We had sailed together with our extended family of seven kids in the Caribbean and the South Pacific, and our close friends, Ty and Helen, had sold everything and were now sailing around the world. We had joined them whenever we could, wherever they were, but only for vicarious thrills. Given my work schedule, we had never even talked about doing it ourselves.

"Let's not judge them or throw them out, just read the list," I directed.

"This is going to sound silly, but I've always been intimidated by foreign languages and I secretly would love to learn to speak one fluently, but I don't think that's possible without living in the country. And, frankly, I think I'm too old," he continued. Mike spoke reasonably good Spanish, and I'd taken four years of Latin.

"Stop. We can do anything we want. Anything that we both decide, we can do. What else?"

"Well, I wouldn't mind spending time somewhere warm, out of the coastal fogbank."

Mike was raised in the Pacific Northwest and had migrated to San Francisco after attending Stanford University; he'd never known hot, lazy summers. I, on the other hand, had lived in a bathing suit, read comic books on rafts, and sat around beach fires long into warm summer evenings in Michigan, along with the mosquitoes. But I could count on one hand the number of times I'd eaten outside in Northern California in more than twenty years.

He had other, mostly individual goals: read more, exercise, spend several months in Paris, try Italy and Spain. Then it was my turn. I started with my travel list, which consisted mostly of revisiting Paris, Tokyo, London, all cities I'd been to many times while working, but had never had enough time to visit. But I didn't want to travel, I'd already done enough hotels.

As I got to the larger ideas, I was amazed by the similarity in our fantasies: I, too, imagined us on a sailboat anchored in Tonga or Sydney. I, too, visualized myself chatting away in French or Italian in a bistro in Paris or a café in Rome, arguing socialist economic theory. (I was an economics major.) But a *palapa* in Mexico would do. And I longed for long, lazy dinners in the warm night air, somewhere, anywhere, although without mosquitoes.

So, sail around the world, live in a foreign country and learn the language well enough to understand the culture, and spend summers somewhere warm were one, two, and three for both of us. I wasn't surprised he wanted to sail, but to learn another language? Live in another country? We had never discussed these ideas before. So we decided to spend our sabbatical year trying them out. We arranged first a sailing trip in the fall, two months in Mexico studying Spanish in the winter, then a house exchange in the south of France in the spring, then back to work for me and to school for Mike.

Our friends Ty and Helen would be in Vanuatu in September and had invited us to join them in exploring the eighty-three islands that make up the archipelago. They gave us an approximate arrival time, dependent on the winds, and we were to check the harbor each morning and evening until they showed. We climbed on a plane in the fog at San Francisco, and eighteen hours and two stops later, we stepped off into the soft air of Port Vila on the main island.

Officially known as the Republic of Vanuatu, population 224,564, this island nation is located some thousand miles east of Australia, three hundred miles northeast of New Caledonia, west of Fiji, and south of the Solomon Islands. In 1991, there were only a few thousand tourists a year. Almost all we knew about the islands was that they were formerly called the New Hebrides, were the primary Navy base in the Pacific during World War II, and were the inspiration for James Michener's historical novel and the musical *South Pacific*. The story was loosely based on a real encounter with a French colonial plantation owner and a nurse stationed at the Navy hospital on Espiritu Santo, one of the islands on our itinerary. And I'd come there to wash my humiliation at being fired right out of my hair and to do a sanity check on the number-one wish on our list, to sail around the world.

This adventure was to kick off our sabbatical, and for the first time since our childhoods we waited, with no sense of time, scanning the harbor for the *Azura*, spending two, three, four days swimming, snorkeling, and exploring the little town. Then, on the fifth morning, with the sun coming up behind her, there she was, anchored snugly off the point. A solid thirty-nine-foot Hans Christian yacht that our friends had rigged for serious open-ocean sailing was to be our home for six weeks. We both confessed to being nervous, not only about six weeks on a small boat with four people, but I had just reread Jack London's *The Cruise of the Snark,* his chronicle of trying to circumnavigate the globe, which is mostly about the boredom of open-ocean sailing. The thought of long hours with little to do frightened me. I might have to think!

We sailed out of Port Vila toward Pentecost, where young men jump off platforms with vines on their feet, then to Maewo to help a stranded yacht, to Ambae on Espiritu Santo, where Hedy Lamarr swam in blue lagoons, and Malakula, where we hiked into the cannibal killing fields. After four weeks, life on the boat fell into a routine. Helen and I played in the mess/kitchen, having cooked together for years. The space was a three-by-four-foot L with a small sink in an island. A foot pedal pumped saltwater from the bay to rinse food, dishes, and hands, and the tap let the precious freshwater flow for drinking and the final rinse of the dishes. Hot water, from a small tank heated by the engine, which was run every night after we moored for an hour to charge batteries, was used sparingly to wash the dishes. Showers were taken outside under a black plastic bag heated by the sun. A turn-your-back understanding allowed for modesty. Bathing suits and other clothes, trampled underfoot as one showered, then rinsed in clean water, served to keep us as clean and salt-free as possible. The deck had a folding table that served for most meals, art projects, and serious card games. When it rained, which it did a bit almost every day, we could go down below to another table with built-in benches. But since the rain was the same temperature as the air, and we were always slightly damp and in our swimsuits, we often just stayed where we were as squalls dumped rain. It was only at night that we felt the need to get dry and salt-free.

We had two separate bunks, but it was often so hot that one or two of us would sleep up top on the benches until awakened by plops of rain. Even at anchor, the sound of the waves slapping the sides of the boat told all we needed to know about the weather from our bunks. If they were constant, the wind had picked up, and if silent, we were truly in the lee and could enjoy the roll of the surge. The rigging also contributed to a stream of information on the state of the boat. The rhythmic clanging of ropes as the boat rolled became a constant white noise in harmony with the inevitable creaking of the wooden hull. (Ty and Helen were particularly attuned to any changes in the background sounds, stopping mid-sentence with ears cocked, then continuing to talk when the change was accounted for.) Under sail, the sound of the water became our music, rushing under the hull, the wind raising and lowering the volume. Only when tacking, as the nose of the boat pointed into the wind and the sails luffed briefly, was there a break in the rush of the water; then *slap*, the boom would come across, the sail would fill out, and the surge of the water would resume its rush against the hull.

To that music, and with many adventures on the islands, time went by quickly, at least for us. I expect Ty and Helen were relieved to reclaim their vessel as they sailed off, having left us in our straw hotel in Port Vila. We had given our first choice on our to-do list a significant trial run. It was actually health considerations that ended the sailing dream. Jack London's adventure ended abruptly in the Solomon Islands when he developed a severe staph infection called "Solomon's sores," and just like Jack, Mike ended up in the hospital with a Vanuatan/Solomon sore and a frightening medical experience in a developing country. (I wasn't spared either, being diagnosed later in San Francisco with viral meningitis due to being exposed to pathogens that my Western European immune system had never before encountered.)

Our last evening, sitting on the beach looking over the horizon, Mike said, "I don't want to go up the mast once a week, and I don't want to have to dive after my anchor in filthy harbors. I'm too old." And I realized that always being slightly salty and slightly damp worked on my disposition in subtle but negative ways. And I didn't want to spend several years rationing fresh water and washing clothes on rocks.

So we decided, reluctantly, to move on to number two on the list: find another country, anywhere with warm weather, a different language, and a different culture. Someplace where, when I was ready to retire, we could live part-time, in the meantime having learned the language in classes in San Francisco. Since we lived on the West Coast, Mexico was a logical choice, close but still foreign. We arranged to spend two months in San Miguel de Allende, where we rented a house and I signed up for intensive Spanish lessons and a sculpture class, while Mike enrolled in every painting, drawing, and sculpture class he could find. Our vision of ourselves in a foreign country had been evolving, and we mutually agreed that we wanted to learn the language and participate in the local community at least well enough to understand the cultural differences, not just be observers.

San Miguel is a beautiful colonial city, with lively markets, bustling restaurants, and shop after shop of local crafts, all supported by gringos coming south for warm weather and inexpensive living conditions that depend on cheap local labor. But the only real interaction with locals that we had was with our maid, Greta, who was struggling to support her three children on fifty dollars a month. (We did spend an afternoon with the owner of one of the art schools, who seemed more interested in raising money than a cultural exchange.) There was a lively and interesting social swirl of expatriates in San Miguel, but most seemed to have little contact with the Mexican people except as domestics, which was not at all in keeping with our objectives, and by the end of our stay, we realized that the sharp division between the wealthy and poor in Mexico would leave us squarely in the middle, with little cultural interaction on either side. We might experience warm evenings, but we would be very much out in the cultural cold.

By the time we packed up to leave, we had refined our search. We knew we were looking for an actual house to buy, in a foreign country with warm weather in the summer, but not in the tropics or Mexico. Since we were contemplating a serious investment, we eliminated a lot of places based on financial risk. Asia seemed too foreign, the Middle East too closed to Westerners, South America even more complicated than Mexico. That left us, somewhat rationally, in the southwest of Europe.

The house that we exchanged for our beach house was in the southernmost part of France, in the Roussillon wine region, but an easy trip into Spain and not too far from Italy. Our primary interest was Spain, since Mike already had a working knowledge of Spanish and our stay in Mexico had left me with a good base. Italy had lots of appeal as a travel destination, but the currency risks and government corruption at the time made it less attractive as an investment. After weeks of two- and three-day road trips across the border into Spain, through the mountains and down the coast, we concluded that years of Franco had broken the spirit and infrastructure of the country and left the people stooped and suspicious of strangers.

And the weather, specifically the wind, was driving us out of the extreme south of France. The tramontane wind that blows out of the Pyrenees across the broad, flat valleys in the Languedoc-Roussillon are as bad as the infamous mistral in the Rhone River valley, blowing up to sixty miles per hour, twenty-four hours a day, sometimes for weeks on end, leaving it impossible to bike or even walk at times. (After all, we were partially trying to get out of the summer wind and fog of the San Francisco Bay Area.) And we found the Languedoc-Roussillon people to be as bent over against foreigners as they were against the wind. To avoid them both, we found ourselves going farther and farther north, across the Black Mountains into the Haut Languedoc with its lush green hills and water flowing everywhere, a complete contrast to the wind-dried valleys in the south. We hadn't really spent much time in rural France, but by staying in small auberges, exploring the gentle hills and villages during the day, and eating rustic country food in friendly surroundings, we met many people, even with our limited French. And the people seemed as warm and generous as the hills were green. We followed the Tarn River farther north and east, moving from gentle rolling hills to steep terraced cliffs dotted with dramatic chartreuse valleys. The people were friendly and curious, and *petit à petit*, we started to feel we might be home. Then, one day, near the end of our stay, while driving through Roquefort cheese country near Millau in the Tarn Valley, Mike suddenly veered off to the right onto a smaller country road marked by an arrow that said Saint-Rome-de-Tarn.

"I don't know why, I just want to go there," he said.

The road changed from gentle bends to sharp curves, and the lush greenery of the lower valley gave way to steep cliffs and abandoned terraces scaling the hills. As we approached Saint-Rome, we could see the pointy towers of a château in the middle of the village. Driving past, we spotted a sign, *à vendre*, in the window. The château was for sale, so we stopped and peered into the open side gate of the grounds. We saw a large yard, which was encircled by a narrow path shaded by climbing roses. A huge stone basin was outside the back door, and we could see black and white tiles, worn to a matte finish, through the window of the kitchen. We looked at each other as if to say, "Why not?" and called the agent from the phone booth on the corner. My two-week crash course in French allowed me to introduce myself and ask if someone spoke English. They did, sort of. While we waited for Monsieur Padot to arrive, we started to fantasize about the future, when we would retire. With all this space, we could have several studios—perhaps Mike's artist friends could come to stay with us—and maybe there could be workshops, galleries? We'd never before considered these possibilities, but the place demanded a purpose. How many bedrooms?

Monsieur Padot arrived in his Renault, parked, and pulled out his data sheets, mumbling in franglais that the château had eleventh-century origins, but that it had been transformed over the generations, most recently into a retirement home for nuns who had then died and floated away (that was the sense of his hand gestures at that point), leaving the stately structure available for its next reincarnation. Monsieur Padot was a full foot shorter than Mike, and while he fiddled with a heavy iron ring with at least ten ancient keys, he kept looking up, as if to make sure that someone could actually be that tall.

The château had entries on two levels, two on the lower and several from the upper private garden. We entered below first, into a twenty-foot vaulted cellar with no apparent connection to the rest of the house. It had probably been a stable at some point, as its worn ceramic tiles in subtle shades of sage green and black had been chipped by hooves. Passing through the other lower door, probably the formal entrance in an early rendition, we were startled to see a large, cast-iron furnace, its vents running in all directions, in the middle of the otherwise elegant stone entry. Monsieur Padot patted its side, shrugging his shoulders: "*C'était pour chauffer les bonnes sœurs.*" "It kept the nuns warm," he explained.

We followed him up the dark circular stairway, the stone steps worn in the center from a thousand years of wooden and leather soles, the limestone walls carved to match the curve of the stairs, arriving at the main level into a formal dining room where the stones switched to linoleum, the walls to asbestos tiles. In response to our surprised looks, he apologized, "It was done to cushion the nuns in case they fell."

A proud stone fireplace was at the end of the room, too clean to have been used recently. "There are seven fireplaces in all; however, the chimneys were cemented in to protect the nuns from drafts." His shrugged shoulders and raised eyebrows in sympathy with our obvious distress at this news.

We continued through the main floor into the enormous kitchen, the only space with the original tile floor still visible, out into the garden. A stone-roofed pigeon coop, big enough for a large slate table, was at the end of an arched rose trellis. Another vaulted cave, at least thirty feet long, entered the earth under the upper road. The garden wasn't large, but it was well situated for full sunlight. Off the kitchen, on the side near the upper road, protected from the sun and prying eyes by a nasty corrugated plastic roof, was a huge, flat washing stone carved from one rock, with spring water flowing from one end into a small waterfall at the other.

Back inside, Monsieur Padot showed us the continuing circular stairway in one tower, then another in another, and explained that the remaining two towers had been filled with bathrooms on each floor, for the *bonnes sœurs*. There was also a grand central staircase, winding up the remaining three levels, the stone steps also glued over with linoleum. The cast-iron handrails had been retained to support the dears. "It can all come off," Padot promised: "*Avec l'argent, tout est possible*," a phrase I was to hear often in the near future: "With money, anything is possible." Above the main floor were two more floors with rabbit warrens of small, cell-sized bedrooms, each with a sink, a bed, and nothing else. There were fourteen of them, separated by thin plaster walls, sometimes dividing one of the many closed fireplaces in half. "Okay, with money, anything is possible," I said to myself, repeating the Padot mantra.

But the pièce de non-résistance was the chapel: a small room perched on metal beams at the very top of the central staircase, its faux-paneled walls and plastic flowers reflecting red from seriously garish stained-glass windows. "Don't worry, it's been *désaffecté*," Padot said quickly before we could groan. He spoke reasonably good English, but he didn't have the word for "deconsecrated," and although we got the gist of what he was saying, we had visions of nuns with cans of Lysol disinfectant walking out the door. We mumbled to each other about structural problems and karma when you take steel beams and a chapel out of your attic.

The thought of stripping the modernity away from this place was too overwhelming for us, given our intentions to return to the work/school-a-day world, so we decided we would come back the next year. If it were still for sale, it was meant to be. If not, we'd keep looking. But we had been seduced. We loved the area, and the freshly hatched idea of having a center for artists became an obsession for the rest of our two-month stay. As we cruised the countryside, we'd brainstorm the structure of it all. I'd manage the gallery, of course; Mike would do his art, and we could meet local artists and truly become part of that community. But not until after I retired. Now, back to the real world.

In the summer of 1992, I was to return to work as planned and Mike was going to finish his MFA and become a working artist. Then the fates, or the capital markets, stepped in. Some of my early investments suddenly became liquid, and I had a choice. If we were careful, we could both retire early, something I had never contemplated. After all, I had liked my work, the stimulation, even the stress.

The lure of an adventure in France was compelling. But the most important influence on my personal decision to give up the high-pressure life I'd been living was my sister, Linda, who had saved my life at least twice: once in my early twenties when I found myself desperate and emotionally bankrupt, and again when, at age forty-six, two years before our sabbatical, her heart suddenly stopped and another series of coronary arrests left her in a coma. The suddenness and severity of her attacks, a family legacy, reminded me that life can indeed be short. And when she did come through, her courage and struggle to recover gave me the guts to get off the treadmill of my high-pressure career—not at a high, when it would have been easy, but at a low when everyone expected another salvo. I'm convinced that without her painful experience I would still be out there charging imaginary windmills and potentially shortening my own life.

During the breaks between our trips to Vanuatu, Mexico, and the Languedoc-Roussillon, I signed up for a few classes at the San Francisco Art Institute and enrolled at the Alliance Française. I fell in love with both. We decided to extend our sabbatical so that I, too, could work on an MFA at the Art Institute. I wasn't sure I would ever be an artist, but I was curious enough to try. As I turned down a job offer, burning my bridges to my past life, an energy permeated my being that would carry me through the next few years.

We returned to France nine months later in the spring of 1993 and called Monsieur Padot in Millau. The château was still for sale, and would we like to see it? After several more visits, we were frustrated by our inability to make a decision. We needed to see more places, the cave that went under the road seemed unstable, the fireplaces would be extraordinarily difficult to fix, and there wasn't room for a proper garden. And we were nervous about the idea of Americans taking over the village château in the center of town, a special place—how would we be received?

Monsieur Padot, frustrated with our indecision, politely asked if we would like to go with an associate of his to see a place farther down the Tarn Valley, a water mill. It needed some work, but the site was lovely and Monsieur Gineste could take us there *tout de suite*. On our first trip to France, we had seen a mill sitting in the middle of small river, a charming building with willows and water lilies dancing in a gentle breeze, and had been completely enchanted. We had even considered several mills in our search, but while they were all beautiful, the idea of being in the middle of a riverbed always seemed precarious in a country that often has big floods, so we decided to avoid them. When Monsieur Gineste arrived, Mike dragged me to the car. "We'll just look," he said.

"Okay, Mike. We'll just look. But we agreed that mills are off the list. Right?"

Gineste, driving twice the speed limit in his car in front of us, led us out of Saint-Rome-de-Tarn, off the main road, through miles of terraced farms, then through the Rance Valley with its burgundy-colored soil. As we followed the Rance River, the cliffs became more gentle, the hills greener. Through Saint-Affrique and Vabres-l'Abbeye we followed the signs to Saint-Sernin-sur-Rance. Suddenly, we turned off, following a blue and white sign pointing toward Plaisance. The roads became smaller, the sheep barns bigger, and Mike's enthusiasm higher. "Stay neutral," he pleaded.

As we sped along, trying to keep up with the disappearing Renault in front of us, we were charmed by the sudden appearance of the church, perched high above the river, and the small village at its feet. A few kilometers past Plaisance, we turned off the main road, high on the valley wall, and started down into a canyon. Less than half a mile later, we slowed for a major curve in the road, and Monsieur Gineste pulled sharply to the right into a gravel drive, presumably the entrance to the property. He waited for us to park, jumped out, tapped his watch, told us where to find the keys, gave us his card, and declared "Goodbye and good luck." Our reputation for wasting realtors' time had evidently proceeded us.

As he sped off, we walked down the drive and stood in front of what we both knew instantly would be our new home. "Oh, my God. It's wonderful," we said in unison. "Look at the bridge, the river, the stones, the terraces." There were several buildings cascading down the hill, some almost in ruins, and vegetation covered all the paths, but the terraced cliffs that held the mill high out of the path of a potential flood convinced us we would be safe at La Pilande Basse. The arched stone bridge and the water flowing everywhere made us overlook the ferns growing from the walls inside the house, the creaking beams, the leaky roof. Then we called Monsieur Padot (Monsieur Gineste spoke no English and a French we'd never heard before) and told him we were interested. Very interested. He told us to keep the keys for a few days and call him if we wanted to make an offer. We checked into an auberge in Plaisance called Les Magnolias, and spent the next two days exploring the mill, the villages on all sides, and especially the river, Le Mousse, its tributaries and its destinations: the Rance River, then the Tarn.

The letters that follow were written to my sister, Linda, my best friend and the only remaining member of my nuclear family. I had sworn at her bedside while she was in a six-week coma that if she'd just come back, I would never again let so much time go by without seeing, calling, or writing her. Even before she came out of the coma I started recording cassettes for her just in case she could hear. When she did wake up, it was clear she would be handicapped, physically and somewhat mentally. She could read, but not write, and naturally she suffered from severe depression. So as she recovered, between phone calls, I began writing long letters to her during our six-month-per-year stays in France, recounting our more humorous experiences in our new life at La Pilande Basse. She enjoyed reading them to her friends, so I kept the letters light, hoping to entertain her and help her travel vicariously out of our hometown in Michigan. There were no responses, since she couldn't write, but I would answer her questions on the phone.

The letters, and later, e-mails, to Linda in this book are interspersed with journal entries I kept at the same time, depicting the more realistic and sometimes darker side of being an American living in rural France. Each year, there is a gap of five to six months, representing our time back in San Francisco.

LA PILANDE BASSE

May 28, 1993
JOURNAL ENTRY
La Pilande Basse

Water sounds fill the air, rushing, slapping against the broad flat rocks, swirling under the stone bridge that seems almost too picturesque, a cliché. Somehow the sound is too loud for the size of the babbling brook slipping under the bridge. The large, flat stones, twenty feet below, could hold lawn chairs and comic books if children were to come.

The lilac branches pushed aside, the door slightly lifted—both Dutch doors together, that is—and a solid bump on the bottom as the bottom door grinds open across the dirt floor of the smallest structure below the main building on the river side. After one human width, it stops, stuck against a pile of metal detritus: worn-out bits of gears and pulleys piled to the low ceiling. White spider skins hang on abandoned webs, hung with dust instead of prey. Water lisps at the base of the little building, and bats, rudely awakened, circle, searching for a safe exit. On the back of the door is a nail, a nail with a cross, a cross meant to warn potential trespassers that someone is watching. And hanging under that cross, a set of keys. Five keys. The agent had said everyone knew the keys were there, but nothing had ever been taken.

There are two large arches on the base of the river side of the big, long building, dark passages into unknown spaces too dark and musky to be welcoming. Closer to the water, the hush becomes more a rush. A crumbling set of stone stairs, made from larger rocks poking out of a stone wall, form a precarious descent

to the river, protected by stinging nettles and blackberry bushes. Near the entrance to the main building is a large, round stone, leaning against the base of a structure with an odd metal screw device protruding from the center. The stone is at least twelve inches thick, with odd symmetrical grooves radiating from the large center hole. Ferns, moss, and wildflowers poke their heads out of every dirt-catching crack.

On the other side of the front door, another round stone is precariously perched atop a small stone pedestal. (In all, eleven millstones would be counted.) A stuccoed annex with moldy straw and chicken-wire doors hanging open on one hinge is nestled in the corner formed by the long, lower mill building and the large, two-story barn.

A huge trellis made of branches perched on thick chestnut trunks forms an entry into the mill building. One old gnarly grapevine seems the sole source of the matted leaves clinging to the trellis, providing shade where people could shelter to wait while their grain was being ground. The keys are as rusty as the lock into which they nestle with some foreplay of jostling and pushing. A musty, humid perfume with hints of ferns and dried mud rushes past us out the door. With eyes accustomed to the shuttered darkness, a floor-to-ceiling structure appears: four large, vertical wooden beams, separated by even thicker crossbeams, stands imposingly in the entryway, a mystery. The water sounds are muffled here, but more intense somehow, more urgent.

At the river end of the seventy-five-foot-long main room, a fifteen-foot window with dozens of small panes forms a mosaic of the green cliffs on the other side of the large creek bed. When we tug it open, the river sounds rush into the room, invading the space even as they bounce off the foundations below.

A large walnut-stained platform in this space holds two huge octagonal boxes and a strange upright metal/wooden screw device that looks as if it can twirl between the two, refusing to play favorites. A sixteen-foot wooden box with the skeleton of a turning structure that clacks with metal weights when it rotates hangs off the stone walls, with little slats crudely carved underneath. Odd bits of furniture, tottering with neglect, hide in the darkness.

The stairs, steep and worn, real miller's stairs, complain loudly of the uncertain feet that test their worthiness. They lead to a musty room with a four-foot flat stone sink, its edge worn from years of sharpening knives against the sandstone. Garish peacock wallpaper covers even the ceiling, a failed attempt to contemporize that has instead a clownish effect.

A thoroughly rusted stove, a relatively new addition to the room, stands beneath a chimney on the other side. Next to the chimney is a large, flat rock built into the wall with two 8-inch round holes carved into it. Below this is a stone catch basin. Another mystery.

To the right, an ill-fitted door leads to what appears to be an attic full of odd metal devices; one, with large fins, leans in a corner, another is a solid cylinder still attached to the beams. Another, even older, is a rusted-out stove that squats precariously in the middle of the room. A large square hole in the floor reveals odd wooden boxes on the platform below. The plank floor is layered with a thick white dust and sags underfoot. Water sounds creep gently into the space when the window, with the same-sized panes as the huge window on the first floor, opens to a dizzying view of the river below.

There are two other rooms, with moldy beds and mossy carpets. No sounds penetrate the thick stone under the plaster walls and wooden ceilings, both covered with garish flowered paper. Paned windows, shaded by the grapevine with its load of still-green fruit, open on the front of the building, with a clear view of the arched stone bridge that forms part of the driveway.

At the bottom of the steep miller's stairs is one of two doors leading out to the back of the building. One door, its shutter mostly decayed but still blocking the light and sound, truly resists. After being nudged and kicked, a muffled *boing* announces its surrender. And there, behind the door, its secret shared, the water is no longer a hush but the constant thundering crash of a twenty-foot-high waterfall one hundred feet from the door and strangely at eye level, with no bottom in sight. Only if the viewer leans over the edge of the cliff can the flat rocks below be seen. The water explodes in a frothy spray, re-forms to flow into a little swimming hole, then whirls around the bend that forms the terraced cliff and slams against the side of the building on its way off and under the bridge, where sounds echoing its power climb back up the sides of the canyon.

From the terrace next to the river, at least four other terraces can be seen. All are etched into the steep tree-covered hill, which towers at least five hundred feet above the mill. Crumbling stone walls, eight to ten feet high, define the levels, the passage from one to the other a mystery. Perched above the main building on the third level, with gaping holes for windows and doors, is another building, a small ruin, impossible to reach as all paths are blocked by dense stands of blackberries and fallen stone hedges—something to be explored later.

The large, two-story barn forms an L with the long mill building. But even from the door of the upper floor of the barn, the water sounds wash the air. The beams sag under the weight of large sacks of feathers and skeletons of chairs. The twenty-five-foot ceilings are draped with stunning undulating spider webs, some detached and flapping in the air. There are holes under the eaves at the end of the barn, with strange small wooden platforms as their sills.

The ground level of the barn is dank, with water running through the large, flat stones that form the floor. A rotting wooden criblike structure, fifteen feet long, leans against the back wall. Darkness hides the rest.

July 20, 1993
Dear Linda,

You sounded sincere on the phone yesterday. Are you serious about coming to *chez nous* in France next year? I'm assuming we will have a roof and a floor by then, but I'd hold out for a toilet if I were you. But start brushing up on your French, since we already have some wonderful local friends for you to meet: Monsieur Roussel, the chef and owner of Les Magnolias, our local Michelin-rated hotel/restaurant; Madame and Monsieur Blanc; and more. But we'll spare you the experience of meeting Monsieur Parnat. He's the one who made minor repairs on our mill for the old owners in exchange for them plucking his chickens and storing miscellaneous *brocantes*, or used furniture, in our barn. The same one who poured cement over the plank and stone floors, and constructed the world's ugliest fireplace of splattered concrete. The very one who is shocked and hurt that we are not using him as our contractor.

On July 16 we signed the final purchase papers for La Pilande Basse, our mill, the origins of its name still unknown. But even before the papers were signed, Monsieur Padot had given us the keys and told us to do what we wanted, so we began to shovel the chicken feathers out of the barn and get to work. We have to find contractors and get bids, all in a language we don't know. Hum, *roof*? *Fenêtres* I know. We're staying at Les Magnolias in Plaisance, a sweet little auberge with an even sweeter owner, Francis Roussel.

When we bought the place we knew we had a problem with what the English call "the rising damp," a phenomenon peculiar to two-hundred-year-old homes built into cliffs. It seems the concept of *foundations* is relatively recent, so the three-foot-thick walls were built directly on the rock of the earth, or the earth of the earth as the case may be. So when it rains, water wicks down or up through the rock into the floors and walls, creating a remarkably constant cool, damp environment. Great for wine and cheese and terrible for rheumatism. Rising damp is the reason God made tapestries and the French took it from there. Rising damp is the reason we have ferns in our new/old wine-cave-turned-kitchen. (This gets confusing, so let me explain the layout: The mill is a two-story building, long and narrow with a two-story barn joining it to form an L. The ground floor used to be the working mill, with stones, and presses and flour sifters at one end near the river, and at the other end, a small lean-to to house sheep and a closed section that served as a wine cave. The second story housed the bedrooms, kitchen and tiny parlor, with an attic above the millstones. The toilet was outside, unceremoniously poised in what was long ago a pigpen.) Eminently fixable, I've been told. Monsieur Padot, Francis Roussel, and everyone who visits says the same thing, "*Avec l'argent tout est possible*," or "With money, anything is possible." We have no idea how, exactly, but we are keeping the faith.

I won't bore you with all the gory details of dead rats under beds, fleas in the barn from the chicken feathers and who-knows-what-else critters, the disgusting mess in the outhouse. No, I'll just say I've spent days dressed in rubber gloves, a bandana, a face mask, and mud boots. A bottle of *eau de javel*, or bleach, was my constant companion. Bats no longer startle me, and I've learned I can pee in positions unknown to womanhood. Nettles—stinging nettles—and womanhood?

While we were working we would fantasize about the day the river would again flow through the house, not just lap at its feet. We had heard that there was an association of mill owners that can give assistance and advice to neophytes, so we were eager to track it down. As fate would have it, the day before yesterday the president of the Association des Amis des Moulins d'Aveyron, or Friends of Mills in Aveyron (the name of our *département* in France), showed up at Les Magnolias, and Monsieur Roussel introduced us when we showed up there for dinner. Monsieur Azéma agreed to visit us a few days later and take a look at the millworks.

Monsieur Roussel had also told us about a Monsieur Blanc, the son of the last miller, who lives in the hills around-here-somewhere. (He was precise, but our French was not.) He would know about the millworks and could give us a history of the house if we could ever possibly find him. And, of course, then we would have to be able to understand him, which is no mean trick for us. Not only do we have serious limitations with our French, but "bunna suppa" sounds more like minestrone to us than French onion, although that's *bonne soupe*, "good soup," in the local accent. *R*'s are sometimes rolled, as in Spanish, not throated as in French. We decided that we would definitely wait to find Monsieur Blanc until our language skills were much better, and when we had pen and paper at hand and maybe even a tape recorder. Besides, we had a lot to do before we could worry about guests and the nuances of a flour mill.

Then yesterday, I was roaming through the main floor all alone, dressed for germ warfare, the front door ajar to hopefully release the clouds of years-long closed-house smells. As I was stumbling around in the dark room (the shutters were stuck shut) mumbling profanities, I suddenly glanced at the door and there was a man, backlit by the morning sun, clutching something in his hands. Startled, I did what any level-headed woman would do: I screamed! It scared us both half to death.

Gaining my composure, simultaneously stripping off a rubber glove and my dust mask, outstretching my hand in the universal peace gesture, I gasped my best "*Bonjour, monsieur.*" You see, I had learned one of the secrets of life in the jungles of Vanuatu: Always Smile at a Man with a Bush Knife. I had never actually seen a man with a bush knife in France, as I had in Vanuatu, but this one definitely had something in his hand. Only when I stepped into the daylight could I see that it was his beret, which he was turning and rolling in his hands like a rosary. I also realized I was at least a full head taller than he and probably in a higher wrestling-weight class. In my best beginner's French, I again extended my hand, saying, "*Je m'appelle Jeudi Hochet.*" He finally stuttered his name: "Monsieur Blanc"!

"Monsieur Blanc? *Oh là, entrez, entrez s'il vous plaît.*" ("Oh my, Mr. Blanc, please come in.")

Backing slowly up the drive toward his car, wagging his finger in front of his face as only the French can do, he responded, "*Non, non, non, merci bien.*"

I realized I had to act quickly or we could permanently lose our mill resource. You have to remember that Americans have baked into our DNA the you-all-come mentality that spells survival in a frontier society. One must yank one's neighbors bodily into the house out of the way of arrows and tomahawks. But in rural France, people are much more formal and require more time to chat, to get acquainted first. So, denying my genetic heritage, I deposited the bleach bottle, took off the other glove and bandana, crossed my arms, and settled down to a calm, casual conversation in a language I didn't speak, outside in hostile territory. Indians be damned.

But as we did the who-we-are, where-we-are-from, I could see he couldn't keep his eyes away from the open door. And when he told me he had actually been born in the house, in the bedroom above our heads, I knew he could be had! I backed slowly toward the door, finally leaning against the stone entry. Chatting all the while, he craned his neck, adjusting his eyes to the dark, searching for something. And there it was: the walnut oil press, just inside the door, a huge, dark-oak memory. When his eyes filled with tears, I realized that he was not just a mill resource, but a kind, sensitive man revisiting his past.

Now was the time. I had to do something smooth and subtle to allow him time to compose himself. Tripping over the bleach bottle, I made my move inside under the guise of calling for Mike, who was upstairs doing battle with mouse turds using an ancient vacuum cleaner. Any semblance of my dignity evaporated when my gentle "Mike . . . Mike . . ." turned to "*MIKE!*" Sensing my urgency, he clambered down the stairs, all elbows and knees as a lanky six-foot-five guy is apt to appear, still clutching the vacuum wand, which had somehow come off in his hand. Sometime that week he had combed his hair, and I'm sure I had promised him I would wash his clothes in the river any day now.

To my surprise, Monsieur Blanc had followed me inside. Now imagine this sweet, gentle man, loose in his place of birth with two huge, filthy Americans: Mike, folded forward to fit under a large beam, tall by anyone's standards, blinking to adjust his eyes to the dark, and dragging his limited French into his consciousness. And me . . . another tall creature with rubber hands and feet!

With my elbow in his ribs, I exclaimed, "Mike, *voilà*, Monsieur Blanc . . . *the* Monsieur Blanc." But of course, Mike, recognizing the opportunity as only he can do, calmly took charge and soon had Monsieur Blanc spouting "that-used-to-be's" all around the house, not that we could completely understand him. Apparently, our temporary dining nook used to be a sheep's pen and our dining-room-soon-to-be-kitchen was *une cave avec un problème d'humidité*. It seems the rising damp had existed even when M. Blanc was a lad, but he, of course, said "*Avec l'argent tout est possible.*"

He was shocked and saddened by the cement poured on the floor and the general disrepair of the millworks. When he sold it twenty-five years before, he said, it had been a working flour mill with two sets of millstones and a gigantic flour sifter, all powered by the rushing Mousse River.

Monsieur Blanc came back the next day and, together with Monsieur Azéma (the man from Des Amis des Moulins), spent hours reconstructing the ways of the mill. Fortunately for us, Monsieur Azéma spoke reasonably good English, and he could explain the nuances of the discussion. It seems that Monsieur Blanc had had to sell the mill after his father's death because his sister, who is married to a Roquefort sheep farmer up on the hill behind us, didn't want to maintain it, and he didn't have the means, so they sold it, and he hadn't stepped foot inside for twenty-four years, although he drove by at least once every day. Apparently he wasn't fond of the old/new owner, who had let the mill fall into a near ruin. As for us, he seemed genuinely grateful that someone was going to restore the place of his birth. But when Monsieur Azéma suggested that we would be able to restore the millworks, he shook his head, "*C'est pas possible. C'est trop tard.*" But Monsieur Azéma assured him that it could be done, it's never too late.

During the rest of our week staying at Les Magnolias at night and trying to clean out the mill during the day, Monsieur Blanc brought his entire family by at various times, gave us some old photos, and invited us for aperitifs several times. He seemed quite taken with us, speaking slowly and without a strong accent, and he should be a good friend and neighbor over the years. As for Monsieur Azéma, he was delightful, a real mill nerd, and will be of great assistance in our project. He invited us to Sévérac-le-Château to meet his parents who, with his help, are in the process of restoring a mill that belonged to his mother's family.

We are sure you will love the people, the unbelievably good food, the street markets in Albi, the closest city, about a twenty-mile drive along the Tarn River, and, of course, our little *moulin*. Our region is technically called the Midi-Pyrénées, and its center, Toulouse, is about an hour and a half away. While it is the fourth largest city in France, most people don't even know where it is. Inside the boundaries of the region are eight *départements*, ours being the Aveyron. While the Aveyron is the largest in area of any of the one hundred *départements* in France, it has the fewest people. It is the center of Roquefort cheese production, and the Aveyronnais people have a reputation similar to our Ozarkians, deserved or not. It is *La France Profonde*. Deep France, in the middle of nowhere. Two hours north of the Pyrenees Mountains and two hours northwest of the Mediterranean, it is definitely in the south of France. But Provence and the Côte d'Azur are usually called the South of France, so we'll just shrug our shoulders and say it is northwest of Montpellier, in a tone of voice that says, "If you don't know where that is, you're out of it."

Our center of the universe is Plaisance. All sixty-two people. Actually, we are between three villages, Plaisance, Coupiac, and Trébas-les-Bains, which provide all the amenities: fresh bread, vegetables, and good butcher shops. The surroundings are bucolic, with bright patches of chartreuse and yellow ochre punctuated with fluid swarms of sheep munching the rich grasses.

For art lovers, there is the Toulouse-Lautrec museum in Albi, the *beaux arts* of Toulouse, a Goya museum, and lots of Romanesque sculpture. The Dordogne, with spectacular churches, prehistoric cave paintings, and, of course, truffles, isn't far. The spectacular cliffs of the Gorges du Tarn, topped by bizarre, stark plains covered with wildflowers, and the caves where Roquefort cheeses are aged are also part of our region.

We expect our nightlife will probably be pretty quiet, with long, drawn-out meals in the warm night air, and no mosquitoes! (We have water running everywhere, except through the plumbing, since we have none, as each rain brings minor torrents down the main road, down our driveway, then trickles under the rotten front door. The surrounding countryside is steep, especially our canyon, so we have no standing water.)

You knew I would get around to the food. Our restaurants aren't all marble, brass, and black tie, but the food is good, the prices reasonable, and the service friendly. And though we don't have many tourists, the dress code is "tourists in travel togs." Foie gras, guinea hen, duck and goose confit, every part of the lamb, and a special purée of potatoes, garlic and fresh cheese called *aligot* are regional specialties. The morning market in Albi bursts with fresh vegetables and fruits, along with hundreds of other foods, a perplexing array of cheeses and sausages, and fresh fish from the Mediterranean and the Atlantic. And the bread, the best we have found in France, big, bawdy *pain de campagne*, comes from Coupiac. There is a bakery in Plaisance, but frankly, *c'est pas formidable*. Not very good. The French lesson for the day starts with the morning excursion to the *boulangerie*, with the ritual "*Ça va? Très bien, merci, au revoir, bonne journée.*" Then I have to remember, is it *une baguette* or *un baguette*? Feminine or masculine?

But the best are the days spent lost in the country discovering the hundreds of beautiful little villages struggling to endure in a postmodern world. Around every curve is a hamlet or a fortified-farm complex, or some other gorgeous pile of old stones, perched on a rocky prominence for protection from the Romans, Moors, Visigoths, English, and Germans. Great vinegars, fresh cheeses, and vegetables can often be found thanks to handmade signs on the road. The people are warm and genuine, speak no English, but are patient and understand hand signals, smiles, and good intentions, so they will love you.

The weather is not unlike that of infamous Provence, with one enormous difference: no mistral, that notoriously insidious wind that can blow forty miles an hour, twenty-four hours a day, for weeks. Consequently, the foliage is much greener, and other things beside wine grapes will grow. It's nice to have four seasons again, rainy springs, hot-dry summers, cool, beautiful autumns with brilliant colors, cold winters with occasional short-lived snowfalls. Summer and late spring temperatures range from sixty to ninety degrees. So, bring layers.

—*Love to Gary, Judy*

July 26, 1993
JOURNAL ENTRY

The summer water sounds are barely audible from the bridge. The flat gray rocks are bleached from the hot summer sun, and in the deeper pools the backs of small trout can be seen weaving among the shadows of the trees on the water. Just before we bought the mill, Coupiac, the village upstream, was inundated with over twelve feet of water that had built up behind a logjam in a poorly designed culvert under the main parking lot in the center of the village. The dam raised the creek level high enough to flood the center of the village, and when it finally broke free, tree trunks, stacks of firewood, water bottles, cans, and other floating detritus joined the river of mud racing downstream, through the mechanic's garage, past the ambulance driver's house, inundating La Creste (the only other mill on the Mousse with vestiges of mechanisms for flour grinding), gathering strength and mass, then flying over our waterfall, slamming against the rocks under the old stone bridge of our mill on its way to the Rance River, finally plunging into the Tarn, its red torrent racing side by side with the green clear water from the Cévennes Mountains.

The wall of red mud and debris flooding the banks left clumps of black plastic stuck in the bushes lining the river. The trash deposited by the torrent mars the beauty of the tumbled rocks, a constant reminder that the water, a mere trickle in midsummer, can be ruthless in a flood. Countless plastic bags of cans, medicine containers, mud-filled fifty-gallon drums, sheets of black plastic from upstream gardens, pesticide cans, insecticide sprayers, plastic foam, music boxes, toys, even girdles are being gathered and hauled up the steep banks on our backs, which are unaccustomed to such physical labor. Although the flood was exceptional, the water came nowhere near even the lowest terrace of our mill, since while the river side of the building's feet are in the water, the first floor is twenty feet above the riverbed. We never would have bought the mill, for fear of inevitable flooding, if we hadn't seen the damage from this flood, the worst in over one hundred years, three weeks before we signed the papers.

We've received three different bids from contractors and are struggling to decide what to do. One, Bernard Guerin, is a self-described hippie-turned-woodworker. He speaks some English, seems quite competent, and happens to be our closest neighbor; his *atelier* is just downstream on the Mousse. The second is a local mason-turned-general-contractor. While he speaks no English, his work is quite good, perhaps too fine for a rustic water mill, and, more importantly, he is the son of Monsieur Blanc and the grandson of the last miller. The third, Monsieur Pollet, we found in a book called *Living in France*, a slightly loving-hands-at-home publication full of advice for Englishmen anxious to make the leap across the pond. His large firm specializes in restorations and has an Englishman, Pearson, who serves as an architect for their clients who are French-impaired. The bids are quite close, but we don't want to hire our closest neighbor or the son of another neighbor, for the same reason one doesn't go into business with a friend: It's too hard to be tough if one needs to be, and we do have a serious language problem, so we're going with Monsieur Pollet and his architect, Pearson. Through him, Pollet assures us he'll have the sandblasting and beam-shoring done by the time we return in October and will have rudimentary living quarters so we can stay at the mill. But we're making reservations at Les Magnolias, just in case.

A BACKHOE IN THE LIVING ROOM

October 30, 1993
Dear Linda,

We're back in France for six weeks to supervise the first round of restoration work on the mill. We have a phone number and an address, although we are camped in the barn during the day and living in luxury at Les Magnolias at night, with Francis Roussel, the chef-owner, preparing one wonderful meal after another for us: croissants and fresh jams for breakfast, a sweet picnic basket stuffed with chunks of pâté and leftover rabbit for lunch, with a starched square of linen thrown in for some sense of civilization in the total chaos at La Pilande Basse. (We still don't know the origins of the name, Pilande, but we've learned there's a Pilande Haute, a high one as well as our low one, whatever a *pilande* is.) Les Magnolias has a *bon repas* designation from the Michelin guide, which means the food is excellent, especially for the price. We are living at the auberge on the pension plan, whereby we have a room and our meals for less than thirty dollars a day for the two of us. We somehow thought we might be able to stay at the house since we had been told the sandblasting would be finished when we arrived. Not exactly. They had just begun, and of course, it would take longer than they thought. Hoping to push the contractor to move a little faster, we keep telling him how unhappy we are at Les Magnolias, how expensive everything is, and how badly we want to move into the mill. Careful what you wish for: trading the comfort of the auberge for a water mill with no roof or windows?

Les Magnolias is in the center of Plaisance, tucked in among several ruins, most of which Francis owns and intends to restore to add more rooms to his six-room hotel. It's a seventeenth-century manor house covered with climbing ivy that has turned a warm fall red for our arrival. When you open the stout front door, you enter into another time: stone pavers, smoothed from walking and washing, lead to the left into the dining room with its warm stones flickering in the constant fire from the foyer at one end. The other end has a walnut bar, with polished copper pans hanging above the work surface. Ten small round tables are comfortably spaced, set with starched white cloths, three crystal glasses per place, and tiny vases, each with a single fresh flower from the garden in the back. Francis has a collection of small stone basins, once used outside the front door of local farmhouses to wash hands fresh from the barns. Most have primitive Romanesque faces carved into them to ward off evil spirits that might otherwise enter. These basins are selectively placed in corners and stone niches, their faces smiling down on contemporary guests.

Climbing up the stairs to our room, we pass a *grande salle* that's used for weddings, baptisms, and wakes. Like most houses in the village, the auberge is set against a cliff, so the second floor opens out onto its own garden, sheltered by one of the stately magnolias that inspired the name. Francis wanted to give us the largest room with double doors and our own patio, but after one night, Mike announced he couldn't sleep in a bed with a footboard, even a handsome walnut one. His very long legs need dangling room, and given that the beds are small by American standards, we spent the night unwrapping his legs from mine, "One, two, three, turn!" The only room with a bed with no footboard is also the smallest, ten feet by ten, with a bathroom so small the bathtub is half size, but high enough to bring water to your shoulders when perched on its built-in seat. Francis wants to move the beds, but we love our small space, and since we spend so little time there, he has given up. We return after dark, soak our weary bodies in the pink plastic tub, and go down to the intimate dining room, which hosts mostly hotel guests except for one balding man who eats there every night at eight o'clock sharp. There we are served by Marie-France, Francis's young wife, and we eat and eat and eat: *soupe au fromage*, lambs' feet, ragouts, lobster in creamy something, and foie gras, and foie gras, and foie gras. (Francis teaches classes in Paris on preparing fois gras, and he's promised, when I finally have a kitchen at the mill, he will show me how.)

All of my plans to go back to work have dissolved, and I can't even remember on what venture capitalist I intended such revenge. We think we can make it on savings and investments if we're careful. We just found out that we have sold our San Francisco place, and not only that, we have to move out before we return from France. Ty and Helen have been living there while they sit out the hurricane season with their boat in Mexico, and they are happy to help us, so we are moving by telecommunication. The movers will pack and Helen will direct traffic, sending everything either to storage destined for France next year or up to the beach house. (Strange how we can remember every item in every drawer from across the ocean, but can find nothing we're looking for when we're there.) We expect to usually spend April through September at the mill and the rest at the beach house, going into San Francisco for some cultural hits, staying at hotels or with obliging friends. I feel absolutely no regret for selling our city house. It was beautiful and had a great view, but no soul. The mill? Full of soul, maybe even souls, as I'm sure there are kind ghosts everywhere. It's odd how we don't have a toilet and can't speak the language, but we are already home.

Our return was almost uneventful. This time, we flew from San Francisco to Amsterdam, then directly on to Toulouse and the *douane*, or customs. Since everything in France is so expensive, I had convinced Mike that we should smuggle in all our electronics, thereby avoiding the customs duty. This trip's bounty included a fax, a telephone and answering machine combination, a boom box, a VCR, a computer, and a printer—everything a rural French citizen should have and blissfully doesn't know exists. Also, since November would be cold, and since we would have no heat, no chimney, no roof, and no floor, I thought an electric blanket, a down comforter, and a quilt might be important. As it turned out, they made good padding for all the electronic gear.

Now, neither one of us is too cool about this smuggling thing, and I had to carefully rehearse my reasoning on why I hadn't declared anything and be sure I had the invoices ready in case we got busted and had to pay something, and I even had on clean underwear in case I was strip searched. So feeling shaky but looking cool, I adroitly piled my share of bags on my cart and walked straight through the *rien à déclarer* or nothing-to-declare door, delighted when the glass doors slid behind me. I turned to congratulate Mike on his first major transgression in France, but he was nowhere to be found. I checked the customs desk, but no Mike. Then, at the other end of the baggage conveyor belt I spotted him, doing a credible Hardy and/or Laurie impression, all elbows and knees, wrestling with the rest of our luggage.

We had stuffed huge body bags with the electronics wrapped in blankets, which tended to fold in the middle with their clunky cargo on each end. When he placed one on top of the other on the cart, it would bend in the middle, shift to the other side of the cart, and slide noisily to the floor. He would run around to the other side, pick it up as if it was a drunken lady, and try to place it securely on the cart, only to be foiled by the law of center-of-gravity tipping the first off the other side. With his third arm, he was grabbing at our last bag riding the luggage conveyor belt around and around, all the time trying to maintain some degree of nonchalance. Two, three, four tries later, one of the last two ladies in the baggage area said softly to her friend, "*Faites attention, je pense qu'il est dangereux."* ("Be careful, I think he's dangerous.") Finally, he managed to wrap his considerable arms and legs around the whole bunch and roll noisily through the door. Even if there had been a customs person around, he would never have stopped anyone who was so obviously an amateur.

By the way, all this stuff is now actually functioning in our barn, plugged into the one extension cord that runs from the only electrical outlet in the mill, out through a window, over the rabbit cage, through the grain shoot, and under the pigeon house to our makeshift twenty-first century. *A Year in Provence*? No, *The Egg & I*, featuring us as Ma and Pa Kettle, chicken feathers and all. *La France Profonde.*

It is the end of October and we have been here three weeks. We are having buyers' remorse every other day, which is driven by the weather and the depth of the mud in the mill. Just when we can't stand it anymore, we are surprised yet again by some wonderful pile of rocks under the briar patch or some sweet new person.

At some level, we feel as though we have come full circle, from immigrant grandparents from rural European countries (we forget how German Grandpa and Grandma Ketels really were) to the States, an education, some level of wealth, and home again. Only this time, we have a choice. As Ty once said to me, "Happiness is having options." Monsieur Parnat's daughter will surely stay and run the little *épicerie*, a tiny food market with only a few products, in Plaisance, as her mother and grandmother have done. Will she be happy? By Ty's definition, she will be as long as she actually chooses to stay there, knowing she could move somewhere else and assume a different role. But has she been programmed by guilt or lack of self-esteem to believe that she has no choice? Will she be a modern-day Madame Bovary, fantasizing about another life in Paris or Rome? We, at least, must be happy, since we chose what we are about.

Here I sit in the *grange*, or barn, surrounded by my computer, a fax, a Minitel (the French version of the information superhighway), and an automatic coffeemaker, while Mike is struggling to shovel the dirt out off the stone steps leading up to the little house on the hill. It's a complete ruin, but he can't wait to explore it. There are dozens of chairs and other *brocantes* from Monsieur Parnat still piled at the other side of the barn from my office, but I can't take stock until we have repaired the beams. In fact, I don't dare move more than a few steps from the door or I risk tumbling through the floor into the old sheep barn below. (The juxtaposition of these ancient walls tumbling in ruin and our state-of-the-art office is disorienting.) The workmen, after their breakfast of sausage, bread, and wine, shake their heads as I stumble off to the gloom of the barn. But there are long-term visit applications, or *cartes de séjour*, to fill out, lists of furniture to pack, floor plans to execute.

Oh, did I mention that after they dug out the floor in the mill we found two springs? That's water springs. In the soon-to-be new kitchen? Or that after they sandblasted everything the beautiful old stone walls glow with same warmth as the surrounding countryside? Or that tonight Francis is cooking up some mushrooms, foie gras, and duck confit for dinner? Life is good. I hope for you, too.

—Hugs, Judy

November 5, 1993
JOURNAL ENTRY

The nettles have been cut back to expose the stone steps leading down to the river at the base of the mill, where the water washes over the top of the last step in its winter rush first to the Rance, then to the Tarn River. The soothing water sounds are overshadowed by chugging machinery, loud shouts of masons and carpenters. There is no refuge, even there. Behind the mill, the waterfall's dramatic crashing feels threatening even from the upper terrace. Four days of downpours have dyed the clear water red/brown from the plowed fields in the watershed above the mill. In the front and back yard, the ground, the greenery, everything is covered with the red clay that used to hold the old stone roof tiles in place, shards of which, along with the mud, are being tossed by the roofers as they dig out the old for the new. Even the tiny ferns that had pushed through cracks in the walls have folded their arms and retreated. Mud—red, gray, and brown—everywhere. Along the bridge's one remaining sidewall are stacks, graduating in size from small to large, of thick, flat roofing stones, or *lauzes*, waiting to protect the mill for the next two hundred years.

We arrived here in October to total disarray. Huge compressors were pumping fluid sand against the oak beams, washing away the whitewash of lime and plaster, antiquing the clinging garish wallpaper. The rabbit hutch between the house and the barn with its chicken-wire doors had completely disappeared. A young stonemason was knocking a hole in the three-foot walls of the front of the mill, supporting the weight with thick adjustable steel beams. I thought he said *mini-pelle* when we asked what he was doing. The hole was much too big for the window we'd planned on putting in, so we ran for the dictionary. It said *mini-pelle* was a backhoe. Surely they weren't going to drive a backhoe into the house? But they did.

Then nothing. They just didn't show up. Two, three, almost five days of no activity, only the architect, Pearson, and his wife, Amelia, coming to discuss and rediscuss the same floor plan as the day before. It quickly became obvious that Amelia is the organized one, taking notes and following through. Pearson talks big about doing the minimalist composer Michael Nyman's summer house in the Dordogne, taking us on field trips to see irrelevant projects, dodging all attempts to get Pollet, our contractor, to see us. We are already in the tough part of the construction process and beginning to ask tough questions. As we were talking about opening windows into a stone wall and the structural problems that that might cause, and asking for architectural drawings, Pearson admitted that he was not an architect in the traditional sense of designing houses and calculating stresses, but that he was something of an interior designer, though actually he had no training in that either. He spoke French, he knew Pollet, and had found his way into the book we had read about living in France.

Over a cozy diner at Les Magnolias, where we were still being spoiled each evening after working at the mill, we discussed how we felt we had been slightly taken, and that we needed to convene a meeting with Pearson, Pollet, and Amelia *tout de suite*. In that meeting, we realized that not only was Pearson not an architect, he knows less French than we do. He pontificates, Amelia rolls her ankles while she tries not to interrupt, and Pollet, with furrowed brow, tries to look like he understands. Finally, with our prodding, Amelia slipped in and explained to Pollet that we had been promised that we could stay at the mill during construction, and that while we liked staying at Les Magnolias, we needed to move to the mill, and that things weren't moving as quickly as we had been led to believe they would. Or I think that's what she said. Monsieur Pollet, sucked his teeth, examined us closely, slammed his hand on the makeshift kitchen table and exclaimed, "*On y va!*" or "Let's go!" Or maybe, "You asked for it," given that the roof is half done, there are no windows, and there is a backhoe in the living room.

November 7, 1993
Dear Linda,

Let's be clear, I'm having a bad mill day. I'm sitting huddled in the attic in every layer of clothing I can find since, unfortunately, we've left the comfort of Les Magnolias, Francis's picnics, and the consistent heat of a radiator. To make a long story short, since the last letter, we have had a "come-to-Jesus" meeting with our contractor, Monsieur Pollet, and are again making good progress. Apparently, the work crew had been pulled off our project to straighten out a problem elsewhere, and when we threatened to be an even bigger one, they came back. We complained about not being able to stay in the mill as planned, so Monsieur Pollet arranged for a temporary shower, a little cook stove, and a long extension cord, saying, "You want it? You got it. But I'd wait for a roof if I were you." We're staying in the river end of the mill, in the old attic, with a bed, a piece of plywood on sawhorses for a desk, and a lamp. We still have to climb down the stairs, walk across the planks to the front door, and down through the stinging nettles to the outhouse for serious business.

We try to draw and write and ignore the noise all around us, but sometimes it is impossible. Last week, as I was writing and Mike painting, less than three feet away from us the workers were demolishing the roof. They sounded like huge rats gnawing their way through the timbers. Finally, after a particularly insulting clunk of junk, Mike threw up his hands and stumbled off to clear more brambles.

But enough complaining. We are choosing to do this, we don't have to. At the most fundamental level, that is the critical point. No matter how cold it gets (coldest fall in Europe in recent memory), we remind ourselves, sometimes hourly, of how fortunate we are, usually while blowing our noses, backsides to the open flame on top of the butane bomb that serves as our only source of heat. First, we have each other. (I never thought I would judge a relationship based on its btu potential, but it's an even match between Mike and the electric blanket.)

We've even settled into a routine: get up early in the morning, go to the *boulangerie* for croissants, and make coffee for us and the workmen before getting into our overalls to start work. Mike brought his Farmer John overalls from home, and I had decided that I wanted my own French *bleus*, the indigo blue French work clothes. And thank God, because I live in them. They are my protection from brambles, the interface with

Mother Earth, extra warmth, and my blue badge of courage that proves I am a working person: I can do things with my hands. Although maybe what we are doing is more with our beaks, you know, like birds nesting. In fact, sometimes I bend my knees a bit, stick out my rump, and wiggle it, just like a nesting hen. Some image, huh? A huge blue hen wiggling her fanny, plumping her dream nest in France Profonde.

I should also add: a large blue hen in green rubber shoes. From the States. I brought a pair of rubber clogs—Smith & Hawken garden catalog, summer 1993—which are shaped like Dutch wooden shoes. Living in a mill, particularly in the middle of a construction site, requires protection of all sorts, starting with the feet. If we are not hauling wood from the river, or wading out through the mud to the WC, which is presently down below the will-be front terrace in the old pigpen, or *porcherie*, we are stepping through pigeon shit at a *brocante*, or used-furniture place. I won't mention the inevitable splattering that comes from the continuing indignity of being a woman without indoor plumbing in rural France, but I have learned one more of life's secrets: "Don't pee on cement." Apparently, Monsieur Pollet's interpretation of temporary living quarters doesn't include a toilet, so our constant evening companion is a little yellow chamber pot. The fact that it's plastic reduces the charm. We've been sleeping in the attic, which is on the river side, with a funky window that needs coaxing to open. In the morning, when the yellow pot is full, out she goes: remember, urine is sterile. During the day, we climb down the precarious stairs across a catwalk over the mud, down the steps to the pigpen, where the outhouse hole opens into a pit that, in turn, is emptied by floods. That is *not* sterile. There's a septic tank in our future.

Until about two weeks ago, I thought myself smart indeed to have brought these rubber clogs all the way from the States. That was before Mike came down from the *pigeonnier*, or pigeon coop, in the attic, dust mask perched on top of his head, with today's find. He had discovered, stuffed into one of the holes in the dovecote, an old shoe from some previous miller. It was carved from wood, brought to a point at the toe, with rounded iron cleats nailed onto the bottom. Tacked to the opening, fragile but still in reasonable shape, was a leather top, laces and all. The real thing: an ancient wooden shoe (called a *sabot* in French and the origin of the word *sabotage*, because workers would use them to fowl up the machinery in sweat shops), of better design and function than those of Smith & Hawken. I can close my eyes and picture the owner of that large shoe, stomping through these old stones. We showed it to Monsieur Blanc, who said, with tears in his eyes, that his father, the last miller, had to come down the stairs backwards, tucking the toes of his *sabots* under each step as he descended.

There are many reminders like that from other centuries: for example, Amelia's father's funeral. (She is the wife of our wannabe-architect, Pearson.) She told us less than six weeks ago that her parents were moving to France after years of service in the British equivalent of the CIA. They hated England and could hardly wait to leave after his retirement. A week later, she told us that her father had been diagnosed with pancreatic cancer but was moving to France anyway since he preferred to be buried in Beauregarde, the little village where he and his wife had bought their retirement home about five years ago. Two weeks after moving permanently to France, her father died. We didn't know him, but since Amelia has become our English-speaking lifeline, we decided to go to the funeral to show her some support. The hour and a half drive northwest from Plaisance wound through many small villages, the architecture changing as we moved from the Aveyron into the Lot department.

The whole village, even though they barely knew her father, stopped work and came to the service—all thirty people. The body lay at rest in the house, unembalmed, while people came to pay their respects. The men of the village went to the house to load the coffin onto the village hearse: a black cart owned by the village, with two huge wheels and crutches on each end to suspend the coffin during Mass. Large white tears had been painted on the sides and were embroidered on the black velvet drape covering the oak coffin. Flowers were stuck into green Styrofoam and placed, somewhat carelessly, on top. Most of the village followed the hearse, drawn by the same men, to the church, a total distance of less than a hundred yards.

The church was small, but the men managed to pull the cart up the steps, through the doors, and down the aisle, scraping the little rush-seated chairs aside, up to the altar where two priests waited to perform the service. One, with a deep bass voice, spoke a little English, just enough to apologize to the English but French-speaking family that he was sorry he couldn't speak English. He sang the musical parts of the Mass while the other priest performed the rest of the ritual. It's usually awkward when the priest or minister obviously doesn't know the deceased, but this old character just loved the communion, relishing the chalice of wine in big gulps with loud smacks of his lips. I thought he smiled a little inappropriately during the ceremony. I tried at first to understand the words, and when I finally realized that most of it was Latin I gave in and let the experience wash over me. It was a visual, aural, and sensuous (cold inside those old walls) feeling. The sound of the chanting, the blues and pinks of the murals—little pointy hats and we could have been in the thirteenth century.

After the service and the waving of the incense, the cart was noisily turned around inside the church and pulled back down the aisle, through the doors, and finally bounced down the path to the cemetery behind. Chrysanthemums from All Saints' Day still covered the other graves. The coffin was lowered by hand, suspended from ropes. After the sprinkling of the holy water, his wife, a tiny woman with cowlicky gray hair, dropped a morsel of earth onto the coffin. Amelia and her sister did the same. Slowly, the whole village filed past and cast their symbolic goodbyes. The hollow clunk of dirt on the coffin echoed again and again. We, like many of the others, had never met Amelia's father, yet we tossed our bit of earth for our collective ancestors.

—*Hugs to all, Judy*

November 8, 1993

JOURNAL ENTRY

In order to complete the sale of our house in San Francisco we had to drive to Bordeaux, the nearest American embassy, to get the papers notarized, a five-hour drive one way. It's a beautiful old city on the Atlantic coast with a brand-new contemporary art museum in a thousand-year-old building. There was a conceptual installation there of a thousand dishpan-sized steel pots on wheels, filled with the debris from the artist's home, which he had built and then lived in for over twenty years, treating it as an art piece before demolishing it and videotaping the destruction. He ceremoniously filled the pots with broken pieces of the white ceramic tile he had built his house with. All these stainless-steel containers, each on casters, were placed in carefully spaced rows in a cathedral-sized room with a glorious vaulted ceiling and buttressed walls. The work was a powerful statement about our time: maybe there's not much worth saving of modern life, but the lying in state of the debris in the grandeur of the space gave it a quiet dignity. A monument to a life's work. I'm anxious to start an art project, but for now, it's the mill itself.

November 29, 1993
Dear Linda,

This is not all fun. I'm typing this with my finger in an enormous bandage capped with a rubber finger cot after smashing it in a window shutter through which I had just dumped yet another load of rubble that had tumbled onto our work table from the roof. We were both sick last week, and have been cold to the bone for the past three. They had to demolish the working part of the fireplace, tear out the floor to expose the millworks, and bust a huge hole in the side of the house to drive in a pneumatic tractor big enough to knock the rock out of the floor so we could deal with the rising damp in the kitchen. So we have had a backhoe with a jackhammer on its business end living under us since. It's too cold to work outside very long, so we huddle in the mill's attic, with our bed, computer, and Mike's drawing table, and listen to Jean-Claude *bruuuum* the jackhammer up, where it slams into the ceiling—our floor—and smashes down into the bedrock, *ra-ta-ta-ta*. There's another, smaller, regular-sized jackhammer at the other end of the mill picking at the cement that covers the entire floor of the millhouse, the cement that Monsieur Parnat poured trying to tame the rising damp. All this so Mike can fit under the beams. Jackhammers in stereo.

Jean-Claude, the backhoe operator, is a handsome man who is emotionally involved in dragging this large hydraulic arm around, dropping it in place, and slamming it against the resistant rock until it gives way. (I'm tempted to fake an orgasm as he rips through another successful fault.) When he's through, he collapses the giant phallus, gently, on the ground with the business end in the middle so he can sharpen and grease it, giving it a pat as he strides out for his pastis.

Our persistence in insisting we move into the mill has created a dilemma, since we don't dare move into a hotel again even though that would be intelligent. We thought threatening to move into the mill would make them move faster. Now, we realize some things can't be hurried. Staying has become a macho thing: Everyone asks us, "*Il fait pas trop froid la-bas?*" "*Pas trop mal, merci,*" I deny the cold, sneaking my hands as close as possible to the heat source of wherever I am. If only we had an indoor toilet so I didn't have to squat on the frozen ground, which splatters as badly as cement. The path down to the *porcherie* is piled high with construction material and is slippery from the clay tossed down from the old roof, so I only go halfway down to the WC when possible.

The little yellow pot is never where I need it. But I have learned another secret of life in this process, however: "Happiness is when your pee don't steam."

In case you wonder whether we are losing it, here's proof: Last week, we were standing in the middle of what I think someday may be a kitchen, trying to decide on the location of the sink. Imagine, there was a hole blasted through the side of the house for the backhoe/jackhammers sitting where the dining room table will be; the floor over the millworks had been torn out in most places, exposing rotting mill wheels from one century or other; a temporary elevator was roaring over our heads carrying a ton of old stones for the roof; dust and diesel fumes were everywhere; a dozen men were bustling in all directions speaking a patois that we didn't have a chance of comprehending, asking us questions about things we didn't understand anyway, when Mike, disgusted with my conventional suggestions about sinks and counters, looked around thoughtfully, and with a perfectly straight face, asked, "Are we missing a chance here to be completely impractical?" I collapsed in laughter, a bit too hysterical I expect.

Another equally ridiculous situation and bad for the American cause: a friend, while taking us to the airport in San Francisco in October, told me to close my eyes for a little surprise. When I opened them, I found a pile of tiny condoms which were, of course, finger cots from the hospital lab where she works, you know, the tiny rolled thin rubber things that professionals use to protect themselves from all bodily fluids? They look exactly like baby Trojans. I stuffed them in my pocket, telling her I was sure Mike would appreciate them although they looked to be a bit too big. We all laughed and drove on. Little did I know that they would save me from a lot of aggravation and perhaps destroy the American myth in one fell swoop.

Last week, after I smashed my finger, I was screaming in agony, squeezing it to stop the blood in the cleanest rag I could find. As I tried to think of some possible way to keep it from swelling and becoming infected in all the filth, I remembered the finger cots tucked in my summer jacket somewhere under the plastic. Mike, recognizing shock when he sees it, shoved me back on the bed and pushed a glass under my nose. "First things first." Of course, a shot of *eau-de-vie*, or home-distilled alcohol, the amazing French moonshine made under careful license, probably lethal in potency but as common as garlic in the pantry. We had a bottle, which our contractor had given us and which he eyed every day to see if we had had our healthy share. We had actually nipped at it once, but with tears in our eyes decided it was not for the uninitiated.

Well, I had been initiated. I slugged back the glass and felt the anesthetic spread. Whoo! I could see how that stuff could become addictive. But it did give me the strength to plow through the piles of filthy clothes to find the lightweight jacket I had been wearing at the airport. After soaking my finger, I bandaged it and pulled the finger cot over all, congratulating myself on my solution to a potentially nasty problem. I would be able to apply pressure to keep the swelling down, and keep the bandage waterproof and clean *en même temps.*

We had been invited to Madame and Monsieur Blanc's house the next day for lunch, when she had promised to show me how to make *soupe au fromage*, cheese soup. When we left the house, I stuffed a few extra finger cots in my pocket telling Mike that I had better be careful not to drop any or the word would be out on him. Yup. You guessed it. I don't have a clue where they went. Maybe in the Blanc's dining room, at the store, the bakery, in front of the mill with all the workmen? Sorry, Mike.

But the lunch? Let's talk about what's important. We started with the soup, a layered mixture of cabbage, cheese, bread, and just enough bouillon to turn the whole thing into a bubbling *gratinée* after an hour in the oven. We had seconds since we were sure it was all there was for lunch since there was no sign of other food on the sideboard. But Marthe (we are on a first-name basis now, Germain and Marthe, although we still use the formal *vous* for *you*) jumped up, exclaiming "*Mon Dieu, j'ai oublié le pâté!*" ("I forgot the pâté!") From somewhere mysterious she pulled out a homemade pâté topped with *trompettes de la mort*, trumpets of death mushrooms, still in its crock with her label on it. I took two slices with the obligatory bread, just to be polite, of course. When she reappeared again from the kitchen with the *magret de canard*, or duck breast, we knew we were in trouble. We were already stuffed, and we hadn't started yet. Curly endive from their garden, home-stewed fruits after the cheese course, and a raspberry cloud inside a cake ring, made by her son the baker with more cream than should be legal, followed. Wine, of course, but not too much, accompanied each course, carefully chosen by Germain to complement the food.

Then the *eau-de-vie* appeared. Germain poured less than a tablespoon for Mike, while Marthe poured an equal amount of *vin de noix,* a liqueur spiked with sugar and walnuts, *pour les femmes.* The nut liqueur was more my speed, sweet, a little like its Italian cousin amaretto. We rolled down the hill to *chez nous* after Germain had finished stuffing bags full of carrots, endive, chard, lettuce, and other winter vegetables from his garden for our dinner that evening, just in case we got hungry later. All that, even though I had told Marthe, "*Une seule feuille de laitue va passer mes lèvres ce soir.*" ("Only one leaf of lettuce is going to pass through my lips tonight.") Given our limited French, I don't know what I actually said, probably something closer to eating only milk and worms. *(Lait et verres.)*

Actually, we had to hurry to be back to celebrate the finishing of our roof. Four men had spent six weeks overhead on the steep roof, hand-cutting the *lauzes* that have served as shingles in this part of France for centuries. Not to be confused with slate, they are layers of the schist that surrounds us in the hills, approximately one inch thick and ranging from six inches to two feet square.

It probably would have been cheaper to use new *lauzes*, which would have developed their own patina in time, but we decided to use roofing stones from old buildings. In other words, Claude (Cloood), the supervisor of the roof work, would go out and "get" old stones from various farmyards. He would disappear and mysteriously, later that day or week, a truck would show up with pallets full of *lauzes*, sometimes with live moss still on them. When we asked him where he got them he would turn his head, cock his chin, roll his eyes, hold his palms up, and shrug his shoulders.

We don't know how he found enough, but one day I was driving back from Coupiac and saw him standing at the side of the road eyeing a stack of *lauzes* near a farm. I beeped and waved but there was no sign of recognition on his part, even though there was no ignoring our bright purple Twingo. To protect us from the crime? Amelia told us they had bought an old building close by that was falling down and that we had paid for everything, but that Claude didn't want the farmer to know he was buying them for those rich Americans. Apparently, all Americans are rich. We just don't know if the farmer owned the building. Those things happen here, you know.

But the roof. Hand chiseled. Hand set. Also a new chimney created by Jean-Pierre, a handsome young apprentice under the careful and noisy direction of Claude. The chimneys in this region have a special top that is created by rocks on the four corners of the chimney face with tables of big flat stones across them. Two or three more layers create an effective wind and spark screen. There is a custom of placing a pointed rock on the top for luck, which is done by whoever created the chimney. It is called a *clucke* in the Occitan patois of the region. It means "mother hen," symbolizing the protection from the elements. Some are carved faces, but ours was more in the shape of a large hen's beak. Since it was the first chimney for Jean-Pierre, he hadn't placed a rock, probably expecting us to ask Claude to do it. But when the subject came up, Claude, with a nod, showed us who should perform the task. Lots of insisting, grunting and "*mais non*'s" later, the lad hoisted the final pointed stone, grinning ear to ear into the camera. Champagne, speeches (Champagne helps my French a lot), and congratulations on the first major section of work to be completed, appropriately, on Thanksgiving. We noticed that the young man stopped his truck at the top of the road and sneaked out to take a photo of the house as he left for the last time.

It's time to go back to the states for Christmas, and I confess, I'm ready to go. We now have no floor downstairs, no windows, no fireplace. It has been spitting a freezing rain for a week, and mud and water is streaming into the hole in the side of the house. Our neighbor, Bernard Guerin, after paying us a short visit, remarked, "God, it looks like Beirut here!" I've tried to be a good sport, cooking in my Mexican poncho and running our new dryer, which we bought for warmth, ignoring the mice and the mud, brushing the dust from the sandblasting out of my teeth and off from my bread. But I've been sick with diarrhea for two weeks, literally crying as I slide down the path to the outhouse, toilet paper in one hand, a water bottle to flush in the other, the flashlight under my chin, colder than I thought possible, my no-longer-charming-green sabots covered with mud.

Well, that's it from France for now. We have to entrust the house to our work crew and pray they can get us a toilet, a furnace, and a shower by next March. It's all I ask. We have been told that if the workmen like the owners, they will put bay leaves in the house somewhere, for luck. Then it will be a happy house. If they don't, the house is cursed for eternity. Time will tell.

I'm trying to figure out how I'm going to serve a going-away dinner of foie gras, lamb, and poached pears with 3 wineglasses, 2 plates, and 23 forks in the middle of our one-room house with one plastic wall, a temporary shower, and a washer and dryer (the one extravagance we've allowed: clean clothes). No refrigerator. We don't need one.

We've accomplished a lot in these cold two months. We decided on a general floor plan for the ground floor which includes under-the-floor heat, improvement of the big stand-in fireplace, and my new Godin gas stove that includes a wood-burning oven as well. There will also be another fireplace on the upper floor, since the winter cold permeated our being up there.

Godin is a French brand of high-end stoves that is priced in the same range as a small car, but since this is my only real kitchen, we decided I was worth it. I priced them in Albi and Millau and then drove to Coupiac, where Monsieur Constantin has a small appliance store. We had bought our dryer from him, and I'm sure the stories were circulating in the village about those wacky Americans. But we decided it would be best to support local merchants unless the price was truly unreasonable. Monsieur Constantin had been a carpenter before he opened his store. It seems he cut all five fingers off of his right hand with a power saw, and though doctors had grafted three of his toes to his hand to form a three-fingered/toed appendage (it's hard not to stare), he was no longer capable of woodworking. He hadn't sold too many important appliances in his new store either, and he was enthusiastic about selling us a Godin. When I asked him the price, he quoted a price somewhat higher than the other stores, so I countered, lowering the price a bit but still preferring to have someone local to do repairs if necessary. He couldn't hide his glee as I wrote him a check, and as I was leaving he said, "You could have done better, you know?"

I shook my head and told him, "No, no, Monsieur Constantin. You need to learn to act as if the customer hurt you with the price you agreed to. Okay?" Again, given my French, I'm not sure I said exactly that, but it was close enough that he agreed.

"*Oh, oh. Bien sûr, Madame O'Shea.*"

Tomorrow, we give the keys to Germain, say goodbye to Francis Roussel, and we're gone.

—*Big hugs, Judy*

November 30, 1993
JOURNAL ENTRY
La Pilande Basse

Germain Blanc was stunned when I gave him the keys to the mill. He lowered his head and looked up at me, shy and yet proud to have been entrusted with the keys to his place of birth. He turned them one by one, his lower lip quivering, the only set of keys to La Pilande Basse—the house where he had lived until his marriage to Marthe nearly forty years before. The place where his mother had died at such a young age and that his stepmother had run with an iron fist, according to Francis. Although he lives only five hundred vertical feet above the waterfall, after his marriage he rarely went down to see his father and had not entered the mill in the twenty-four years since he sold it after his father's death. There were only five keys when the former owners, a bourgeois French couple from Graulhet, took over.

The wife of the couple who bought the mill had loved it, but the husband did not want to spend the money to preserve the millworks or even the roof. The wife hired Monsieur Parnat to fix up the place and watch over it when they weren't there, which was most of the time, but like many *brocanteurs* he had pilfered what he could, and instead of putting in proper drainage and double walls, he'd poured eighteen inches of cement over the entire stone floor on the lower level. And instead of plaster, he'd whitewashed the stone walls and chestnut ceilings in the main mill room. The new owners had wallpapered everything upstairs, even the ceilings, hoping to hide the scars left by pulleys, chains, and powder-post beetles. The wife had added indoor/outdoor carpeting in the bedrooms, which became soggy with the unresolved humidity. Parnat, with virtual free rein over the property, had slowly filled the barn with chicken feathers, sacks of wool from old mattresses, and strangely, fifty-four disintegrating chairs. Twenty-four years of neglect had crept into every crack in the walls of both buildings, leaving tiny ferns as keepsakes.

Germain kept bouncing the keys in his large calloused hand, counting the keys carefully. Although everyone knew the keys to the mill were kept in the *porcherie*, behind the door on the nail with the cross, he had never dared go back after he sold the mill. And now he had been given six keys, including one for the *porcherie* itself.

Driving from Germain's to Les Magnolias, I thought about the first time Francis Roussel had told us about Monsieur Blanc, who is much older than Francis. But it's Francis's eyebrow that quivers all the time now, a tic that shows up when he's tired. He has gout and limps around in the kitchen, beads of sweat forming on his forehead and dampening the gray roots of his dyed-brown hair. He closed Les Magnolias for the winter yesterday, all the family festivals and All Saints' Day over, the summer people long gone, the grinding eighteen-hour days done with until next spring.

Francis has helped us so much during our stay. First with lodging, then feeding us, but also giving us tips on everything from appliances to handmade tiles for the bathroom to spotting a claw-foot bathtub in a field. He was quite pleased that we weren't going to remove the scars/patina of time or otherwise sanitize the rustic charm created by generations of frugal millers. We wanted the bathroom to slide into its space by using recuperated materials if we could, tile and tub. He told us about Raujole, a tile-maker in Creissels, near Millau, where they still cast tiles and apply the enamels by hand, taking the clay from a cliff where the Romans made pots for hundreds of years and shipped them throughout their empire. The clay is so pure it doesn't need processing, so each tile has its own delightful impurity, created when the bits of organic material burn off in the kiln. We chose a golden yellow and brick orange for the bathroom, knowing the enamels would melt and flow in varying puddles of color, perfect in their imperfections. The floor tiles will not be enameled, just stay the color of the clay, enriched with coats of linseed oil to protect the surface.

He had seen the tub while on the way to Millau, just before the Roquefort caves and right after a small village, Moulin Neuf. (I have no idea where the mill is in that town.) The road winds through the Rance Valley, giving spectacular views of the limestone cliffs of Roquefort jutting out of the deep red soil of the valley, quilted with greens in every shade. We pulled off to the side of the road and walked out into the field to examine the tub. It was perfect: no cracks in the enamel, and an impossible-to-duplicate dripping rust patina underneath. It was being used as a watering basin for sheep by one of the local Roquefort cheese farmers.

We stood beside it calmly, arms crossed, knowing by now that the five-minute French rule would prevail. Wherever one goes in rural France, into the deepest woods or on the most obscure country road, if one stops, say, to paint or pee, within five minutes the owner of the property will be there, sometimes cruising casually by on his tractor, but usually demanding politely, "*Puis-je vous aidez?*" ("Can I help you?")

The price was negotiated at about one hundred dollars, and the farmer couldn't help smiling the Monsieur Constantin smile. But we were smiling, too, since we got the tub and the satisfaction of not having to pay an outrageous price to another farmer who had miscalculated our naiveté and had started way too high. "*Vous nous prenez pour des Americans, monsieur?*" "Do you take us for Americans, monsieur?" (This phrase is a pejorative, usually spoken only by one negotiating Frenchman to another.) Francis taught us this, too, and even with our minimal French we enjoyed the shocked look on his face when I said it, walking away from the first potential deal. But we knew that the second farmer got a fair price, since we'd been to many *brocantes*, and we were happy, too, with our discovery.

When I arrived, Francis was pulling the ivy, still red from autumn, down from the window ledges at Les Magnolias, wrapping the vines nervously around his hand. His young wife, Marie-France, round with her first child, his third, the other two now young adults, arched her back against the cold and blew breath-rings in the crisp air. She stuffed the ivy packages into the plastic bag crackling with the cold, not smiling. I felt as though I'd interrupted an argument.

At his request I followed Francis into the kitchen, where he brought out the last of the *soupe au fromage* and his favorite Madiran wine from the restaurant's cellar for our final meal at the mill that night. As I left, a single light in the kitchen reflected on the stone pavers, lighting the hallway to the dining room. Chairs with their feet in the air signaled Francis's time of rest. After a shoulder-patting *bon voyage* and *bisou*, he pulled the thick wooden door behind them as they entered into the gloom of the empty hotel.

March 17, 1994

JOURNAL ENTRY

The past three months in the States were spent sorting through boxes from our move, finding an exporter to pack and ship a container of furniture, frantic French lessons, long weekends with our children, who weren't sure that we hadn't lost our way. We discovered Mr. Schwartz, an exporter in South San Francisco who sells American appliances with 220-volt wiring. He has all the plug adapters, transformers, reducers— things we didn't even know we needed. We packed and he stuffed a shipping container that we hoped would arrive not too soon and not too late the next spring.

We also ground through the process of acquiring the special visas we would need to apply for our *carte de séjour,* which is needed for stays longer than three months. Police checks, eight copies of financial statements, medical insurance documents, marriage licenses, birth certificates, divorce papers—all to be translated by official translators. This would need to be done every year for ten years, at which time we could stay for five more years before starting the process again. We weren't sure we needed all this; we could always slip into Spain and back and beat the residence requirement, but we wanted to do it right. Besides, we wouldn't have to pay duty on our furniture, now tucked away in Mr. Schwartz's warehouse.

The road from Toulouse is boring, especially at night, flat and uneventful, and it takes forever to start seeing billboards that feel French: La Carroserie, Leader Price, Lille-sur-Tarn. We usually take the road around Albi since it's faster, past the race track, the new McDonald's, and the urban sprawl sprouting poorly constructed metal structures with bright paint and no charm. We could be in Sacramento, California. And then the towers of Sainte-Cécile appear, towering over Albi, glowing from beneath, up-lighted like Toulouse-Lautrec's showgirls in his Parisian brothel paintings. (Those paintings and lithographs, including the original lithograph stones, are housed in the museum next to the church. His mother offered all his work to the Louvre when he died, but they refused, probably because of the subject matter, so she installed his work in the bishop's castle, next to the imposing cathedral.)

Mike decided to take the high road from Albi toward Plaisance, staying out of the fog that we knew would be blanketing the valley. We passed through the villages of Villefranche d'Albigeise and La Croix Rouge, then the quiet center of Alban. Five kilometers on the other side is the road that starts down into the valley in 108 curves. I stared at the road and tried to count to avoid getting carsick, but then, just after the last curve, my stomach in my mouth, I saw, lit through the leafless trees, the hexagonal bell tower of the church in Plaisance high on its rock, glowing through the fog covering the Rance River, our welcome home. We crossed the stone bridge and wound through the darkened streets.

Plaisance is a sleepy little village with a total of sixty-two permanent residents and another two hundred on the outlying farms who have Plaisance as their address. It is in the *canton*, or county, with Coupiac, Saint-Sernin-sur-Rance, Martrin, and a few other hamlets. According to Francis, its church is considered a classic example of original Romanesque architecture and has been carefully restored. There are traces of commerce in fading paint on some buildings, but other than Les Magnolias, Madame Parnat's tiny grocery store, and the bakery there are no shops. The mill is about two miles on the other side of Plaisance toward Coupiac. The road stays high on the hills all the way to Coupiac, but well before that, off to the left toward Solage, another curvy road descends, following the course of the Mousse, our river. Down, down, to the sharp curve, on the right, sits La Pilande Basse, snuggled down in the river canyon.

We could barely see our old bridge (ours, because it was traded to the former mill owners when the main road was rebuilt in 1988), which forms the semicircular drive in and out of the mill property. A thick fog clung to the river bottom, climbing up the schist cliffs and the stone walls of the mill and hiding the arch of the bridge.

We were excited/nervous to rediscover the mill and what we might find. Pearson, our so-called architect, had been evasive about the stone floor and the bedroom layout, which didn't bode well. The crunch of the newly spread gravel under the car tires was the first pleasant surprise. (We had left behind rivers of mud and plank walkways into the mill.) Under the glare of our headlights, we pulled up under the trellis, now bare, only the skeleton of the old vine arching up the support beams. The car doors thunked in the night, echoing against the stone. We strained to hear the Mousse, but the water sounds were tucked into the blanket of fog above the riverbed.

March 31, 1994
Dear Linda,

We arrived mid-March, in the dark. We were cold, had lost some luggage, and got stuck with a bad car, and when we arrived at the mill, there was no key where the contractor was supposed to have left it. It was too late to bother Germain, but we hoped we would find Francis at Les Magnolias and that he would still be up and that he could find the key we left with him in the fall. We banged on the door, bedraggled, bewildered, and bejetlagged, and although they were not yet open for the season, we were lucky enough to stumble into a "light snack" Francis was having with some friends. There had been a wedding at the auberge the day before, and they were dealing with the leftovers. Trust me, two more chairs around the table made no difference. We started with a double fish *fumet*, which is a silky bouillon made with fish bones and herbs, then reduced twice before adding chunks of lobster, followed by an elegant sufficiency of sausage from Truel, a little *soupe au fromage*, and a plump guinea hen plopped in the middle of a steaming vegetable stew. Naturally, the cheeses included two or three kinds of Roquefort and other *brebie* (sheep), *vache* (cow), and *chèvre* (goat) cheese in various stages of aging, then a touch of *crème legére*, a supposedly lighter rendition of *crème fraîche,* but made with Roquefort and served up in a tiny plop like a scoop of ice cream, and a little *eau-de-vie* with a chubby, drunken plum in the bottom. We were home.

But then we had to go back to the mill and try to make up a bed. We knew we would have a furnace—they were to have turned on the switch that day—a bathtub, a toilet, and my new Godin stove. At least we were going to be warm, and no more slippery-slidey down the garden path to *faire pipi*. By the circle light of our flashlight (we don't yet have lights), we saw that everything was covered with plaster dust, mortar, and/or sawdust. We climbed the miller's stairs, the body bags leaving a slug track in the dust behind us. We unrolled our thin, slightly damp mattress in the cleanest dirty place we could find and fell sound asleep. Well, actually after we tried out our new indoor plumbing. Our new bathroom was the second delight of the evening: new/old tile from Raujole, the claw-foot tub, the old kitchen sink now a bathroom fixture, and, most importantly, a radiator, a warm wall in the dark.

In the morning sun, we checked out the newly defined upstairs rooms. We had had to tear out all the plasterboard interior walls to make room for the first bathroom in the mill, so we elected to completely reconfigure the floor plan. We had gone round and round with Pearson about the main bedroom. We wanted two large suites with baths and a shared family-room-type space in between, with a fireplace, that could form a third bedroom. We also wanted the washer/dryer in a dressing area/bathroom with no tub but a serious American shower. There had been a lot of tooth sucking (lips pursed, tongue clacking behind the teeth, usually with a finger wagging a no, no, no) on the part of Claude, the foreman of the work crew, when Pearson asked him about our idea: "Hum, water, leaking, should be in cellars, and showers should be little plastic upright stalls, hermetically sealed." In other words, he didn't approve of our wants. So, in spite of dozens of faxed drawings of different configurations, we had had to rely on his judgment on our judgment. In short, we have the biggest bathroom you've ever seen and the tiniest bedroom, and a radiator in each one, hot in the bedroom and cold in the bathroom. Not the best surprise, but partially our fault.

The *grenier*, or attic, where the grain was cleaned and dried, was to be the second guest suite space. We wanted to keep all the old millworks, close up the hole in the floor, close the pigeon holes with glass, and put a window under the eaves and in the back north wall so guests could watch the waterfall in their jammies. The biggest decision was whether or not we would replace the chestnut floor, which was extremely distressed by sacks of grain, the scraping of machinery, and the falling of stones from the roof repair. In fairness to Pearson, he insisted that we have an industrial cleaner come in and try to get to the bottom of centuries of abuse before we installed a new floor. We were stunned at the beauty of the wood, although the planks undulate a bit from the uneven beams that hold it in place, and one or two have reinforcing stays from below in the mill room.

The common room in between is still rough, with no fireplace, but held the worst surprise of all: the stone basin that was next to the old fireplace had been filled with cement for no apparent reason, just filled with cement. All cooking used to be done in fireplaces until wood-burning stoves became available/affordable. In the fireplace there would have been a big hook and a chain that held a large round pot for soups or boiling potatoes. But slow-cooked dishes like *pot-au-feu* or pot roasts were done on thick stone slabs with saucer-sized holes in them. *Braises*, or live coals from the fireplace, were placed in metal grills below the holes in the stone and then the pot over the hole, hence the origin of the term "to braise" meat, or slow-cook it over low heat. The hot ash fell into a stone basin below and was then used for soap and candles. Efficient. And now impossible.

Danders up, we crept down the stairs. By the light of day we could see that the downstairs floor was covered in thick black plastic. What was it hiding? We had commissioned Thierry Vigroux, a young man from the nearby village of Coupiac, to quarry and form a new stone floor, which he was supposed to have distressed to look old, but hopefully not too hokey. In spite of several faxes asking Pearson how it looked, he hadn't offered any comment, which I had interpreted as a potential disaster. When we lifted the corner, there were pools of condensed water on the stones from the new cast-into-the-cement-floor-but-under-the-stones furnace, and our hearts sank. (As it turned out, the damp was deliberate, to allow the mortar to dry slowly so the stones wouldn't crack. Vigroux knew the plastic would keep the newly poured cement, in which the stones were placed, from drying too quickly and cracking.) We found a scrawled note from Vigroux telling us we could remove the plastic *tout de suite*. When we did remove it, the puddles dried quickly from the heat of the furnace coils embedded beneath the stones, and the floor was gorgeous. We began to think Pearson hadn't even seen it. And my stove, the Godin, actually two big side-by-side stoves, one gas with an electric oven, the other a wood-fired oven with a solid cast-iron top, so polished it looks like steel. The bases are steel but enameled a gun-metal blue, with brass railings to open the ovens and the wood-burning stove. Monsieur Constantin was wrong. I couldn't have done better!

Now, if I just had a kitchen sink. We've decided to have Vigroux make a new/old stone sink like the one in the bathroom but with a regular sink below it, but that will take months. But time we have. Redoing a house in France seems to be different than in the States. We had tried to set realistic expectations about the work that might have been accomplished, and to be fair, most of what the contractor had promised had been done. The exterior walls are three feet of stone and mud, and the sewer chase had to be buried in those rocks. That meant they had to pull out some of the old stones, hollow out the drain, and then replace the rock, trying to keep the same mortar color and the somewhat rustic stacking of stones that is an important characteristic of the mill. In some cases, they succeeded.

Unfortunately, there were other things that were major disappointments, not just the little stone basin being full of cement, but a sewer drain in front of the front door,

and the occasional downright sloppy stonework. What confused us was that one half of a wall would be beautiful and the other just horrible. Another mystery. I'm off to bed.
—*Love to all, Judy*

April 4, 1994
JOURNAL ENTRY

We have to do something about the uneven quality of the workmanship. When we asked Pearson why we had a storm drain on our front-door stoop, he gestured to the stone wall enclosures around the opening as if it were obvious that we would have standing water after a storm, since the front door of the mill is directly downhill from the main road and the runoff would have nowhere else to go. Because we had lowered the floor in the mill with Jean-Claude's backhoe, the entry to the house was three feet lower than it had been, so there were new steps going down to the front door. Instead of providing an outlet to send it farther down the hill, the workers had built a little swimming pool in front of the main entry door! When we asked him, somewhat heatedly, what would happen when three leaves clogged the drain, or exactly why are there walls all around and no diversion before the steps or after, he blushed, shrugged his shoulders, and hung his head. We'll never know what they were thinking, but the drain and the potential runoff disaster there and another behind the house became the second item of a list of must-fixes. Pearson was the first. Either he was present and agreed with these mistakes and isn't competent, or he wasn't there and is irresponsible; either way, it must be fixed. But we needed his minimal language skills, at least for a while.

We followed him silently, taking notes, gushing over the good, glowering over the bad. Fortunately, the good outweighed the bad: the lovely new oak floor on the river side of the long room in front of the millstones, the new window that replaced the opening for the backhoe and that brightens the other end. With the sun low in the spring sky, shafts of light spread across the stone floor and warm the gray/brown/blue of the schist stone walls. The new terrace that opens off from the oddly proportioned little new bedroom upstairs should be inviting when the drainage problem is solved; right now it's another potential flood basin since there's no way for runoff to escape. The upper floor of the barn, with new beams and oak flooring, at last accessible, took our breath away. With twenty-foot ceilings, the cavernous space, free of feathers and decaying chair frames, was stunning. The warm stone walls are lightened by the new skylight and larger windows, making a perfect studio space for Mike and guest artists. The lower barn, my studio space, with its low ceilings and one tiny window, was less charming, with its fresh cement floor, bright blue furnace, and water heater. But the toilet tucked back in the corner, a real luxury in a studio space, was some compensation.

The little house high above the mill, which when we left still had a roof, was a bad surprise, the only one that Pearson couldn't have prevented. Over the winter, the weakened planks supporting the stone roof had collapsed, spilling broad slabs of stone down into the shell of the house. It had been the main dwelling at La Pilande Basse for at least two hundred years and then was abandoned for the larger mill. Half of it fell down when Germain's father took the *lauzes* off that part of the roof to put up his enlarged barn, and now the second half threatened to do the same. Pearson said we'd have to do something quickly if we wanted to save the beam structure. Even though they've stood for three centuries, the walls will tumble in just a few years without a roof to protect their fragile mud jointing. (Before cement was affordable, most old stone buildings in rural France were constructed with clay and were meant to have a thick layer of stucco on the outside and plaster on the inside to protect the walls. Renovations usually include what is called jointing, or pointing, with contemporary mortar. The mill building is a conglomeration of crumbling stucco, mortar and mud, but we don't like the overdone look of uniform pointing.)

But the biggest disappointment was the way the crew treated the cleanup, dumping their wine bottles, chicken bones, and unmentionables into the tunnel, which was the waste hole from the old outhouse, but which we wanted to return to its original function as another millrace under the *porcherie*. (Before this building became a pigpen and then an outhouse, it held another set of millstones used to grind corn for animals. The water ran from the river, behind the mill, through the main millworks, then out through the tunnel running under the pigpen. Every drop of water was used twice.) We both decided, without even speaking to each other, that there had to be a change of crew, a major restoration of the worst problems, and, at best, a probationary period for Pearson.

We insisted on a meeting *tout de suite* with Monsieur Pollet and Pearson. When they arrived the next day, we followed Pollet around, babbling/complaining in French as well as our/my emotional, jet-lagged state would allow. His face grew redder and redder until he arrived at the door to the *porcherie,* where the clogged tunnel could be seen. He turned on his heel, his face in mine, "*Avez-vous fini?*" ("Have you finished?") He then turned, without waiting for an answer, glowering at Pearson, and said "*Plus tard!*" ("I'll deal with you later!") I wasn't at first sure what that meant, but when he turned back to me his demeanor changed back to his congenial self.

"*Ne vous inquietez pas. On va tout refaire. Bernard sera ici demain.*" ("Don't worry, we're going to redo all that. Bernard will be here tomorrow.") His ire was obviously directed at Pearson, who should have been supervising the work and hadn't, or who had simply made bad decisions. Pollet packed up his things and left, handshakes around except with Pearson.

Then, and only then, did I notice the yellow primulas. Everywhere, at the river's edge, in the cracks in the *porcherie* walls, by the footpath: shimmering wild primroses, welcoming us home.

BERNARD PIERRE

April 15, 1994
Dear Linda,

It's been a tough couple of weeks, but we finally resolved our problems with our contractor after a long come-to-Jesus meeting. Hurly, Curly, and Moe were fired, a new crew came on the job, and quickly and willingly redid all the bad stuff, and we have a new hero, Bernard, the stonemason. (Don't confuse him with Bernard, our woodworking neighbor, the other potential contractor, or Bernard, Germain's baker son, or the other two hundred Bernards in Plaisance.)

Bernard the stonemason was sent by Monsieur Pollet, our contractor, to repair both the work and the relationship: he's a master at both. By way of introduction: the work crew arrives each morning after 1 1/2 hours on the road in a large van that carries all their tools and equipment. They unfold their legs, stretch, and walk directly to the cliff face that forms part of the entrance to the driveway. Then, all four or five of them line up and pee against the rock cliff. Although their profiles are visible from both the road and the house, they just turn their heads so they can't see *me*, figuring, I guess, that if they can't see me, I can't see them. Then, after greeting us and accepting a welcome cup of coffee, they work straight through until noon, wash off most of the dust from their hands in a fifty-gallon drum of spring water, yell out "*Bon appétit!*" and haul off to Les Magnolias, where they eat a hearty prix fixe meal paid for by Pollet, or, I suppose, us. They're back at one thirty and continue working until five, when they clean their tools and load back into the van. They wear khaki work pants with lots of pockets, T-shirts, and vests with more pockets. There's no eye or ear protection, helmets, or steel-toed boots, no dust masks, no gloves. The mere suggestion of any of these is greeted with guffaws.

After our meeting with Pollet, we were anxious to see Bernard and crew emerge from the van and line up. There were four of them in their standard-issue clothes; two of them were Claude and Olivier, from last fall's crew, but the other two were strangers, one young, and the other forty-something, shorter than the rest, with a khaki mason's cap. One thin circle of cigarette smoke curled up above his head in the cold morning air. As they, almost in unison, did the unmistakable male hip-roll and zip, turned, and strode toward the house, we could tell Bernard was the one in the mason's cap. He checked every detail, sizing up the house, the steps descending to the storm drain, and us, shivering in the open door. We shook hands with everyone and invited them in for coffee.

We had actually been able to understand Pollet clearly, probably because he was used to dealing with clients with limited French, so he spoke slowly in monosyllables, but the work crew is different. They all speak rapid-fire French with a strange accent, full of slang terms, or argot, none of which is in the dictionary or in use at the Alliance Française. Eventually, Mike and I looked at each other and shrugged, and stopped trying to follow their conversation.

After one cup of coffee, Bernard said something unintelligible, which we assumed meant, "Show me the problems." We started upstairs with the stone basin next to the fireplace. He stared, obviously stunned by the stupidity of the former crew. He sat back on his heels, cocked his head, knocked on the stone, then tapped on the cement. Bernard shook his head, grimaced, lifted his shoulders and said, "*C'est possible, mais pas sûr."* He pointed to a place in the slab that he thought, from the sound of his knocking, might break when he tried to pick out the cement. *"On verra."* We'll see.

The drains in front of the front and terrace doors left him speechless. By the time Pearson showed up and was bumbling along in his tenseless, article-free French, Bernard ignored him completely and through hand gestures and a few words explained what (we thought) he was going to do. He summoned Patrick, his apprentice, and they went to work. Pearson presented his bill and left.

Since then, I confess I find myself watching Bernard and Patrick more often than I should. Partially because they seem to be everywhere at once, partially because they're *bien foutu*, or buffed, in a way that comes from honest physical work, not gyms and steroids, and partially because of the layout of the mill. The mill sits with its feet in the river on one side, and its back up against the cliff wall that forms an upper terrace. There is a narrow passage between the barn and the cliff, but you can't pass with anything larger than a garden rake without going through the house. Wheelbarrow after wheelbarrow of cement bumps down from the bridge, where the cement mixer lives with the fifty-gallon drum of water used to mix the cement and wash hands and faces for lunch. (The sand and cement drop quickly to the bottom of the drum, filtering the spring water to crystal clear!) A thick plank forms a catwalk down the front steps onto a wide strip of plastic in the house, which catches most of the overflow plops, protecting Vigroux's stone floor. At noon, the wheelbarrows full of cement are parked in the living room so the concrete doesn't harden in the sun. No matter where I am in the long lower room of the mill, I can see them coming and going, and no matter how many times they pass, they always turn and smile and I do the same. I sometimes wonder if it's me or them that perpetuates this ritual. I can look, can't I?
—*Hugs, Judy*

April 20, 1994
Dear Linda,

You asked how my French was coming. It's improving every day. We study hard, but trying to communicate with the construction crew, using a peculiar vocabulary not taught at the Alliance Française, is challenging. They speak no English at all and use their own street talk, with lots of colloquial terms that aren't in our dictionary. Most of the time we are clueless.

But I do know that I've learned a lot about communication strategies. There seem to be three different schemes for people who are trying to be understood in a different language. The most desirable is to shorten a phrase to key words and keep searching for a synonym until the other person gets it. Hand gestures and body language are important. The second strategy, less helpful, is to speak *ever so slowly*, repeating the same mysterious word over and over again, wearing down the other person until he or she gives up. The third strategy is to just speak more loudly until it gets through the other person's thick head. Bernard is a shouter, and, given that he's the most difficult to understand, there's a lot of shouting. I can spend fifteen minutes in the dictionary searching for "How many wheelbarrow loads will it take to do the back steps?" only to get a rapid-fire, unintelligible answer, pushed out through the Gauloise hanging from his lips. When I say, "*Comment?*" or "Huh?" he just speaks more loudly, like I'm totally deaf. When I say "*Doucement*" to try to get him to slow down, he throws his cement-covered hands in the air and says the French equivalent of "Oy vey": "*Oh, putain, c'est pas possible,*" or "Damn, she can't be that dumb." That's when I run back to the dictionary. Eventually, we get through to each other, and I never forget the new word.

Claude, who oversaw our stone roof last fall and is back for the carpentry this spring, is equally hard to understand. He speaks with a strong Midi accent, which more closely resembles Italian than my Alliance Française French. And he has no strategy to communicate whatsoever. He just shrugs his shoulders and continues what he's doing, as if to say there's no use in trying. In the absence of any response, I go ask Bernard, having researched the words carefully. Naturally, I can't understand him, and he ends up shouting, nicely, but shouting just the same. Finally, one day he dragged me over to where Claude was working and pointed at him and hollered, "*Lui, bois,*" or "Him, wood," then pointed at himself and said, "*Moi, pierre,*" or "Me, stone." He continued to alternate between the two of them: "*Claude, bois, moi, pierre.*" It finally sank in. I'd been asking him questions about window frames and Claude questions about jointing the stone around those frames, although Claude was the *bois* boss and Bernard the master of inorganic substances. And just as the interface of those two different materials is antithetical, so are Bernard and Claude, two alpha males who are often chest to chest, with pointer fingers high. The rivalry between them is legendary, according to Patrick, Bernard's apprentice and the easiest to understand: he uses key words and keeps searching for a synonym. He also explained the odd, uneven quality of the original workers' stone walls. As it turns out, the three stooges who were doing the stonework would do a careful job in the morning, then go off to lunch, which included all-you-could-drink wine. They would then return and try to build our walls, heads bobbing, eyes half-closed. They were well known for doing the same thing on other jobs, too, according to Patrick.

I've been taking furious notes in my studio journal during this process, because someday I want to make some strange tools out of contradictory materials, such as scissors with stone handles and wooden blades, large and ridiculously out of scale, but with wood and stone together showing the impossibility of the transition. But no other projects for now. Focus. (I can't find a word for that in French.)

—*Hugs, Judy*

P.S. Our stone basin next to the fireplace upstairs has been restored to its original beauty. It took Bernard a whole day of careful chipping to avoid breaking the thin stone. He earned his pastis that day.

THE BREAD OVEN

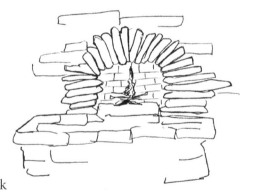

April 22, 1994
Dear Linda,

I have a new toy: *le four à pain*. Every farm and hamlet and usually every mill once had a brick oven, used primarily to bake quantities of bread, meat, and beans. Because it could take hours of waiting for grain to be washed, dried, ground, and sifted, people would bring their dough with them to a mill and cook it during their wait. For safety reasons, these ovens were often a free-standing configuration, but occasionally one was attached to a barn or outbuilding. The structure was sometimes rounded in back to follow the igloo-shaped interior. For farms and mills, the stone building was usually six to twelve feet in diameter, with a slanting roof of stone or slate that started about waist high in the back and ended at about six feet over the arched opening. The chimney was in front of the door to carry out the smoke of the cinders used to heat the interior. The opening usually had a forged metal door to guard the heat after the coals were scraped from the inside into the bucket. Vast quantities of wood, and all the work that that entailed—cutting, chopping, stacking—were required to heat the entire structure, so as soon as traveling to the local *boulangerie* became easier than firing up the oven, it turned into an anachronism—except to old romantics like us.

I was quite disappointed that the mill didn't seem to have one in spite of our searching, and Monsieur Blanc couldn't remember one from his youth, either. Then, one day last fall, in one of his slash-and-burn states, Mike discovered a little lean-to attached to the back of the barn. The roofline was at waist height, but since the whole complex tumbles down a steep cliff, it was impossible to tell what might be in the other part that disappeared into the back of the barn. And since the beams in the barn were so rotten, we couldn't get to that part to see exactly what was on the other side of the wall, which was hidden behind the piles of old chairs that Monsieur Parnat, the local *brocanteur*, had left behind when he hauled off his sacks of chicken feathers.

But when we returned this spring, the crew had repaired the beams and installed a new oak floor so we could get to the far reaches of the barn. We showed Bernard the strange little roof sticking out from behind and asked him if he thought there might be a bread oven there. From the low roof level, he led us along the side, then into the barn, walking through the narrow passage between the building and the cliff, keeping his hand running along the stones at the same level. He entered the barn, still running his hand along the wall. At the far end, he stopped, pointed at a vague outline of a chimney, which we hadn't noticed before, and nodded knowingly. Then we asked him if they could knock a hole in the old wall just to see if there might be a *four à pain* behind there. After careful, Gauloise-sucking consideration, he told Patrick to start "*là.*" "There" happened to be an enormous rock, which I thought threatened to stymie the whole project. When I asked why he didn't pick an easier spot to go in, with much rolling of the eyes he patiently shouted that if he were closing the door of an oven, he would start with the biggest rock he could find and fill in around it, but that if I wanted to risk knocking a hole into the delicate brick formation of the roof of the maybe bread oven, so be it!

I hate it when Bernard is right, which is most of the time, but he was right. After an hour of chiseling, Patrick had created a hole big enough to peek through with a flashlight. We had expected a total disaster, since why else would a miller of flour brick over a bread oven? We shined the light to the back of the space, and there it was, a perfect igloo-shaped brick dome. The salts in the brick had crystallized enough to pearlize and diffuse the light. The only sign of disturbance was one small lacy root of the ivy that had hid the oven roof for sixty years. Perfect shape! *"Rare, rare, rare."* The whole crew nodded and shook their wrists, snapping their fingers in agreement.

The only sign of damage seemed to be the lack of the brick arch that usually frames the oven door. When Patrick opened it a bit farther we could see a neat pile of bricks, obviously carefully stacked, which corresponded to the number required to rebuild the opening. Germain Blanc's sister, who is fourteen years older, told him that when he was about four years old, their father had wanted to connect the grain barn with the then-independent bread-oven building to make a much bigger storage space. Since it would be impossible/dangerous to fire off a bread oven in a barn full of flour dust, he tore down the chimney and built a stone wall over the opening, but not before he had carefully removed and stacked the first layer of bricks inside the oven, in effect saving them for a future generation. Thank you, Monsieur Louis Joseph Blanc. Germain's son, who is a baker, told us it will take us two weeks of a slow fire to dry it out the first time. That's just to let you know that we're not overly romantic about the practicality of a bread oven. But if we were completely practical about anything, we wouldn't be here at all! But *"de temps en temps, pourquoi pas?"* "From time to time, why not?" But first, Bernard will have to rebuild the chimney in front of the oven door.

And the bay leaves. Do you remember last year when I mentioned that workers sometimes put bay leaves in a house as a gesture of goodwill toward the owners? Well, when we arrived, one craggy wall of the house had been carefully stuffed with bay branches. It's a happy house, but full of ghosts, all friendly, all hanging out to see what those Americans will do next.

—*Big hugs, Judy*

THE CHAIRS AND OTHER NEIGHBORS

April 26, 1994

Dear Linda,

When we first bought the mill, Monsieur Parnat, who had been storing used furniture and bags of chicken feathers to be made into mattresses in the barn, had come to remove his things, all except The Chairs. He told us that he had left them since they were too rotten to be of value and that we could use them for kindling in the fireplace if we liked. For some time, the chairs served as a French lesson. In trying to tell French friends why they were there, it was necessary to say "If they had had any value, Monsieur Parnat would have taken them with him." Past-pluperfect conditional?

But one day, inspired by my desire to install our first conceptual art piece (and anxious to claim his studio space), Mike dragged the chairs from the now-safe barn, where the catwalks that went from beam to beam had been replaced with a new oak floor. We lined them up, all that could stand, in a row one behind the other in a gentle curve following the lines of our beautiful old bridge. Fifty-four of them. They took the place of one of the side walls on the bridge, which was removed when our driveway was part of the main road. It seems modern tractors couldn't pass its narrow channel. We eventually tried turning the chairs so they formed a theater row facing the river, but it wasn't the same. Somehow the emotion wasn't there, the sad, silent vigil, the dignity. In the sun, they were full of anticipation, and in the rain and clouds they paid their respects in spite of the weather. I called the installation *Les fantômes du Moulin,* or *Ghosts of the Mill,* but mostly they were known as The Chairs.

I only found out this week about the young lad that was killed in 1948 on his bike at the spot where the last chair rested. The narrow little bridge, now on our property, had been the commune's main road until five years ago. It seems a big tractor forced him off the side onto the rocks below. Usually, there is a cross, a monument of some kind for those struck down on the road. But just after the war, there wasn't enough money for this boy. Maybe that's why this silent memorial touched everyone so much.

We left the chairs there for over a month, watching the neighbors slow and point as they came around the curve on the new road, which overlooks the old bridge. We took dozens of pictures, and when we had them developed in Albi, thirty miles away, the young man at the photo shop said, "Those are the chairs near Coupiac, right?" (Coupiac is our other little village.) We're famous. We thought everyone would think we were just crazy Americans, and while there are those who do, most are genuinely moved by the chairs, without understanding why. We've watched as fishermen, in their normal trespassing mode, push through them, loaded with gear, only to gently re-form them, sometimes righting one that the wind had blown over. Our workmen often needed the space and moved a few aside for a while, but they were always put back where they had been, sometimes tastefully adjusted a bit to get the spacing just so. The chairs also moved themselves. Those with legs too crumbled to stand for long would just lean back and rest on a stronger friend for a while. I sometimes left them that way, and sometimes propped them up with a piece of *lauze* left over from the roof.

One day, it was time to move them. Don't ask me how, but I knew they were tired. They had said what they had to say to everyone who would listen. They could have picked a better day, since it was hot and I was sick with a guest's cold. But I couldn't have waited another day even if they had let me. I put on my rubber boots and began moving them up the river path overlooking the waterfall. There was no thought of smashing them for a fire: the violence of that act was unthinkable. I decided that while there might be other sites for them later, for now they would be our silent guests looking across the little river into our backyard. I got so I could carry three at a time, slogging through knee-deep mud on the path that leads to the waterfall on the other side of the river, my boots sucked off every time just above the last big rock. Only thirty-nine chairs survived the transport: thirteen trips in all. The others either came unglued after sitting all summer in the sun or collapsed from powder-post beetles chewing on their feet. I decided one had to be kept behind to be thrown out since its metal springs and upholstery tacks would be inappropriate if it should tumble into the river. One of the workmen followed me down the path, helping me carry the last few. *"Elles sont vos amies, n'est-ce pas?"* It was true. They had, in fact, become my friends.

And there they sit as I write. I can see them from the attic window, in the rain, their feet stuck in the mud formed by the dozens of little springs that run down the hill behind them, wildflowers climbing up into their laps. There are worse things that can happen to an old chair.

—*Love to Gary, Judy*

April 26, 1994
JOURNAL ENTRY

Over the weekend we went to Aix-en-Provence for a meeting of the national association of Des Amis des Moulins, or mill geeks. The trip was suggested to us by Jean-Pierre Azéma, the president of Des Amis des Moulins de l'Aveyron, who introduced us to the idea that we might be able to make the millstone turn again. The meeting was in a conference room, with long rows of tables and an official-looking head table, where Monsieur le Président was surrounded by the guest speakers, professors of sociology and archeology. After several hours of business-meeting-like agendas with no conclusions that I could make out, and no potty breaks, I was squirming in my seat like a six-year-old, shoulders dropped, thighs squeezing my clenched fists, glancing at the sixty or so Frenchmen and women in the audience.

"Do they ever pee?" I whispered to Mike. The answer is hardly ever. Nor do they squirm or look around or doodle or daydream. (Even French kids, little kids, in restaurants don't leave their seats, they don't cry or whine, they sit and eat course after course of wonderful food. No hotdogs, macaroni and cheese, or corn dogs, but salads, fish, stews, and spinach.)

But even I, when the lectures finally started, sat up straight and scribbled furiously in my journal, looking up from time to time, hoping to fool everyone into thinking I actually understood what was going on. My journal notes are more doodles than writings.

Un moulin is pronounced with the lips pushed forward and with the *moo* and the *lan* sounds echoing in the channels of one's head. *Mool* is "to grind" and *an* means "place" in patois, the old dialect closer to Latin than French. *Meule* comes from the same roots, meaning a millstone, the round, fat, heavy, rough, gritty gray ultimate white elephant one can't throw away. *Meunier*: a miller, the man who manages a *moulin*. *Grain*, finally a word I know, inedible without *meules* and *moulins*. Mills transform grain to food, facilitating life, like art. Like art, we cannot live without them.

In the old days, when the *meules* still turned, everyone had to come to see the art, and they brought their animals and wine for a brief respite to watch the miller work, a chance to be a spectator not a worker. (During the occupation in WWII, millers weren't allowed to grind grain for anyone but the German army. So the farmers came at night, Monsieur Blanc (who finally asked us to call him Germain) told us, sacks on their backs, across the waterfall, and Louis Blanc ground their grain, transforming the tiny seeds into digestible flour. How did he hide the noise—the song of the mill—from the Germans?)

Why are we here? We don't belong, we barely speak the language, we don't understand their problems, we haven't paid the price. We're just dilettantes, superficial, playing at being adventurers. But we share a common root, so we must have something to give. Maybe we can save La Pilande Basse.

Back at the conference, the sociology professor was explaining what the everyday life of a *meunier* and his family was like before steel-rolled mills took their place in the early nineteenth century. (Our mill, however, functioned as a working flour mill up to 1964, when Louis Blanc died. It was one of few stone-grinding mills left, barely profitable, supported by the farmers for whom he'd ground grain during the war.) Before then, every village had at least one, sometimes several mills. Since France has over thirty-six thousand villages, there had been at least that many water-powered mills, some grinding flour, others sawing wood, stamping metal, spinning thread, stamping rags to make paper, and turning small stones for sharpening knives. When electric motors, steam engines, and steel rollers became economical, the mills disappeared, some falling into ruin, some making electricity, others converted to homes or factories, depending on their size.

Since flour doesn't keep too long, the oils in the bran eventually becoming rancid, and wheat or rye as grain is relatively easy to transport and filter out the pests, peasants would bring sacks of grain every six weeks or so to their miller, who would weigh it, clean it, and grind it. Then the miller would pass it through a large flour sifter to remove as much bran as possible. It would be bagged and reweighed for transport. The miller was paid a percentage of the weight of the grain in grain itself or in *troc*: an equivalent amount in animals, fabric, salt, etc. Millers weren't always trusted to be honest with either the scales or romantic advances, so they were watched closely by their clients. They were also highly regulated, at one time not being allowed to have a bread oven or sell flour, lest they monopolize the staff of life.

The professor, who was interested in publishing a serious sociological review of mills, then handed out a series of questions that the audience was to either fill in there, if they were descended from a milling family, or complete with any elderly neighbors who might have memories of their local *moulin* and/or *meunier*. Someday, maybe, our French will be good enough to interview Germain.

There were several site visits, one of which was to the Moulins de Barbegal, one of the oldest known mill sites in France. Constructed by the Romans in the first century A.D., the mills were activated by water from the aqueducts, which turned one set of millstones, and as the water continued downhill it would tumble onto another wheel and stone, and another, until sixteen sets of stones were fully activated by one fall of the water. But as we stumbled through the ruin, out in the middle of a field, far from any village, only the bases of the millstones could partially be seen. Well, at least they could be seen by the archeologist who was leading the tour. As the group scrambled among the rocks, I found myself occupied by a charming man, Monsieur Rolland, who was curious about our presence as the only non-French in the group.

"Pouvez-vous tout comprendre?" He was hoping we couldn't understand everything, as he wanted to practice his rusty English. He's a recent widower and a physics professor in Paris. I explained, as best I could, our mill and asked him if he owned one. He smiled and shook his head, obviously wishing he did. When I asked him why he was a member of Des Amis des Moulins, he poetically extolled the virtues of mills, their beauty, the engineering of falling water and blowing wind. He was ecstatic to be there, standing at the site of perhaps the first true factory in the world.

We then went off to the famous windmill of Alphonse Daudet in Fontvieille, the source of his most famous work, a book of short stories called *Lettres de mon moulin (Letters from My Windmill)*. Daudet describes the sound of the windmill when the mistral, a ferocious wind that blows down the Rhône Valley, was blowing:

> I wasn't able to sleep last night. The mistral was angry and the howling from
> its booming voice kept me awake 'til morning. The entire windmill cracked,
> the torn sails swaying in the north wind whistled like the rigging of a ship.
> The tiles were torn from the roof leaving it in ruins. From far afield the
> thickly planted pines, which cover the hills, thrashed and rustled in the dark.
> I could have believed I was on the high seas.

The lecturer explained the mechanisms of the windmill, basically the same as those of a water mill except that instead of a turbine being turned by the force of the passing water and thus turning the millstones from below, the sails of a windmill, stretched over wooden frames, catch the wind and activate, through a series of gears, a set of millstones below. The entire capped roof of a windmill rotates according to the direction of the wind. Climbing the rigging, setting the sails, taking them down in storms—all were dangerous activities. A water mill has its own challenges, building and repairing dams and the inevitable floods. But both kinds of millers had stones to dress and grain to clean, grind, sift, and bag. They both had occupational hazards related to the white dust in their lungs and eyes.

We left the conference, clutching our questionnaire for Germain and pages of addresses from the attendees, with lots of good intentions to follow up on both. We decided to stop in Aix-en-Provence for a picnic lunch and go off to Saint-Victoire, the mountain that is the subject of many of Cézanne's paintings. We parked in front of a *boulangerie*, jumped out of the car, bought a baguette, and came out to find that the lock had been punched in on our rental car, the interior was in total disarray, and no one was in sight. We'd been warned about leaving anything of value, so nothing was taken, but the incident took the glow off our experience and we decided to get on the other side of the Rhône River *tout de suite*. We were anxious to get back to La Pilande Basse with our new appreciation for its historical value.

May 1, 1994
Dear Linda,

Happy Mom's birthday. I always get weepy on May Day. Here in rural France, people bring one another a small pot of lilies of the valley to celebrate/commemorate the day. My French is good enough to ask why, but it isn't quite good enough to understand the answer. I plant them anyway.

You asked how we decided to bring American artists over to the mill and work with them so you could explain it to your friends who are confused by our seemingly sudden plan. I wish there was a one-two-three logic to that decision, but it happened more organically than rationally. Let me explain. While we were back in California these past two winters, Mike was continuing work on his master's degree at the San Francisco Art Institute and I was taking some prerequisite undergraduate classes to be able to do the same. Last winter, I asked him how much it was going to cost. When he told me, I remarked that it would be cheaper to bring my professors over here, give them their own house and a car for a month or so, and watch them work. I'd learn much more doing that than in the twenty minutes or so one has with a professor in the course of a regular class. I said it half-jokingly, but the more we talked the more reasonable, no, exciting it sounded. I don't need another degree, just working experience.

But even a few months ago, our plan was somewhere in the future, when we could afford to redo the little house. But because the roof caved in, we had to decide right away what to do. We've been working all month on getting bids to get the work done before next summer. I hope to invite Dan Pillers as our first artist-in-residence, assuming we can get the little house together by then. He's been my studio mate since the first class I took at the Art Institute, a sweet man unfortunately starting to become quite ill with AIDS. I think we need to get him over here before it's too late. We'll start there and see how it feels.

You also asked about Monsieur Parnat and what a *brocanteur* is and why I think you don't need to meet him. *Brocanteurs*, people who collect junk and resell it elsewhere, sometimes to antiques dealers, are often accused of stealing furniture or linens from abandoned houses and taking advantage of widows in mourning by offering low prices for priceless objects. Germain, who watched Monsieur Parnat take care, or rather not take care, of the mill for the past thirty years, told us he thought many millwork pieces were missing and that he was positive Parnat had stolen them. Apparently, he even accused him of this at a village fête last winter.

Last week, we were in the mill with Germain, at the end near the river with the window open, the sounds of the water climbing up, over and around, and deafening us to all else, when a *"Coucou,"* or "Anybody home?" echoed down the long room. At the door were Monsieur Parnat and the mayor of Plaisance, Monsieur Tournier, whom we had not yet met. I was surprised that Monsieur Parnat had entered a no-exit room with Germain in it, but then I realized he wouldn't have been able to see our features well, backlit as we were by the brightness of the window. And when the *messieurs* were close enough to see that Germain was there, it was too late. Clueless to the dynamics, the mayor strode over and held out his hand. We completed the niceties, thinking surely Germain wouldn't do anything rash with the mayor as witness. Without so much as a hello to Monsieur Tournier, Germain strode angrily over to Monsieur Parnat, his shorter round belly under Parnat's rounder but higher one, shouting his accusations of theft, specifically, the millrace doors, *les vannes*. Mortified that blows might follow, the mayor separated the two and Germain stomped off, a dismissive hand in the air, "*Bof, bof, bof.*" Embarrassed, all four of us re-exchanged greetings, and Mike took the mayor on a short tour of the mill.

The next day, Monsieur Parnat came over and presented us with what he called a "gift," a bronze *vanne*, which, incidentally, fit perfectly into the opening of the sluice gate, obviously its original home, in the *chambre d'eau* where the turbine will be installed. Hmmm . . .

—*Hugs, Judy*

May 15, 1994
Dear Linda,

You were so sweet on the phone last week. I'm glad you're enjoying our stories. We have been working such long hours I hardly have time to write. I fall exhausted into bed every night, and even my journal's pages yawn at me, empty. I have a lot to tell you, mostly about neighbors we've started to meet. As I wrote, we will be bringing American artists over to work with us, but it looks like we might have a local social life as well if we can get our French to another level, above grunts and hand signals to accompany our limited vocabulary and grammar. So far, having an English speaker around is still important. Francis told us about someone named Suzie, an American woman who's married to a Polish man who lives up above Plaisance and teaches English to adults in Albi. I called her to introduce myself and ask if she would help us with our French. She's agreed to come twice a week for a while, which we hope will give us more confidence. In our first session, it became clear that we would also be good friends. She's about my age, as is François, her "Polish" husband, who was born in France, his parents having been recruited to work the mines after World War I, but to the French he's still not really French. He's a retired miner she met while he was taking an English class from her a few years ago. They recently got married, and he hasn't spoken a word of English since. She's been here for over twenty years, first living in Aix-en-Provence, but moved to the Aveyron when she was divorced from her first husband. François came by the mill during our second session, curious, I suppose, to meet us. It turns out that in his retirement he has turned into a serious mushroom hunter, as is Mike, and they arranged an early-morning hike to look for *cèpes*, which are the same as porcini. The hunt wasn't successful, but the bonding was.

Last week we went to Brigitte and Bernard Guerin's house for dinner. He's the woodworking Bernard (Bernard *bois*) who bid on some of the work for our mill, but understood why we needed someone who spoke English to coordinate the workers and translate for us. They live just downstream from us in a hamlet called Le Mousse Bas. Brigitte, one of the most beautiful women I've ever seen, is a visiting nurse, traveling from farm to farm, giving injections, changing dressings, and making lots of men's hearts skip beats, I'm sure. Bernard speaks some English and Brigitte seems to understand a bit as well. He has a sister, Claire, who teaches English in a high school in Millau, and she was there with the father of her two young children, Mick, a Scot who is a photographer and vociferously anti-American. "The food is terrible, it's dangerous to walk down the street. Everyone is fat." He says he lived in Berkeley, making it sound like he went to school there, but seemed to back down when we pushed with questions. He and Claire did live for a year on the East Coast while she taught school. They also included their neighbor, Max, who is a bachelor in his late forties, and one of the original owners of one of the houses in their hamlet. Max was very shy, spoke a little English, but seemed better informed about politics and life in America than the others and countered Mick's rantings better than we could have, certainly in French.

They asked us questions about our family, and when we talked about our adult children, who are starting to get married, since it will soon be time for them to start families, they all seemed shocked. Neither couple is married, and both have two children each. Mick went off on a rant about how puritanical and unsophisticated Americans are that bordered on being truly offensive. Rather than push any more of his buttons, I changed the subject to the food on the table and how wonderful it was. Brigitte served a crab, grapefruit, and avocado salad, while Bernard sautéed duck breasts and roasted some potatoes, followed by the inevitable cheese course. The Bourgogne wine stood up well against all that yummy fat. And I, who never bake anything, brought a pie that left them speechless. I had tried to think of something uniquely American, and then I found a recipe in my tattered *Joy of Cooking* for bourbon pecan pie. An American visitor had brought me five pounds of pecans from Costco when she visited in April, knowing pecans can't be found in Europe, and I thought they would last at least five years. Brigitte insisted on the recipe and a supply of the nuts.

The Guerins have been very generous in introducing us to their extended group of friends, as have Suzie and François. At Francis's suggestion, we went to meet a ceramic artist, Jean-Michel Prêt, who has a splendid studio in the middle of the woods above Coupiac. (If someone visits his studio and he's not there, they can take an object and leave the money in a little chest. He says he's never had anyone cheat.) He's my age, is extraordinarily sensitive, and is a dead ringer for Willie Nelson, ponytail and all. His young children giggled and ran through his legs as he talked, and we're to meet Eveline, their mother, as soon as she returns from her parents' house in Montpellier.

Suzie is going to introduce us to some friends, Didier and Clémence Poli, who went from selling insurance in Paris to buying an entire hamlet, completely in ruins, and are moving in this fall to start work on it. Apparently, Didier has a very large jazz collection, for which Mike has an equal passion, Clémence loves to cook, and they speak some English. Should be interesting. Suzie also told us that Max, the Guerins' neighbor, drives a truck making deliveries all over France for the local charcuterie, Bories, in Plaisance. He listens to France Culture, the equivalent of our National Public Radio, probably the best-quality, most balanced programming available in France, on a variety of subjects. That's why he's so knowledgeable. I'll keep you informed as I learn more. *Au lit.* My bed is calling.

—Love, Judy

June 1, 1994
Dear Linda,

You seem to enjoy the details on our increasing cast of characters, so I have to introduce you to Christelle, but I have to start with Maran, her husband, who was recommended by Francis as someone who could help us battle the overgrown shrubs, ivy, blackberries, and stinging nettles that covered everything when we first arrived and threaten us still. (While Mike had cleared the main paths, we still couldn't go up the terraced land or even get to the waterfall because of the impenetrable jungle that flourishes thanks to the combination of sun and falling water.) We had met Maran at Les Magnolias when we were staying there last fall, because he was a *pensionnaire* there. That is someone, living alone, who contracts with a restaurant for lunch and/or dinner. In fact, Maran has eaten there, lunch and dinner, for twenty-eight years, retiring to his tiny apartment only to sleep. He always sits at the same table, at the same time (8 p.m. sharp), always with a two- or three-day growth of beard, but not the fashionable kind.

Since we shared the dining room for over a month, we always acknowledged each other, often shook hands, and spoke banalities. He wasn't much taller when he stood up, as he is just over five feet tall, built like a oak stump, and balding, with the one-side-grown-long-and-slicked-over-the-other-side comb-over, most of his teeth, and a sweet disposition. It was impossible for us to understand him since he spoke with such a thick, rapid-fire patois accent. (Even Francis said he has trouble understanding him sometimes.) We just nodded and agreed with everything he said. We knew he worked days at the local charcuterie and did brush and tree cutting after work until dark and/or dinner at Les Magnolias.

In spite of the language barrier, we were pleased to have him come this spring, every Sunday, to help us clear three of the upper terraces and the path to the waterfall on the other side of the river. Each time, he cut a forked branch of a tree to hold the brambles and nettles away from himself while he whacked at their roots with a large scythe. He would then pitch the tangles into a big pile and burn them, tossing that week's forked branch on top. After accomplishing more in one day than we thought he could have done in two weeks, he would tap on the door, grinning broadly, covered from head to toe in bits of leaves, dirt, and sweat, knowing a healthy dose of pastis would soon be poured by Mike's heavy hand. At the end of April, after he gladly slugged back two pastis and started up the path dragging his chainsaw behind him (ours was too wimpy for him), I thought he mumbled something about not being able to come the next week because he was getting married.

When I asked Francis if my French had completely come undone, he said, no, Maran had decided at fifty-five years of age that he wanted a wife, and since there weren't a lot of Frenchwomen willing to marry a tiny, not-all-that-tidy fifty-five-year-old French peasant, he had ordered up a mail-order bride from Madagascar. Francis explained that this is not that unusual in rural France, where there aren't many women left willing to put up with the life of a *paysane* in a countryside where the good still die young. But in Madagascar, a large, desperately poor island off the east coast of Africa, everyone dies young, and because of the misery, especially for a woman, some elect to come to France and marry someone, never having met him, and try to earn money to send back home to their families.

Madagascar was formerly a French protectorate, so everyone learns French in school, and while they don't have French passports, people are given deferential treatment for visas. Francis said there is a whole network of women from Madagascar in the Aveyron. These arrangements are usually made by the mayor of the village, who must promise to assure the safety and welfare of the woman involved. The mayor even goes to Paris to marry the new couple, so there can be no hint of scandal when the bride returns to her new home.

I first met Christelle the day after she arrived in Plaisance at the *mairie*, or town hall, where we had both gone to get our *carte de séjour* so we can legally live in France for more than three months at a time. Since I had never seen any other black person in Plaisance, I was pretty sure that the tall, striking woman in the room was the new bride of Maran. I introduced myself and told her she was welcome to come and see us at La Pilande Basse whenever she liked.

That evening, they both arrived, and Maran was beaming, introducing his bride in much the same way one might show off a new toy. Actually, he was cute, obviously more than just a little smitten with this lovely lady, unconsciously rubbing her lower arm with his finger and saying shyly, "I think she may kind of like me." She, on the other hand, was obviously in shock. Her eyes were as big as saucers, and she avoided contact with Maran for more than an instant. She sat perched on the chair, her knees together and ankles apart, twisting her feet and hands nervously.

Madagascans speak French with a lilting melodic accent, but she said little, and Maran's thick patois is still very difficult to understand, so after an agonizing hour, they pushed away from the table. I couldn't resist asking Maran if he had any time to help us some more. With a wordless French gesture, lips pursed, head tilted, and eyes upward with the slightest nod, he told me "What, you think I'm crazy enough to leave this sweet new wife all alone to come and work for you?" But she jumped at the chance. "I could help you. I can learn anything!" So somehow, hand signals and shy glances later, we arranged to have her come and help me around the mill, but only when she was settled.

She came the next day. The first thing I asked her was to help me clean up the piles of sand and dust that Bernard, Claude, and their crews had dragged through the house the week before. I got out the shop-vac and took off to get more cleaning supplies for us both. When I came back a few minutes later, she was still standing there looking at the R2-D2-sized vacuum cleaner in amazement. I first thought she might not have ever seen a vacuum that big, so I started to show her the hoses and how the plug was stored beneath. But when the frown didn't move, I realized she had never seen *any* vacuum cleaner before. When I plugged it in to demonstrate and started to go after the piles, she jumped and grabbed the broom. "*Plus efficace*," she said. And in her hands, it *was* more efficient. After she had swept everything, she washed down the stone floor with bucket after bucket until the water ran clear. She came every day that week, and even agreed to tackle the vacuum to get into the cracks in the walls, but she still jumped every time it whined into action.

As for the *carte de séjour*, I can see this will be an annual ritual. The French are master bureaucrats, and they fill out four forms for everything, which must each be stamped with some official-looking seal. For us, we have to have everything translated by an official translator, with their seal in blue, and all initialized with the date. When we called to introduce ourselves to our officially designated translator, Madame Gibelin, she seemed delighted and curious to meet us, insisting we shouldn't worry about paying her, she'd send us a bill later. Why she was so sweet and trusting? Then I realized that for the next ten years she will be translating the same marriage license, two birth certificates, letter from our accountant on our financial solidity, and our medical insurance policy, and charging us about $200 each time. We're a guaranteed couple of grand for her, with practically no work but stamping and signing. Sitting in the office of the mayor's secretary, I shuffled all the official papers we'd been instructed to bring: in addition to the above, a police report, an electrical bill, our closing documents on the mill, an official eighty-dollar stamp, four photos each, and copies of our passports. The mayor's secretary has worked there for years and always will, since he has one of the coveted *fonctionaire* positions: a highly sought-after post, similar to one in our civil service, but with more job guarantees. But he's very high energy, helpful, and confused by our French. (He belongs to the wrinkled-brow-and-look-confused school of language differences. When I tried to speak in my best French, he leaned forward, his eyes started to squint, his eyebrows crunched, and it was clear he didn't understand a word I said, and since he speaks no English and fumbling through isn't an option, I now bring a dictionary to our meetings.)

We got to the very end of compiling the dossier, which he was to send off to Rodez to the Office of Immigration, when he saw that my last name on my birth certificate didn't agree with our marriage license. (Tracking through our two divorces seemed insurmountable.) He insisted that we had to have someone reissue the marriage license. When we pleaded with him, telling him there was no way anyone would do that, he reached in his desk drawer and pulled out a bottle of Snowpaque, their version of liquid paper. He held it up and said in French, "Do you know this stuff?" He then walked out of the room, shaking his head.

"Oh, oh. Of course. Who cares?" I mumbled as I changed the marriage license to Ketels, blowing hard to dry it completely before he returned. Because the French are such bureaucrats, they have developed a special disregard for bureaucracy and talk openly about *système D,* their method to *se démerder* ("get oneself out of the shit"). My first lesson.

—*Hugs, Judy*

June 15, 1994
Dear Linda,

I learned a big lesson yesterday: the French, or at least Marthe, hate spices, almost all spices unless they're salt, pepper, or herbes de Provence. Cinnamon is acceptable in desserts, but be careful. I learned this lesson because I had been so eager to invite Marthe and Germain to the mill for dinner that I didn't take the time to ask if there were things they didn't like. I wanted to prepare something new and adventurous, since that's what *I* like. They were expecting *souper,* the simple evening farmhouse meal, which is usually just soup, not the multiple-course meal at noon, so I fixed chili, thinking it would be different for them. I was careful to not make it too hot, and it tasted delicious to me, and I thought I was brilliant.

They arrived, Marthe with a sweater in hand and a scarf around her neck against drafts, even on a hot June night, and Germain in his summer beret and sandals, loaded with lettuces and a big bunch of asparagus from their garden. When I announced we'd be having Mexican food, he was thrilled and asked lots of questions, but Marthe held back, wrapping her sweater around her, as if to ward off evil foreign invaders.

The first course, a salad with corn bread, went quite well, probably since it wasn't too strange, but the chili? Marthe took one bite and all but spat it back in the bowl. Too spicy for her. My homemade tortillas were a major disaster, since I hadn't thought of a backup plan of regular ole bread, even for the cheese course. Fortunately, cheese I had. Lots of it, from the Saturday market. My German pancake was eaten, but I shouldn't have said it was German, or it might have been enjoyed.

Live, learn. Live, learn.

—*Hugs, Judy*

July 21, 1994
Dear Linda,

Une femme de ménage, a housekeeper. That's what I've become after my stellar career as a biotech guru. I do love it here, but can we talk frankly about dust? Someone wrote a wonderful book called *French Dirt* about gardening in France. Well, I'm going to write a book called *French Dust* about housekeeping in France. If you take an old stone house that is used to having a river run through one end and springs dripping down the bare rock on the other, then you put in drains and false walls and dry it out with a new, powerful furnace, what do you think happens to the mortar that is mostly mud? Bingo, dust. And if you take the natural little tunnels formed in three-foot rock walls made from irregular stones and blow a cold north wind through them, what do you get? A duststorm. I could see small clouds of it coming off the rocks every time we had a little breeze. I used to cluck my tongue when I saw someone putting stucco over beautiful old stones. There's a reason God made stucco (called *crepi* in French). He hadn't yet invented the Dustbuster.

Fortunately, we have since found a way around plastering over the old walls by filling the larger holes, then applying a magic product, a breathable, transparent coating that Thierry Vigroux will spray on after we've blocked most of the holes. Most French people plaster over everything, which leaves a sanitary but sterile-looking surface that changes the character of the building, and overly even jointing can make a lovely old wall look mechanical and lifeless in its regularity, so we wanted to be sure the crew didn't overdo. So Bernard *pierre* told us to put a strip of newspaper in the small crevices we wanted filled. We noticed one stormy night that we could actually feel the wind coming through the walls with our hands, but that our cheeks were more sensitive. So we went over every square inch of the walls, putting our noses close to the stones and inserting a small strip of newspaper in the significant cracks, Mike on top, me near the floor, sniffing and stuffing, so Bernard could fill them.

We didn't have enough vocabulary to explain the fuzzy wall to the mayor of La Bastide Solages, the tiny village on a cliff overlooking the Tarn River, when he stopped by to invite us, in person, to a village fête to taste the "succulent paella cooked over a wood fire." He is a sweet man, curious about what we're doing, especially with hundreds of white strips of paper sticking out of the walls. His curiosity is probably the real reason he stopped by in person. After much nodding and handshaking, we struggled to understand what he was saying, but he has such a severe speech impediment, coupled with our language impediment, that it was impossible to understand him. But more importantly, he suffers from Ekbom's syndrome, a neurological condition that causes uncontrollable movement of one's limbs, usually a leg. It was sometimes called "jimmy leg" by old-time comedians before that became politically incorrect. Monsieur Bel, while seated at the table, sipping his pastis, tried in vain to control his right leg, which was hopping violently, his foot tapping the floor loudly, by pushing on his knee until the leg slowed down and stopped for a few minutes. It wasn't funny, he wasn't laughing, but he didn't seem too embarrassed either. We felt like he'd brought along an alien over whom he had no control, which made it hard to concentrate on what he was saying, none of which we could understand anyway. Fortunately, he left a yellow flyer with all the important information on the fête.

By the way, I'm not denigrating *les femmes de ménage*, either. I'm not sure what I'd do without Christelle constantly sweeping up after Bernard and his crew. We also have a woman named Natalie come in once a week to help with the laundry and teach me how to take care of my Godin stove. She loves to wax and polish, and Christelle loves to sweep and iron. I'm completely spoiled, except for digging out muddy tunnels, painting bathrooms and fences, and stripping wallpaper. We've been working overtime to receive our first real guests, Charles and Sandra Hobson, who will be staying in our *grenier* turned guest suite. Charles is a book artist who has been very helpful in Mike's change of career, and we hope he will come here as an artist-in-residence some day. Sandra is a mystical presence, sensitive and knowledgeable about otherworldly things. She will be able to see and feel our friendly ghosts, but not until she has a bed!

(We finally received our container from Mr. Schwartz, and I've been unpacking the essentials to outfit our new rooms.)

Since we've been here we've had only one near disaster: Mike tried to kill himself, or the ladder sliding out from underneath him in the attic did. He fell about ten feet on his head and back. I saw him hit and was positive his brains would be seeping out over the floor. He was unconscious, eyes rolled back, hands jerking spastically. He, too, had been working in the attic getting ready for our friends and was completely exhausted. I started into the room, wrapped in a towel after my evening shower, when I saw the ladder slip. I couldn't find my glasses to find an emergency number, but remembered Germain and Marthe's. *"Mike est tombé, il est blessé tellement qu'il ne bouge pas."* ("Mike fell, and he's not moving.") Germain called Dr. Vianez, then he and his neighbor Monsieur Sureau jumped in the car.

Bottom line: he's fine. But he was out for twenty minutes, couldn't move for two days, and will be badly bruised in all my favorite places for weeks. We were amazed at the quality of medical care he received. A physician arrived within five minutes of the phone call, crash boxes under both arms, ready for anything (probably hoping for something exciting, since he generally takes care of the people in the old folks' home in Trébas-les-Bains). One one-hour house visit, three prescriptions, and another one-hour complete physical later, we were out eighty dollars. The doctor was embarrassed because we would have to pay him "so much" and then have to wait to be reimbursed by our insurance company. A similar incident in the States? How much?

More next week.

—*Love, Judy*

RÉQUISTA AND CHER

July 30, 1994
Dear Linda,

We are continually struck by the contrasts in our life here. Last week for example, at the recommendation of Germain and Marthe, who have all but adopted us, Mike and I went to a monthly farmers' market. Not a market where farmers bring their goods to sell to city folk, but a market where farmers go to buy their chicks, their ducklings, seedlings, tractor chains and odd bits of mysterious hardware, their rations of sweets and breads, and also clothes, shoes, girdles, jam pots, and rubber boots. They also sell their live rams, pigs, and cattle there.

We climbed out of our beautiful, rocky valley to the high mesa, to the village of Réquista. Now, Réquista has not one single redeeming feature as far as we can tell. No château, no cathedral, no *bastide* fortifications. The old stones have long since been covered with rough stucco against the harsh wind that blows on the uplands, and modern (read *ugly*) villas surround the village and its huge metal barn that serves as the regional animal market. The cobblestones are being replaced with modern brick and asphalt, neon signs are everywhere, and the town hall has modern toilets with slippery, shiny pink tile.

After an hour of wandering through the market tents, looking at stall after stall of polyester aprons, orthopedic shoes, and bric-a-brac galore, we decided we had had enough. The place seemed deserted except for the traveling merchants, and nothing was particularly interesting in spite of our neighbors' insistence that we would definitely enjoy the experience. As we turned toward our car, we detected a strange buzzing noise that grew louder as we approached a newish cement-block building with the regulation corrugated metal roof, its rolling doors wide open. We poked our noses around the corner and were slapped in the face with the smells, sounds, and sights of another century.

The people we had thought would be strolling the streets going through the merchants' stalls were all there behind that wall. The men were dressed in French *bleus* and wearing black berets, the women in dark dresses, with bandanas tied tight beneath their chins for protection against the wind. They stood, legs spread, backs bent from years of hard work. They were cheek to jowl, waving their arthritic fingers, negotiating the price of the ducks, guinea hens, chicks, and rabbits that were stacked to the high ceiling in handmade crates. Wings and paws flailing, the unlucky ones were being hauled kicking and screaming into strangers' cages. There were hundreds of people, kissing the air next to the cheeks of their neighbors, nodding and bobbing, cocking their heads to the side, eyes raised, shoulders shrugged, palms up, cheeks full, bottom lip pushing the upper to the nose, ready to *bof bof bof, pfuff* in that classic French expulsion of *je ne sais quoi*. The debate was in patois, which is still spoken by most older people in the south of

France as their first language. They all seemed to be the same age: old. The young have disappeared, along with farming as a lifestyle, leaving the last generation to kill the one remaining chicken. You feel as though they are all going to die at once, and only the stuccoed-over village will remain, its neon flashing.

We walked slowly through the crowded building, fully exposed to "the French stare": a look that doesn't pass judgment and doesn't welcome or reject, but is just curiosity in its purest form. It asks who we are, and what in the world are we doing there? That look comes from years of lifting the head when a cart, now a tractor, passes by, usually pulled or being ridden by a neighbor, sometimes a relative. The look is ready to change into a smile or a frown, depending on the occasion. But with strangers, neither happens. And strangers we were. I didn't exactly rummage in the closet looking for the perfect outfit for a day at the animal market, and my jeans, cleanest dirty shirt, and jaunty little sun hat were decidedly out of place. In spite of dressing down, my cityness was stuck to me like my sweaty blouse. Mike's two-meter height is always good for a look, so the two of us were quite a show. We finally decided to relax and enjoy watching each other being watched. As we passed, the din would fall silent in our immediate vicinity, then return to normal after the obligatory turning of the heads for the stare.

We watched as a particularly solid old lady strode toward the door in front of us with four ducks, two held by the feet in each hand, wings flapping. What was she going to do with them? Eat them, raise them for sale, breed them? I wouldn't have had the slightest idea how to proceed, in any event. I suddenly felt terribly alien in their world. A real city slicker. I wanted to apologize and assure them that I hadn't come there to mock them or feel superior, I was just curious. And I would be leaving now.

As we drove down to the mill from the high plateau we kept making references to life as we know it in California and life as we are discovering it in rural France. I reminded Mike that Cher was supposed to call us any day now, and we chuckled just imagining her at the *Foire de Réquista*.

Cher? Réquista? Let me explain: Shortly after we arrived home in San Francisco last December, still questioning our presence in that other world, a friend of mine who lives in Beverly Hills and is married to "the" plastic surgeon of the stars called to gossip. It seems that Harry Belafonte's daughter is getting married in her garden, and so on and so forth. And, oh, by the way, Cher is going to call me because she is interested in a house in the south of France and I can tell her what to do and not to do.

As an aside, in the past, it would never have occurred to us that Cher might actually call us. We had been to too many cocktail parties with too many "Oh, you should call a friend who blah, blah, blah," with all the requisite exchanging of phone numbers and good intentions. But we have found that living in the south of France or maybe any foreign country is different. If someone is going to the south of France, they tend to actually take the conversation seriously, almost as if they are looking for a lifeline, or a friend in a foreign place, you might say. Consequently, one tends to accumulate a strange array of shirt-tail acquaintances. Fortunately for us, this has not yet been a burden, since we have no place to put anyone, but we have met people here who seem to spend all summer entertaining the Great Aunt Harriets of so-and-so. The best advice we've heard and so far have stuck to is "If friends come and you are excited about showing them your little corner of the world, by all means do so, but if you are planning to show them around out of guilt, don't do it." Makes for a few awkward moments, but how many times can one see the Toulouse-Lautrec museum already?

So a week or so later, Cher actually called, or more accurately, her manager—let's call him Bernie—telephoned to say they were in London and would be in France in a few days. Now that is the bottom line of two much longer conversations that took place under the following circumstances: Marthe Blanc, my mom/sister, had decided that I needed to "put up" some pâté. We had picked a day, and she had instructed me on how to call the butcher and order the neck, the liver, and God-knows-what-else ground to order, salted, and ready to can. When she asked me how much I wanted to make, I was fully prepared for at least six jars just to show my enthusiasm. When her jaw dropped at the suggestion that we would go to all this trouble for only eight pounds of pâté, I quickly doubled my order, thinking I had better like this stuff or we are deep in the larder with *mauvais* pork fat.

So, on the morning of the great event, off I went first to Coupiac to the local hardware store, or *quincaillerie*, to buy the *bocaux,* or mason jars. First, I had to have the requisite discussion with Jean-Paul, the owner, and everyone else who came in about how much of this and that fat and liver versus a breath or not of Armagnac versus Cognac versus foie gras or not. Finally, totally confused, the jars tucked under one arm, I arrived at the butcher's to find the ground meat *toute prête*, ready in an immaculate white pan, which I should borrow and return when I had a chance.

In the meantime, *chez nous*, there were our two regular fishermen working their normal holes in our little river. They still come two or three times a week, before six in the morning, always park carefully in public property, but charge right down our little path, which is carefully marked, for insurance purposes, "*Privé*." The old man is less than five feet tall, gnarly in the best sense of that word, has at least six teeth, and loves to fish for hours. His companion is half his age and obviously physically and mentally impaired. He is quick to tell you about his accident, which left him in his sorry state, as he asks for permission to trespass. Since he walks unsteadily, lurching with one quivering foot after another, his cane worthless due to all the fishing gear he's carrying, he always asks if he can pass by means of our old stone stairs, and he carefully picks his way through and over the rocks to the other side of the river. But his attention span and stamina are minimal, so he ends up waiting in the shade of their old car (a beetle-shaped Citroën called a *deux chevaux*, or a "two-horse," after its tiny engine), usually thirsty and anxious for the safety of his older buddy.

He first came to our door asking for help, certain his friend must have been hurt since he had been gone so long. Naively, Mike and I climbed up and down the steep riverbanks searching for a smashed body in the rocks. When we returned, the old man was leaning on the fender of the little car, smiling through his minimal teeth and rubbing his wicker fishing basket, as if enjoying some private joke. We'll never know if his friend had really been worried and the older guy liked to tease him, or they had conspired to see the inside of the house of those Americans.

But I digress. When I returned with the meat for the pâté I went off to pick up Marthe. With armfuls of flowers, more lettuce than we could eat in a week, and the smallest canning vessel she owned (twice the size I would need), we returned to *chez nous*. On my new stone sink, she arranged the pan of ground meat and a glass of hot water with two soup spoons inside, next to all the scrubbed canning jars. She then showed me how to pack the meat into the clean *bocaux*. (The hot water is to keep the meat from sticking to the spoon.) We were well into the gossip about Maran and Christelle when the phone rang. It was Bernie—you know, Cher's manager? They were in London, and did I know why he was calling? Yes, but, well, the invalid fisherman was at the door worrying about his friend again, and Marthe was up to her elbows in pork fat, and, frankly, she didn't think we should let this guy in, and where was Mike when I needed him?

As I tried to listen to Bernie's questions, the fisherman, in his wet boots and dragging his fishing poles, dashed through the door and past me, slapped two still-flapping trout on my new/old stone sink right next to the pan of freshly ground pork, and then thanked me for the glasses of water and our search-and-rescue efforts. I put Bernie on hold and thanked the young man profusely, as Marthe harumpffed her disapproval at my side. The fish jumping, Marthe harumpffing, and Bernie plumping his importance, I pleaded into the phone, "Do you think you could call back in a few minutes?"

Meanwhile, Marthe, who has never heard of Cher, and I went off to find some rocks to weigh down the pâté jars inside the enormous canning pot. Now, our rocks are generally not clean enough to put in sterilization equipment, so we were cleaning off the mud with the hose from the *source* under the bridge when Bernie called back. When he asked where I was, Mike said, "Well, she's out washing some rocks, shall I call her in?" I think Bernie was relieved to talk to someone a bit calmer, so as Marthe and I lugged and hefted the huge pan on the stove, weighted down with river rocks with a now-dead fish sliming my new stone sink, Mike had a fifteen-minute phone conversation with Cher. At first, I was a little jealous, but when it was obvious she was asking him what our astrological signs were, I thought, "Not to worry. But, please, stay out of the Aveyron."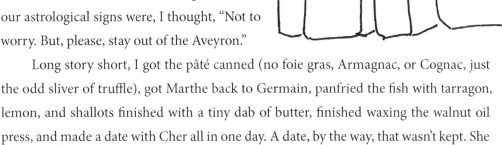

Long story short, I got the pâté canned (no foie gras, Armagnac, or Cognac, just the odd sliver of truffle), got Marthe back to Germain, panfried the fish with tarragon, lemon, and shallots finished with a tiny dab of butter, finished waxing the walnut oil press, and made a date with Cher all in one day. A date, by the way, that wasn't kept. She didn't call, she didn't write. That's rude where I come from—wherever that is. Seems she wants a château with a view of the sea, not a rustic mill with a river running through it.

Well, enough already. I have to save something for the next letter. I hope you are well and not spinning too fast. Or at least if you are, you're yelling "Wheeee" all the way.
—*Love, Judy*

WHAT ARE WE DOING HERE?

August 14, 1994
Dear Linda,

I hope you are getting your passports like you promised. We should have some three-star accommodations by next spring. We will talk more when we get home, sometime at the end of October or the first of November, depending on how all the work progresses here.

As for us, this is the "What are we doing here?" letter. We wanted a warm place to spend summers, right? Well, it has been so hot since the end of June that we can hardly breathe. I am writing sitting in front of the fan sucking in the air from the river, fantasizing that it is a little cooler. I have nothing on except my reading glasses, and they would go if I could see. All of France has been paralyzed by the *pas normale* heat wave. We have been swimming every day in our swimming hole, including the entire work crew—before their pastis—so you know it's hot. But even though we are suffering a bit, when I walk down the path and see the water splooshing over the waterfall, careening through the rocks and out under our old stone bridge, I just can't believe we could be so lucky as to have found this place. When we sit out at night at 10 p.m. savoring the last morsel of *brebie* cheese, washing it down for the *deuxième goût,* or second taste, with a sturdy red wine, I remember the fog in San Francisco and the mosquitoes in Michigan.

There are some downsides to being in the country with limited language. We're sure there are people here with similar interests in art and music, but until we can communicate better, we're at a disadvantage. But I do love this place, and I still don't know why. It's partly because we are so strange here that we can be exactly who we are with no ramifications. People have been kind to us, welcoming us into their homes, even though they don't necessarily understand us. No one expects that we know "the right thing to do," so we are forgiven for our sometimes insular, sometimes odd behavior.

The mill is progressing, but what a project. I have a friend named Mollie who is building a multi-million dollar estate in California with three houses, barn, studios, etc. And she just points her finger, throws some money at it, and it's done. Whenever we get into something really uncomfortable, we laugh and say "Mollie wouldn't like this." Like sleeping on the floor for months on a rubber mattress, wide open to the attic and the outside. Like having rocks continually falling out of the old walls. Like chasing bats out of one room into another. (They're all gone now, Linda.)

But even she would like finding stuff for the house, and you would go nuts. We are deliberately going slowly, savoring each purchase. We can go to one village to watch the last real coppersmiths make sets of heavy, zinc-lined copper pots. In another, tapestries, in another, lace. Handmade knives, embroidered linens, wooden garden baskets. Cheese keepers? Never heard of them, right? (One isn't supposed to put cheese in the refrigerator, but in one's wine *cave* in a screened case with several shelves.) And the regional flea markets, or *brocantes*, are extraordinary. The old folks all shake their cocked heads and say, "*Mais oui, mais pas comme autrefois.*" It may not be like it used to be, but for us, it's a "the worst you gave me was the best I ever had" sort of thing.

I consider the whole project to be an education, and I'm taking Sculpture 101 from the workers. I hang around Bernard and Patrick, the stonemasons, while they're carving lintels and building stone walls, and climb up on the conveyor/elevator to watch the carpenter fit the stone roof on the little guest house. I'm getting good at bucking wood with a chainsaw, which absolutely blows them away. The first time I picked up a Skilsaw they hovered around me, looking for Mike, fingernails at their teeth. They couldn't believe that the major-mother Swiss Army knife—always within reach—was mine and not Mike's. Now, they know better, giving me the ultimate tribute by calling me *costaude*, or tough and strong. (It can also mean *chubby*, but I refuse to accept that.) We know from Francis that the crew likes working here (he feeds them lunch), mostly because we get as nasty and dirty every day as they do, hauling rocks and digging up lost garden paths. They are accustomed to tony Englishmen who arrive, throw money around, and leave, complaining about everything when they return. They are protective of Mike and me in a strange way, since they are so sure that we are going to do something dumb, usually because we do from time to time.

Workman's comp and protection laws have not hit rural France, and when Bernard needs to get something done, he just does it. He can match the color of old mortar with charcoal from the fireplace or carry tons of rock up a cliff face. Claude's team can cut eighteen-inch beams with a chainsaw and connect the joints perfectly. Then they turn around and negotiate the purchase of a ruined barn for the stone roof.

They seem genuinely happy with their lot, proud to have chosen their trade and of having achieved specific levels of workmanship based on quality of work, not seniority. The chief mason and woodworker always have an apprentice who follows them like a puppy, while the "old man," sometimes patiently, teaches him. The apprentices sometimes get stuck with the dirty work, but often not. Yesterday, after six weeks of insufferable heat, I noticed Bernard hauling one wheelbarrow of cement after another. (I noticed this because the only way to get from the cement mixer in front of the house to the waterfall in the backyard, is through the finally finished living room. Mollie wouldn't like.) When I asked him where Patrick, his nineteen-year-old apprentice, who usually schlepps the cement, was, he shrugged his shoulders and said, "*Il fait bien trop chaud pour le petit.*" Bernard had recognized that Patrick, unaccustomed to working so hard in the heat, was fading. When I went out to the waterfall, Patrick, knee-high in the cool river, was putting the finishing touches on the masonry with a little coaching from the *bien* sweaty Bernard, who was lowering buckets of mortar down to the riverbank.

At the end of these hot days, they run to the river, whooping all the way, dunk each other in the swimming hole, then join us on the front terrace to suck down a Gauloise cigarette, slug back a few glasses of pastis, race to the van (the last one in has to drive the two-hour commute, and I've seen them sit there for five minutes, no one budging, when there is a photo finish), and roar off in the ramshackle truck.

Did I say it was hot?

—*Hugs, Judy*

August 15, 1994
JOURNAL ENTRY

There are two paths on the opposite sides of the river; one goes down then up to the waterfall, and the other goes up and up to the hamlet Le Bousquet, where Germain and Marthe live, then continues to the top of the ridge one thousand feet above us. It's a *chemin rural,* which belongs to the commune of Plaisance, but it hasn't been cleared in decades. When it was maintained and her family was young, Marthe carried a five-gallon can of milk—forty pounds—on her tiny back, down three hundred feet, across the mill's bridge, then up past what is now the Guerins' place to the intersection of the road toward Plaisance. There used to be a *crémerie* there, where they collected cows' milk to be made into cheese. (She and Germain raised seven children by maintaining six cows, their own vegetable garden, a rabbit hutch, a chicken coop, and a gaggle of ducks. Today, most local farmers have two or three hundred sheep and profitable contracts with the Roquefort cooperative; tankers come to take away the milk.)

At the *crémerie*, Marthe would fill her milk can with the whey from the previous day's production, carry it down the road past the Guerins' place, over the mill bridge, and up the steep path to the top of the hill and her barn, where she would mix it with other nutrients to slop the pigs. She did this every day, twice a day. In this heat?

The other path that takes off from the end of the bridge follows the base of the cliff on one side and the course of the river on the other. The path starts a vertiginous thirty feet above the rocks with no guardrail, then descends to follow the *ruisseau*, or little river, up to the waterfall. Stone walls, built by some past miller, maintained by many more, follow the rocky contour of the riverbed and keep the path from washing away. From the middle of the bridge looking back, the mill and its attending buildings can be viewed together. Looking down into the river, the scene is surrealistically picturesque: the cascading rocks form little waterfalls of their own, playing with the water as it sashays through the V's between obstacles, ducks into eddies to stash dried leaves, swirl, and continue down to the Rance River, then the Tarn, the Tarn to the Garonne, to Bordeaux, and finally the Atlantic.

Starting down the path, the water sounds change from an echo off the base of the bridge to a babbling as the path approaches the rocks. About halfway to the waterfall, there's a swampy patch where water from multiple springs cascades down to join the Mousse. There's also an easy way down to the flat rocks in the riverbed from there, as rock sitting isn't a mud-free experience. A red folding chair, if it's wedged just right, allows for reading in the shade with the small August trickle of water over the falls to cool throbbing feet and wash away the rich mud from green gardening shoes.

I look down at my forty-nine-year-old hands resting on my tattered journal: number four, starting with Vanuatu. My nails are broken, and a permanent brown stains my knuckles from painting, planting, cleaning, cooking, and my fingers seem fatter, more muscular, my wedding ring sunk in the flesh, tiny scratches in the gold. Marthe's sixty-one-year-old fingers are already twisted, the joints bent outward from years of digging, stripping corn, picking, cleaning beans, plucking eggs from nasty hens, plucking feathers from the same, pitting cherries and plums, and carrying seven children down the path on the other side of the hill to the barge that would ferry her over to Trébas to the doctor when noses were too drippy and before there were bridges across the Rance and Tarn Rivers. She performed these chores every day, from the time she was old enough to help on her family's six-acre farm until she retired at sixty-two years of age.

I put my fingers in the cool water to wash off the shame and dried them in the sun. Leafing through number-four journal, I see that from March to the end of August, we've made progress: in our language, the house, our circle of friends, and finding the perfect flat rock, one that supports a red canvas chair and lets a foot trail in the flow from the waterfall.

August 21, 1994
Dear Linda,

We have some strange decisions to make, as every day we have a new, unusual problem. Like, should we put reinforcing bars through three-foot-thick rock walls? What does one do with an old millstone buried under the floor, anyway? Should we dig out behind the dam and make a natural swimming hole while we're repairing the top? Should we destroy the old battered, bleached, rotten, iron-studded stable door? Where do you want your water from the spring to arrive, under the old stone bridge or near the arches of the millrace? Do we tear down a one-hundred-year-old grapevine because the wooden frame threatens to collapse and kill someone? Most of the time, we ask Bernard *pierre* or Claude *bois* what they would do. Their advice is usually right on, and the few times we have done it our way against their advice we have been sorry.

Like The Windows. Now, the French have developed windows to a fine art. They last for hundreds of years, and close as solidly and perfectly as the door of a Mercedes. *Clunk, clink,* they're sealed and locked. And, of course, they always open inward, so you can deal with The Shutters. Every house has shutters, often instead of curtains, as protection against prying eyes, the cold, the heat, and presumably summer-house burglars. (Our neighbors, the Guerins, have never locked their house, not once.) They can be shut completely, or held open slightly with a beautiful metal handle to allow a breath of fresh air and enough light to avoid low-lying beams. And together, The Windows and The Shutters form a sensible, synergistic totality that has taken hundreds of years to refine. Now we had two windows, which for reasons I can't remember, we wanted to open out instead of in: something about being above a stone sink or a buffet and how all the stuff I would put there would be in the way. Lots of teeth-sucking later, we had our windows. Beautifully articulating, nicely appointed with all the hardware, the works. Well, naturally we are sorry. We can't have The Shutters since we can't reach them from inside, and we need them in The Cold and The Heat! When it rains, we can't open them, so the room is intolerable. God, I hate it when they're right.

But once in a while we are dead-nuts on. (Man oh man, it feels good to talk American instead of French or English English.) Like The Sink. All of the old kitchen sinks in our region are carved from slabs of sandstone usually about three feet by five feet and about eight inches thick. The slab is incorporated into the wall so that the water drains outside the house through a hole—a four-inch hole in the wall, big enough for squirrels, mice, and the biggest black slugs you can imagine to pass through. The basin, or the sink part, of the sink is usually only a few inches deep, more like a drain board.

Well, we have three of these wonderful old hunks, one in the kitchen-turned-bathroom upstairs, one in a little sheep pen-turned-gardening-corner, which served as our temporary kitchen, and one in the guest house on the cliff. I wanted one in the new kitchen, but I also insisted in having a sink-sink that we could polish, one with a garbage disposal (we compost, so it's just to make cleaning easy), so we had it made: the latest in old stone sinks. Everyone said we were nuts: too big, too heavy, too expensive. Well, they were right on all points, but what a handsome piece of sculpture. Even the doubters inhale their "*Ooh là là!*" and flip their wrist while snapping their fingers *en même temps* as only the French can do. It's about 6 feet long by 3 1/2 feet wide, and about 6 inches deep. The drain board is carved into it at a slant, running into a large hole with a barely discernible stainless-steel sink mounted underneath. It sits on two stone pillars, with old bleached-out shutters from the barn as doors to hide the dishwasher and disposal. Using a big handmade bristle brush and organic soap, I scrub it every morning—it's one of my favorite rituals. Then I pile huge baskets of fresh fruits and vegetables on wicker plates all over the drain board, turn on the halogen spots to bring out all that color, and cook my brains out!

We don't know yet whether they will be right about the shower. Time will tell, but we have a five-tooth-sucking bet (one tooth-suck is a minor difference; five, the worst) that we will replace our French doors, the wood protected by marine varnish, with proper glass panels within a year. We had a hard time convincing the cabinet maker that maybe Americans know a little more about good showers than the French. It's their only serious deficiency in the building trades that I can find. After all, it's only been since the fifties that most people in the country started to install indoor plumbing, much less showers.

We had two drains put in, since theirs are much too small, and, scandal of scandals, two showerheads, one permanent and high enough for Mike and a removable one for me. And, *mon dieu*, I didn't want a bidet. Trying to explain that the removable showerhead was just as effective and a lot more fun without getting graphic was tough. The cabinet maker insisted on coming to the house to install the shower himself, which is unusual, because he wanted to meet these crazy Americans. And when he showed up—I'm not kidding: Little Abner. Six foot four, built like a brick shithouse, sleeves rolled up around great chunks of muscles—real ones from lifting beams and pressing wood, not from a health club. The most handsome young man I have ever seen, ever. He was getting ready to install a new pigeon-landing shelf with a pane of glass behind it to keep the pigeons out of the bedroom in the *pigeonnier*-turned-sleeping-loft in the eaves of the attic-turned-guest-room. Instead of pulling over the ladder to the loft on the far side of the room, he just jumped up in the air, grabbed the closest beam, hauled himself up, and walked across the rest of the exposed girders to the far wall. And I don't think he was showing off. *"C'est normal, madame."*

It took me months to get them to stop calling me *madame*. I told them in no uncertain terms that while working at the mill they were on American soil and were absolutely forbidden to call me that. I tried to explain the meaning to an American woman: either we're just old or we run a *maison de putes,* or whorehouse, and I wasn't that old and whorehouses are illegal in the States. By now, all the other workers call me Judite or Jeudi (the word for Thursday in French), which is the closest they can come to my name. Except for Claude. He just can't do it. He blushes, drops his head, and turns away every time we talk about it. He doesn't mind at all, however, if he hauls out his *bitte pour faire pipi* in front of me. That's different. *"C'est normal, madame."*

As I write, Bernard (Beaarnaar), Patrick (Paatrweek), Claude (Cloood) and Daniel (Dannyelle) are carting rocks down to rebuild the wall along the *porcherie*, which was damaged during the installation of our water treatment plant. Now, these rocks came from somewhere down the river, I don't actually want to know from where. All I know is that when they hightailed it into the drive and dumped another huge pile of rocks there was a lot of "You're the one that should have been watching! How was I to know the English guy was there?" In other words, we've got a lot of hot rocks. Not that France is short on rocks, don't get me wrong. It's just that the French are so good at borrowing them from one ruin to fix another, and from the English, no less.

Also, as I write, Mike is working on his garden, or watercolors, or doing interesting things with Polaroid transfers. But when the work is done, the studio finished, no more excuses, then what? Lest we vegetate, grow roots and turn to seed, we are making plans for the fall and next summer. We are going to do some formal invitations for collaborations and have a mini-show in conjunction with an open house at the mill this fall. Having deadlines is important, keeps the old stress level up. We've also heard of several local artists, but our French needs to improve before we can adequately communicate about art philosophy.

So, why are we here? We're still not completely sure, but I know at a visceral level we are doing something we were meant to do, so I have to have confidence that the real meaning will develop. I do know we are creating a space for artists to come and work. We have worked hard to develop not just the physical part, but also the spaces for some spiritual expansion. We certainly haven't been doing much art, unless you will accept that this whole business is a conceptual installation. So far, I must say, we're pretty unclear on the concept.

But the quiet strength and dignity of our aging neighbors is starting to inspire us. Through them, and partly because of them, a major project is beginning to gel, interestingly enough, through The Chairs. Before I moved them up the path over the waterfall, our neighbors would stop, look, and ask questions about them. But what they actually wanted was to see the mill again, and of course, they had heard by now that there are some odd Americans living there who sort-of speak French, who seem to like to have people stop by, and they'll even show you upstairs, and wait till you see the size of the bathrooms, and they've got a shower with two showerheads and two drains! But they all have stories about our mill and how they carried the grain on their backs across the waterfall in the middle of the night during the war, and how they still miss the music of the mill and Monsieur Louis Blanc. And "Oh, by the way, what are you going to do with those chairs, anyway?" Then they ask, *"Tournera-t-il encore?"* ("Will it turn again?")

Somehow, some day, we must make the millstone turn again. This means that everything, the mill wheels, dams, water chutes, sluice gates, millstones, everything, must be redone. Mike is already doing the drawings. Also, we are trying hard to learn enough French now to interview everyone before they die to make a limited-edition art book on the mill. Maybe saving one old building in rural France is why we are here. Frankly, it's a hell of a lot more important than most other things I've done in my life.

Time for pastis!

—Hugs, Judy

LATE SUMMER AT THE MILL

September 1, 1994
Dear Linda,

It's time for harvesting all that's left of Mike's first garden. Right now I live and breathe and think Beans, Tomatoes, and Zucchini.

Beans: We have learned a lot from our first little *potager,* or garden, not the least of which is the difference between tough ole string beans and newer varieties without that string. As Gary knows from tending his mother's garden, stringless beans are tender, requiring only a little labor to clean by popping their ends before plunging the beans into boiling water to be blanched for eating cold in a salad or stuffing in the freezer. The variety given to us by Germain could be strung together and used as fire ladders for our attic. There are enough of them, and they are that tough. We have tried everything, from picking them while they are young (three minutes out of the flower) to waiting until the seeds are mature enough to dry them for *cassoulet.* The former technique doesn't seem to matter, and getting into the seedpod for the latter requires a black belt. We got the seed from Germain, and only packing them in *bocaux,* then cooking them for hours, tenders them into stringy army-green things for a cold winter's night. I'm voting for the compost pile, but my Mikey, as only he can do, sits patiently in front of

the *télé*, pullin' and strippin'. You'd think they were the first vegetables he ever grew—
and they are!

Tomatoes: *beaucoup trop en même temps*, too many at once. Scads of them. Baskets
full. Big, brawny, yellow-hipped, sweet, juicy, drippy, squirty all over. But *beaucoup trop
en même temps*. While Mike rips and pulls, I plop and peel. Seeds running down my
hands, old recipes for anything you can think of lined up. Grandma's sweet chili sauce. I
can hardly wait. Another Claude, one of the stonemasons, couldn't believe that I would
make a *confiture*, or a jam, out of red tomatoes; green, yes, and he'd like that recipe,
too, *merci bien*. It seems he has too many tomatoes now as well. Everyone in the south
of France has too many tomatoes right now and too many beans. It's a bit of a status
thing, actually. When you go into the little local market and someone is actually buying
lettuce, tomatoes, or beans, you say to yourself, "I guess they don't have a garden. What
a shame."

Zucchini: we have only one plant and we are overrun. But the surplus has made
me more adventurous in my cooking. I started stuffing the flowers with a little shredded
Cantal cheese, *tomme fraîche* (another mild cheese), and a hint of Roquefort, then
grilling them and serving them with fresh *concassé de tomates*, diced tomatoes with
vinegar and spices. To die for. Which is what I thought might happen to the plant if
we didn't allow the squash to develop. Wrong. It just sent out dozens more flowers and
zillions more squash. Up to our zucchinis in *courgettes* we are, and the plant has turned
into a man-eater.

On the other hand: Finally, in my lifetime, I have enough great green gobs of
garlicky pesto. I feel positively rich every time I clip the basil tops and grind them
in the mortar with fresh violet garlic from Lautrec. Even pine nuts can be found at
Madame Bertrand's little grocery store on the main square in Coupiac, although they
are certainly not local. Parmesan cheese is more problematic, but I've found an old
salty cheese that crumbles into the sauce and is almost as good. No one here grows
much basil, mostly because they don't know what to do with it (*pistou* is actually a
Provençal herbal mixture unknown in the mountains of the Haut Languedoc, where we
are), and I've become a local hero by introducing people to pesto, mostly for, of course,
the tomatoes.

And speaking of social success, my reputation is dependent on bringing a pecan
pie to every event, since after the dinner with Bernard and Brigitte, our neighbors

downstream, word spread that at least one American might know how to cook so you should ask her to bring that pie. We've been invited to several other dinner parties with new friends who always request the pecan pie. I mean, literally, I don't think we will be asked back when I finally run out of pecans. In any event, I believe my cooking has improved a thousand percent here. Maybe it's because everything is so fresh, the cheeses are so flavorful, the confit so perfect. Or maybe it's just that everything eaten outside in the sunshine washed by the sound of our little waterfall just tastes better?

It isn't all perfect though, I must say. Let's get one thing clear: I don't like red currants, and I think canning jams and jellies are one of life's over-rated pleasures. And I blame the same American friend who brought me the little Trojans and the pecans for one of my more trying culinary experiences by introducing me to the questionable practice of stripping fresh, ripe red currants from their cluster through the teeth, fresh from the bush. After I spat them across the room and unscrewed my face from the jaw pain, I said that they were an acquired taste that, like learning another language, was best left to the young. It never occurred to me that I might be soon facing not just a mouthful, but milk buckets full, with no way around conserving them in the dead heat of the summer.

What happened? When Marthe called to ask if I'd like to pick some *groseilles*, I said, "*Bien sûr, pourquoi pas?*" or "Why not?" Not that I had any idea at that time what they were. It was just an excuse for an outing and a good French lesson. When I arrived at Marthe's house, it was clear she was going to give me some recipe to make some kind of jelly from some kind of berry we were about to pick. She pulled out a cookbook, in French of course, which was written in 1932, the year she was born. The brown pages were clean but well used, and the binding was held together with cracking brown glue. She painstakingly wrote out the recipe for *gelée de groseilles*. We were going to her daughter's house, where she had *groseille* bushes, ripe and ready to put up. When we pulled into the drive and climbed up to the bushes, much to my horror, I saw row after row of, yes, red currants.

As Marthe, her daughter, Geneviève, and I picked red currants, high on the hill in the hot sun, Marthe prattled on about this person and that as they passed by in their cars. I confess, I found myself doing the same, following the turn of Marthe's face, at least a head and a half below mine, as friend, enemy, cousin, or child passed below us. Most of the time there was a raised hand and a "*Woohoo!*" But occasionally a distinct snub. The story of some old feud, with a lopsided explanation of the circumstances, would follow, with an unstated expectation that I would continue the enmity as well. (I confess I'm beginning to scan passing cars myself at *chez nous*, and at least 30 percent of the time I know who they are. In fact, while we intend to build the wall and hedge to hide the road, I'm a little concerned I'll miss my neighbors passing and woohooing.)

As we finished and prepared to leave, I assumed we'd split the proceeds. But no, it seems neither one of them can stand red currants either, and I was doing them a favor by taking all the berries we could pick, which was a lot in two hours! So after hours of picking, the plucking of spiders and bits of leaves, washing, stemming, cooking, and stirring, I ended up with four, count them, four, small jars of the foulest jelly I have ever tasted. When I told Marthe it was not a culinary success, she shrugged her shoulders and told me she couldn't understand at all why I bothered, and she doesn't want any of the jam either, can't stand the stuff.

Even when you don't ask me, I ask myself. What are we doing here? The bottom line: we still don't know. My French is slightly better than Mike's and he is suffering a bit from the isolation of the language, but instead of grousing around, he is studying hard by reading newspapers while surrounded by dictionaries, watching television, and picking up words here and there. Suzie's twice-weekly sessions have helped him as well. He understands almost as much as I do, but he's much shyer and leaves the talking to me. But we both can get through a short evening of just French guests quite easily now, although we're exhausted at the end from such concentration. As for me, I honestly feel, for the first time since I was a little kid, that I am completely happy. Unconditionally, nothing to prove to anyone, doing what I want to do. The feeling is so rare, yet so familiar. Remember?

—*Love and miss you en même temps, Judy*

FLOOD AND FÊTE

September 28, 1994

JOURNAL ENTRY

Francis had agreed to cater our party to celebrate the first round of work. We wanted to be inclusive: Pollet, all the workers—the metal workers, the stone cutters, the painters, and their wives—the housekeepers, and the Blanc family. That added up to about eighty people, and we couldn't count on warm weather or clear skies. Francis arrived this morning about ten, a tan sports coat over his head, not much protection against the downpour that had started a few days ago. We decided we had to seat everyone in the mill itself.

He wanted to serve the same thing that the old miller would have prepared a hundred years ago: roasted onions and pâté with chunks of foie gras, then a little *soupe au fromage*, followed by fire-roasted *sanglier*, or wild boar, with *cèpes*, and Roquefort cheeses finished off with a traditional apple *tarte Tatin*. We decided to have a great long table in the barn with aperitifs, along with music imported from New York City (son Derek). Francis paced off the room, made circles in the air, pulled imaginary chairs out and back, all the while noting in a worn journal how all this could happen. "*Pas de problème*," he announced, then he dashed out the door, estimate in hand, to fix lunch for our workers back at Les Magnolias, the same damp coat slumped over his head.

September 28, 1994
Dear Linda,

We were lucky enough to have all of our seven kids schedule visits between August and mid-September. What fun to see rural France (renamed Rural Fuckin' France, or R.F.F., by them) and the mill through fresh eyes. We're so close to it we've lost touch with reality. Most of the construction—terraces and bread oven—on the mill house and barn is finished, with major construction underway on the little house over the waterfall. Right now, instead of a ruin, it's a ruin with a new/old roof and windows. We're working hard to get it ready as our "official" guest-artist house for next summer.

Just when we're feeling relatively civilized, however, we have some major event that reminds us we are not only living in rural France, but in a deep canyon that is part of a complex watershed. Last Friday was such a reminder. There had been a cyclone on the Mediterranean, along with 120-kilometer-per-hour winds in the Cévennes Mountains, which feed the Tarn River, the ultimate dumping ground for our little river. The winds missed us, but not the rain. Normally, when it rains, it takes about twelve hours for the watershed to start dumping into our river, and then we get a few hours of muddy, milky runoff that quickly returns to its normal clear, cold self. By Friday morning, we had had two days of torrential tropical rain. The river had risen a bit, and was a little cloudy, but was not out of the ordinary.

At noon, the work crew left for Les Magnolias for their daily ritual of a four-course lunch, with all the wine they could drink. I checked the slightly more cloudy river as I wished them *bon appétit* and returned to the house to finish preparing our more modest lunch. Five minutes later, I decided to try some of my Marthe pâté as a first course. I glanced at the creek as I walked to the barn where I keep our preserves, and in that short time, the level of the water had mounted at least six feet, had turned a deep, blood-reddish brown, and was raging out of its banks. I yelled for Mike to get his camera, thinking that this storm might be more exciting than the one we had seen in the spring, and then I went behind the house to admire our newly refurbished dam/waterfall in action. In absolute terror, I yelled for him to forget the camera and get some sandbags, as we would soon be in deep water, literally.

To explain: Ordinarily, even in big floods, we are not threatened. Huge walls of water can crash over the waterfall, swirl around the little cliffs and run under our bridge. The bridge and the first level of the house are twenty feet above our river, which is three hundred feet above the Tarn. Our canyon is quite steep, so even in a flash flood our little river wouldn't be likely to rise twenty feet. But, due to some silly circumstances, we ran the risk that day of the river washing through the back door of the house.

There is a complicated system of doors, tunnels, and water canals that allowed the old miller to divert water from the top of the waterfall, down a chute, which is at the same level of the house, and then pour down onto the waterwheels under the house. In order to redo the millworks, we basically have to repair that whole system. The first step was to dig out all the dirt from a tunnel that connects the river to a canal that brings the water to a reservoir behind the house and the mill wheels. Mike, along with the kids, had just finished clearing the tunnel, with just a flimsy temporary dam to stop or divert an excess of water from running through it and down the chute into our back door. And excess water we had. Plethoric redundancies of it.

In Mike's defense (I've promised no public I-told-you-so's on this one, even though they are due), it hadn't rained for so long, we got lulled into thinking that there would never be too much of a downpour and that we had lots of time to construct a system of doors and traps to divert the water into its proper reservoir behind the house.

His temporary dam of iron and plastic, which he thought would suffice, didn't. In less than ten minutes, a wall of water, mud, and debris came down the river and seriously threatened to wash out all the work that he had done, leap the tunnel connection, pass through the chute and—if we didn't do something fast—slam against the back wall and into the main room of the house.

We started carrying buckets of sand and rock to build a temporary dam, but it was obvious we couldn't do it ourselves. Ordinarily, we have six to eight *costauds* ready to help. But horror of French horrors, it was lunchtime. We called Les Magnolias and asked if the crew could come back to help us. Now, these guys had left a relatively calm river thirty minutes before, and when I said, "*C'est une urgence, le ruisseau est en crue, pourriez-vous nous aider?*" ("It's an emergency, the river is flooding. Can you help us?"), they couldn't believe that what I was saying was true, so I got a fork-in-hand, painfully hesitant, "*Maintenant? Tout de suite?*" They elected Bernard to return to help the hysterical Americans deal with what they thought would be a simple little flood.

Once Bernard arrived and saw the river, he was wide-eyed and apologetic for questioning our plea, yelling above the noise of the waterfall: "You were right, this is crazy." He grabbed a demolition sledgehammer, the one I can barely carry, climbed over the edge of the water chute and, clinging to the branch of a tree with one hand and smashing the huge hammer into a stone wall they had just finished that morning, managed to knock down enough of the water chute to divert the water away from the house. Fortunately, the cement holding together the three-foot-thick wall wasn't completely cured, and it gave way under his assault. When he had finished, we all climbed above the waterfall to look down at the wall of water, mud, and huge trees shooting into the air, then smashing into the rocks below. I think we all realized what could have happened if Bernard had slipped or if the old wall had given out. It was a real-life watermill experience. Germain told us that someone was killed a hundred years ago trying to prevent the river from taking out a small bridge he had built. There is no arguing with the river, the power, the sheer force of water, the suddenness of it all.

Our best guess is that a bunch of logs got jammed upstream and blocked enough water and mud to create a flash flood *chez nous* when it finally gave way. All our neighbors and half of Plaisance stopped by to see if we were all right, to check the level of the river, and to tell us that the Rance River was threatening Plaisance, that everyone in Coupiac (our upstream village) had moved to higher ground, that another twelve feet of water was coming down the Tarn, and that the road to Albi had been closed. Lots of "Where were you when?" stories, muddy shoes, pastis, and strangers touching strangers. Germain Blanc told us later that we had finally seen the river *en colère*, angry. Another badge earned in R.F.F.

We were supposed to go to Paris that afternoon on the fast train, the TGV, for my birthday and all the grand fall art openings, but nerves jangling, we stayed home to protect our little corner of the world. All the rivers have settled into their slightly soggy slopes now, and we've returned to our routine: *moi* painting walls, writing, and managing the work, and Mike completing a series of intricate watercolors of ethereal millworks. Our TGV tickets are still on the windowsill.

—*Hugs, Judy*

October 10, 1994
JOURNAL ENTRY

The fête is over: *apéritifs* in the barn, food cooked in the newly redone bread oven, tables set with white linens in every space in the mill—even around the wooden cases covering the millstones—eighty people seated and fed lavishly. Derek sang, Ty and Helen decorated the tables with chunks of *lauze* tied to pale purple heather from the cliffs above Le Bousquet, and Francis, thoroughly exhausted from two days of preparation and cleanup, watched at a distance. He had baked the *soupe au fromage* in the bread oven in the barn, and was dripping with sweat from the heat and the transport up and down the stone stairs, so by the time the event wound down to the inevitable game of *pétanque* on the bridge and driveway he dropped into a lawn chair, his arms hanging at his sides.

We had compiled a "before and after" photo album, including everyone who had done any work on the mill. I think they were pleased, but how do we know? Language, besides smiles and banalities, connects people, then pushes or pulls them together or apart. But without it, nothing. No judgments can be made, no conflicts can erupt, no pain can be shared, no mutual joy. After a year working closely with these people, I'm not sure we know them at all. I know Francis is suffering; his broad hand with the half a thumb from some unknown accident shakes when he talks. His smile doesn't match the lines between his brows. But I don't know how to ask him why.

LE BOUSQUET

October 16, 1994
Dear Linda,

Okay, you don't call, you don't write, but I don't give up. I need to write to someone about what happened yesterday. In person, I don't think I could talk about it or even try to explain. But it happened. Nothing out of the ordinary in R.F.F., but for those of us who think we have life figured out, it was unique.

Last week we took Germain to the train station so he could go to Vichy and Paris to visit friends and relatives for a week while Marthe stayed at home to wrap up the fall work in the garden and recuperate from the scars of being together too long with the same mate. She had called earlier in the week to say I needed to harvest their excess red peppers, and I told her that I would come up late Saturday afternoon. As usual, I went to Albi in the morning to the flea and food markets, strolled through the shops in the pedestrian center, and did all the stuff that is better done *toute seule*.

I arrived home, market baskets full of duck breasts, *crème fraîche*, a little pâté, fresh oranges from Spain, and roasted beets still warm from the farmers' market. I decided to take a little nap before I called Marthe and had just settled in when there was a sharp knock at the door. Snapping to, I slid down the stairs and opened the door to find my little fisherman friend, still lisping, twitching and rolling his *r*'s, asking me how I was and did I like the fish he had left a few weeks ago. I told him how delighted we were with the trout and how happy we would be to see him next March. A few minutes after he left, I was settling back into my fetal position when the door was again assaulted. I shouted to Mike that it was his turn. I could hear a conversation with an obvious stranger, and when Mike mounted to tell me that the cheese man was here, I raced downstairs to check out *le fromage*. He turned out to be a cheese maker from a nearby village who passes by our house every Saturday to make deliveries, and he wanted to show his wares. He had bags full of fresh *vache* (cow) cheese, which is roughly the equivalent of mozzarella, as well as hockey-puck-sized dry cheeses that had been salted and laid up in immaculate crates to age: the older, the more expensive. Who could resist? Not me, when such a cute, enterprising young man can stop by *chez nous* every Saturday when we have need.

Cheese keeper full, and realizing the futility of sleep, I decided to call Marthe and go get the red peppers. Roasted, with refreshed salted anchovies, lots of garlic, olive oil, and a touch of reduced balsamic vinegar? A little fresh *vache* cheese and bread? Climbing out of the car in front of their house I realized how I had come to take their modest home, smack dab in the middle of a real hamlet, for granted. In rural France (all through Europe, for that matter), dating from feudal times, people built homes extremely close together—for protection, and for shared resources such as water and bread ovens. The Blancs' hamlet, Le Bousquet, dates from some time close to that. In a space of less than 150 feet by 150 feet, there are at least five homes shared by four families. The paths in between the buildings were footpaths three hundred years ago, and only a small French car can pass and turn in such quarters. In the most spacious driveways, side mirrors are at risk.

There is nothing special about Le Bousquet. The old stones have been stuccoed against the weather, and telephone poles and electrical lines mar the spectacular valley views. In the winter, when the leaves are off the trees, the Blancs can see down the five hundred feet to *chez nous*. Marthe's parents were born there, as was she, and when Germain married her and sold our mill, he eventually became the *patron*, taking care of Marthe's mother as well as raising his large family there. Over time, Marthe has shown us her kitchen, dining rooms, and the wine *cave*. But only last week did she decide to show me the upstairs, where she had raised seven children. In three bedrooms, counting theirs. There was a boys' room with three beds in a space of ten feet by twelve, and a girls' room that was somewhat smaller. The bedspreads were hand-stitched, and the mattresses were stuffed with lambs' wool, also stitched by hand in the spring after the lambs were shorn. She was matter-of-fact in her narrative and downright proud of what she had done with what little she had. A tiny room attached to their bedroom, less than six feet by eight, had housed her beloved mother until her death in 1962; Marthe planted a rose bush where her mother had fallen. In order to go to bed, her mother had to pass through the bedroom of her daughter and her husband, in order to sleep in what was, essentially, their closet.

Downstairs, the main room is about ten feet by fifteen feet, with a large farm table in the middle, a wood-burning stove that serves to heat the house, and an aging gas stove on one wall. There is an armoire and a large wooden barrel that a well-meaning son converted into a rolling bar, seventies style. The third wall has a couch covered with an old throw, the fourth wall is the stairs that mount to the sleeping quarters. The bathroom is reached by going outside, down the front stairs and into the cellar, to find the toilet, the shower, a vegetable sink, and a huge wine vat. Off from the main room is a dining room, complete with a permanent long table set on the diagonal to maximize the number of seats. Connected to the main house is a barn turned second dining room for the other half of the twenty-eight people Marthe feeds every Sunday. To enter the house, one has to walk up a flight of stairs, which hides the entrance to the cellar/bathroom. There is a large storm drain under these stairs, and the stoop up top is connected by a cement catwalk to the adjacent barn/dining room. This space was to become the scene of today's activity. And I have to be graphic, because this was a graphic event.

When I arrived, after my four big, sloppy *grosses bises* (we had graduated from the normal three cheek kisses for friends to the four used only for family), Marthe offered me the obligatory choice of Muscat, Cassis, water, or whatever. The real objective, of course, was to sit and gossip a bit since I hadn't seen her for a week. Suddenly, another Bernard, the Blancs' youngest son, appeared, arrived, fired off his usual rapid-fire monologue, and disappeared just as quickly. I never know what he says, since he speaks so quickly, and Marthe told me once even she can't always understand him.

As Marthe and I walked to the garden, she told me that he had come to kill the lambs he had been pasturing at Le Bousquet out by Germain's garden, and she asked me if I could stay and help. These were the same lambs that our kids had fed this summer when we took them up to meet the Blancs, having called them over with their American *baaaa*'s and handfuls of grain. I answered honestly that I wasn't sure I could. She genuinely needed me, as Germain wasn't there and she wasn't strong enough to assist Bernard alone. I decided then and there that I couldn't selectively participate only in the pleasurable parts of my adopted family. They had given us so much and now they needed me. So, my heart in my throat, I said, "Yes, I will help."

While Marthe and I talked, I watched Bernard prepare the site for the event. It was to be in that space just under the front stairs of the house. A hook, usually adorned with an old pot full of flowers, was emptied, and a cable with a strange rig descended to the ground level. There was a hand crank for raising and lowering a trapeze-like bar, which had two removable metal rings on each end. He laid out a heavy wooden mallet, a hacksaw, a large cleaver, and several knives of various shapes and sizes in a surgeon-like manner. Two large, heavy plastic sacks were close by, as well as a crate with heavy twine, two large white tarps of heavy linen, and, oddly, a small air compressor. Marthe carried two buckets out of the cellar/bathroom, one full of water smelling strongly of bleach and the other empty, and carefully placed them by the steps.

Marthe and I walked the hundred yards to the barn near the sheep pen, while Bernard drove the old Renault. He backed it in close to the pen and placed cardboard in the trunk. We walked through the barn, which was loaded with drying tobacco hanging from the ceiling to chest depth and slapping our faces. I inhaled the smell as my fear mounted. What was I afraid of? Fainting, throwing up? That I might like it? I kept reminding myself that this is a natural part of farming, that these people are subsistence farmers. They are poor and have to grow everything they eat, including their meat.

My heart was pounding as Bernard reached down and grabbed one front hoof and one back hoof, flipped the ten-month-old lamb, already a hefty one hundred pounds, on its side on the ground, lassoed its feet, and loaded it into the car in less than a minute. I was grateful for the short walk to the house with Marthe. She asked me if I was okay and whether I was sure I wanted to go through with this. *"C'est pas la peine."* It wasn't really necessary, she said. She could try to find her neighbor up the hill if I couldn't do it. She remarked how even her farm children couldn't watch a pig being slaughtered since they cry so much, and she herself had to hide when it came to cows. I told her that I believed I should follow through, but that I couldn't promise I wouldn't have to leave, sit down, vomit, or all of the above. She understood.

When we arrived at the front steps to the house, Bernard had already positioned the lamb on its side on the cement stairs, feet folded under it, Bernard pushing it against the steps. Marthe donned a tattered apron, obviously saved for such tasks, and assumed the assisting position beside her son, without discussion, *comme d'habitude.* The mother-to-son banter stopped as she and Bernard moved quickly to make the animal's final moments as fast and painless as possible. The empty bucket was positioned under the head that was hanging over the edge. Marthe pushed against the lamb with all her weight, holding the animal as best she could against the stairs. She motioned for me to do the same. Bernard took the mallet and, with one fast, heavy blow to the skull, knocked the animal unconscious. He slit the throat and we held on fast while the blood pulsed into the bucket. It became obvious quickly why I was needed when the natural reflexes of the lamb jerked and its body pushed with all its considerable strength against the stairs. It took the three of us to hold it still while we watched its life drain away. I can still see my hands buried in the wool on its back.

After that, things started to happen so fast I didn't have time to think. I had assumed that skinning the sheep would be next and that it would take some time and some very sharp knives to separate the connective tissue. But instead, Bernard quickly untied the animal, made a small slit in one leg, and, using the compressor, blew air into the space between the skin and the flesh. The hide quickly separated from the carcass, making the sheep blow up into a Macy's Day Parade critter, with strange sighs coming from its lungs. It went from being a creature of God to a freak, and then in one horrible, grotesque gesture, it banged flat like a balloon. If I were going to lose it, it would have been then. I looked at Marthe in time to see her looking at me closely, those wise old eyes trying to judge if she had made a mistake. When I shook my head and held my hand over my mouth in a mock vomiting gesture she began to laugh. She said reassuringly, "*Ça va vite passer.*" ("It'll pass.")

Then we went to work. Bernard moved quickly to free the hind feet of skin and hooves and hung the carcass from the hook on the trapeze. With skill, he skinned the animal while his mother moved beside him, putting tension on the skin so he wouldn't accidentally pierce the flesh. He carefully cut around the anus, washed the knife in the bleach water, and slit the belly from the throat to the opening. Marthe held the large plastic bag while Bernard carefully separated the intestines and let them tumble into the sack. A musky, bloody odor, along with unexpected heat, emanated from the pouch, and when Bernard grunted to his mother to move it because he didn't like the smell she reminded him that it was only warm innards: "*C'est normal.*" I will never forget that smell.

Marthe and Bernard exchanged sharp comments, as only mothers and sons can do about the importance of septic technique, and every few minutes she ran to the sink to wash her hands, while Bernard continued to use the bucket with bleach in it to clean his hands and knife. I could only hold the trapeze still and rotate the carcass as needed, my legs spread to avoid the constant washing of water/blood down the walkway into the storm drain. The kidneys, the liver, the *ris* (sweetbreads), and the heart were saved as choice pieces of meat, as were the hooves, destined to become one of the treasured dishes of the region, *pieds d'agneau*, lamb's feet. The lungs and other organs went into the sack with the intestines.

After he had finished, Bernard washed everything thoroughly and wrapped the carcass in the immaculate tarp to be hung in the cellar for a few days of drying and curing. I was relieved to finish and quite proud of myself that I hadn't needed to abandon my comrades. Then, just when I thought I had succeeded, Marthe asked me if I had enough time to help them with the second lamb. So after struggling through my first real slaughter experience, I had to do it again, right away. Walking out to the barn the second time was worse than the first, and I couldn't look at the remaining sheep in the pasture. But I did assist, twice.

The bottom line? I had either assisted in the murder and dissection of two lovely lambs, or I had helped two farmers complete an important autumn task, depending on your perspective. In reality, I felt more like I was watching important partnerships in action. Mother and son, man and animal, life and death. I was there, but I was detached enough to maintain my perspective, and at some level I feel I've survived another test. I'm not a hypocrite. Maybe I can survive in the face of a disaster. I can do what is necessary to feed my family, and, yes, I will still eat lamb. I know, Gary, you've done this many times, but for me it was a first.

I staggered back down the hill, still shaken after the experience, and tried to collect my thoughts in my journal before they, too, were cold. Instead, I decided to write someone. Don't ask me why you got stuck with the news.

Close to leaving time . . . getting nervous.

—Love, Judy

CLEAN DAYS AND DIRTY DAYS

October 28, 1994
Dear Linda,

Packing to leave. I have such mixed emotions. I want to see the kids and our close friends. I want to sit in the hot tub and watch the seals and cormorants fight over the herring run. But I am not ready for pierced nipples and O. J. Simpson. And I'm totally unprepared to wear city clothes and carry on in cocktail conversationese.

And I'm going to miss the Clean Days and Dirty Days. Each morning when I wake up here, I have to decide whether or not this is a Clean Day. If so, was yesterday a Dirty Day, and did I take a shower last night or in the morning, and if it is going to be a Dirty Day, do I want to start out clean or just go for the grime? If I have to go to the market first, I have to stay relatively clean until I return. So do I want to put on the clean work clothes for the market, or try to be somewhat feminine in my clean-day clothes and then change, or just screw it all and use the dirty work clothes from the last time if I have to finish a seriously dirty job that day, and let everyone know in town that I work, too, dammit.

It is virtually impossible to stay clean here unless I head for the big city of Albi and get out of the construction site and away from the mill and off somebody's farm. And when I arrive in Albi, I am always conscious of how dirty my clean shoes are and how short and broken my nails are and why hadn't I seen the grass stain on my slacks, and how come I was overdressed when I left and now I'm too casual next to the city folk? Where's my lipstick, and how did that glob of mascara get on my cheek? Don't I have a mirror *chez nous*? It has been months since my bag matched my outfit, and I'm down to one pair of shoes I can wear in public.

If I stay home (notice I said "home") on a Clean Day it's only a matter of time until I give up and go for the grubby. I try, I do. But in just the ten steps to the barn there is another pile of lost iron objects that the workmen have retrieved from whatever is happening. How can I resist sorting through them? Or there are the odd weeds that need pulling before they turn to seed again. Or I realize that if I could just stain that windowsill before lunch, I could be done in that room. Or someone comes to see the little guest house and the path is muddy and the bread oven is dusty, and how can one draw in charcoal without a complete mess? And then Germain shows up with a two-year supply of carrots covered in mud, and the mud splashes off from the stone sink in the sheep-pen-turned-gardening-corner.

Sometimes I have to decide twice a day whether to stay clean or not. If there is a grubby morning and a shower before lunch, by midafternoon there can be another temptation to lure me back to the stained side of life. Sometimes it's just getting tomatoes out of the garden, and while I'm there I might as well carry some of the old stone roofing tiles out front, and how the hell did I get mud all over my boobs like that? I remember shaking my head in wonder when my perfectly clean kids would return in ten minutes covered with goo. Now I understand. When you're a kid the whole world is a construction site, always with something to be done, usually involving dirt, trees, hammers, saws, and paint. Anything but clean water.

Mike, too. He has a pair of Farmer John overalls that are a dead giveaway for the dawning of a Dirty Day. And if he puts on his mud boots, I know he's going for broke. He'll be knee deep in the water and dirt, digging out the millrace before his coffee kicks in. On those days, he's forbidden to come through the house to the barn. He has to take the back path, which is a tiny passage between the barn wall and the cliff. Tough if he's got a wheelbarrow. Clods of mud stick to those boots of his. There'll be cow-puck-sized plops all over my stone floor if I'm not careful.

Remember when we were kids and we got two pairs of shoes in the spring and two in the fall and we wore them out completely? And the same with our clothes? How our good clothes went from good to casual and then to play clothes? Remember when Mom or Grandma declared the school slacks could now be used after school? Well, I'm happy to say I'm a kid again. And *I* get to pass judgment. But instead of two pairs of shoes every six months, it's two pairs every two. Worn to a frazzle by the time they hit the *poubelle*. And my best slacks have long since turned to paint clothes. Even my French blue overalls are getting close to retirement, turned gray with paint and grease.

There is something liberating about crossing the line between clean and dirty. Something that lets the kid out, that makes you jump in the puddles rather than try to tiptoe around them. The old "Oh, well, why not go for it?" and you wipe your hands heartily on your clean fanny and settle in for a good, grubby time. It's usually hard physical work, and there's nothing better than that coming in, stripping off the now-work-clothes, and standing under a steaming shower, arms crossed, rocking under the water, I-don't-want-to-get-out kind of tired. Self-righteous, even.

But soon we have to go back to California. I don't make the clean and dirty decisions there. And I don't understand why. Maybe we are too settled, too comfortable, and the mud's all gone. I confess, if it weren't for the kids and our close friends, I would be tempted to stay here full-time. Nobody has an earring in their lip, and there isn't one advertisement in the local rag for a body worker. I'm not sure yet, but I think the mill is turning into our home and the beach is becoming the second house. Mike is less sure than I, mostly because he still feels isolated by the language. He's making good progress though and is even out hiking today with François, Suzie's husband, looking for fall mushrooms.

In the meantime, all of our new-found French friends have been inviting us for goodbye dinners, the average number of courses being five. Yesterday's meal at Clémence and Didier's hamlet, as much a construction site as the mill, started with *ris de veau* with mixed greens and vinaigrette, then salmon and leeks roasted in parchment, followed by fresh *cèpes* and a potato *gratinée*. Just when I couldn't eat another bite, the duck came out, followed, of course, by an assortment of increasingly aged *vache* and *brebie* cheeses. The "not-too-rich" pear cake, dripping with coffee-flavored whipped cream and topped with hand-picked pear halves and shaved chocolate, was impossible to resist. Four "farewells" down *comme ça*, and four to go! Enough already!
—*Hugs, Judy*

October 30, 1994
JOURNAL ENTRY

On her last day at the mill, just before we were to leave, Christelle took my arm and pulled me down to a chair at the dining room table. She blurted out, "*Il pue*," or "He stinks." "My-skin-is-black-but-it's-clean-and-he-has-hot-water-coming-out-of-the-wall-so-there-is-no-excuse-and-he-won't-let-me-wash-the-linens-and-his-socks-haven't-been-changed-in-weeks-and-he-NEVER-washes-his-hair-because-it-wouldn't-lie-down-over-his-head-and-he-thinks-that-I-am-wasting-water-by-washing-the-floor-be-cause-there-will-be-mud-again-and-his-mother-agrees-with-him-that-washing-the-sheets-more-than-twice-a-year-will-just-wear-them-out."

She twisted her bandana into a thin rope while she complained about other, equally complicated problems: he won't allow her out of the house, or give her money even to buy groceries, or allow her to learn to drive, and he drinks too much. So except for coming to our house two days a week, she is forced to sit in her tiny, dark house in the middle of a village of only sixty-two people, the big outing being going to the butcher's truck and the *boulangerie*.

Slightly stunned, I suggested she try talking to his sister; maybe she could talk some sense into Maran. She told me that his sister changes her sheets once a year! She collapsed onto her hands on the table, her back shaking. When she raised her head, one gray hair in her blue-black head was stuck to her forehead, and her nose was dripping from too many pent-up tears and suppressed anger. I pulled out a tissue and offered it to her. *"C'est gentil, Judy."* But I wanted to be more than just kind to her.

After exploring several options, Christelle and I agreed that, at a minimum, she was not to sleep with him unless he took a bath. Then she and I made a list of all the things Maran must do, and she was to take the list, along with Maran, to see the mayor of Plaisance, who had arranged the marriage, and their priest, and tell them that if Maran didn't change she would go back to Madagascar. But I told her she had to be ready to leave. She couldn't utter hollow threats.

She folded our list into a tiny package and stuffed it in a little leather bag I had given her last summer. *"Je le ferai."* I'm not sure she's got the nerve, but she says she'll do it.

ANOTHER UGLY FRENCHMAN

February 5, 1995
Dear Linda,

We're back in France. We arrived groggy and grumpy at the Toulouse airport, again with our body bags stiff with treasure. Each time, Mike swears he will never again load all this junk, and why is it that we can't just come like everyone else, just slightly overpacked? Each trip, I have a different list of I'll-die-withouts. The first time it was Peet's coffee. Pounds of it. (French-roast coffee doesn't exist in France. In fact, if the Italians didn't sell coffee here, no one would drink it.) This time, it was eight 5-pound bags of pecans, five packages of flour tortillas, microwave popcorn, brand-new thick, rich towels for Marthe's new bathroom, and, of course, Germain's answering machine.

I'm completely intimidated when I have to cook for friends in France. They make everything look so easy. I intend to continue with my pecan pie success, hence the pecans, but I need to keep coming with something new and different, hence the flour tortillas. I'm struggling to tell you exactly why I brought them, since I've never in my entire life actually made a burrito as I can get a great one in any neighborhood in San Francisco. For some reason, in France it's *à la mode*, which has nothing to do with pies, to try Mexican food, and nobody knows how to make it, nor do I for that matter. While I can find some scary Mexican boxed tacoy-looking things at the Géant Casino Supermarché in Albi, flour tortillas are unknown. I figured if I bought some at the last minute, stored them flat, and popped them in the freezer as soon as I got here I could have a burrito hit at least once a month, even though I've never wanted that before. That shows the quality of my thinking: twelve packages of tortillas on top of 180 pounds of luggage. Mike was beside himself. "How do I explain those tortillas to the customs guys?" I kept trying to tell him to visualize the pleasure of *carnitas* squirting out the fold in the tortilla and down his shirt. (I don't know how to make that either.)

And the popcorn here just doesn't pop, and since I live on popcorn and am sure watching a movie without it is unhealthy, I've tucked boxes of Theater-Style Orville Redenbacher Popcorn, lite, of course, in all four corners of all bags. Popcorn in France can only be found pre-popped, and it is slightly sweet, always soggy, and full of half-cooked kernels. I love to tear open a steaming packet of microwave popcorn and serve it as an aperitif and watch the French tentatively take one bite to be polite, then realize it's not sweet, in fact it's salty, and damn, it's good. They can't help themselves, and they dive for the last bite. Maybe some day the markets here will have microwave popcorn, and when they do I will be perfectly plug-compatible with R.F.F.

We are spoiled in America with certain things. And our dense, richly woven, affordable towels are one of them. The French, of course, have good towels, but they are expensive, and there are no washcloths as we know them. (They have mitts, which never quite dry and smell moldy after a day or two.) I knew that Marthe's sons were building her a new bathroom, upstairs, next to her bedroom. So at sixty-two years of age, she will no longer have to go down two flights of stairs, outside, and into the cellar in the middle of the night. (If that wouldn't train your bladder, what would?) So I overdosed on a peach-colored selection of hand, face, bath, and even a couple of American-sized bath blankets, which turned out to be a good foot taller than Marthe!

Now, there were lots of other essentials in our baggage, too, like antiperspirant, Good Earth tea, Skippy's super-crunchy peanut butter, my papermaking supplies, Mike's watercolors, our sterling silver, and wasabi, most of which is subject to duty. The last two times we landed, there was only one lonely soul in customs, as tired as we were, sweet and full of questions about why we chose the Aveyron and why a *moulin* and so forth. This time there were eight of them, fully alert, with dogs impatient to find something evil, and while we flew in from Paris on a full flight, we were the only international passengers in the Toulouse airport, so we were segregated off to one side to face the phalanx. Even I was a little intimidated.

Mike loaded his cart much more quickly than I and plunged ahead without checking with the official customs-story person (me). They had no choice when faced with two people with two huge body bags each, a three-foot square cardboard box, six other miscellaneous pieces of luggage, two carry-ons, a computer, and at least one camera bag tottering on the luggage carts. One of them held me back while another went through one of the smaller, less incriminating pieces with Mike. My guy asked me what was in all these bags, and I decided being somewhat up front was in order. I started with "gifts for French friends and a few things for the kitchen that are hard to find in France." I figured that covered just about everything but the bourbon. By his pained look I could tell that he didn't want to go through all these bags.

"What kind of gifts?"

"Well, towels, nuts . . . " Ouch, I said the *nut* word. Agriculture rural France doesn't like nuts in the land, something about the potential for introducing rare diseases like phylloxera, which came from America in the mid-nineteenth century and almost destroyed their vineyards. They were finally saved by grafting their vines onto American disease-resistant ones.

"But sealed, sterilized, you know how we are, hah, hah, hah." He luckily decided to ignore us and we were waved through with huge sighs of relief on everybody's part.

When we were at least twenty yards out the customs' door, mentally clicking our heels together, we heard someone running down the corridor after us. One of the customs guys came up beside me, leaned over and checked the address on the big cardboard box. My heart sank until I heard a thick Midi accent ask, "You are the Americans who bought the water mill near Plaisance, aren't you?" It was the sweet man from last year who remembered us and wanted to know how the work was going, and were we enjoying France and how long were we staying, and be sure and stop to say hello the next time through. Another ugly Frenchman.

Have I told you what that means? "Another ugly Frenchman." We have several friends who say they have had bad experiences in France with snobby, rude people. Usually it has been in Paris, which is, after all, another big city like New York, full of snobby, rude people in a hurry who are sure they live in the only civilized part of the world and anybody else is a hick, or *plouc* in French. Those same friends haven't spent much time in the countryside, but they assume all Frenchmen are the same. We have never had a bad experience, even in Paris, but in the countryside, away from the obvious tourist centers, the people are usually genuinely sweet, curious, and most of the time, love Americans. Still, we have one friend who insists that all of France is horrible and that instead of *The Ugly American*, she's going to write a book called *The Ugly Frenchman*. Frankly, our friend has a problem everywhere she goes, but we continue to keep an open mind and try to do research for her book.

We loaded our gear into our leased Twingo, a cute little Renault that should be the next VW bug, but the French don't quite get marketing yet so you'll never see one in Detroit. It is tiny, drives like a dream, has enough room for Mike's legs and another person in the car, the seats fold up and down and out, it gets great mileage and is inexpensive. The only problem is the colors. They are generally bright purple, electric green, or vibrating blue, which is echoed in the upholstery. The knobs and buttons are also in bold colors and generally much bigger than necessary, suggesting a Fisher-Price approach to product development. In fact, one of our kids called our Twingo "Our First Renault." But this year was our second Renault Twingo; the exterior was a sedate black, but inside, the same brightly colored knobs and dash—a nice welcome home.

We drove the hour and a half to Le Bousquet to fetch the keys from Marthe and Germain. Since we had called from Toulouse, when we arrived there was a full table set, pictures of the latest flood, tears, and hugs. Marthe was wrapped up in several layers of conflicting patterns of *tricots*—sweaters—battling the second or third cold of the winter, like a little sausage with arms, bits of Kleenex sticking out at the ends of her sleeves. Her bedroom slippers, straight from the farmers' market at Réquista, were partially zipped up over wool socks. Okay: a clear rich duck broth with tiny noodles for the soup, crudités, cold leftover ham hocks and mustard, crusty bread with homemade pâté, cheese, of course, and chocolate éclairs. I tried to demur, but what's a sleepy girl with no self-discipline to do? Be rude? After Marthe went to so much trouble, in her condition?

It wasn't until we had unpacked a few days later that we could enjoy watching her with her new towels. She had invited us to the weekly family dinner on Sunday with all the kids and grandkids there, twenty-eight in all, seated around the permanent U-shaped dining table in the converted barn. Okay: endive and egg salad, *soupe au fromage*, roast duck, potatoes with mushrooms and parsley, cheese, my pecan pie, Bernard's (one of the Blancs' seven kids and a pastry chef) *oreillettes*, and Dominque's (son-in-law and *boulanger*) *choux*.

Oreillettes are delicious, light, flaky pastries deep-fried in duck fat and sprinkled with sugar. A million of them weigh less that an ounce. A *chou* is a golf-ball-sized cream puff filled with pastry cream. They sometimes build houses and churches using *choux* as building stones and then pour hot caramelized sugar over them, sticking sugar-covered almonds on for roofs—the French equivalent of gingerbread houses. Sébastian (grandson) is studying culinary sciences in their equivalent of high school. He usually serves the *apéritifs* and the wine, carefully uncorking, wiping the rim on a bleached cloth, and gently sniffing the cork, even with *vin ordinaire*. Taking food seriously is a passion with the French, and even Germain can tell you the menu from last week's communion meal at his son's house, and all seven children have a space, the basement, garage, or a special room, that is designed to seat all twenty-eight for a sit-down dinner. They would never consider a buffet and balancing a plate on a knee.

A small gift of some kind is a ritual, particularly at a meal, but for us the towels and an answering machine were a thank-you for keeping an eye on of the house for us. Two or three times a week, Germain goes down the hill, takes his keys out of his pocket, and makes the tour into the dark house with all its shutters closed tightly, makes sure the pipes aren't freezing and the mice aren't eating too much, and waters Mike's tubs of geraniums sitting on a bench under the only unshuttered light, the twelve-foot paned window at the end of the mill near the river. He must slip through the small passage by the barn to see what's going on behind the house. I imagine him reliving some events of his youth, perhaps thinking of his mother. But my French isn't yet adequate to glean the nuances of emotions. Some day.

I took Marthe aside in the empty dining room to give her the towels, wanting a little private thank-you session. As usual, she was like a little kid and could hardly wait to tear open the package. She was absolutely thrilled. Grabbing them all, wrapping herself in as many as she could without dragging them on the immaculate floor, she ran off to show them to everyone, "*Joli, joli, joli, mais c'est trop.*" ("Pretty, but it's too much.") She always says that, "*C'est trop,*" no matter what the gift, a simple cup of coffee, even. But she always says it with that slight grin that means "Keep those cards and letters comin', babe." Sometimes I tease her and reach for the gift saying, "Okay, if it's too much I'll take it back," and she lightly slaps my hand with a little "I know you don't mean that, but don't touch it anyway" smirk on her face.

As for the answering machine? Another hit. They are still expensive in France and consequently little used except in businesses and big cities. In R.F.F., people are where we were about fifteen years ago: "I'll never speak into one of those things. Never." (Of course, now we're mildly annoyed that we have to actually talk to a person should they answer and not just leave the essentials and split.) I thought he might resist, but when he opened it in front of all his kids, they were so excited that he got into it. They kept telling him how often they call or don't call because they know he's in the garden or she's in the barn and don't want them running to the phone. Now they can leave messages guilt-free.

Germain was absolutely adorable making the answering recording in a total monotone: "You, have, reached, Chez, Blanc, Le, Bousquet, de, La, Bastide, Solage. Leave, us, a, message, *vous, êtes, bien, chez, Blanc. Laissez, nous, un, message, s'il, vous, plaît*, after, the, tone, which, follows. *Merci*." Remember the first time you had to do it? And were you sixty-seven years old? And were you French and in order to talk did you have to turn and tilt your head, lips pursed in embarrassment, palms up, gesturing that gesture at least six times, knowing full well the recorder couldn't record French sign language?

But I'm ahead of our return. We had hoped we could have the furnace turned up before we came back, but Germain had been so confused by the newfangled technology the first winter that we decided to skip it and just suffer for the first few days while the house heated up. I had put sheets over most of the furniture, but I knew the floors would have a thin layer of stone-wall dust, the dormice would have eaten the caps off the Champagne corks, and the cold would have permeated to the core of those old stones. Even with those expectations, we were thrilled to see the outline of the grape arbor reflected in our headlights, and when our outdoor motion lights blinked on, we were home. The best surprise, however, was that when we pushed open the door, we could feel the gentle heat and clean smell of a warm, freshly scrubbed house. Germain had somehow figured out the furnace, and had called Natalie and Christelle to come and clean before we came. He had even put fresh pussy willows and dried flowers everywhere. Another ugly Frenchman.

Monsieur Pollet, our contractor, and Bernard *pierre*, the stonemason, came by the next day to schedule the work for this year, without Pearson. Seems they finally fired him, not just off our case but all projects, much to our relief. My French, painful as it is, is much better than his anyway. So we're flyin' solo here, no linguistic copilot.

But the news isn't all good. The sister of our neighbor Bernard Guerin, Claire, thirty-five years old, has an aggressive breast cancer. She is halfway through her chemotherapy, has lost her hair, strength, and a lot of weight, but seems to be the strongest of her family right now. Her two small children don't understand what's happening, and her partner, Mick, wants to put her on a macrobiotic diet because he doesn't know what else to do, her mother and six siblings are hovering but not helpful, and friends who are uncomfortable with illness have deserted her. She was visiting Bernard last week, and we invited her to stay in our attic-turned-guest-room next to the river because there were so many people *chez* Guerin. She jumped at the chance but, after four days of rain, the river started to flood about 6 p.m. and instead of a gentle little stream-song rushing by that evening, there was a heavy-metal rock-slamming river, smashing the foundations of the house, and clouds of mist and foam rising from the crash of the waterfall dripped down the windowpanes. She slept for twelve hours, ate everything in sight the next morning, and said it was the first time she'd slept in weeks!

But now it's my turn . . . *bonne nuit!*

—*Love, Judy*

FRANCIS AND OTHER SORROWS

February 12, 1995

JOURNAL ENTRY

I stopped by Les Magnolias to see Francis and to invite them to the mill for dinner. (I couldn't just call. The telephone is still too scary in French. I can ask a question, but I don't necessarily understand the answer, and dates and times are too difficult.) The auberge isn't open yet, and Francis, shadowed by his now almost two-year-old boy, Franc, was doing some work on his own house, a small ruin carved into the rock face behind the hotel/restaurant. Francis's parents owned Les Magnolias, having bought it after the Second World War. His mother was a self-taught cook and his father a stonemason who restored the rambling manor house when money allowed. Francis learned to cook from his mother and how to cut stone from his father. Now he does both, cooking from spring until fall and rebuilding parts of the hotel in the winter.

I was stunned by how ill he looked, beads of sweat on his forehead even at a chilly forty degrees, the gray roots of his hair longer than the dyed-brown part, his hands shaking. Marie-France, his young wife, after the obligatory *bisou* stood in the background wringing her dishtowel and watching Franc's every move. She seems even more aloof than before, more cold than timid. Jealousy? I wonder if the second wife, the one for whom the husband leaves his much older wife, is always on guard around other woman, especially foreign, therefore exotic, women?

We've pieced together the Francis and Marie-France story from various people. They've only been married about five years, Francis having left his first wife when Marie-France came to work at the auberge as an intern hostess, fresh from the culinary arts program in Toulouse. Francis's betrayal of his first wife, who now lives high on the mesa above the Tarn Valley in Alban, a rather miserable wind-twisted village, turned much of the local community against him, and there are fewer weddings and baptisms in the *grande salle*. In a village of only sixty-two people, any ostracizing would be experienced daily, painfully, as he walks to the post office or *boulangerie*.

He said he was ill over Christmas. He thought he'd had a heart attack, but now they think he had some horrible bacterial infection. His doctor thinks his problems are psychological, like those of Francis's mother, who committed suicide by jumping off the bridge into the Garonne River. He is still visibly weak, his normally cheery demeanor has changed drastically, and his gout has forced the constant use of a cane.

They, Marie-France, Francis, and Franc, came for dinner the next day. I was nervous about cooking for a Michelin *bon repas* chef (restaurants that offer excellent food at reasonable prices are listed in the Guide as "good meals"), so I pulled out all my old no-fail standards: *apéros* of caviar with *crème fraîche* on flat green beans; first course of cream of mushroom soup made with homemade stock and fresh wild mushrooms; *plat principal* of salmon, cooked in my Swedish smoker with a mango, black bean, tomato, and cilantro salsa, and twice-roasted potatoes, with reduced balsamic vinegar drizzled around; and for dessert, my German pancake folded around fresh homemade raspberry jam, dusted with powdered sugar. Was divine, and even I can say it.

Francis was, I think, genuinely impressed, since the American reputation for terrible food is alive and well in 1995, and even among people who should know better. He was curious about the smoker, and we made a date to try smoking fresh foie gras. He's quite an expert on fresh and foie gras pâté, even gives classes in Paris on it, and promised to bring his special salts, which he swears are the secret to successful pâté.

He's upset about the village elections, which are in April. Everyone knows who's voting for whom even though politics are never discussed, because a list of candidates is drawn up by those on the left, another by those on the right, then everyone votes for their list and the elected group, in turn, elect a mayor. In such a small village, everyone knows who's on which side of the electoral equation through years of analyzing the lists. Voting takes place at the town hall, using an old wooden box with a slot. Pierre, the secretary to the mayor, pulls the mimeographed ballots out one by one, calling out the names until all one hundred (including farms and hamlets in the hills, there are about three hundred people in the total commune of Plaisance) or so votes are counted, the winners taking all. And there's a lot at stake. The mayor has the power to determine tax structures for repairing or not roads and water systems. Francis is on a new list with a much younger candidate for mayor in competition with the present mayor, Monsieur Colomb, who has been in that position for years. He's afraid that if his group loses, Monsieur Colomb will be vengeful when it comes to setting Francis's taxes and permit fees, and repairing the damaged roadway leading up to Les Magnolias.

As they left, Francis lifted the sleeping Franc and hoisted him over his shoulder to transport him to the car, a completely natural gesture for him. Maybe it's just my imagination, but he looked so weak, wincing and limping from his chronic gout up the gravel drive.

RURAL FRANCE AND CALIFORNIA

February 14, 1995
JOURNAL ENTRY

Christelle arrived early this morning, and tapped timidly on the front door. I opened to see her standing there, head down. She looked dreadful. Her first cold winter had changed her so dramatically I feared for her sanity. Her beautiful black skin was dull and gray, her eyes vacant. She had gained at least twenty pounds, and she walked with her arms gripped tightly across her chest. Though only forty-two years old, she looked sixty, and she talked without expression about her children. (She has, or had, three girls in Madagascar, one of whom, a sixteen-year-old schoolgirl, was killed by a rejected suitor, which was considered justifiable homicide in their male-dominated courts.)

Over the winter, she says that, thanks to my counseling, she pulled together enough strength to give Maran an ultimatum: "If I don't have the freedom to come and go as I please, and if I don't have a right to the money you earn as a wife keeping your household, then I must be an employee or a slave. And since I'm not your slave, if I work for you, you must pay me. You paid eighty francs a day (about fifteen dollars) at Les Magnolias, so you must pay me eighty francs a day also. You can pay me by the day or by the week, but I want it in advance!" Thanks to her toughened stand, coupled with some good counseling from other co-conspirators (Francis and the mayor had some serious talks with Maran) and his fear of losing Christelle, Maran has begun to change his habits, but very slowly. He is taking baths when he's horny, washes his feet at night, and has given her full access to their money. He still won't let her learn to drive. so before we give up our rental car, we're going to the gentle slopes of the Tarn to let her strip the gears.

February 14, 1995
Dear Linda,

Here is where our split life gets hard. Mike's older daughter, Eileen, had a baby girl, Kaitlin Clair, yesterday, almost on Valentine's Day, February 13. We are having trouble internalizing this new little person without seeing her even though we heard her cry a bit on the phone. Mike is going back the end of March, but I have to wait until the beginning of June to see and believe that this tiny O'Shea person exists. We don't get to see Eileen much even Stateside, since she's in Seattle, but I wonder what I'll do when the local kids have kids. Will I be able to leave the States for France guilt-free? But now, another first: sleeping with a grandpa.

But a clean grandpa. We've been trying to help Christelle educate Maran as to how often men bathe and shave and change their underwear since apparently his parents never did, so he's had no role models in his fifty-five years. Try to imagine the four of us around our kitchen table, not speaking the same language, trying to be casual and not preachy about how often we bathe. When Mike said he took a shower every day and always washed his hair when he did, Maran could not believe it. His eyebrows shot up (this didn't budge his glued-down hair) and he cocked his head, snapped his fingers against the palm of his hand while uttering the unmistakable "Eeuuuhhh!" that means "Not for me." Good try.

After they left, Mike said, "I want you to remember I could be negotiating deals in

Tokyo or London,
schmoozing with the
hotshots on Wall Street.
But no, I'm spending my
time in rural France
trying to coach some filthy little guy
who speaks undecipherable French
and no English when to change his
underpants." I have a feeling this
has more social value than any financial
deal we ever did.

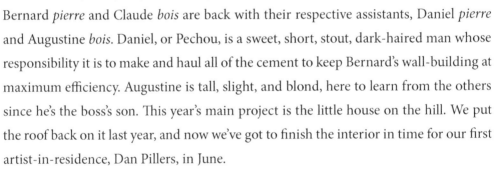

   Our new crew showed up today, with
the cement mixer, or *bétonnière*. People say
"If they don't bring the *bétonnière*, they don't
intend to stay, they're just leading you on."
Bernard *pierre* and Claude *bois* are back with their respective assistants, Daniel *pierre*
and Augustine *bois*. Daniel, or Pechou, is a sweet, short, stout, dark-haired man whose
responsibility it is to make and haul all of the cement to keep Bernard's wall-building at
maximum efficiency. Augustine is tall, slight, and blond, here to learn from the others
since he's the boss's son. This year's main project is the little house on the hill. We put
the roof back on it last year, and now we've got to finish the interior in time for our first
artist-in-residence, Dan Pillers, in June.

   To get to the little house—we call it La Ruche ("The Beehive") since we found an
old hollowed-out trunk in front of the door in which Germain's father kept his bees—
one has to climb the stone steps to the upper barn, then take a steep path that climbs
at the edge of two terraces, about sixty feet up from the main house. All of the building
materials must be taken up those stairs and path. Last year, to lift the big stone roof
slabs, they used a crane, then an elevator to load the stones on the terrace above the
roof of the house, and built a catwalk from the terrace to the roof. But this year they're
going to cover the stairs beside the barn with dirt and build a temporary steep road to
La Ruche, and when all is done, they'll dig it out and rebuild the stone steps going up
the path. Well, that's the plan.

—*Hugs, Judy*

March 5, 1995
Dear Linda,

This is a weird letter. I am just going to tell you what's happening straight from my journal because I can't allocate space relative to the importance of the event. My usual objective is to tell you about our life in rural France, and I usually devote pages and pages to that, but something happened back in California that has left me devastated: Hayden, my sweet, gentle son, was mugged in San Francisco last Tuesday night. I tried to call you, but I guess you're traveling. I expect you'll have this when you return, and maybe writing about it will help. They threw him against something hard enough to break his pelvis and snap his arm. No reason, no robbery that succeeded, anyway, since he was found clutching his wallet. They say it was a skinhead initiation. He gets out of the hospital tomorrow after five days of morphine-muffled pain. Horrible decisions about going back or not. He says absolutely not, he has a wife, he's a man, Mom. He would feel guilty. What does he know? He's on drugs.

My baby was attacked by someone and I can't do anything. I feel like a caged animal. Caged by distance, yes. But also by ignorance. Who can I hurt? But I'm also locked out by the harsh reality that my son not only doesn't need me there, he doesn't want me there. Not because he doesn't love me, but because he has his own independent support system now. A wonderful wife, friends, siblings. He grew up and went out into the real world, and I'm redundant. When did that happen? I guess I did the job I was supposed to do, but I hadn't come face to face with the fact that some day I would not be needed anymore. We talk to him every day, sometimes twice, and he seems to be well taken care of. He doesn't need surgery, he's home in a hospital bed, and while the pain is bad, the constipation from the painkillers is worse. I told Seana, his new bride, "Remember two things: bedpans will test any marriage, and urine is sterile."

But the violence. I've started keeping score: In the past two years, I've had a friend murdered, our car was stolen once, broken into and vandalized two times, and now our son has been viciously attacked. All this in a supposedly low-crime city, San Francisco. But it happens even in France, like in Aix last year and then just last week when we went to Albi, parked our car by a carnival, and when we returned, someone had punched our lock and stolen my raincoat. In Albi! It isn't exactly Rural Fuckin' France, but almost. I used to think it was the media that was causing all the problems by overstating the crime, but it's hard to rationalize when I look at our own statistics. What's worse is that our children are growing up hardened to the violence through such culturally enlightened films as *Pulp Fiction* and *Reservoir Dogs*. O. J. Simpson has captured the hearts of America, and Geraldo Rivera features serial killers on prime time. I'm sorry, but the whole goddam world is sick and getting sicker.

I decided I had to do something or I would go insane. Do you remember The Chairs? Well, I had left them on the path overlooking the waterfall, thinking that might be a nice way to leave the world, wildflowers in their laps and mist from the waterfall accelerating the rot. Suddenly, the chairs became my outlet for my frustration. Yesterday, I picked them up, all that could stand, and carried them to the new side wall of the old bridge. I wedged them on the wall, seat and straight back at a forty-five-degree angle, hanging precariously over the river so that the only thing that kept them from tumbling to the rocks below was their not-so-solid back legs. Of the twenty-five that survived the trip from the path to the bridge, thirteen tumbled within an hour, their remains washed away to the Tarn River. I was pleased with the violence of their fall, their smashing against the rocks and drowning in the angry rain-swollen river. My first installation piece. Some peace/piece. Art can do that.

Mike has been very supportive, dragging me out of the construction mess to change the scene. We went to Coupiac last night to have dinner at the Hotel Renaissance, run by Lynne and Robert (*Lean* and *Rowbearrrr*), an odd couple. She's English, he's French, in their forties. She is too thin, with a ruddy blond complexion from too many cigarettes and constant wine sipping. He's dark and round-bellied from eating her French fries cooked in duck fat. He holds court behind the bar at the Hotel Renaissance, while she runs the kitchen for the little café: the café where no locals will eat since it's not possible for an Englishwoman to cook, of course. Everyone says the building is cursed, and there have been three owners who have tried but failed to make it work. Not enough rooms for a hotel and not enough diners for a restaurant. At least they speak English.

I don't think they'll last much longer, however, since she told us a rumor is being spread that she is a prostitute, *une pute*. Apparently, any woman who would hold court behind a bar with her husband, and drink and smoke as much as she does, must be one. When Mike and I stopped laughing, we noticed that she wasn't. The night before, a local bachelor, an unshaven, unwashed hermit who earns a living by mucking out neighbors' sheep shit and is obviously mentally retarded, sat at the bar all night twiddling a twenty-franc note, about six dollars. Finally, when he was adequately sloshed, he slid the bill across the counter and stammered, *"On y va!"* or "Let's go!" She became apoplectic with anger and humiliation and chased the poor soul into the street with a broom. She thinks their mayor is trying to run them out of town, and it looks like he might succeed.

At least I'm outta here tonight.

—Hugs, Judy

MILL STORIES

March 8, 1995
Dear Linda,

Hayden is doing much better, my anger and frustration has waned, and I'm still waiting for the rest of the damn chairs to fall.

In the meantime, we continue to marvel at the sheer joy that Germain exudes when he comes to see us. (It's never with empty hands—he brings gifts like eggs, cabbages, cuttings for our nonexistent garden.) For him, no matter what we do, how much we change the mill, we are saving his birthplace from total destruction. He tries hard not to interfere, but he can't resist saying, *"C'est pas chez moi,* but in the old days we would never have put a window in a north wall." He always starts by reminding us and him that it's not his house, but . . . with every detail of our project. But when we knocked an opening in a wall to the north in his old bedroom, he approved. *"C'était toujours trop noir."* It must have been very dark indeed with no windows at all.

We certainly get double the pleasure every time he sees something that we've dug out of the muck, or yet another stone wall uncovered. He often just runs his fingers over the bolts and worn spots in the old scarred beams, sometimes recalling some piece of long-gone equipment that hung there. But more often he has a little anecdote from his youth—usually recounted with some mist in his eyes. (Now, if only our French was good enough to understand the nuances—dictionaries, drawings, gestures all help.)

By now, we have stories from virtually every corner of the mill. Like the time the old owner took the chestnut doors off the huge flour sifter, *la bluterie,* and put them out on the road for the garbage man. Germain took them and has been storing them in his tobacco-drying barn for the last thirty years. (I wanted to ask him if we could buy them, but that didn't seem right.) Or the wedding of his older sister, Maria, on the terrace, the reception in the upper barn, and how his mother passed the food through a tiny door in his bedroom that connected the two buildings, long since bricked over.

One day he stopped by to chat and I asked him about some strange dark swirls that I found in his old room, under the wallpaper that the previous owner must have loved, since she put it everywhere, even on the ceilings. He blushed and burbled something that sounded like *potato* and *chicken feathers*. I kept saying "*Comment?*" or "Huh?" until he finally gave up with a wave of his hand. He came by that afternoon with a potato that had a dozen chicken feathers stuck in it. He then dragged me upstairs to show me how the feathers, if dipped in paint and lightly brushed on the wall, made those traces of his youth. His family was too poor to have wallpaper, and he wanted to have some decoration in his tiny cell. We kept the marks on the wall, of course, but the potato started to rot, so I took some of Bernard's cement, formed a rough potato shape, and stuck the feathers in at odd angles, and it sits on my desk as I type.

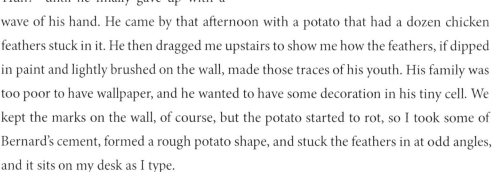

This morning Germain stopped by for coffee. Seems that Marthe (who has asked us to call her "Martou," which is like someone named Martin asking you to call him Marty) has decided that coffee is bad for her digestion, so Germain has to sneak it on the side. While I was tamping the coffee into our little espresso machine, he suddenly gasped, "*C'est pas possible. Où t'as trouvé ce truc-là?*" Pointing to an odd fifteen-inch-long U-shaped metal bar with sharp end-points bent out perpendicularly to the U, he asked where we had found it. Mike had discovered it digging out the *porcherie* and had hung it on a large spike sticking out of our stone walls in the kitchen, the same spike holding the cross that we had found behind the door in the *porcherie* when we first saw the mill. He grabbed it, dragged Mike by the arm out the front porch, across the bridge, down the path on the other side of the river, and up to the top of the waterfall.

Every watermill has a dam or a weir that diverts the river into a reservoir so that the miller can control the flow running over the paddlewheel that turns the millstones.

Most dams are a few feet high, and as the water flows over them, they form a small cascade of water. We have a unique situation in that our dam is over twenty feet high, and our main reservoir is behind the dam. The overflow of water forms a spectacular waterfall. But the top of the dam had been damaged over the years, and we were in the midst of repairing it, so we had diverted the water away from the dam through a special canal. Years of mud and debris had backed up behind the dam, and we were stumped as to how to get it out.

Germain, now at the top of the dam, pointed at the base where there is a large square hole cut into the six-foot-thick stone wall, with what appears to be a wooden wall holding back the muck from winter floods. Water drizzles constantly from the cracks between the planks. Frustrated by our still-primitive French, Germain was jumping up and down, "*Avec ça vous pouvez nettoyer le barrage!*" Apparently, we had found the key to cleaning out behind the dam: a unique tool that he and his father used to pull out the planks that form the clean-out door so that the flood runoff that filled the reservoir behind the dam could be washed downstream—after they dug down twelve feet, by hand, in freezing water and weather since it has to be done in early March when winter runoff is at its peak. Mike and I exchanged the "Well, *I'm* not doin' it!" look and tried to share his enthusiasm.

Meanwhile, Bernard and Pechou are schlepping more and more cement through the house, up the path, and down the path. They have a little tractor that chugs up to La Ruche, and they are like kids, arguing over who gets to drive it. Whoever wins jumps behind the controls, and the other tries to balance on the sloped engine hood, legs held high. The slope is so steep, I'm afraid it will tip over backward. While the *pierre* crew plays with the tractor, the *bois* crew is stuck up in the little house, walking across beams and putting in new chestnut flooring. Claude *bois* and Bernard *pierre* are at each other's throat again over something, probably because Bernard seems to be having too much fun. In any event, I'm staying out of the way of both of them.

To get enough stone to build new walls and stairways, Bernard and Pechou spent two days tearing down another house to rebuild ours. I think it's the same one that supplied our *lauze* roof. I now know they/we bought the ruin first, so we're not as naughty as I had feared. It's been pouring rain, so when they return with the truck there's lots of splooshing of mud, and grunts of "*putain*" hang in the air. It's the first time I've seen either Bernard or Pechou complain. As for Claude, he always complains, now that I can understand him, and Augustine just whines. A whine is a whine, even in French.

Part of our reason for coming here was to learn a new language. We're making progress, enough so that we can expand our circle of friends to those who speak no English at all. We met an artist in that category, Jean-Michel Prêt, last year, and last week he and his partner and mother of his two children, Eveline, invited us over for dinner. She made the most delicious leg of lamb I've ever eaten: cooked for four hours with a bottle of Montbasillac and a whole head of garlic with the pot sealed with bread dough. Heaven.

He's a potter with the biggest hands I've ever seen and makes the pots with a simple and stunning Japanese esthetic. His demeanor is similar, simple and sensitive. She takes in foster children, and they always seem to have at least four kids running around somewhere. They live in a mostly restored pile of stones called La Souyrol up on a hill above Coupiac. (He's the one with a small gallery there, which he leaves wide open, and if some passerby sees something he likes, that person puts the money in a jar and takes his pick.) We met him the first time when we ventured down the rutted dirt path, and he shyly came out of his studio, slapped his clay-covered hands on his apron, and shook our hands with enthusiasm.

We've met another clear-speaker, Odette Soulier. She, along with her husband, bought a farm on the top of the ridge above Coupiac and is slowly transforming it into a bed and breakfast with horse-riding facilities. She had heard of us and stopped by while I was painting the iron fence out front. She's a lovely woman, dark hair, French thin, and seems genuinely interested in meeting new people who might have similar cultural interests. Her passion is music. She invited us over for an *apéro* to meet her husband, Jacques.

She, Eveline, and Jean-Michel speak French so clearly, without any Midi accent, that I sometimes forget they're speaking another language, and I have been known to respond in English, forgetting language is an issue at all! I am still amazed that I can say these French words, these strange sounds resonating in my sinuses, and they understand me.

Like *bonne nuit, ma cherie . . .*

—*Judy*

March 9, 1995

JOURNAL ENTRY

Bernard, our stonemason, after months of working with us, has become a good friend. He confided in me yesterday that his wife is bipolar and on a real downswing. She tried to commit suicide over the weekend, which she does with some degree of regularity, never coming very close, but enough to have to call ambulances and the police. When she's up, she spends every dime she can on clothes, cars, and classes. The first class was to work in a nail salon, then to be a medical secretary, but she can't stay with anything long enough to do it. She has been the target of many scam artists as well. The latest was a plan to open an art gallery in the Toulouse airport. All the crook asked for was thirty thousand francs, everything they had in the bank, so he could renovate the space and they'd be rich. He hasn't been seen since. Over the years, Bernard has lost his own house, his father's house, which he inherited when he died, and every dollar he ever had, which she spent in her manic phases, along with most of his *joie de vivre*, thanks to her depressions.

Bernard said he only told us about Gabrielle's problems to explain why he'd like to work weekends at the mill to try to make up for some of her follies. Apparently Monsieur Pollet doesn't mind, so we'll maybe get a leg up on digging out the tunnels that bring and take water to and from the mill.

In my romantic view of France, people don't have these sorts of problems: no mental illnesses, no child abuse, no alcoholism, certainly no scam artists. When you can't speak the language very well, what you see is what you want it to be. But as my French balloons, my fantasies deflate.

THE CHAIRS AND DUCK CONFIT

April 15, 1995
Dear Linda,

Now that Hayden is almost completely healed, I have to deal with The Chairs. Thirteen of them stayed in that excruciating position teetering over the rocks and the river. I wanted to move the survivors, but I was afraid of the number thirteen. So I waited for a storm. Nothing. Since most had tumbled at random, I decided to fill the spaces of departed chairs with those at the ends, wedging them less tightly than the others, thereby making certain at least one more would tumble. And it did. I turned the remaining twelve at the same precarious angle, but toward the roadbed of the bridge where a tumble wouldn't be fatal, just slightly embarrassing, but all of them survived that change.

Over the next six weeks, I moved and photographed them in every position imaginable: flat on their backs on the bridge, side to side, stacked on each other like a house of cards, and finally, with some lined up as judge and jury in a mock trial. I declared them all guilty and condemned. We were in the middle of cleaning out the river but, of course, we had a steam shovel to clear the riverbed instead of digging it out by hand as Germain used to do. I had spent four days with a chainsaw, cutting down and piling the trees and roots that catch all the plastic during floods in the center of the cleared riverbed. I doused the pyre in kerosene, and when the flames were cracking ten feet in the air, I burned the chairs, one by one, tears streaming down my face. One for my Hayden, one for me, one for my Hayden, one for me. He loves me, he loves me not. He loves me.

So now you know . . .

—*Hugs, Judy*

April 18, 1995
Dear Linda,

Last week I was working in the upper-barn-turned-Mike's-studio when an American voice matter-of-factly asked, "What are you doing here? Are you just romantics or are you hiding from something?" I turned toward the voice and saw only a silhouette against the bright sun at the door, the tallest, thinnest woman I've ever seen. After she introduced herself, she went on to explain that she has a theory that people who move to rural France, whether French or foreigners, are either one or the other. Her name is Shirley de Condomine, a striking American who's been married to a Frenchman, Berteau, for over twenty years. They have two beautiful, very French daughters, Catherine and Andrée, live in Paris, and spend summers at their large farm-turned-summer-house on the other side of the Rance River overlooking Trébas. Les Peyrettes Hautes, the name of their place, is their summer home, and since many French people spend a good part of their summers at ancestral properties, I guess she's neither a romantic nor in hiding. She had heard we'd bought the mill and wanted to check us out. My quick response to her somewhat impertinent question, given what we've been through, was that we must be total romantics and that she should consider adding "just plain crazy" to her list of possibilities. We made a date to get together, and after she left, I began to wonder. Am I hiding from something? Should I have gotten back on the work horse? Her theory's a good one, worth considering.

I keep asking: Why are we here? Is a sense of adventure baked into our DNA? Is this like camping—in the woods but with the car nearby—just to show we can survive? I like to think that here I'll be free to make art, and learn to be internally driven instead of always doing what I think others want. And, because we're so exotic/weird here, given our language handicap, at least for a while we can do what we want, saying "*J'ai rien compris.*" (Maybe even after I can understand, I can pretend I don't?) I don't have a clear answer yet, but I do know that by being here we make the locals prouder of their village and culture, since they think we could have gone anywhere in the world and we chose La Pilande Basse and Plaisance.

Last week I sprained my ankle running down the catwalk Pachou uses for the wheelbarrow, trying to get to the phone. The plank was covered with plastic to keep cement plops from staining the front landing and the interior floor, and I misjudged the edge. I did a complete ankle foldover, then I went all the way down, hitting my ribs against the stone wall. I was afraid my ankle was broken: it was swollen badly, and the pain was excruciating. The next day we decided I better get it looked at so we went to the hospital in Albi, but X-rays didn't show anything. They put a removable plaster cast on it and told me to keep all weight off it for at least four weeks. (The entire hospital experience, including the X-rays and cast, was two hundred dollars. They didn't know how to take money since they are paid automatically by their excellent government health-care system, and they asked us to come back since they don't have any administration dedicated to collecting money.)

Coincidently, we were to dine with Jacques and Odette Soulier that night, so we went, although the skin above and below the cast was a deep black/blue and my whole leg was throbbing. What I didn't know until we arrived is that he's a doctor-turned-pig-farmer, an M.D. and an osteopath, physicians who take a more holistic, less mechanical approach to the body. When he saw the cast, he asked me what happened. When I told him, he said "Take all that off and get over here." He rubbed a whole tube of arnica gel onto the joints in my leg, and while he manipulated my knee and ankle, he explained that unless a bone is broken, the pain usually comes from muscles or ligaments that have been stretched, torn, or dislocated, and if they aren't put back correctly, it can take months to heal. When he'd emptied the tube, he told me to walk normally. Stunned, I was sure I couldn't, but I tried, and damn, it didn't hurt much at all.

It was actually our first meeting, and because of Shirley's comment about why people leave where they are and settle in rural anywhere, I asked them why they had decided to come to the Aveyron, leaving Montpellier, city life, and profession behind. She replied quickly that she was Aveyronnaise, that her family had owned the château in Combret, and she felt she was home. His answer was a bit vague, something about changing their lifestyle, starting over again. "The French have a word for us, *les recyclés*." That's one of those *faux ami* words, or a word that sounds like an English word, but has a totally different meaning. In French it really means "to be retrained or to change jobs"; in English, of course, it's smashed soda cans in a pile. But now I can't meet anyone without asking myself: Are they romantics or hiding something?

In any event, I am glad they're here. He loves to teach us French, and she speaks clearly and slowly, giving us hints when our faces show panic as we search for a word. (I've since learned that she used to be an English professor at the university level.) He slaps his knee when we try to say, "*C'est la fourrure d'un écureuil de Eulalie.*" It doesn't matter what it means, it's just impossible to pronounce.

At dinner, every fifteen minutes or so he told me to get up and walk around, which I did with minimal discomfort. When we left, he said to call him if I couldn't walk completely normally in a few days.

As for me, this smashed can is in bed.

—*Hugs, Judy*

April 20, 1995
JOURNAL ENTRY

My ankle is almost healed; it went from the blackest blue to the yellowest green in a few days, and remarkably, I had no pain other than swelling after Jacques manipulated it. Then yesterday, my ankle froze, I couldn't bend it at all. I called Jacques and he said to get over there, *tout de suite.* When I arrived, he cleared the dining room table and told me to get up there and lie flat on my back. After asking a few questions and testing my ankle, he swung my leg, bent my knee, crossed my leg and crunched down hard. *Crack.* He did the same thing to the other leg, *crunch, crack.* He sat me up, crossed my arms in front of me and, from behind, lifted me off the table, *crack.* He then slapped me on the back, and apologized, "I forgot your back. Everything gets twisted when we fall!" The pain is gone now and the ankle bends normally. Remarkable.

Bernard and I made some handsome cement counters last week for the kitchen and studio spaces in the guesthouse using a special cement, pigments, and a very liquid mix of concrete and gravel. We weighted the poured concrete with heavy Plexiglas and all the big rocks we could find, which forced the cement up against the Plex. When we removed the weights, we were left with an equally smooth surface with natural swirls in the pigment, which closely resembles stone. I can't wait to try the same technique in some sculpture pieces I'm working on in my head.

I've learned so much from working with Bernard on all our projects, mostly about using what's on hand. I tend to run to the hardware store to buy a tool when I'm stuck, but he just improvises. We needed heavy, even weight on the Plexiglas, but just putting stones on top made it wavy. He grabbed long, steel beam supports, laid them on top of the Plexiglas, put sheets of plywood on top. and then put the rocks on top of that, leveling the surface as he went. The beams distributed the weight of the stones evenly.

One day I was trying to make a perfect circle to cut some fabric for a table, which was over six feet in diameter. After watching me struggle and swear, he took some five-foot strips of plywood, bolted them together at one end, drove a nail in at the other end, clipped the head off another large nail with bolt cutters, leaving the sharp point, drove another nail in at the bottom of the second strip, then pulled it out and rammed a pen in the hole, showed me how the arms would articulate at the bolt, and walked off. He'd built a six-foot geometric compass, all in less than ten minutes.

Bernard is installing temporary handrails for Linda, who can't manage the irregular stone stairways without a banister. Since her heart attack and stroke five years ago, she falls so easily. Gary has to do everything for her, get her bathed, clothed, and fed. He is a wonderful support person, but he's so nervous about coming to Europe for the first time that I'm going to meet them in New York to accompany them to Paris, then drive them down to the mill, château by château.

We're trying to finish La Ruche so that our first guest artist can stay there at the end of July, but it's too far up for Linda. The house was built into a stone cliff, and the rock face still forms the back wall, which means water runs down the rock after big storms and someday we will have to decide whether to put in a French drain, which is another wall, usually of brick then plastered, with about a six-inch separation between the wet wall and the brick one, with small vents to let air pass. This system solved the rising damp problem in the mill, and it should keep the main structure of the little house dry. But the rock is so beautiful, and it has a large flat stone sink built into it. Bernard is going to try to dig a trench around the rock. We'll see.

We've decided to put the bedroom on a mezzanine level so as to not block the light from the new skylight. We're building the bathroom sink into an armoire and making two telephone-booth-sized cabinets with glass doors, one for the toilet and one for the shower. Mike is designing the tile for them, and we'll have them made at Raujole, near Millau. One of the brothers at the tile factory is an artist who does large public works in ceramic. He's thrilled to have Mike come and work with him. He'll help him choose the glazes and do trial firings for him, so the colors will be true.

April 21, 1995
Dear Linda,

Mike is off to see his new grandson and I'm here alone holding down the fort. Well, me, Germain, and Martou. (Martou is a diminutive of Marthe, as I think I told you, so our relationship has gone from madame to Marthe to Martou.)

They decided that I needed to learn to make my own duck confit, and now that I'm on the other side of that experience, I can tell you, buying it at twice the normal price is more intelligent. I had seen large hunks of duck in every butcher shop in Albi, sometimes encased in plastic, always covered with a thick layer of fat, and finally asked Martou what it was. First, she made me taste some, hot from the oven, the skin crisp and the meat dry but delicious, like duck carnitas, not at all greasy like I had imagined. Then she explained that, *autrefois*, in the old days, before refrigeration, in order to preserve their ducks they would salt and cook the meat in its own fat and then put the confit in large ceramic crocks, pouring the fat over the pieces and storing the covered jars in their *caves*. To eat it, they simply pushed back the congealed fat, took what they wanted, and then spread the fat back over the rest. Because it was salty, sterile, and covered with a protective coat of grease, the meat would last for months.

Confit is basically any meat cooked slowly in its own fat, and duck confit is not sweet little baby duckling confit, but a fully mature, twenty-pound, three-foot duck (as big as a goose), which we don't see in the States. You buy, or raise and force-feed the ducks as Germain and Martou do, slaughter and pluck them, cut them up, and salt them for a few days, then you cover them in six quarts of duck fat, then cook them for forever, then can them in mason jars, or *bocaux*. The process takes about four days.

But I didn't know that, so I speedily agreed to their tutelage. Martou told me where to go to find the best ducks, Monsieur Bonnafe at Frayssines, just on the other side of Plaisance. I called to order them, *tout prêt à faire cuire*—all ready to cook— per Martou's instructions, which I now know basically means "dead." I arrived at the farm, driving through the inevitable mud mixed with straw, animal feed, and chickens, all protected by mean dogs. There's something unnerving about arriving at a farm. Everything is big—the tractors, the barns, the hands of the farmer, and especially his wife—and everything is dirty, but honestly dirty, soiled in the name of food. I hadn't worn my rubber sabots, so as I tiptoed through the goop, I was concerned in a citified way about the conditions under which my precious (read expensive) ducks may have been slaughtered.

Giving up on my shoes, I slogged after Madame Bonnafe in her rubber boots to the back of the barn and stepped through a door that led into a bright room, surreal in its contrast to the entry. Everything, the floor, the ceiling, the walls, was in white tile, scrubbed with *eau de javel*, or bleach, and hanging from hooks along the wall was an array of big naked dead ducks. They were slightly obscene, their bellies swollen with the fattened livers that would soon be my own fresh foie gras. She unhooked two large specimens and slapped their bottoms as she plopped them into large plastic sacks, saying, "*Ne les laissez pas dans le plastique, madame.*" Leaving meat in plastic is a no-no in France, where most meat is air-dried, or wrapped loosely in parchment paper. I staggered back to the car with over forty pounds of duck slamming into my legs while I tried to nod and wave with as brave a smile as I could muster.

Back at the mill, Martou and Germain had arrived with a large white linen roll (the same that had come out for the slaughter of the lambs), with pockets for cleavers, knives, and bone-cracking scissors and were lining them up on the new terrace by the bridge. I naively rolled up my sleeves and said, "*On y va!*" Germain wagged his finger in front of my nose saying, without words, "Not yet, my dear." Martou held each duck as he carefully cut out the backbone and separated the fattened liver from its various attachments, especially the veins that run from the bile sack, a process that took over a half an hour. One false move and the entire liver, at fifty dollars a pound, has to be tossed. The foie gras, each weighing at least four pounds, was divided into lobes, wiped, wrapped in waxed paper, and popped into the freezer for later processing into either pâté or utterly delicious raw slices quickly sautéed in a pan with a slightly sweet wine reduction and light dusting of crunchy *fleur de sel* at the table. (Apparently, freezing the liver actually improves its texture.)

Once that was achieved, the gross-motor cutting started. Germain placed the duck on a large wooden block, pulled out an Alfred Hitchcock–sized cleaver, and with a few swift whacks cut the duck into manageable sections, while tiny Martou, with her severely twisted arthritic hands, deftly disconnected joints, cracked large bones, and cut the duck into serving pieces. I was actually helping by the end of the second duck. Martou had brought a huge, shallow pan in which she spread a layer of coarse salt, then arranged the duck pieces on top and sprinkled another ample layer of salt on top of them, and told me to put it in a cool, dry place until the next afternoon. She said she'd be back with the duck fat and spices for the next stage. She looked around at my new kitchen sink and my new Godin stove, sucked her teeth and asked me, "*Va-t-on le faire ici?*" But I didn't understand why she wondered where we were going to cook the ducks.

Every house in rural France, no matter how modest, has two things: a garden and a "summer kitchen." Since everyone cans vegetables and fruits from their gardens, and makes all manner of jams, jellies, and pâtés, often in five-gallon pots, they need an eighteen-inch burner attached to a gas bomb to preserve all their bounty. The burner sits on the floor in case of catastrophes, and spillovers are part of the process. So they turn part of a cellar or *cave* into a permanent big-messy-job kitchen. I've been in

Martou's, and while off-season it's neat and clean, the floor is stained with boiled-over black-currant jam and the ceiling is sticky with duck grease from years of putting up confit. But, after all, I had managed to make pâté with Martou—and Cher, Bernie, and the fisherman—in my regular old kitchen-kitchen, and it wasn't too hard to clean up. So what if it took a few days to get the grease off the stone sink and I had to take the stove apart if the cooker boiled over?

The next day started out simply enough, with Martou waddling down the drive, carrying a sauté pan that was easily thirty inches in diameter. We made two more trips to bring down the *bocaux* of duck fat she offered as a gift. She deftly dusted the salt off the duck pieces and spread a generous layer of duck fat on the bottom of the pan, which was big enough that it covered all four burners on my sparkling Godin stove. Martou alternated the duck and the fat, tucking bay leaves, juniper berries, fresh thyme sprigs, and peppercorns between the cracks, ending with a layer of several more quart jars of fat that she had saved from the dozens of ducks she cooks each year. With a final plopping spoonful—which splashed on every kitchen surface—she declared "*Ça suffit.*" ("That's enough.") It took almost an hour just to get the whole greasy mess up to a simmer, and then we watched it carefully for another two hours, moving the pieces around, and with every poke and prod pushing more and more fat onto/into the burners, the air, my clothes, my hair, and my disposition.

I calculated the number of servings of this rich protein from two large ducks and decided fifty-four portions would last me a very long time. I had visions of me dumping yucky, greasy, spoiled hunks of it from the bridge at midnight, when Martou couldn't see me, when the duck went "off." But no, Martou had other plans. It seems now, instead of cooking it for forever, we cook it for forever minus an hour and a half because we pack in *les bocaux* and cook it again for that hour and a half and then it will keep forever. At that point, I couldn't bear to think of eating any, ever.

So just when I thought we were through, we/I had to wash and dry thoroughly a couple dozen quart-sized mason jars, pick out the meat and spices from the molten liquid, separate the fat, pack the mason jars with duck, repack them with the grease, then wipe, seal, and boil them in the huge canning pot, which would only take six jars at once. By this time, Martou had graduated me to complete sous-chef status and was holding court at the kitchen table while I dripped duck fat down my arm/leg/sink/floor/counter into the *bocaux*. When the mason jars were full and sealed, they went into the canning pot, which I filled with gallons of water, put river rocks on top of the jars, and then stood watch to avoid spillovers on my Godin. Then I had to fish out the hot *bocaux*, put in another six, and so it went, on and off, on and off, while she told me the latest gossip about the couple at the farm above us called Le Carassier.

Martou has a spitfire French that I can barely understand. She speaks very quickly, laughs easily at her own jokes, and doesn't seem concerned when I chuckle in what I think are appropriate places. She said a lot in those hours, and as near as I can understand, it seems that the monsieur at Le Carassier has a problem with the pastis, and his wife put up with his evil tongue and nasty disposition for over forty-five years. But everyone knew she had been having an affair with a nice man in Plaisance for some time, and this winter, at the age of seventy-two, she left her husband to be with her lover. They moved to Réquista to avoid the social ostracism of rural culture. The story almost took my attention away from the ugly mess I was making, but when Martou suddenly asked me if she and Germain could come with me to Toulouse when I went to pick up Mike so they could see the planes landing and taking off, I stopped, wiped my hands and gave her a real American, slightly ducky hug, "Of course, you can!"

But that evening, Martou long gone, after the last duck *bocal* was placed in our cellar, as I scrubbed the burners, the floor, the sink, the hood of the stove, my shoes, and my pride, I decided never again would I "put up" confit except on the middle of the bridge or in my own summer kitchen—and that there is a reason God made butchers.

You asked about what to wear. Don't bring everything you own. Just a few bags!

—*Love, Judy*

RESTORING THE MILLRACE

May 1, 1995
Dear Linda,

Happy Mom's birthday/May Day!

I took Martou and Germain with me to the airport in Toulouse last week to pick up Mike, early enough so they could see some planes landing and taking off. Martou, clutching her purse, stood with her nose to the window, eyes wide. Germain, always

curious, bent down low to see the belly of the planes. They've taken trains to see relatives in Vichy, and Martou takes the "cure" at the baths in the Pyrenees, but they, and no one they know, has ever taken a plane. I wonder if they would ever dare to come to see us in San Francisco? No, that would be *trop, beaucoup trop*.

I was anxious to have Mike see all the work that had been done while he was gone. He had left me to supervise the first part of the restoration of the dam and the canals that will eventually bring water out of the river, into the reservoir behind the mill, and then through the house, turning our millstones and grinding our flour. The first step was to dig out the tunnels that bring water from the river, which we did last summer, bucket by bucket. After that, any wall under or behind the house that would have water in or around it had to be reinforced and *crépie*'d. Then the reservoir behind the mill had to be repaired with layers of cement and a final coat of *crepi*, which Bernard and Pechou have been carrying through the living room, wheelbarrow by wheelbarrow. Germain's son, Yves, had hurried to install five new sluice gates to control the flow of the water from the river, down the canal or millrace, to the reservoir.

The millrace ends just at our back terrace, theoretically, in a horizon-pool double waterfall on each side. To repair it required a precision that had even a veteran mason, Bernard, sweating for days. He didn't want to initiate it without Mike, so when we arrived from the airport, he was standing in the doorway, turning his khaki *crepi-*splattered mason's cap in his huge hands. *"Venez, venez le voir."* ("Come, come and see it.")

Mike, standing on the terrace where the millrace ends, bent over to check the level of the two sides of the canal, and asked, "Will it work?"

Bernard shrugged his shoulders, took a deep drag on his Gauloise, *"On verra."* ("We'll soon see.")

We *would* soon see, but after Mike admired the rest of the work. He reached over and pulled on the small sluice gate at the end of the chute, admiring Yves's ingenuity in making the opening variable with a simple hole-and-peg system. He then walked slowly along the newly rebuilt millrace wall, the one Bernard had to break down during our flood last year. As Mike strolled the narrow passage twenty feet above the rocks in the river below, I made a mental note to get Yves to make a handrail along that path. Mike tried the other two small gates, one for irrigating the garden, the other for emergency diversion, then stood in front of the two winch handles, one to lift the heavy metal clean-out door, and the other to open the flow through the tunnel, down the millrace, and hopefully fill the chute to the edge, then overflow gently into the reservoir. He had no idea how much to open the door, so he conservatively did two small turns on the wheel, the steel door slid open ever so slightly, and we held our breath as the stream of water ran down the bed of the canal and slowly filled it to its brim. Bernard had spent hours calculating the pitch of the canal and the length of the depression in the border, but there was no way to know if he was right. A wave of water rushed down the chute, crashed into the end, swirled back, then settled in while it filled the full two-hundred-foot length of the canal. The level inched up slowly to the top edge, then, at exactly the same time and in one motion, the clear water spilled over the two sides and splashed into the reservoir below, forming a dramatic two-sided waterfall. Bernard jumped in the air, hat in hand, *"WAAAAAYYYY!"* (That's how *oui* sounds in a French high-five: "Yeeeesssss!") I actually cried. And Germain's usual teary eyes flowed over freely when he came by later that afternoon. He's brought each of his seven children and all available grandchildren over since, and tears flowed each time.

But all that seems like child's play compared to the present project: the repair of the dam and the much larger reservoir behind. The millrace and its waterworks control a very small flow of water compared to taming the entire river. Dams or weirs in wide, shallow rivers may only be a few feet high, but in the steep canyon where the Mousse cuts deeply into the schist cliffs between Brasc and the Rance River, there's a 20-foot-high dam, in need of repair but mostly intact, and about 7 feet thick at the base, across a 40-foot narrow in the river. That's our dam! In the spring when there is abundant water, the overflow from the dam forms a spectacular waterfall that crashes down on wide flat rocks that form part of the wall of the dam itself.

When we started, the reservoir behind the dam was full of mud brought down by years of flash floods and neglect. The top of the dam was damaged in the 1993 flood, and the water flowed mostly off to the right rather than forming an even cataract. Years of erosion have exposed crevices in the seven-foot-thick stone wall of the dam, which, when we've finished, will be filled and a layer of *crepi* put down to keep debris from collecting in the cracks. To do that, we had to dig out all of that mud and debris with a bulldozer, and before that, Bernard and Pechou had to rebuild the path on the other side of the river, making it wide enough to run a small bulldozer down and up behind the dam/waterfall.

What we were doing with a bulldozer and three strong young men, Germain and his father used to do, every spring, with a shovel and a pick and an odd U-shaped tool with pointed hooks bent at a right angle at the tops of the U, the same one that hangs on the hook next to the oil press along with the wooden cross from the pigpen, the same one that brought tears to Germain's eyes when he saw it again after thirty years. He and his father would divert part of the river through one of the sluice gates, then wade into the icy waters of the Mousse, dig down through eight feet of mud and leaves to the top plank of the clean-out door, and bang the prongs of that U-shaped tool into the board. Then, one pulling from the top of the dam, the other waist deep in cold muddy water, they would wrench, tug, lever, and finally yank out the first plank and watch the river sweep away the dirt down to the top of the next board, then yank, step back, yank and step back, until the bottom of the dam was exposed and the water ran clear. For Germain and his father, the timing was delicate, since there had to be enough water to clean out the mud but not so much that the river couldn't be redirected through the sluice gate. Then they had to rebuild the clean-out door, every year. Under perfect conditions it was a cold, dirty, and sometimes, dangerous job, as it was shaping up to be thirty years later.

For that long overdue clean-out, the decision had been made to chop through the plank door from in front rather than try to wrench the planks one by one behind the dam. The possibility of a major cave-in, or tons of rock and mud crashing too quickly through the opening, had been thoroughly discussed, and Bernard and Pechou decided that the risk was worth taking, given the cold and dirty alternative. They decided to have a rope around a tree to quickly pull themselves out of the way if necessary, however.

The next day, leaving the rusty tool on its hook, Bernard and Pechou, each with a logger's axe, slid down the bank to the flat rock that forms the base of the dam where the main clean-out door, closed by the old chestnut planks, could be accessed from the front. Pechou shivered in a rain slicker, while Bernard stripped to his T-shirt, throwing his clean khaki work shirt back up onto the path while they waited for a signal from Jean-Claude to break down the door. Behind the dam, working in the riverbed in his bright red bulldozer, Jean-Claude had managed to divert the water, making the entire river crash down on the rocks off to the side, the mist billowing up and condensing on faces, hands, and axe handles. Finally, Jean-Claude signaled to Bernard with a mimed swing of an axe that it was time to go after the planks.

The opening is about seven feet high by six feet deep, with the thirty-year-old chestnut planks, water trickling through them, barely visible through the drizzle. Bernard and Pechou, dragging their axes, disappeared from our view from the terrace into the mist. A few minutes later, hollering with mixed fear and pleasure, they came flying out, grabbed the rope, and pulled themselves up to the path, while a small river of mud oozed out the opening. They gave Jean-Claude the signal to let 'er rip, and thirty years of debris, mud, rock, and gravel washed by the free flow of the river through the base of the dam on its way to the Rance River. Bernard and Pechou, whoo-hooing all the way, climbed up the path, then dropped down behind the dam to the now visible broken planks and pulled them out easily, one by one. Somehow, Bernard managed to stay relatively dry, but Pechou was shaking as he waded up to his waist in the freezing water to pull out another board. (I couldn't stand it any longer, so I drove straight to Coupiac and bought him some waders, size short.)

Things progressed more quickly after that, that is until we heard a loud, angry voice: "*Qu'est-ce que vous foutez là?*" ("What the fuck are you doing?") It was Monsieur Colomb, the mayor of Plaisance, shaking his fist in anger. It seems we had picked the opening day of the fishing season to clean out our dam, and our thirty-year stash of mud and rock was flooding and muddying first the Rance River fishing holes, then the waters of the Tarn all the way to Ambialet, thirteen miles downstream.

I hastened to apologize profusely, stammering in my pidgin French, to tell him how *bête*, or stupid, we were to pick such a day and, without taking a breath, tried to explain to him how we were trying to repair the fishing holes in our communal Mousse River, and how the fishermen could come up the path to find larger and larger trout in the new reservoir, and that he and they were welcome any time, and how this would never happen again, ever, we promise, and we're so sorry, and how can we make up for it, and would he have a pastis while we talk?

There is a natural tension between millers and fishermen, since weirs and dams tend to block the migration of fish, so fish ladders are theoretically required in any remaining mill dam. The mayor started to remind us of that until he looked again at the twenty-foot-high structure and realized the futility of any fish making it up that distance, even with a ladder, shook his head, took the pastis, threw it back, shook our hands, and split.

And now, *moi aussi*.

—*Hugs, Judy*

May 10, 1995
JOURNAL ENTRY

We had a small fête to celebrate the dam and water canals and the departure of Claude *bois*. He had put the final touches on the new stairs and the cabinets in the little house and won't be back for a while, so Bernard *pierre* is quite content to have the full command of the mill project. We served pastis in the barn, with little pizzas from our new/old bread oven. Since we gave Claude a Laguiole knife and had given Pechou new waders during the dam breakdown, we thought we should recognize Bernard even though he has a few months of work left to do. I had been collecting his crumpled packages of Gauloise cigarettes since the beginning of the project, and I put them in a gift box and wrapped it, bow and all. When he saw the package, Bernard was quite touched until he opened it. As he dumped them all onto the oak floor, the entire work crew fell out laughing, including Bernard. We'll see if it has any long-term impact on his littering habit.

We had dinner last night at Les Magnolias, and I'm worried about Francis. His hands are shaking more and more, and he's obviously physically exhausted. When I asked him, "*Comment vas-tu?*" instead of saying he's fine, as usual, he replied slowly, brows furrowed, his half-dyed lock of hair stuck to his forehead, that he thinks he's deeply depressed. He had told me once that his mother had had emotional problems and had finally committed suicide by throwing herself off a bridge in Toulouse into the Garonne River. His doctor, a close friend who knew his family history, told him his problems were all in his head.

Watching the cool exchanges between him and Marie-France, I'm beginning to believe that maybe the doctor's right: marital problems could be contributing to his overall stress and fatigue. But he has classic symptoms of cardiovascular disease: gout, fatigue, even pressure in his chest.

As we left the table near the fireplace in the small dining room, we talked about Francis and his family coming over for dinner on Mondays when they could, as they did last year. We had been talking about smoking some foie gras, and now that I've got four big lobes in the freezer, I'm anxious to do it. But he says he no longer has the energy to go out on his day off. He's fifty-four years old.

LINDA'S VISIT TO THE MILL

May 15, 1995
Dear Linda,

I hope your bunion surgery will be well healed by the time we arrive in Paris. We'll take it slow. We'll have a good time at the mill in any event. Bernard promises to put some handrails on the paths going up to the terrace above the waterfall, where I expect to whomp yo' butt at cribbage.

I know you're nervous about meeting our French friends because of the language. But they're all quite patient, speak trickles of English, and love to play the professor. We'll avoid Monsieur Parnat, and most likely the lady from La Bonne Rive, a farm on the road between La Pilande Basse and Coupiac. It's hard to describe her house, but imagine a house built on the side of a steep hill, with the wall of the second story of the house right on the shoulder of the road, so you look down into the courtyard formed by the house and the barn. If you drive slowly enough, you can catch a glimpse of rural France from another era. The muddy yard, delineated by the house on one side and the low back wall, allows a view into the steep meadow below that is capped by a stone cross. The square courtyard is closed on the fourth side by a huge stone barn, its *lauze* roof falling in, and decaying stacks of hay bales holding the side wall in place. An old rusty tractor, one tire gone, is in the side yard, grass growing up between the wheels. The courtyard is full of chickens and empty bottles saved for some purpose, laundry hanging rain or shine, multiple cats, and one very mean-looking dog. A single light bulb hangs from a wire by the front door.

The first year we were here, we had some brave friends come to visit us. We took off in our Twingo to go into Coupiac to have some of Lynne's duck-fat French frics for lunch. Just as we were passing La Bonne Rive, an old woman, babushka tight around her head, her purse jammed up to her elbow, jumped out in front of the car, frantically waving both hands to get us to stop. When I did, she ran to the passenger side and pushed our friend into the middle of the car where there was no seat, shouting, "*On y va! C'est l'heure de la messe.*" Apparently, we were to give her a ride to Mass. I asked her somewhat naively if she usually walks to the church in Coupiac, about three miles one way. But with a crooked finger wagging, swollen joints pointing forty-five degrees to her right, she exclaimed, "Never, there's always someone I can stop." I've since picked her up a few times, hoping to wrangle an invitation to see her house, which apparently hasn't changed in over a century. Her husband died forty years ago in a tractor rollover accident, trying to plow that steep meadow below the house, a common cause of death for farmers on the steep hills of the Aveyron. Since then, she lives alone in a house with no plumbing and two light bulbs, one in the kitchen, one outside.

I usually drive past her house slowly in case she needs a ride. With her white wiry hair, thin and wild around a prune face with transparent, vacant blue eyes, how old must she be? She's at least seventy-five. Then last week I saw her walking along the side of the road, not toward Coupiac, but on the stretch between Coupiac and Plaisance. When I pulled over to see if she wanted a ride, she said, "*Oh non, madame,* I was visiting my mother in Plaisance and I'm so pissed off at her I need to walk off my anger!" So if she's seventy-five, what does that make her mother? So remember, duck fat and red wine are good for something.

—*Hugs, Judy*

June 4, 1995
JOURNAL ENTRY
Mid-Atlantic

Yesterday, my beautiful baby girl Jenea walked down the aisle! She received her diploma from Harvard, threw her cap in the air, and ran through the streets of Cambridge with her classmates toward their future. I'm so proud. Now I'm on my way to New York to see Derek and then to meet Gary and Linda at the airport in New York so we can fly together to Paris for a few days before we drive down to the mill. Since Linda's problems began, she's had four different surgeries, all trying to ease the pain from contracting muscles caused by nerve damage during her stroke. The last was only five months ago for a bunion on her dragging foot, but because of her poor circulation, it's been healing very slowly. I'm afraid she won't be able to walk through the arch into the grand courtyard of the Louvre. I want to see her face light up like it used to. Neither Linda nor Gary has ever been to Europe, and they're both worried about the currency exchange and getting cheated and pickpocketed. That's better than being shot, which is what most Europeans worry about when visiting New York.

June 10, 1995
JOURNAL ENTRY
Paris

Linda and Gary met me at JFK in New York. Linda walked down the ramp, clutching her purse, deep furrows between her dark brown eyes, watching the ramp in front of her carefully. John Hoffensberger, her hometown stylist, had obviously just cut her thick brown hair into a contemporary, him-hoping-Parisian hairstyle, and her shoes, purse, and coat were carefully coordinated. I, in my New York black, felt underdressed for her grand voyage. Gary hovered at her elbow, nervously looking around at the multicultural diversity of New York on his first visit there. English had already been replaced by strange grunts and clicks of words from people of every color elbowing their way into the territorial space of two solid Midwesterners. They couldn't see me through the crowd, so they followed the black rubber mat toward the unknown.

Gary is a remarkable man. He's always up: a glad-you-stopped-by kind of guy, positive, funny, well informed, curious, and incapable of sitting still in quiet contemplation. The second of seven sons, as a teenager he took care of his father who was dying of ALS, put his brothers through college, married my sister, and is now taking care of her, helping her to bathe and dress herself, arranging an active social life, cooking, and until last month, working full-time. Linda gets upset with him, sometimes pulling her arm away when he is trying to help her, then getting angry when he hasn't anticipated some potential problem. Strokes do strange things to personalities, but Gary had read all the books, so he knew. When I look shocked at her apparently inappropriate outbursts, Gary shrugs, "That's the stroke talking."

As they made their way down the ramp, I watched her pull away from his hand at her elbow, then grabbing his as the crowd closed around them. Then Linda saw me, and her face lit up as tears filled her eyes, "I can't believe we're really going to Paris. I'm terrified! I brought everything I own. I can't walk very far. I want to see everything!"

Our arrival at Charles de Gaulle was uneventful, and the taxi ride to our hotel in the Marais could have taken place in Chicago, and I could see Gary realizing that the two countries are more alike than different. At our little hotel, one of the two gay owners asked for our passports, a holdover from another time. I felt he would rather not host Americans, especially straight ones, but Gary and Linda didn't seem to notice so I kept quiet. We took a taxi immediately to the tourist bus stand on the rue de Rivoli, and Linda struggled bravely up to the top of the bright red double-decker bus. My reluctance to be such an obvious tourist disappeared when the bus turned onto the street toward the place du Carrousel, stopping for the best view through the Arc de Triomphe on the right and the Pyramid and the Louvre to the left. Linda leapt to her feet and clung to the handrail. I choked back my tears, then slapped Gary on the back, "I'm glad you stopped by."

The rest of our stay was joyous but heart wrenching. Linda refused any wheelchair proposed at the Louvre or elsewhere, and navigated the narrow steps to restrooms in the brasseries. We went to Fontainebleau and pretended to be riding white stallions, clop-clopping our tongues as we held imaginary reins high in our supposedly kid-gloved hands, pushing our imaginary bustles aside as we demounted our imaginary steeds, laughing and ignoring the stares of other visitors. But she tripped so easily, and the cobblestones were impossible for her to navigate for long, so we retreated to the gardens with crusty sandwiches and screw-top splits of wine.

Back in Paris, she stumbled on the steps leading down to the little park on the nose of the Ile de la Cité, and her enthusiasm began to drain out, along with her energy. We skipped most of the museums and just enjoyed the parks, and, of course, the food markets at place Monge, Raspail, and Grenelle. She never tired of moving through the stalls of olives, Moroccan spices, pigs' ears, anise biscuits, cheeses, sausages, strange fish, and the paella steaming in huge flat pans. We picnicked almost every day so she could try that one and that one. "Oh, no, that one, too."

From Paris, I decided to take three days to drive to the mill. I had found some special small châteaux and planned the trip around them. I had this fantasy that Linda could enter some escape place, like our childhood princess play-castles, where she would forget all her pain, crack out of her invalidism, and emerge the old/new Linda. The first night we stayed at a charming little château near Poitiers that had only six rooms and lots of little pointy towers. She was visibly enthralled with the beauty of the gardens, and she insisted on walking all around to see the towers from every angle. But her foot would drag with every step if she didn't concentrate, and she was exhausted by the end of her tour of the grounds.

In our few days together in Paris, I began to suspect that Gary might be doing too much for her and that maybe that was impeding her progress. Then, at the hotel, Linda called my room to ask if I had a hair dryer. I said, "Sure, come on down and get it," thinking that's what a normal person would do, and I so desperately wanted her to be normal. I waited and waited, until a full thirty minutes later, she knocked on my door. "Where the hell have you been?" I asked before I noticed that she had my room number pinned on her shirt. Only then did I realize that the stroke had left her short-term memory so bad that she couldn't remember, from one floor to the next, in a six-room hotel, my room number. She had tried, but if Gary hadn't finally written it down, she wouldn't have made it at all. To be sure she could make it back, she was also clutching her own room key, the number engraved on the wooden knob. I hugged her close, hoping she wouldn't see my tears of realization, then walked her back out the door toward her room.

The next day we drove south, taking the back roads through one beautiful little village after another. Our next stop was in Brantôme, where we stayed at the Moulin de la Gorce and ate at the Moulin de l'Abbaye, trying to prepare for our arrival at our own mill. Linda, who was working on a Ph.D. before her multiple problems, had a hard time understanding how a mill works and why they're necessary. Short-term memory is necessary for learning new things, and while she seemed to understand at the time, she couldn't remember the basic concept the next day. (I guess I'll have to forgive her for forgetting to tell me that our grandmother died six months ago. Gary thought she had, and there is no one else left who could have.) She was definitely forgiven when we arrived at the mill and she said, tears in her eyes, "I feel like I know it already. Where's the bread oven? Where's Bernard and his wheelbarrow? Can we eat tonight at Les Magnolias?"

June 15, 1995

JOURNAL ENTRY

I feel as if I'm finally grieving for my sister. It's been six years since she had her heart attack and stroke, and while I thought I knew how handicapped she was, I kept thinking she could improve. I saw her whenever I was back in the States, for short visits, but never like this, out of her home, confronting new concepts. In my mind, in my absence she was continuing to improve, but seeing my room number pinned to her blouse on our trip to the mill made me realize how futile her recovery was. My sister is gone: the verbal banter, the hard lobs she used to hit when we'd fight—those things are missing. There's a new person there who looks like her, talks about our parents, and can pull up old memories with no problem—a sweet fifty-two-year-old lady who loves to flirt with Bernard and Pechou and play cards, even though she can no longer add or subtract.

When her heart stopped the first time, she was in Reno and I got there before Gary did. From her hospital bed, she reminded me that our mom, when she herself was dying at forty-six years of age, had told us that nothing ever happens that's truly "bad" unless you don't learn anything from the experience. Mom was always under too much stress, which undoubtedly contributed to her early demise, and our father smoked heavily until a major stroke struck him when he was forty-eight, which left him, too, with the mentality of an uneducable child. Having witnessed his crushing loss of dignity, Linda and I made a pact that if either one of us ever had a debilitating stroke, the other would help the first commit suicide if she wanted it. For three years after Linda's stroke during open-heart surgery, she begged me to fulfill that promise.

"You promised."

"I lied. I didn't know you, too, would be only forty-six. I can't. Please let it go."

Last week, sitting on the new terrace above the waterfall, Linda admitted she hadn't learned from our parents' experiences, and that she had continued to smoke and continually put herself under enormous stress in spite of warnings from doctors and friends. I explained to her that her suffering had been important in the decision that Mike and I had made to change our lifestyle, and that I had been on that same stress train and could well have gone into the same tunnel. I told her this again yesterday and she said, holding back tears, "Thank you. That means it wasn't all a bad thing. I'm proud of you, and please keep sending me your letters. I read them to all my friends. It makes them so jealous!"

I tried to explain the other benefits of our move to France, how we feel, maybe for the first time, more in touch, not only with people here, but with ourselves. By examining our differences, we see our similarities. We're required to explain our politics and our social system, which makes us look at our own values and culture much more closely. I tried to explain how privileged we feel to be here. Not everyone has the luxury to do what we're doing. She knows we worked hard for what we have, and that we feel a need to pay back by bringing American artists here who might not be able come on their own.

But I don't think she understood. Not really.

OUR FIRST GUEST ARTIST

June 27, 1995
Dear Linda,

I can't believe you came and went so fast. I knew Gary would figure out the money thing and you'd take off and you did. But Nice, Monaco, and Italy? All in two weeks? So, were your friends appropriately envious?

Hayden has declared himself 100 percent recovered. While number-one son Derek is getting ready to get married! They've decided the wedding will be at the beach house in Inverness, so get your ticket. We'll be coming home early, getting ready for the wedding, then probably coming back to the mill for a month or so in November.

Mike has his first show in France at a beautiful gallery in a fortified barn up on one of the broad plateaus, called *les causses*, above the Roquefort cheese caves. It's a group show, with about twelve local artists, and a chance for us to finally start to network with the art community in the Aveyron. The gallery space is the home and studios of a Parisian couple, Elizabeth and Claude Baillon, who moved here about twenty years ago to work and show the work of others. In spite of being completely *perdu* in the middle of nowhere, they usually have about three hundred people at every opening, or *vernissage*, and they have a respected national reputation. We had seen Elizabeth and her daughter's work in a show at the château in Coupiac and were quite impressed by the quality of their paintings and textiles. Jean-Michel, Eveline, Mike, and I went up to meet them, then invited them to the mill to see Mike's paintings, and they asked him to join the group show next month. Now, he's into serious framing.

He will be showing his drawings and etchings of the old men in Latour-de-France, where we stayed when we first started this adventure. When you retire in France, you can no longer work, or at least be paid for working, and every village has a bench in the center of town with a changing array of half a dozen retired men, bored, dumpy, staring at passersby, with an equally ratty pack of dogs at their feet that follows them from home to the bench, to lunch, to the bench, to dinner. Sometimes, the old men play *pétanque*, a form of lawn bowling, but mostly they just wait. It's that silent waiting that makes them so haunting. Mike surreptitiously, somewhat compulsively, photographed and drew them until he knew them, maybe too well. At fifty-eight, maybe he feels some camaraderie, or perhaps revulsion at their total lack of curiosity, or energy, or *joie de vivre*. In his etchings, he abstracted their forms, putting hats from other centuries on them, their nasty dogs peeing on their legs, showing their physical inertia through static images. He used many of these images in his M.F.A. show last year at the San Francisco Art Institute (the Toot). It will be interesting to see the French reaction to this cultural statement about aging. His work will be even more engaging when shown against the stone vaults of the gallery.

In art school we often talked about wall people, painters and printmakers, and floor people, sculptors. I'm convinced their brains work differently. Mike, a wall person, can see a photo composition that I will never see. But he can't hang the painting or photo on a wall, since he doesn't consider the space around it. It usually ends up at eye level, which, since he's six foot five, no one else can see. I, however, can't even start to work on something unless I know the space it will occupy. I start there and then build something.

But, for now, I have to get ready for Dan Pillers, our first artist-in-residence next month. I met him in the welding studio at the Toot a few years ago while we were both compulsively trying to learn to weld while constructing weird and wonderful things. We were also the senior citizens, he being about fifteen years younger than me and fifteen years older than the rest. He was in his pod phase and I in my making prototypes-that-didn't-work phase. Neither is worth explaining. Thankfully, both phases passed quickly, thanks to the constant nagging of Adrienne Mendel, our sculpture professor at the time, who is also coming for a week this month.

Dan has become a good friend, and as one can do with gay guys, we talk about everything us girls talk about: sex, clothes, makeup, art, parents, and lovers. We were going to wait to invite him next year, but he has AIDS and his health has been deteriorating. I was afraid if he didn't come this year it might be too late. Bernard is going to give Dan and me a weekend stone-cutting class, and I can't decide what I want to make. (I confess I learn more about sculpture and building things from Bernard than I ever did from Adrienne at the Toot.) Dan can help me set up the sculpture studio, pick out tools, etc. What's better than cruising a *quincaillerie* (a hardware store)? Buying tools, that's what. Their tools are so elegant. Their hand tools, I mean. Oh, don't you go there . . .

—*Hugs, Judy*

July 14, 1995
JOURNAL ENTRY

Dan Pillers arrived for six weeks, full of enthusiasm and pain. It's been one year since his last lover died of AIDS. He's lost four partners and countless friends in the past seven or eight years. He has put together a body of work from that pain that won him the outstanding-student-of-the-year award at the Art Institute last year. Much of his work is performance, such as sitting in public spaces and tearing red fabric into small pieces and handing them out to people. Other works are more ephemeral, figurative forms on beaches that are destroyed by waves.

Dan is quite shell-shocked, but remarkably upbeat about life in general, and his observations about our life here are enlightened. He's already noticed that people here in the country use everything, like wild dandelions in salads and omelettes, and whey, or *petit lait*, in cakes and custards. They stuff the neck skins of ducks with sausage and nuts, save the luscious duck grease, give peelings to animals and compost the rest. He wants to try it all. He particularly wanted to taste rabbit, which is served in rural France as often as chicken, so we took off for Brousse-le-Château, which has a little restaurant on the Tarn River that always serves a *lapin à la moutarde*. As we toodled along the river, an animal truck pulled out in front of us, loaded with rabbit cages. We followed them for a few miles, their little faces poked through the wire, noses twitching. Finally, I asked him if he was sure about tasting a dead one. He asked me how to say "too bad" in French, and when I told him "*tant pis*," he rolled down the window and shouted, "*Tant pis*, Fluffy!"

July 26, 1995
Dear Linda,

The week that was: guest artist from hell. As you know, we intend to invite artists to come to stay with us at the mill for a minimum of three weeks to a month, for selfish reasons. It's cheaper than a semester at the Art Institute, and I think I'll learn more from watching them work than I ever could in a class. They will have their own little house, and we'll rent them a car. Life will be great. But since it's a fairly intimate situation, we decided, as a rule, to have them come visit for a short time the year before so we can check them out.

Dan Pillers, my studio mate from the Toot, is here for six weeks this summer, but no need to check him out since we've been welding together for some time now. But one of our professors, Adrienne Mendel, invited herself for "the short visit," when Dan was going to be here. She's not my favorite professor; she's judgmental and not supportive, but I do respect her work, so I said yes. She has won awards primarily for large public installations, often including water elements, such as sculptures that can turn into kids' sprinklers on hot New York days, and the mill seemed a natural setting for her.

She's been here a week, and I'm going to kill her. Well, maybe Dan's going to kill her first, that is if Mike doesn't beat us to it. Dan and I set up an itinerary, including a stone-cutting workshop with Bernard *pierre*, a trip to a local forge, a visit to Jean-

Michel's ceramic studio and one to see Mike's show in the fortified-farm-turned-art-gallery, a trip to the source of the Midi Canal with its dam and a park designed to celebrate the waterworks, and a day trip to the cave in Pech Merle, which has paintings that are about thirty thousand years old.

I won't go into how she dragged a chair down and up the path to the waterfall on the other side of the river to ensconce herself on the big flat rock where the water crashes down and refused to participate in the stone cutting with Bernard, because she'd been there, done that. Or how she walked into the forge and turned around and walked out, saying the same thing. How she dismissed Jean-Michel's work as amateurish and called the work of the artists on the plateau "craft." How she, who claims to be the master of water-articulated public art, showed no interest in going to the source of the Midi Canal, even though Mike had purchased a rare book explaining the unique articulation of the water source. Or how she screamed at me when I put some of my own clothes in my own washing machine along with hers when she needed to do some laundry. Or how she spent hours telling us and retelling us how she and her husband haven't lived together for over twenty-five years because she still is angry at him for some transgression or other, and that her daughter is trying to recover from doing speed and hasn't spoken to her since Adrienne stopped speaking to her husband.

No, the final blow was the cave of Pech Merle. It's about a three-hour drive from La Pilande Basse, and we got an early start since the number of visitors allowed for the day is limited. She sat in the back seat and lectured Dan and me the entire trip about how important her work was in New York circles, while Dan and I made monster faces in the front seat. I was sure the cave would be a major disappointment, like everything else, so I was ready for whatever foul thing she might have to say.

At the cave, you descend into the darkness through a small, somewhat oppressive tunnel, with a guide and a few other visitors. We stayed near the back so I could translate the discussion, and we sometimes found ourselves a bit left behind. The ochre lines of strange beasts emerging out of the dark, the red and black outlined hands, some with missing fingers—injuries or signatures—always touch me in a way no museum ever has. Whether those images are religious icons or idle graffiti doesn't matter to me. But the footprints, actual impressions of a small foot in the clay floor of the cave that have kept their perfect shape for so long are what still startle me most. Adrienne was strangely silent through the entire visit, and when we finally emerged out of the dark into the hot July sun, she surprised us both when she exclaimed, "That was stunning. Unbelievable. That man made art before he made tools!" And then she turned and started in on me, "THIS is where we should have started my visit, not wasting five days on trivial projects. THIS is what art is, THIS is where it started!"

I looked at Dan, he looked at me, and I said what any red-blooded, scolded American child would say: "I need some French fries."

"Me, too," said Dan, both agreeing to some silent, undefined conspiracy.

We didn't ask her but went to the little concession stand next to the entry to the cave, and she had no choice but to join us. We sat down on sticky plastic chairs at the sticky plastic tables topped with a faded blue Orangina umbrella, with our hot, crunchy fries tumbling from a paper cup. It was almost August, and as in all hot, dry countries, a wasp beelined, or wasplined, to the food. Then two, three, dozens of wasps, in swarms they lighted, hoping to cut out a small section of our *pommes frites*. They landed on the fries at first, then our hands and arms. Dan and I, in an unspoken complicity, acted as if that were completely normal as they covered the table, her fries, her hands, then our faces, then hers. Dan was as cool as I needed him to be, no gesture of concern, which gave me courage to roll my eyes and talk about the drive back, should we take back roads or the *péage*? She flailed, they came, we sat still as they went after her food, until finally she shrieked and ran, and we sat and laughed and laughed, a little too hysterically, but what pleasure to terrify the "terrifier." She said not one word on the long drive home.

I don't think the "short visit" will be followed by a "long visit" next year.
—*Hugs, Judy*

July 31, 1995
Dear Linda,

I'm glad you met Bernard *pierre* while you were here so you can envision a bit of our past two weeks. He spent two weekends showing Dan, Mike, and me the basics of stone cutting: picking the rock, how to move it without getting hurt, making a pattern, or *gabarit*, of the ultimate image, plucking plumb lines around the rock, then how to hold the basic tools, how to make them bounce gently over the surface of the stone to dress it, or use single sharp, vertical whacks to split it into large chunks.

Picking the rock was the easiest/hardest part. Easy, since we have a sandstone quarry at Coupiac, and hard because we had to load them into Bernard's truck, transport them, and get them onto a workable surface. We picked sandstone since it's available and relatively easy to shape. We had some granite chunks that we had brought back from the Sidobre (a large granite quarry in the south of France), but Bernard said granite has to be worked within days of coming out of the ground since it's quite soft when first quarried but quickly becomes, well, granite in full oxygen and is impossible to cut, even with a diamond wheel.

We started at the quarry, watching Bernard assess the stones: first a hammer tap to test for major faults, a foot rocking to assess the weight, then the crowbar roll to the truck. Dan guessed the larger rocks weighed at least three hundred pounds, which Bernard, all by himself, moved from the ground to the truck bed by building a stone staircase with smaller stones to allow him to lever and flip the larger rocks up toward the bed of the truck, shimming the lower edge as he hoisted the boulder with a crowbar. Dan and I were not allowed to come anywhere near him during this process, since Bernard didn't want any amateurs around in case the rock or the staircase slipped. He wanted to be able to get out of the way and fast. It took almost two hours to load, then, with the back end of the truck almost scraping the ground, we crept out of the quarry, driving ever so slowly back to the mill, down the gravel driveway, across the bridge. Bernard then angled the front of the truck up onto the bank of the ditch at the base of the cliff, forcing the back of the truck almost to the ground. He jumped out, picked up the crowbar, and tumbled the huge boulders onto the ground, slapped his stone-dusty hands against his khaki work pants, and declared in his signature gap-toothed grin, "*Simple, n'est-ce pas?*"

Then came the tool lesson. Now, I love tools. They teach in art school that form often follows function, and it is true. It's also no wonder that many important sculptors often start with their basic instruments, abstract them, change their materials, and then blow them up into marvelous, graceful shapes. The back of Bernard's truck is usually his toolbox, overflowing with stone chisels, elegant blades with graceful handles that were developed over centuries. He had lined up the tools on the bridge before we left for Coupiac to get the stone, and they were waiting in silent vigil when we returned. Bernard started at one end of the array for our lesson. The tools come in all sizes and shapes, and he's color-coded the handles so he doesn't have to scrounge around in the back of the truck for the right chisel or hammer. The large red one with the four-inch flat blade is for scoring, the orange one with teeth is for rough dressing, and the little gray one, the only one light enough I can use for more than five minutes, is for defining the shape. The hammers range from small tack-hammer size to twenty-pound sledgehammers, which I can barely hoist over my shoulder.

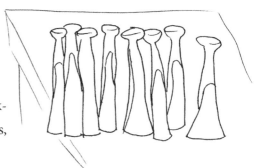

He took one of the smaller rocks, about three feet by two feet, and began chipping a small cleft into the full length of the surface. He turned it ninety degrees and continued the line. Again he turned it to the third side. He then took out a medium-sized hammer and the large, flat chisel and, with one smart crack on the top, took exactly one-third off the shoulder of that rock. He took a smaller chisel and started rounding the cracked edge, making tiny taps, bouncing the chisel off the stone. He then took the serrated blade and chipped the flat side to take away the "broken" quality of the surface. As he was demonstrating, Bernard talked about the signature markings on stones in cathedrals and other important buildings. The mason who dressed the stone would always leave his particular sign or initial on one face. He talked about cutting 6-foot-wide, 18-inch-thick millstones out of a quarry, and how a 10-foot-square block of rock could be cracked precisely by making slits around the square and driving wooden wedges into the slits. Water was dripped onto the wood, and the slight swelling would pop off a two-ton slab that could be formed into a thick, round millstone with ease.

With ease? As we watched for about a half an hour, Bernard tapped the stone with an eight-pound hammer about sixty times a minute, or almost two thousand times. Dan, who is a landscape gardener in his day job, had no problem with this. He picked his rock and his hammer and, with minimum instruction from Bernard, started on his bushel-basket-sized stone, the head of a three-part piece he'd sketched out. He had the edges knocked off in no time. Rapping, rocking, and bouncing the chisel, he whistled a happy tune.

I, who can do three reps of eight with a ten-pound weight at the gym, was good for about thirty seconds. I tried the smaller hammer, which didn't seem to make much of a dent in the large, flat stone I had chosen. I had decided to make a door for our bread oven, like I had seen in some book. It looked beautiful and insular, and besides, I'm incapable of making something without knowing where it will go, and it seemed practical. Bernard told me I had chosen the most difficult thing he could think of to start with: a three-inch-thick by three-foot-square block that had to be perfectly flat. I showed him the picture, he shook his head and said, "*D'accord.*" "Alrighty, then."

Now he went for the real tools. He pulled out a twenty-pound grinder with a ten-inch cutting wheel, something only he could lift and control, and told me to stand back. He wedged the stone, put one foot on top, and went at it . . . *eerrrooooonnnnnnn.* A sound I'd never heard and an explosion of stone dust spun out of the wheel. I could no longer see Bernard, who wore no ear or eye protection, much less a dust mask, his Gauloise hanging from his lip behind the screen of floating sandstone. Coughing and choking, I ran to the lower-barn-turned-my-studio-space for a dust mask, earplugs, and goggles. By the time I had collected the "necessary" equipment, Bernard was done. The odd-shaped stone had been cut down and formed into a reasonable facsimile of the shape of a bread oven door, and he was tapping the serrated edge of the stone chisel against the smooth surface, softening the precision cut of the grinder.

"Okay, are you ready to do some art now?" he asked sarcastically.

"Yes, I want to make *this*!" I said, holding up the first tool I could find in my work apron, which happened to be a pair of scissors. I was as surprised as he was—I usually agonize over decisions about what to make. "Just the handles, but big, of course."

"Okay, but I'll do one side and you do the other, or I'll be here until next month!"

He pulled out my smaller grinder, the size used by metal workers to finish welding joints, and quickly changed the metal-

grinding wheel for a stone-cutting wheel. He showed me how to hold it, and warned me about kickback, which can happen if the spinning surface comes in contact with the stone from the wrong direction. He used his monster machine to rough-cut two large stones into the approximate size while I drew the details of the handles on kraft paper to the scale I wanted. In spite of my impulsive, almost petulant decision to make the scissor handles in stone, I was already envisioning the blades in plywood, and then cut on an angle to expose the layers. Rock, scissors, stone. I guess I'll need some paper, too.

When I showed the drawing to Bernard, he quickly retorted, "*Moi pierre, toi bois*," recalling the distinction between him and Claude.

He showed me how to make a temporary "sand table" using a wheelbarrow full of sand. He wedged it against a big rock so it wouldn't tip and so I could push the stone's edges down into the sand to absorb the shock of the cutting and tapping to avoid shattering the soft sandstone. I was thrilled. I had my tools, my work apron, my dust mask, my ear protection, and my glasses, and I was whaling away with my little stone-cutting grinder, which he sarcastically called *mignon*, or cute. Bernard, in the meantime, had his huge grinder, the ground for a work surface, and his Gauloise. The four-finger part of the huge stone scissors, Bernard's side, was finished in less than two hours. While he worked, he showed me how to measure the stone, how to make templates to form the round border, and how to dress the cut edges to remove the saw marks. And, of course, he was running back and forth between Dan, Mike, and me, giving the appropriate lessons to all.

In the course of three hours, I had rough-cut a three-foot circle to form the thumb handle of the stone scissors. As I started to dress the stone, just as Bernard was telling me not to tap the thin band of the circle at a ninety-degree angle with the stone chisel, I did, and it shattered, neatly, into several pieces on the sand in the wheelbarrow. I didn't cry. I wanted to, but I didn't. Without saying a word, Bernard disappeared behind another cloud of dust and buzzed up another circle, wedged it in the sand and handed me my *mignon petit* grinder.

Dan, while we were making giant scissors, had finished all the basic shapes: sphere, square, and triangle, had dressed the stones, and using a different texture had formed the outline of his own hand on each piece, à la the red-outlined hands at Pech Merle. He wanted to stack them to simulate a somewhat figurative five-foot statue. While I carefully dressed my second handle, Bernard drilled holes in Dan's already shaped stones with a percussion drill, cut some metal bars, put them in the holes, and had *Les Mains* securely installed on the terrace overlooking the dam. He smacked his huge calloused hands together and asked, *"C'est l'heure du pastis, n'est-ce pas?"* He'd earned his pastis.

—Love, Judy

August 6, 1995
JOURNAL ENTRY

Dan's gone, and he's entrusted me with an exceptional sculpture up behind the little house. He often constructs temporary pieces in riverbeds or on the beach below the tide line, knowing they'll be gone in nature's time. Most of his work deals with his pain, either from childhood taunts of "faggot," or more recently from the loss of so many in his community to AIDS. Early in his visit here, he found a pile of vine clippings in an abandoned vineyard and lugged them up to the little house. Every time I would go up to see him he had a new small stick structure, wrapped with rough cord, resembling shamanistic fetish figures. But when I went up to help him bring his things down to the car to leave, he showed me the result of those small figure studies.

When you walk through to the back door of La Ruche you are on a stone terrace perched on a cliff that looks over the waterfall. A high retaining wall, partially in ruin, joins the back of the house in an L to enclose and warm the pavers of the patio. A new iron railing runs along the edge of the cliff on the other two sides of the rectangular space. Everyone, without exception, walks over to the far corner of the terrace and leans out over the railing to get as close as possible to the water sounds, and Dan sculpted that gesture. In the exact place where people position themselves, he constructed a life-sized figure woven from the vine clippings. The ends are tied discreetly, seemingly held together by the air, the hands positioned on the railing, the body leaning out to see the water rushing over the waterfall below.

"He's handsome, your faggot man, Dan. But he's fragile and ephemeral. What do I do when he slips and falls?"

"What are you going to do with me when I fall?" he said. Stunned, I shook my head and stepped back into the house.

GIFTS FROM BERNARD

August 30, 1995
Dear Linda,

The wedding plans are advancing. I'm quite pleased Derek and Kristie are getting married at the beach house. Our plan is to come home in late September, arrange the wedding for the tenth of October, then return in November until mid-December or so and be back in the States for Christmas.

Our first guest artist stay with Dan Pillers was successful: stimulating, fun, and exhausting. My studio is supplied with all the sculpture toys, and we're ready to invite the next artist. Dan talked me into inviting Larry Selman, a fellow sculpture student from the Toot, and Michael Strom's girlfriend, Alma, whom I don't know at all, but Dan says she's okay. Michael was a fellow student of ours, twenty-three years old, shy, serious, sensitive, and slightly effeminate, though not gay. And talented. He was stabbed to death near the projects in San Francisco last December trying to help a woman who was being mugged. A single puncture in his heart. Just two days before, Mike and I had bought one of his pieces—three long lances, capped with gold leaves and tiny bells—and I had invited him to come to France to work when he finished school next year. He wrote a letter to Alma, which didn't arrive until two days after his death, in which he described how thrilled he was. Alma read the letter at his memorial service. In it, he called me his guardian angel.

Incidentally, we did hang Michael's piece at our house, and in fact, we had a show of his work where many of his friends also hung their own art commemorating Michael. Work about their pain, their anger and paranoia. The woman whom he was trying to help when he was killed came. She said it helped her to heal. Art can do that. But as for inviting Alma to the mill, after our experience with Adrienne I'm not too sure about having people we don't know at all. Larry I know from working with him in class, but we only met Alma briefly at the memorial service and show. We'll see.

Bernard came last weekend to work on the millrace behind the mill, since we have small leaks that water the garden, but a leak is a leak to *meunier* Mike. We hadn't seen Bernard all month since he went up to sell his father's house in the Creuse region between here and Paris. It was the only thing he had left from his inheritance from his father, but he needed the money to pay off the mounting debts of his bipolar wife. I'm always stunned when he tells us about his weekends at the hospital and his sessions with the police when she gets out of control. He promised her father on his deathbed that he would take care of her and he is: selling everything to pay off her debts. I've noticed this summer his usual two pastis are up to three before he jumps in his truck.

He came loaded with gifts he had brought from his family home, telling us that we were the only people who appreciate old things, which of course isn't true, but it's his excuse to overwhelm us with personal treasures he can't bear to throw away. The first was a four-foot zinc tube with a tight-fitting cap that his father used to protect the undeveloped blueprint paper he used in his contracting business. Bernard had already told us about how that concern had passed to a cousin instead of him when his father died, a crushing disappointment for him. When he was telling us this over the evening pastis, his shoulders folded inward and his eyes dropped to examine his outstretched cement-hardened fingers. Bernard says he performed badly at school and disappointed his father who thought he wasn't capable of taking over the business. He is severely dyslexic, and as a child, before dyslexia was diagnosed and treated, he struggled, stalled, and never finished school, choosing to apprentice as a stonemason at the age of fourteen. Now we can admire his uncanny conceptual intelligence that allows him to imagine the shape of a stone before it's cut and placed.

Perhaps because Mike admires Bernard's work so much, Bernard in turn worships Mike, calling to him to look at his latest creation, speaking slowly so Mike can get his meaning without furrowing his brows—the sign that says, "I didn't understand a word you said." "He's like the big brother or father I never had," Bernard told me once when we were digging out one of the tunnels.

But his eyes still fill with tears when he talks about his father. He has been ostracized by the rest of his family, mainly because of his choices in wives, Gabrielle being the second. The first had problems with drugs and was knowingly pregnant with another man's child when they married. Bernard embraced the child as his own, as he has done with Gabrielle's son, Titi. The first wife, whose name he won't utter, finally just disappeared, taking their daughter with her. When Bernard talks of this broken family, his eyes wander, checking the air around as if there might be a signal to their presence if he could only find it.

He also brought us a package of books, or actually only the inserts, as they used to be published without the hard covers, so the masses could afford them. This bundle was the entire *oeuvre* of Victor Hugo, stacked and bound together with a rough cord. The publishing date was 1866, and the imprint of the letter press embosses the words on the reverse side of each fragile page, leaving a ghost of the previous thought. Bernard is convinced that Mike has read every important book ever published, though perhaps not Hugo in the original French.

Bernard then pulled a fist-sized stone from his sack, holding it in his hand, palm up, his thumb crossed on the surface. Carved on the smooth face was the outline of a cross in the Templar format, four even-length T-shaped ends; one end, where Bernard's thumb rested, was worn and shiny. He said it was a pilgrim's stone, one that some penitent, possibly in the twelfth century, who had been forced to walk from northern France down into Spain as punishment for some sin, would have carried for luck and protection. His thumb would have rubbed the end of the cross smooth as he walked down out of the Pyrenees to Saint-Jacques-de-Compostelle in Spain. His father had found the stone while excavating at a work site and displayed it in a place of honor in his home. Bernard wanted us to have it, knowing we would treasure the history and that his wife would only sell it in a manic burst of enthusiasm.

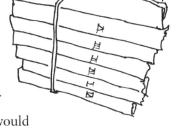

But the prize was a beautiful bowl-shaped crystal chandelier that had hung in the entry to his grandfather's restaurant in Decazeville, where Bernard was born. It has three cups that would once have had crystal bonnets, long since broken. He looked off into the space where his lost family resides, to find his grandfather, the chef, who would lift little Bernard onto the zinc work counter and show him how to make flaky pastry with ice-cold butter, unsalted, of course. Bernard's glances into his past usually bring pain-scrunched shoulders, but this time he blossomed with a gap-toothed smile, never losing the Gauloise bobbing in the corner of his mouth. He *boffed* away our objections to this gift, declaring his fear that it would be sold off, and besides, he wanted us to put it somewhere in the mill where he could visit it. I think we will hang it over the dining table, an elegant contrast to the gnarled old walnut oil press right next to it.

Bernard asked about you as he drove off last weekend. You ol' flirt, you.

—*Love, Judy*

ENTER MONSIEUR CHARRIER

September 4, 1995
Dear Linda,

We continue to meet people, sometimes being introduced by friends, sometimes at a village event, but most of the time they just appear at our door. Such was the case last week when a handsome gray-haired man, I'm guessing about fifty years old, presented himself just after Dan left.

"*Je m'appelle Jean-Paul Charrier et je suis artiste,*" he declared, and while he wasn't wearing a cape, I swore he grabbed the edge of one and threw it over his shoulder. He didn't have a top hat either, but when he bowed, one seemed to tumble down his arm and he neatly caught it by the rim. He continued to speak, his body in profile, his head turned and cocked in a theatrical gesture, his speech flowery and effusive. One of the biggest differences between artists in the States and here is that here artists don't usually call themselves artists: they believe that is presumptuous, that it is up to the community at large to call them artists, and that they are mere artisans. "I sculpt, I paint," etc. So when someone announces "I am an artist," I'm on high alert.

As he toured the mill with Mike and me, the imaginary cape was swung with each declaration of "*Chapeau, chapeau, bien fait.*" ("Well done, well done.") He told us he'd almost bought the mill himself a few years ago, but decided it was too much in a canyon—he needed space and vistas around, he said, arms flung wide to the sky. He'd settled on an abandoned farm complex called Les Sanges, including twenty acres stretched across the hills high above a village on the Rance River called Balaguier, about eight miles upstream from us. He ceremoniously invited us to dinner to meet his wife, Anne, and his young son, Christian, and then he strode off after one final cape-throw, arms swinging straight almost military style. I couldn't help but wonder, à la Shirley de Condomine (remember, her theory is that if you come to rural France to live, you're a total idealist or hiding from something), if he was as romantic as he appeared or was he concealing something beneath all that bravado.

We followed his directions the next evening, through Plaisance, climbing up out of the valley destined for the ridge that overlooks the Rance, through La Fon-del-Mas, past Suzie and François's Rieucros, past the turnoff to Jean-Michel and Eveline's Le Souyrol, into new/old country, at least for us. From the top of the ridge, we could see numerous farms in various shades of autumn sienna, speckled with herds of sheep enjoying the fresh autumn air.

When we finally found the "Les Sanges" sign, Mike remarked, "*Sang* refers to blood, doesn't it?"

We had been warned to park at the top of the drive since there's no turnaround and backing out after dark would be precarious. Jean-Paul greeted us halfway up the long pine-lined drive, his toddler son, Christian, a safe distance behind him, and led us down in front of the house to a magnificent view of the entire valley, aglow with the fading sun. As he *ta-da-ta-dahhhed*, his wife, Anne, a pretty blonde at least twenty years his junior, floated down the steps to greet us. She is thin, equally theatrical in voice and gestures, her broad smile revealing empty spaces behind her six front teeth. She looked almost horse-like when she laughed heartily at something Jean-Paul said, throwing her head back, mouth wide open. Eventually, he presented his son, Christian, a toddler about three years old.

"I'm too old to have such a young child. He drives me nuts," he declared several times in various ways, with the child well within hearing range. While we were standing in front of the house, I saw another child's face in a window on the third floor that pulled back quickly when I looked up. I asked who he was, and Jean-Paul, with a flip of his hand, told us that was Zacherie, Anne's child from a previous marriage, and that he was bit crazy, a declaration made by pointing his rotating index finger against his temple.

Anne retreated to the kitchen while Jean-Paul gave us a tour of the surrounding buildings. The main house had been handsomely restored with taste and respect for the stone. Between the house and the barn was another large building, fallen into ruin, which would become his studio when he finished. With him marching in front, we admired his garden, an old carriage collection in another sturdy barn, his temporary studio, and Yanko, his donkey, purchased to keep some of their twenty acres cleared of brambles and stinging nettles. Yanko bared his long teeth and brayed menacingly as we approached, oddly recalling Anne's earlier laugh. I wondered if owners and their donkeys resemble each, like they do their dogs.

The entry to the main house led to a stone dining area with a small kitchen behind a massive oak door. Another door led into the main salon, the walls of which were covered with Jean-Pierre's paintings, every square inch of hangable space from floor to ceiling. They were colorful, expressive land- and seascapes from the north of France to the south. He seemed to have lived in all the regions for some period of time. At the end of the room was a beautiful harpsichord, Anne's prize possession. She's a nurse who trained in Quebec, speaks some English, and works with our neighbor, Brigitte, making visits to the local farms, giving shots and taking blood, but music is her passion.

We moved *à table*, and since the evening was so warm, we sat outside beneath a huge chestnut tree, admiring the vista and the soft night air. Anne had prepared a lovely four-course meal: crunchy fall garden salad, roast chicken with rosemary and lemon, chunks of Roquefort, and a peach cobbler presented proudly as her Anglo rendition of a classic French tart. We chatted late into the warm fall evening, finishing with candles and sweaters. Christian ate quietly with his head down, avoiding too much contact with his father, who shushed him at the slightest sound. French children are taught early how to behave at meals.

Mike seemed content to meet another painter, and they brewed plans for a show together next spring. Throughout the evening I looked up to see the face in the window, then watched it snap away. Suspicious, I am.

—*Hugs, Judy*

October 26, 1995
Paris
Dear Linda,

You were a smash at Derek's wedding. That black and taupe suit was the pièce de résistance. Did you get that in Paris? I can't remember! I must say the forest fire above Inverness added a bit of drama to the days before the event. I'm glad we didn't end up changing the venue from the beach to the city given how close the fire was coming. The week after the wedding, Derek and Kristie actually rode their bikes up into hills and said it looked like something out of *Apocalypse Now*.

We have stopped in Paris on our way to the mill, a bit of a change of plans. But some good friends who lost their house in the fire needed a place to stay, so we offered our beach house to them. Sounds noble, but it was just a self-indulgent early start to our trip back to the mill, so we can spend a few days here on the way. We'll be staying there through mid-December, although Mike may go back to the States sooner than me for a show he's got coming up. We've been cruising all our favorite museums here, filling journals full of unrealizable ideas. My personal favorite is the Musée des Arts et Métiers, a tool museum. It has such wonderfully crafted tools, most of which I haven't a clue as to their original use, but don't care. Others include stilts that shepherds used to see into the herd, an odd pronged device to pick berries, salt rakes, pegs, and wedges of all sizes that are so beautiful it makes me hurt.

Tools are figurative, in the same sense as the chairs I used in my first installation. Someone was there, someone held them, the oil from their hand smoothed the handle. And I've learned, for me, there are three kinds of art: the first makes me embarrassed to be part of the art world, the second is so sublime that I'm discouraged because I could never make something so divine, and the third just makes me want to run to my studio and play, experiment, and build something. And those tools do that for me. I feel an almost manic crush of creativity.

When I was at the Toot, my sculpture professor, Richard Berger, was almost attacked by the women in his class when he proclaimed that women do sculpture differently than men, with a disclaimer about not being worse or better, just different, more ephemeral. He actually said that because he thought the men could learn something, be less assertive, more sensitive. But it made us women all so mad that we decided to counter. One young woman spent weeks welding a monumental heart, valves and all. I was doing some research and discovered that a Quaker woman had built the first table saw. I couldn't help but wonder how many prototypes she had built before she perfected the design. Consequently, I launched into several projects building crazy prototypes that couldn't possibly work: Rube Goldberg sorts of sculpture. My favorite was a wind-powered saw that sat on a lawn chair. All of which, by the way, were very assertive and not at all sensitive. But all these precious museum-displayed tools in Paris must have had a series of prototypes, and I wonder where they are? I've got a whole notebook full of possible tool prototypes, mostly relating to the millworks, and I can't wait to get there to try them out. I want to use stone and wood, *pierre et bois.*

I'm also ready to get out of the big city. I have too many ideas I want to work on in my new studio. We've never experienced the rude Parisians we hear so much about, but I think, if there are any, it's due to the same attitude one finds in New York. People who live there can't understand why anyone would ever live anywhere else and can be quite dismissive. There is one thing I can't stand, however, and that's when somebody hears us speak French and they immediately launch into English. Some of them just want to practice their English, as we want to practice our French in San Francisco, but others seem to be inferring that our French doesn't come up to their standards. So I've adopted a new strategy. When someone in a store or museum switches to English after I've tried my best French and it's clear they're being a snob, I screw up my forehead, frown deeply for a few seconds and respond in my clearest French, "*Excusez-moi, monsieur, j'ai rien compris.*" ("I didn't understand a word you said.") *Bammm,* we're back in French in a hurry. However, they usually reply in rapid-fire colloquial French, so I have to *fous le camp,* or get the hell out of there in a hurry. Besides, we want to be at the mill. Like right now . . .

—*Hugs, Judy*

November 29, 1995
JOURNAL ENTRY

We've been almost a month at the mill, trees bare, short days, big fires, huge meals. Why, when we are so active in the summer, for many more hours, do we eat only salads and fruit and then in the winter, when the world shuts down at four in the afternoon, do we pull out the pot roasts and potatoes, slow-cooked guinea hens and potatoes, venison and potatoes, pheasant and potatoes? And why do we grow so many potatoes?

I invited the Charriers over to dinner this week, and as all our friends here do, they brought their child, in their case the petit Christian, not Zacherie, however. About 11 p.m., Christian was quite tired and starting to fidget, which annoyed his father. So I offered to put him on our couch and turn on some cartoons, hoping he might fall asleep. When I was scrolling for something with the remote, he said, as might any tired little boy, "No, not that one," in a cranky voice. I smiled and turned around to assure him I could do better, just in time to see Jean-Paul jump up from the table, cross the room, and slap that tiny three-year-old face so hard I thought Christian might sail across the room. I was so stunned I couldn't say anything and looked for Anne to step in. Instead, she shrugged her shoulders, "What can I do?" I tried to make it clear that that was unacceptable in my house, "*C'est pas correct, ça.* He didn't do anything." But my protestations fell on deaf ears. I was red with rage after they left.

The next day I called Odette Soulier, who knows the Charriers, and asked her what I should do. She was quite upset also, and told me that she had had a similar experience and had not seen them since, admitting that it was a cowardly act but she didn't know what else to do. Discouraged, I decided I had to talk to Anne directly and tell her what I thought. He can't be allowed to treat Christian like that. Who's going to protect him?

Part of our stated objective for being here is to live in and speak the language of another culture so we can understand it, which by definition means seeing the underbelly of a society as well as the positive public face. Even so, I'm still surprised to see child abuse so blatantly displayed with no apparent reaction, or known public organization to call, even by the wife of a physician. And even if there were, because of our language limitations I feel impotent.

FIRSTBORN

December 8, 1995
JOURNAL ENTRY

The phone rang at eleven o'clock three days ago. It was cold outside and Mike had left for the States to work on his show, leaving me to entertain Martou and Germain on my own. A long evening was closing down. I thought it was Mike, so I *ahhhlllloooed* in my worst French accent. But it wasn't Mike. It was Kristie, my son's bride of two months, calling from New York where they're living, she a struggling artist and he a musician. "I just took Derek to Beth Israel Hospital, and they don't expect him to live," she said in a voice deep with shock and terror. She had found him unconscious on the floor of the apartment when she came home. "I don't know what happened. He's dying. Please come."

Somehow, I got the number of the emergency room, promised I'd be there as soon as possible, and told her to call Mike in California. After I spoke to the emergency room, confirming that my son, my firstborn, beautiful baby boy, was in intensive care and the prognosis was not encouraging, the next eighteen hours happened in slow, agonizing motion . . . nothing in focus, nothing clear. Direct flight from Toulouse? No, the fucking French are on strike. Closest flight Barcelona, a five-hour drive.

Friends came to the mill from nowhere and everywhere, Suzie and François, Brigitte, Dominque. Dishes done, details worked out. Mike to meet me in New York. Bernard *bois* arrived with a friend and his son to drive me to hell. And over there, my son was dying.

Black Mountains, Lodève, Béziers, Narbonne, Perpignan, Pyrénées, Figueres, the Dalí museum I love. How frivolous and irrelevant. The airport, the waiting, the descent to Lisbon, the four-hour wait on the tarmac, and the terror of arriving in New York. No calls, no information, only the worst fears boiling up. "If Mike is there to meet me, that will mean that he's dead. If not, there's hope," I told myself and the woman next to me, who, a total stranger, never let go of my hand over the ocean, got my bags for me, and waited while I searched the crowd for my love, whom I didn't want to see.

December 10, 1995
New York
Dear Linda,

Even though I called you, it helps me to write. The extent of Derek's problem is only now becoming apparent. At present, he is extremely weak in every muscle. He is now able to control his arms and hands, but he cannot walk due to a total failure of parts of the quadriceps muscles in his legs. The neurologists are cautiously optimistic that he will regain some control; however, they are urging us think in terms of months, not days and weeks as we had originally hoped. We can only wait and see.

As for the cause? We may never know. He had a severe case of pneumonia that apparently got out of control fast. When they aspirated his lungs, they found a bit of a pine needle that he must have inhaled when he and Kristie rode their bikes in the fire zone in Inverness after their wedding. The worst is the cramps in his legs. We took turns holding and rubbing his legs through five days of hell, not knowing if his kidneys would hold up or whether he would ever be able to walk again if they did. There is no way to describe that hell. A crazy jumble of pain, anger, prayer, and damnation. Hours of it. Days of it.

Mike is now here in New York with me until at least after Christmas. We have found a studio apartment not far from the hospital and are huddled up for an unplanned, prolonged visit to the city. We are exploring every museum and gallery, drawing, painting, and trying to enjoy the holiday lights and sounds and counting our blessings. Derek's very scared, but working hard. He will be in physical therapy, trying to relearn how to walk, for months it seems, and I expect I'll be close by until the future is less cloudy. Kristie has been an absolute rock. She's there encouraging him, joking, reading to him, holding him close. Their apartment is only half a block from the hospital, so she can come and go easily.

Somehow, I thought adult children didn't need their parents, but I realize now how wrong that is. And I never imagined there could be so much pain in a mother's heart. Any spare prayers, positive thoughts, or the odd piece of paper are greatly appreciated.
—*All our love to you all, Judy*

January 7, 1996
New York
Dear Linda,

I'm still holed up in New York, and I expect I'll be here a while. Mike is going back and forth to San Francisco to work on his graduate program show, so I'm here trying to support Kristie, who is trying to both work and be at Derek's side. I walk to the hospital every day, trying to take a new route each time to keep from thinking too much. The good news is he's getting a tiny bit better each day and his attitude is good. The bad is that this will take months of physical therapy, and we still don't know how much of the nerve damage in his legs is permanent. The irony is that the doctors who saved his life caused the nerve damage. His veins had collapsed by the time he got to the hospital, and they tried everything to get the IV lines in him. In doing so, they damaged the nerves. I switch constantly between "thank you" and "damn you."

Mike came back just in time to witness the three feet of snow the day before Christmas and walk with me through the empty streets of the city, which was completely closed down: people cross-country skiing in the streets, no buses, just Christmas lights in windows and huge drifts of snow. A stunning experience. Maybe it's just the contrasts in life that count. For Christmas, we did a stocking for Derek, full of little silly things, and asked the nurse to hang it from his IV stand when he fell asleep so it would be there in the morning when he woke up. He was genuinely touched by the gesture.

A few days before Christmas I called Germain and Martou to thank them for closing up the mill and to give them an update on Derek. Germain told me that Bernard *pierre* had come the weekend after I left to help him. Bernard thought he should take down Dan's stone sculpture since he didn't think it was stable enough on its perch above the upper terrace. He decided to move it to a corner of the terrace by the waterfall. But in taking it down, he slipped and the large stone fell and broke his leg. I was almost physically ill when Germain told me this. How much worse can things get?

I then called Bernard to tell him how sorry I was, and Gabrielle answered the phone. She was positively pissy and demanded I pay Bernard thousands of francs for his pain. Of course he will actually draw his full salary from the French disability payments while he's mending, but we need to do something else for him to show him we care. She wasn't even going to let me talk to him and told me I'd have to deal with her. When I firmly told her that we would deal only with Bernard, she reluctantly gave up control.

The tone of Bernard's voice said it all. He was embarrassed, sad for us, sad for himself, and *ras le bol*, or completely fed up with Gabrielle. I wanted to be supportive but I didn't know what to say. I assured him that we would help him in any way he needed, financially or otherwise. I was shaking when I hung up.

Two days later, I was getting ready to walk down to the hospital, and I started to see double. I panicked since, given Grandma, Dad, and, well, you, I was afraid I was having a stroke. I ran to the hospital, told them our history, and they gave me an MRI *tout de suite*. I won't bore you with the details, but I was basically having a real nervous breakdown, not a swooning-on-the-couch-with-my-corset-too-tight-and-my-skirts-over-my-head kind of spell, but a physical reaction to weeks of tension. But in the MRI process, quite coincidently, they discovered I have a tumor at the base of my brain. "Nothing to worry about," they say, "probably an identical twin that never developed." If I had learned I had a tumor under any other circumstances, I think I might have panicked, but given what's happened this last six weeks, what the hell. I've decided to call him Bill. That would make him your brother, too. I know, it's not possible for me to have a guy identical twin, but I like having a brother to call on, 'cuz this ain't fun. I do have to follow up for several months when I get back to California, just to be sure it's Bill and not something else. Will you PLEASE take care of yourself?

—*Love, Judy*

MY MEN

February 14, 1996
En route to San Francisco
Dear Linda,

Happy Valentine's, my dear. Even though we just talked on the phone last week, I can't remember what I've told to whom at this point. I'm on a plane between New York and

San Francisco, with some time to reflect about all that's happened. First, Derek is still at NYU's physical rehabilitation hospital, getting intensive physical therapy, walking, swimming, and lifting weights. He's in a ward with mostly older people recovering from strokes, and just the thought of getting out of there is pushing him hard. Kristie's there every minute she can be, and I'm flying back and forth now every week. They both insist that he's coming home to their fourth-story walk-up, but since he'll most likely be in a wheelchair for several months, I don't know how they'll manage. Kristie said she can carry the chair up and down and it will be good physical therapy for Derek to pull himself up the stairs!

I talked to Bernard *pierre* and Germain last week, and Bernard seems to be healing well. He said he's been making drawings of stone sculptures he'd like to do at the mill. I was quite surprised, since he's never done any art before, well, other than every rock at the mill! Again, art helps healing. Germain told me not to worry at all about the mill, "Oh, except for the terrible freeze we had and the burst pipes in the attic and all of the radiators that froze solid." But François and Didier came over and carried them downstairs onto the front terrace so when they melted, they wouldn't leak rusty water all over the house! And Didier Colomb, the plumber that we fired last year the same time as we showed Pearson the door, said he could come over and replace all the pipes and radiators, *tout de suite*. I wasn't sure I understood everything Germain was saying, but I, of course, told him to go ahead.

Oh, by the way, I had my head rescanned in San Francisco and, sure enough, there really is a tumor there, but the neurologist is sure that it's just the sibling we didn't know we had. How strange is that? Bill seems glad to take over when I need him.

Enjoy your sweets, my sweet!

—Judy

March 11, 1996
San Francisco
Dear Linda,

I'm writing out all the things I told you on the phone so you can show this to Gary to let him understand what's happening. I'll be direct and probably too graphic, but that will save some explanation time. Bottom line: Mike's right sinuses are filled with a tumor that is called an inverting papilloma. It is usually not metastatic, meaning it shouldn't go to other organs, but left untreated it could encroach on the brain itself, and it is already large enough to have caused some mechanical problems with the bones in his skull. The tumor has damaged the bone in all three sinuses on his right side, but the most complicated is the frontal sinus. There is a thin bone, which has been badly damaged, between the cavity and the brain, and it seems his brain is actually sagging into this space.

They treat these tumors aggressively, since if they don't they recur and usually with complications. They will go in from two fronts: from the top of the skull and from an opening made by an incision beside the nose for direct visualization. A neurosurgeon will go in from above and take out the bone that is left, pack the frontal sinus with fat, and put in some cadaver grafts. Meanwhile, a head and neck cancer surgeon will come up from below to remove the tumor itself, take out all the bones in his maxillary and frontal sinuses, graft and repair the damage. Kaiser has a special neurosurgical facility in their Redwood, California, hospital where he'll be in the operating room for seven to ten hours.

The neurosurgeon assured us that this is not that complicated a surgery. They are not cutting into the brain, just pushing it around a bit. He will, however, lose his sense of smell, since they have to cut the olfactory nerve, which at first seems a small price. But with that loss goes much of your taste. Fine wines, pecan pie, great cheeses, and other delicacies will lose some of their appeal. I guess he'll just have to eat more. He won't be pretty for a while and none too comfortable either. Also he will have several months of internal healing before he is perfect again. They say it is not an emergency, but Mike would like to have at least the summer in France, so we asked them to schedule the surgery as soon as possible. After he leaves the hospital, it will be another six weeks before he can travel. I will probably go back to France two weeks earlier to open the house and keep our projects on track. (In between trips to New York.)

No one knows what caused the growth, but it is probably viral. (Putting frogs up his nose, I guess.) Because of the location, it wasn't obvious until his breathing and snoring got so bad that I bugged him until he finally went to the doctor. See, it pays to be a nag after all. Mike seems quite relaxed about it, probably in shock or denial, and I'm trying to hold myself together, but honestly, I'm exhausted and terrified.

We have a friend whose husband had to have major surgery, and she passed among his friends a rock for them to touch and absorb their positive thoughts. Mike liked that idea so I am asking all his friends and the kids to make a braid of some material representing their positive thoughts, love, and prayers and send it to me. The braid can be of any material, from guitar strings to plastic bags, little or big. I'm intending to show them to Mike the night before the surgery and braid them all together while I'm in the waiting room.

Why a braid? We had visited an old rope factory in Mystic Seaport, Connecticut, while driving back to New York from seeing Jenea in Cambridge. We were both struck by the tiny threads that were twisted together to make something strong enough to anchor a ship. I'm hoping all the thoughts woven into individual braids can be made into something forceful enough to get through this challenge, because frankly, I can't do this alone. So braid away.

—*Love, Judy*

March 21, 1996
New York
Dear Linda,

You're right . . . first Hayden, then Derek, now Mike. All my men are broken . . . I'm still commuting back and forth from San Francisco to New York, hospital to hospital. I confess my nerves are shot.

Derek had another test for his nerves yesterday, and they are still convinced he will eventually be able to get around better than now, but most likely he will always need some mechanical support. He's bummed but not giving up hope. "I'm young, you know, Mom!" he says somewhat sarcastically, since everybody always says that when they can't think of anything else to say.

He finally left the hospital last week after twelve weeks of intensive physical therapy at NYU. They live in a four-story walkup, and he has to literally pull himself up the stairs with his arms, using his legs as only a means of being upright. Kristie follows him, chatting about this and that, lugging his wheelchair up behind her. I don't know how she is able to cope with all this. She just won't let him wallow in self-pity, and she's always encouraging him to go here and try that. I seem to have to help him make every move in my head and am as exhausted as he is after twenty minutes of going up four flights of stairs! It was easier the first time he learned to walk—he didn't have so far to fall.

We got him a computer so he'll have something to keep his mind busy while he mends, and he is already anxious to start some classes to learn more about graphic design or maybe advertising. I admire his will, much stronger than his mom's, for sure. But he has gotten the best care, and now it is up to time and a lot of hard work.

I talked to Mike, who's back in San Francisco, this morning, and his doctor saw the final MRIs and said they're sure that his brain is not involved in the tumor and that while they still have to move it around a lot—nine hours of surgery in all—it shouldn't cause any permanent damage. Also, they have to take out his eye for a bit! A bit? An eye is an eye, even for only a bit.

God, this is hard. Fingers crossed, please.

—*Love ya, Judy*

April 20, 1996
San Francisco
Dear Linda,

Mike is doing extraordinarily well, and I'm convinced it was because of everyone's collective goodwill. Except for a railroad track across the top of his head and a slightly drippy nose, you can hardly see what all they did.

When the surgeon came out at the end of nine hours, he seemed quite relieved and a bit nonchalant, nibbling on a candy bar. But when he described in detail the removal of Mike's right eye from the socket and the rearrangement of the ligaments to get the grafts in place, I, who have spent hours watching surgery in the operating room, almost fainted.

I passed that long day with Katie, Jenea, and Naomi in the waiting room (Hayden came over that evening to go into the intensive care unit with me), weaving over sixty feet of individual braids into one big fat one . . . it is wonderful. Friends who didn't know each other were cheek-to-braid with total strangers, foreigners even. I could tell without looking at the card who made what. A photographer friend braided some rolls of film, Eileen braided our first grandbaby's pajamas, Francis, our chef friend in France, braided some bread dough, Bernard Guerin, our woodworker neighbor, steamed and braided some wood. An artist friend shredded all our French postcards and braided them together. Another friend who builds clocks braided a watch fob that connected a small timepiece with a silk dragonfly, which resembles both his and his wife's personality and temperament. A musician friend braided threads of gold with sheet music. Our doctor friend turned horseman braided horsehair and silk ribbons. Other people sent similarly amazingly creative braids. And people say they're not artists. I think we all are, deep inside. There's an art project here somewhere!

I was extraordinarily nervous driving Mike home after only six days in the hospital, but getting back to the beach house was the best thing for him. He still can't use his eye, but that and some fatigue are about the only things slowing him down from a fairly normal life.

You asked me how I could stand it. (Frankly, you are my hero, after all you've been through.) How I could put one foot in front of the other through the last five months? I confess I've gone Zen on you. I started meditating at the suggestion of the neurologist in New York, when I was coming undone. He said he'd seen people living my nightmare learn to find an inner calm that surprised him given the problems they faced—people with children with a much worse prognosis than Derek's. I once did some consulting work on some cardiovascular recovery programs that included meditation and other forms of stress management without drugs. So as soon as I was let out of the hospital in New York, I went down to the bookstore and bought a book on stress management that included meditation and, book in hand, sat down on the floor and learned to go into a quieter place inside myself.

A dear friend who lives near us in San Francisco is a therapist and Buddhist priest. We've been sitting together, and I've been going to lectures and reading everything I can on being present and not going too far into the future or the past. So, you see, I've gone completely California candles and sandals on you.

In a month, I leave ahead of Mike for New York to see Derek and then to the mill to get the physical part of opening the mill out of the way before he comes. We will stay there for the summer and then go to Paris for a month. (We did a house exchange with some Parisian friends.) We have my sculpture professor, Richard Berger, coming for three weeks in June to give us a real dunking in art history, and two of my fellow students—and, yes, one is Alma, Michael Strom's girlfriend. Derek and Kristie are planning to come for his birthday in June. Hopefully, some of the other kids will be coming in August. So life is full.

—Love, Judy

May 21, 1996
La Pilande Basse
Hi Linda,

I spent some time in New York with Derek and Kristie before coming back here to the mill. Derek had a friend who had smashed his knees in an accident and was told he'd never walk right again but who had gone to the Pilates center (not the hard-belly-bimbo Pilates, but the physical rehab place that was created after World War I and is now used by dancers and others with serious injuries) and was walking quite well. Derek talked them into taking him, and in one short month he's walking much better. He actually walked about one hundred feet in Washington Park with a cane. He had to sit down for fifteen minutes afterward, but he's confident that he will walk unassisted sometime in the future. Kristie has to help him up and down the stairs, get him on the bus, get him to his sessions, then go to work herself. These kids are amazing.

As for me, it's one month to the day since I arrived at the mill. I'm off this morning to pick up Mike, and I feel like I'm going on my first date. I shaved in places I'd forgotten for years. I've been terribly lonesome for everyone, but I thought Mike would never get here. I confess, however, I have enjoyed the time alone . . . I could lick my wounds in private, meditate in any position in any condition, rise and shine or sit and sulk with impunity (whoever she is). But a month. It seemed like two years.

I hope his trip is less eventful than mine was. I had a horrible layover in Paris, which included a bomb scare with an eventual detonating of somebody's luggage. A further insult to my nerves. A friend met me at the airport and drove me from Toulouse directly to the Blancs' house for the keys and the inevitable pâté, along with salad and farm-fresh chicken—and cheese, and yummy little cookies. First day, and there goes the diet. I unloaded my stuff, started up the cook-stove fireplace and started to cry. Somehow it seemed appropriate. I was happy to be here at last, with everyone more or less safe.

Since then I've eaten with just about all our friends, with three more to go this week . . . then, of course, we have to start all over when Mike arrives, but that's okay. Everyone is so curious to see the results of the "braids." I am so glad that I did that project: not only was it therapeutic for Mike and me, but it brought people together, even here, who had never met each other. Everyone wants to know if it is an American custom or just a passing fancy. I explain to them about our friend whose husband had had surgery, etc., and they universally think it was a grand idea: they can hardly wait until they get sick! In all, we had over twenty families in France that sent braids. Some of them took a whole weekend together as a group to make them. I get tears again and again.

Bernard, the stonemason, is a bit of a wreck, however. After he broke his leg taking down Dan's sculpture, he spent most of the winter at home with his wife nagging him about money. By law, in France, he received full pay for his disability, but he usually works every weekend in addition to his normal work week, partly to get away from her, but also to earn extra cash. The French health care system, of course, is excellent, paying for all his care, plus disability, but we're going to make sure that he gets that extra. He will come in August and work more on the millworks with Mike, now that we've decided to redo the mechanisms to make the mill turn again. Did I tell you that? I had been encouraging Mike, and he was always a bit "*C'est trop!*" Then one day he said yes. This will be his project for a few years, finding the experts, supervising the remaking of all the turbines and the mill boxes, not to mention the waterworks and the millstones. You may not remember that before Mike got his M.F.A. from the Toot and his M.B.A. from Stanford, he finished an undergraduate degree in industrial engineering. All things mechanical fascinate him. He's been making hundreds of drawings, spending hours poring through old millwork references.

In the meantime, I'm doing the garden. Now don't get me wrong, I love Mike a lot and I would do anything to make him happy, but I never thought I would be on my hands and knees for so long for him. One nice thing about admitting to having never planted a garden before is all the advice one gets and how contrary it all is. But because I was so helplessly lost, Germain decided to give me the "garden secret." I'm sure that Mike doesn't even know that there is a *bonne femme* on the other side of Villeneuve-sur-Tarn who sells seedlings of everything. What an experience: greens of every shade and hue imaginable, hundreds of rows of the tidiest, sweetest smelling sprouts of this and that. I went there all alone, of course, and told her I had never planted a garden in my life (not quite true) and could she give me some lettuce with training wheels. Although I only spent a grand total of fifteen dollars on plants, she gave me all the secrets of tomato plants, lettuce, onions, and eggplants, but, "*Bof,* the basil this year is going to be difficult." I have no idea how she knows that. I thanked her profusely, telling her she must think I'm extraordinarily ignorant. But she shook her head and zigzagged her finger in that nobody-but-a-Frenchperson gesture and told me that even the "old ones born in the country" don't know what I just learned, mostly because they refuse to listen.

So for two weeks I've been doing the garden thing: twelve tomato plants, two 20-foot rows of onions, lots of lettuce, only three melon plants (Germain says they'll never take), and a couple of zucchini for flowers to stuff, and then I seeded some spices for spice, all tidy like the pictures with little stakes with pictures from packages. Now mind you, this garden (*potager*) is only one-tenth the size of most gardens here, and I can hardly walk. Yesterday the geraniums, and tomorrow the dreaded stinging nettles.

One more food story before I go: at seven this morning, Martou called to tell me they were coming by with a freshly killed rabbit and they wouldn't take "no" for an answer. So first thing, before I even brushed my teeth, I had a dead, albeit skinned, rabbit, eyeballs, tongue, and all, plopped down on my stone sink. Martou ran out the door telling me she forgot to wash out the mouth so I better be careful when I cook the head. Cook the head? Okay, so how does one brush the teeth of a rabbit?

Dinner tomorrow with the Roussels at Les Magnolias, Thursday with Shirley and Berteau at their summer hideaway Les Peyrettes Hautes, Saturday with Didier and Clémence at their little hamlet, and Weight Watchers on Monday.

—Love, Judy

REAL LIFE IN RURAL FRANCE

June 1, 1996

JOURNAL ENTRY

I'm afraid Martou has gone a bit balmy. She had some kidney problems this winter, and they gave her fairly massive doses of steroids, which often makes people a bit paranoid, and now she's imagining all kinds of lumps and bumps that just aren't there. She's always been a slight hypochondriac, but it's gotten serious. Germain, who is never patient with her, is even more dismissive than he used to be. Even her children are worried.

But it's Francis Roussel who has me the most concerned. I stopped by as usual when I arrived, and he was huddling in their private space next to the kitchen, the big leather chair folded around him, his gouty foot up on a stool. His hands were shaking, and he said the gout just wouldn't go away and he can hardly walk. Marie-France gave me a perfunctory *bisou* and left the room, the air chilled by her passing. Les Magnolias is looking rundown, since he didn't have the strength, or the will, to work this winter on normal maintenance while they were closed for the season. He just shook his head when I asked him to come over for dinner, his eyes filled with despair. I touched his shoulder and told him he could come anytime to the mill and we could sit quietly together and just relax.

I finally went for a walk with Anne Charrier last week to tell her what I thought about Jean-Paul slapping Christian last fall. We walked along the hilltop above her house, the valley spread out beneath us. The sun was hot and we stopped under a tree for a rest. I didn't expect her to actually listen to me, but I needed to release my responsibility in this drama, so I asked her to tell me more about herself first. She bent over and picked up a piece of straw and folded it into a tiny package before she answered. Choking back tears, she said that her own mother used to tell her that she should never have been born. Her mother had said that she was too old, forty-three, when she got pregnant, and that she would have had an abortion if she had known how difficult it would be to have a child. Anne dropped the straw and picked up a small smooth stone that she rubbed and turned while she talked. She said she'd wanted to be a musician, a pianist, but her mother told her she had no talent so she went to nursing school instead. She said Jean-Paul encourages her music, even buying her the harpsichord.

I asked her if her mother's words were hurtful and how they had affected her life. She didn't answer immediately, gazing at me with a "I know what you're trying to say" look. When I asked about Zacherie, she dropped the rock and held herself closely in a self-embrace. He is her son from her first marriage, a difficult child who she said had had scarlet fever when quite small, an illness that left him mentally handicapped. When I asked why he was not included in their family affairs she said Jean-Paul didn't tolerate him well. Zacherie's father had been an abusive alcoholic, and by comparison Jean-Paul treated her and Zacherie quite well.

I told her I had to speak frankly and she almost cringed, as though she knew what I was going to say. We walked slowly down the hill, entering a pine grove with pine needles underfoot. I said I was sorry that she had had such a difficult time as a child, that her mother's comportment was terribly sad, and that she must have been lonely in her own home. Her tears had already started when I had to tell her that slapping a small child was not normal behavior and what I had witnessed was child abuse. I also said I thought a mother, a real mother, had as her first priority the safety of her children, all children, healthy or not, both mentally and physically. I also told her I thought telling a child he wasn't welcome was a form of abuse maybe more insidious than physical punishment. I then suggested she might consider counseling, first for herself, then Jean-Paul if he would agree. By the time we reached the end of the pines to the gate to her home, Les Sanges, we were both in tears.

June 8, 1996
Dear Linda,

Not much to report on Mike and Derek. Progress is progressing at its own pace, not mine, but progressing nonetheless.

Odette Soulier came by today, I thought to just say hello, but it's clear she's having major problems. Jacques, her osteopath-turned-pig-farmer husband is in trouble with the gendarmes, and she's getting dragged into the mess. He was helping a couple from Paris, a retired hairdresser and his young wife, redo their house, arranging for the plumbers, electricians, and masons and generally supervising the work. Apparently, he was also "supervising" the young wife, and the retired hairdresser is taking revenge. He "denounced" Jacques to the gendarmes, and they ended up in court this spring over who said what to whom. The word-for-word court discussion was reported in the local newspaper. When the husband accused Jacques of seducing his wife, Jacques responded by asking why in the world he would want to seduce someone with plastic tits. I think the husband could have rested his case there, but it's still going on.

Odette is such an elegant woman, poised and articulate, and she is being humiliated in front of the whole community by her spouse. This apparently is not the first time he's strayed, and, in fact, he has had many affairs throughout their twenty-three years of marriage. They moved here to the Aveyron to try to start over, and it's clear that it isn't going to work. As soon as the court settlement is over, they are separating, and the divorce papers are already in the works.

Shirley de Condomine's theory of people moving to rural France either because of pure romanticism or because of having something to hide is proving more and more valid with each passing story.

On her way out, after sharing this sordid tale, Odette told me she had a friend she wanted me to meet. A sweet woman whose longtime companion had just died of cancer, and Odette thought I could help her with some of my newfound self-communication techniques. I had told her about my meditation with my Buddhist friend in San Francisco, and Odette thought I might be able to help her friend relax. Confused as I was by that introduction, I met Bernadette Rolland, called Nadou, the next day. She is a tiny, shy woman who is trying to make a life for herself in her home, Les Balkis, which she and her common-law husband had built together over the past fifteen years as a getaway from their *maraîchage*, or truck-farming business. They had bought an old stone barn with a tiny bit of land and had restored it, bit by bit, until he was diagnosed with cancer. She wanted to try to stay there permanently, hoping to have enough money to get by without having to work with his brother in the business. But now she was embroiled in a tax dispute with the French government, and they were about to take her house away.

In France, under Napoleonic law, if a couple owns their home jointly and one of them dies, the heirs of the departed, not the spouse, now own his half of the property. Even if there are no children, as was the case with Nadou, the property will go to a mother or brother, even distant nieces and nephews, before the surviving spouse, and the inheritor has to pay taxes on their inheritance. Often, they can't afford to do so without selling the place or taking out another mortgage, which they sometimes can't pay, which forces the sale of the house, which dislocates the surviving partner. I can only assume that this was instituted to protect children from a first marriage from losing out on everything if a parent remarries. There is a document that a couple can sign that gives the surviving spouse the use of a property until his or her death, which, fortunately, Nadou and her spouse had signed.

She and Claude, who had never married and who had no children, had had time to make what they thought were all the necessary arrangements. They signed the papers in both their names, so she owned her half clear. She also owned a third of the vegetable business, which she, Claude, and his brother had built over the years. Claude had even taken out a life insurance policy that would pay the taxes on his half of the inheritance, which, by law, went to his closest next of kin, his mother. He had drawn up a paper attached to the insurance policy instructing his kin to pay the taxes with the proceeds so Nadou wouldn't have any concerns about losing her house. Theoretically, Nadou would be secure and could live on the proceeds of the business. Except for one small detail. Claude's mother refused to use the proceeds of the insurance policy to pay the taxes. She said Claude had never told her to do so, and she didn't see why she should pay all that money for the taxes when it wouldn't benefit her or her other children for a long time, only Nadou. Neither fraternity, decency, civility, morality, or that old French standby, solidarity, ever entered into her thinking.

In the meantime, Nadou had been forced to sell her part of the business to the only person for whom it had any value, Claude's brother, to pay the taxes that Claude's mother owed. He paid her ten centimes on the franc of what it was worth. since he knew she couldn't keep her house any other way. Some family. Then the government heard about the sale of the business to the brother and sent her another tax invoice for the income tax on the sale of the business, the proceeds of which she had just paid to the government to keep her house. She was desperate to find the original insurance policy document, hoping she could shame her mother-in-law or convince the government that she had been swindled.

Somehow, Odette thought I could help her in that quest. Now I know I've gone candles and sandals on you by meditating to maintain my sanity, but I'm surely not a channeler, guru, swami, or even sage. But I do think, if we're calm, we can sometimes find answers inside ourselves to particular problems. Being calm and staying with a thought when we're desperate is tough, but sometimes just being quiet in the presence of another person is easier. So I thought I could sit with her, as my Zen friend had done with me, and help her look inside for the solution. She came to the mill, we shook hands in introduction, went straight to the terrace above the waterfall, and closed our eyes. Tears of relief, sadness, and anger welled up from down inside her. I handed her tissues, she wept; more tissues, more tears. Much later, she opened her eyes and declared she knew what she had to do and strode off with confidence, not having shared her conclusions.

I called her the next week to see if she was doing better, and she told me triumphantly that her plan had worked. During our session, something inside of her told her to write down her story, with as much documentation as she could, including some nasty letters from Claude's mother and brother, and go to Rodez to sit down with a tax person. So she did. She showed him the papers and sat quietly while he read through her dossier. She said he kept shaking his head in disbelief but finally looked her in the eye, reached over, and took the tax invoice he had sent, ripped it in two, and told her she owed nothing. See, being centered does help sometimes.

Off to bed . . .

—*Love, Judy*

ART AT THE MILL

June 15, 1996
Dear Linda,

Derek and Mike are healing nicely. Derek and Kristie are coming next week for his thirtieth birthday. Mike is puttering in the garden, arranging his studio, and, in other words, fixin' to go to work since he has two shows this summer.

We're expecting Richard Berger, my sculpture professor, who is coming for the short visit this year to see if he would like to come next year for a longer stay. I admire him enormously, but he intimidates me somewhat, probably because I think he can do no wrong. He's over six foot five, completely bald, has five earrings in each ear, and huge, muscular hands. At the same time, he is a talented piano player, is easily moved by poetry, and is a soft touch for a student's excuse of not being ready. "I was never ready either," he'd say. He admires Ezra Pound, telling me to forget that he was a Nazi sympathizer and just read his poetry. He has taught at the Toot for over twenty years and has hundreds of students who worship him and his misanthropic inclinations and the jazz rap he uses in his lectures.

He is presently teaching a class called The Care and Feeding of an Idea, a class that requires one to start the semester with a concept and follow it through to the end, à la Duchamp and his *Green Box*. Duchamp published his notes and drawings for his best-known piece, called by most students of art *The Large Glass*. He wanted to sell a limited edition of the boxed notes to make money, but Richard wants his students to show him proof that they actually started with an idea, followed through several iterations, leading to a final work. Students usually stall around until the last week of a class and then poop out some "brain-boogers," as Richard calls them, and try to call it "art." If they have to document what they did, he thought they would be more present for the whole semester. I love the idea, since I often like my journals with my studio sketches better than the final work itself!

Off to get my studio in shape.

—*Hugs, Judy*

June 30, 1996
Dear Linda,

Mike is still doing well. His eye has a tendency to wander off when he's tired, but other than that, a boxer's nose, and a ridiculously short haircut he's come to love and I hate, he's the old Mikey.

Derek and Kristie came for his birthday, and I confess I cried with happiness much of the visit. Mike picked them up in Toulouse, ordering me to stay put and plump pillows. I was pacing and puttering, nervous to see Derek after more than two months. I had cut some red roses from Germain's mother's bush for an opulent bouquet, which I intended to put in their room. I was arranging them on the front terrace, and when I heard the car I rushed into the mill, backing through the bamboo fly curtain, which closed behind me, pulling the petals from their stems and scattering them in the doorway to make an unplanned red carpet for my son and his queen. When I looked up, I saw Derek, without so much as a cane, walking down the gravel drive. He stepped somewhat gingerly down the entry stairs and gave me the best hug ever, grinding the rose petals under his feet.

They stayed for a week, then went off to Lourdes for the day. That evening, Derek showed me how he could move his legs higher than before they left that morning. I asked him if he'd gotten some religion in this experience, and he said he'd learned to accept any and all forms of help, something some of us never learn.

Except for you, my dear . . . good night.

—*Love, Judy*

July 10, 1996
JOURNAL ENTRY

Germain came by this afternoon with an odd wooden bucket filled with an assortment of metal spikes, two long wooden handles with spatula-sized paddles carved out on the ends, and a thin one-foot-square piece of smooth wood with a hole to one side, shaped like an artist's palette. He presented the paddles to Mike, explaining that they were the very ones that his father used to reach down beside the millstones, inside the wooden boxes that protect them, to push the flour along toward the opening, in case it backed up while being ground. He pulled the removable panel off from the big chestnut box that encases the millstones and reached over to the side, as his father would have done. Germain told Mike that his father was an artist, too: "*Voilà sa palette!*" The palette, with "Louis Blanc, '46" burned onto the surface, was passed by Germain's father through the stream of flour as it fell from the stones into the wooden bucket. He could tell by looking closely at the powder if the stones were the right distance apart to grind the grain finely enough, but not too finely, so that the bran could be separated easily when it passed through the giant flour sifter, or *bluterie*, hanging on the wall on the other side of the mill room. He promised that when the first flour came out of the stones, he would come down and show Mike how to use these tools, and said there were more surprises to come.

Then, with his head bowed slightly, he turned to me and shyly pulled another handle out of his back pocket, this one much shorter than the paddles and with a golf-ball-sized round cast-iron head at one end. There was a square hole through the metal. Smiling, he reached down into the bucket and pulled out a thick four-sided spike, about half an inch in diameter at its base and about six inches long, narrowing to a four-sided point. He slipped the tapered square end into the hole in the metal. He reached through the still-open millstone panel and tapped the stone sharply with the pointed end of the hammer. Sparks flew, and he laughed out loud at our shock. He explained that his father used that tool to dress the millstones, making them coarse enough to grind the flour. He had seen me cutting stone and decided I needed one of his father's tools as well.

July 18, 1996
JOURNAL ENTRY

Didier, Clémence, Suzie, and François had dinner with us last night. For us it was a thank-you to them for lugging our radiators out last winter while we were back in the States dealing with health issues. The two couples are close friends and eat together almost every week, summer and winter. We've been included several times in the past, but our French is now finally good enough that we understand more of what is being said. Clémence has a constant large-toothed smile, through which she mumbles and laughs her words, but Didier speaks quite clearly, stroking his scruffy blond beard and laughing at his own jokes, many of them plays-on-words or puns that we don't understand. Usually he is quite jovial, but last night, after a bit too much to drink, he started teasing Suzie about being an American, sympathizing with the capitalist political structure, and thus being a member of the *bourgeoisie*. At first we were shocked and even thought we had misunderstood him, but when I was alone with Suzie in the kitchen she confirmed my suspicions about his latent anti-Americanism. She said he often starts in on her like that and that François usually joins in, but in deference to us, he was staying quiet.

"Does he think that's funny?" I asked.

"He thinks he's being clever," she shrugged. "In the country, you take what you get. There aren't too many choices."

Later, as my pecan pie was served, Didier started in on religion, talking about how scary the religious culture is in the United States. When I tried to point out that not everyone thinks that way, he scoffed, and spouted statistics on church-goers, quoting comments from political leaders, and saying how stupid and ignorant people are who believe in a higher being. I tried to point out that believing or not is an opinion; nobody has a right to judge or dismiss them just because you don't agree with them. He became nastier and nastier, to the point where I crossed my arms and kept my mouth shut, thinking to myself, "I don't have to put up with this again." François kept quiet, looking down at his huge miner's hands in his lap. Clémence was still smiling through her teeth, and Suzie was simmering as she pushed the crust of her pecan pie around her plate. She actually stayed back and apologized for him as they were trailing up the drive to their car, "He'd had a bit too much to drink, I think." I don't know what surprised me more: the vitriolic tirade or Suzie's passivity. We know there's an anti-American mentality here; it's obvious in the French news and their television humor, but we'd never experienced a direct onslaught before. But Suzie seems resigned to it.

August 15, 1996
Dear Linda,

Sorry it's been too long between letters. I'll try to catch up with this e-mail. We're delighted you're "online." This redefines the "haves" and "have-nots," but I confess that we rarely write letters anymore except by e-mail. There's something less intimidating, more immediate, and—dare I say it—fun about checking in daily with kids and friends. And with a letter, of course, there is finding the clean sheet of paper, and one should do a little drawing or something, and the blue ink doesn't work and, shit, I just misspelled the person's name, and the envelope and then stamps take on a life of their own, and by the time they get this I'll be home, and why bother?

Derek, now, in August, in spite of the fact that in April the doctors told him he would never walk unassisted, has thrown his cane away, is riding the subway in New York, and recently even rode his bike! He bumped into his neurologist, the one who told him he'd never walk unassisted. Naturally, the doctor was shocked. So much for doctors and averages. Derek's taking computer courses to build a portfolio to go back to school for a graphic arts thing. He and Kristie may even move back to San Francisco. But he told me he needs to leave New York on his own terms.

Mike is finally rid of a horrible cold and infection in that vast space in his head. Scared me, he did. But he is now painting and painting and painting and framing up in his stone studio. He's had two shows this summer and will probably have a big one next summer. Except for the odd headache from time to time, he is almost back to normal. Considering the nine hours of surgery, his eye being taken out and replaced, and all of the bone being removed on one side of his head, you'd think he'd look and feel a little peaked. But I take more naps than he does!

As for me, I've been painting our new forged-metal fence, bar by bar by bar. It was deftly installed by one of our three local blacksmiths, Pierre. So now we have Bernard *pierre*, Claude *bois,* and Pierre *fer*, or "iron." One of Germain's sons, Yves, is one of these *forgerons,* but he was too busy with his projects for the local mines to do the work, so

Pierre *fer* (not *pierre*) assembled the sections of the fence mounted on the low stone wall built by Bernard *pierre* along the cliff overlooking the river. Pierre *fer* is a dashing young man with hands like the steel he bends meticulously, and in his spare time he does sculpture so he's very interested in what we're going to do at the mill, volunteering his help in any way.

Richard Berger was here for almost two weeks and was totally taken by the place and what we're trying to do. While he was here, I started work on the tool series that began taking shape when Bernard *pierre* and Claude *bois* were still here working together. The interface between the hard and the soft, the strange scale of all the millworks, and my trip to Paris to the tool museum started to coalesce around some very large wooden and stone tool forms.

Berger saw me flailing away cutting stone for a huge hammer, still balancing my act in Bernard's wheelbarrow filled with sand as I cut and grind. Berger told me that when he was a kid someone had given him a saxophone after hearing him play. The person told him that he played well enough that he deserved to have something to play. Saying the same thing to me, Berger went off to the building supply store and banged together a massive, solid sand table, a 4-by-4-foot elevated sandbox where I can grind away without killing my back. Of course, I have to get the rock up there, but that's where my metal-working buddy Pierre *fer* came up with a beautiful lift system with an articulating arm that turns on a bearing so I can lift a heavy stone onto the table with a winch. The whole space at the end of the bridge *qui va nulle part*, the bridge to nowhere, has been transformed into a little playground. I can leave my compressor out there with a tarp over it, and I've run a wire for power, so all I do is plop everything I need for the day into the wheelbarrow and toddle on out. I put the umbrella stand there for hot days, and since the wildflowers have grown as high as that elephant's eye, I'm well hidden from the road. (It's funny during tourist season when cars stop and people get out to look at the mill. I can hear them talking about the house before they see me.)

I use the table for everything. I know you shouldn't use a sand table for woodworking. But I had a huge laminated hammer handle to plane and wrestle around to go with the stone head. So I put a thick but supple tarp over the sand, used the crane with some pulleys to move it around, and used the sand and some wedges to stabilize it while I planed and sanded. I've been welding small things there, too, like stands for the larger pieces, and lampshades, thanks to my new MIG welder, since I can stick things in the sand and I'm not worried about fire or people accidentally staring at the spark. I found a beautiful old table vise at a *brocante* that was used for metal working, and I mounted that on another leg for simple metal bending and a vise for grinding. When I asked Pierre if it would be damaged by the weather, he just looked at me like the neophyte I am and said, "Not in your lifetime, sweetie." A kid in her sandbox, I am.

Every night after our dirty-day showers, Mike reads to me while I cook dinner—mostly short stories. It is marvelous. Some things are better "on the air." W. S. Merwin and/or John Berger, both of whom have lived in rural France and have a writing style that captures the sense of timelessness of country living, for example. While Berger *prof* was here, we read e. e. cummings and Ezra Pound in spite of my Pound prejudice. I hate to admit it, but Pound is pretty good on the air, and I like cummings's lectures out loud, though I prefer to read the poetry to myself. But the best part about Berger's visit is more difficult to articulate. I just learned a lot. About physical stuff, yes, but more about thinking about and implementing projects. Berger says everything we make is a self-portrait, and that we have to look there first when we're making decisions, either esthetic or mechanical. I am intrigued about his "care and feeding of an idea" class, and I've decided to try it myself.

I had already finished my stone scissors (the handles Bernard and I carved last summer), making the blades of finely finished laminated plywood, and a hammer called *Miller's Stone Pick Turned Paintbrush.* The piece is over eight feet long, with a handle shaped like a paintbrush, the head carved in stone in two pieces and a point in the shape of a traditional metal point that fits in between the stone pieces like an interchangeable head on a hammer, but pointed like a pick. I wanted to make several points in different colors and different materials, but I'd been blocked and was almost ready to dump the whole project. Using Berger's technique, I started to document the project—my motivations, the influences, what I was trying to say. I had thought it was about transformation, young to old, businessperson to artist, mother to friend, stone-dressing hammer to paintbrush, but it was also about the interface of the materials. A real self-portrait, since I am often the interface in relationships: children and fathers, friends and enemies, men and women, even *pierre* and *bois.* And interfaces of materials are as difficult as those in relationships. I wanted to put wood to stone, paper to stone, metal to straw, even cement to plastic and make it work. I already had the wood/stone scissors, and I went to work on the other points I had to make.

I scrounged in Mike's wastebasket for his rejected watercolors, and I made a recycled pulp of them and shaped a paper point, building a tall, thin box as an armature. I then went through my journals and reproduced my watercolor drawings and comments on the piece. I then "dressed" the head with the hammer that Germain had given us, the one his father had used to rough up our millstones. I put ten coats of varnish on the laminated handle and assembled the whole thing so the hammer lay on its handle and head with the paper point straight up in the air. To me, it assumed a quiet and personal presence: the symbolism of the tools, the extensions of humanity, a monument to the artists and millers who influence me, the synergy I feel when I work with Mike, and the private pleasure I get from my own drawings in journals—God, that was fun. Now two more points to go.

Richard Berger is coming back next year with a grand scheme to turn our *porcherie* into a meditation site—a fantasy I've had since we began. He was intrigued with all the traces of the generations of millers who have lived here, but since we had spent most of our energy restoring their work in the form of the mill, we left few of our own marks. He's going to take one of my fingerprints and one of Mike's and interweave them, blow them up, and transfer them by stencils onto raw clay tiles using enamels, so we can create a tile floor in the pigpen. We'll fix the walls and put windows in the side that looks over the river. It should be a tranquil place when we're done. We went to Millau to the Raujoule tile guy, and he is going to hand-make the tiles, and his brother, also a Richard, will help Berger with colors and enamel choices. He will bring the raw tiles back to Mike's studio to transfer the design and paint on the enamels; then we'll take them back to Millau to be fired.

I learned more in a few days of observing Berger than I ever did in a whole semester of his classes. His concept of "the care and feeding of an idea" came to life before our eyes. One morning, a few days before he was due to leave, he sprang the idea of the fingerprints, we loved it, he started. He wanted to see the space empty, something we'd never done, since the *porcherie* was literally filled to the ceiling with mill parts and other junk that we couldn't bear to throw away. That meant that to empty it we either had to find room in other dark corners or make decisions about what to keep and what to pitch. Berger decided not to wait for us and started tossing everything out onto the front lawn. He was a cross between a jolly green giant and an art critic in the pigpen. He heaved and tossed for three days. Under years of accumulated iron bits and firewood, the little building that was used as an outhouse in Louis Blanc's time had already become a quiet space, with the cracked base of a millstone tottering over a tunnel exit for one of the millraces at one end and a dirt floor on the other—empty and waiting until next year.

As Berger was leaving, I asked him for a critique of the work I had done so far. He was gentle as always, and suggested that I try abstracting the tools a bit more, be less literal. I asked him how does one know when the viewer of a piece has enough clues to "get it"? He responded by handing me a copy of a T. S. Eliot essay written about poetry. Berger maintained that some *soupçon* of the original shape of the tool should be integrated into the final piece, since such clues were, as Eliot wrote, "like a bit of nice meat for the house-dog so the burglar can go about his business."

The two young artists I had mentioned earlier, Larry and Alma, Michael Strom's girlfriend, are with us now. Larry is quite talented, and is going into Stanford's graduate program next year. Alma is, like too many young art students, suffering from past parental abuse and drug use, in her case leading to prostitution and other things too painful to recount. Michael had been her first real, or at least first gentle, companion. Larry and Alma have been mostly working a little here and there at the mill and wandering the countryside and sport-fucking up in the little house, which, given that I invited her because of Michael, leaves me somewhat conflicted.

They have done some pieces. Alma a nice bench made from chestnut planks we found under the house, and Larry a carved demon's head that he feels is his alter ego. It wears the same kind of Joseph Beuys–style fedora that Larry wears everywhere. He put the head on top of a stake with an LCD solar-powered light that has a motion detector attached. He wants people wandering over the bridge at night to be surprised by this troll, in spite of the fact that no one walks over the bridge at night. He refuses to protect the wood, which means in the misty mill weather it will last less than one winter. It isn't the ethereal quality of the object that makes him so stubborn, it's just that he's stubborn and doesn't want to spend that much time on the piece. He was taken by Bernard *bois*, our neighbor and woodworker, who helped him cut a fine chunk of oak for the piece, and frankly I learned more from Bernard's reaction to the process than from Larry himself. Bernard wanted to know everything about the piece, why he was doing it. Larry is pretty good at "art speak," which is what artists and critics write and say to appear intelligent in front of a statue made of horse manure. It was like being back at the Toot watching a student tapdance when he or she hadn't thought about anything until the night before the critique. I didn't tell Bernard it was all horse manure.

Larry had asked if his father, who was going to be in France at the same time, could come and see him. We told him of course, not realizing that his father is a "travel user." It became clear over the first cup of coffee he was trying to hit us up for a longer stay, calling himself an artist and a good handyman. When we didn't bite, he started telling Larry about someone he'd just met who owned a barge, and that if he played his cards right, he, the father, could get free lodging for the summer: "Imagine your ole man on a *péniche* in the Midi. I won't have to do much, I don't think." And so on. His behavior explained a lot of Larry's, and in general, we feel slightly used. In the future, we have decided to stick with professors, who will, by definition, be a bit more mature as artists and offer us a bit more, too.

We decided that when we have guest artists here, we won't change our routine with our French friends, which meant Berger, Larry, and Alma had to suffer through some long French-speaking meals, but Suzie gave them a few lessons, and I think they picked up a little of the language.

Dan came again for a week, but unfortunately is not doing too well. He has been sick a lot lately and is starting to address the inevitable outcome of being HIV positive. He gave me a doll he'd made last year, white, with a small red button for a heart. This year, he made a limbless amorphous doll from tarpaper with crossed red threads for eyes.

Going to go close mine—

—*Love, Judy*

JEAN-CLAUDE ET FAMILLE

August 20, 1996
Dear Linda,

You asked me how we meet people. It's never the same way, almost always by accident, so I'll give you a "for instance." Larry and Alma wanted to see more of the countryside, and while we offered them our car, they were nervous about taking off by themselves, so Mike and I went off with them for a short drive up on the plains above Coupiac. As we came up over the hill, we saw a quaint pastoral scene, a shepherd with his two dogs and a rather sizable herd of sheep clumped in one corner of a big field, with large cumulus clouds grumbling with their heavy, wet load and rolling over their heads. Larry asked me to ask the shepherd if he would make his dogs work the sheep like he'd seen in the movies. So we screeched to a halt, I jumped out of the car, leaped over the ditch, and hung precariously onto the fence while the man sauntered over, all the time looking at that menacing cloud. I started with the salutary "*Excusez-moi de vous déranger, monsieur*," the obligatory "sorry to bother you" needed anytime one asks something of a stranger, and then explained my young friend's request. The man's expression changed, first from a furrowed brow of total suspicion to a broad grin of recognition (he'd been in line at the *quincaillerie* one day while I was waiting in line in my tool belt and had been told by Jean-Paul that I was a Californian), then to that "huh" look you get when someone doesn't understand a thing you've said. I thought I had trotted out my best French, but he responded with a rapid-fire string of rolled *r*'s like we'd stumbled into Spain without knowing it. I tried again, slowly, enunciating each syllable, "Is it possible to see your dogs work the sheep, monsieur?"

He looked at me for a long time and then responded, with a big smile, equally slowly, with every word finishing with an *r* rolled tighter than a Gauloise, "Ahhh, *non*, see those clouds over there, it's going to pour rain, and sheep are so dumb that if I interrupt their dinner they'll never finish before the storm sends them in all directions, and I'll never get home tonight! But I'll show you our little farm if you'd like. *Je m'appelle Jean-Claude Fabre, mais appelez-moi Jean-Claude.*"

So we all, shepherd-turned-Jean-Claude included, hopped in the Twingo, dogs standing guard after a brief command in patois, and bumped down the hill to Moussac, his "modest little farm."

As we came down the drive, we could see fifteen or so brown cows grazing near a large pond. When I asked Jean-Claude if they were for milk or meat, he smiled sweetly with a big grin, "I just like them. Well, actually, I like fresh milk for breakfast, too." Then he added, rubbing his thumb against the first two fingers in the universal sign of capitalism, "And when we need a little quick cash, we can grab a calf and run up to the

Monday market at Réquista." He didn't slap his knee at his cleverness, but his whole demeanor said he would sooner or later.

We pulled past two large agricultural buildings into a farm courtyard with a long, three-story building on the left with three front doors, each with a different date on the lintel. At right angles to the living quarters was an equally long structure with open parking below and a wooden barnlike building on top that could be entered from a road higher up on the hill. Below, in the parking area, was a huge green and yellow combine with long, delicate spikes pointing in all directions, two small tractors, a tiny bright-blue Renault truck, a camping car, an old motorcycle, and an old rusty animal-transport truck, all in a tidy row along with an assortment of attachments that went with one or more of the vehicles. On the right was a staircase leading up to what seemed to be a garden surrounded by huge pine trees.

As we poured out of the car he shouted, "*Monique, Monique, c'est les Californiens!*" His wife, Monique, and their three adult daughters, Beatrice, Sophie, and Florence, four of the most unconsciously beautiful blue-black-haired women I've ever seen, ran out the door of the farthest building, panic on their faces. Their panic morphed into relief, which was quickly replaced with genuine enthusiasm, and the hereditary and/or contagious smile of Jean-Claude filled the faces of Monique, Florence, Beatrice, and Sophie. (Larry couldn't speak French, but it didn't matter; he was speechless when confronted with such voluptuousness, and Mike later told me he himself felt like Little Abner confronted with four brunette Daisy Maes.)

They were all in dirty-day clothes and garden shoes, their hands—no gloves here—covered with dirt. As we completed the obligatory *bisous* forty-eight times (four of us times the four of them times the three *bises* customary in the Aveyron), an older woman, elegantly dressed, her hair recently done, and her head cocked to the side, appeared in the doorway of the middle house. "*Maman, venez rencontrer les californiens!*" Jean-Claude shouted. Already, the formal use of *venez* told us this woman was different, since it's rare today in France to *vouvoyer* a family member. She extended her hand briefly to each of us and then disappeared into the gloom of the middle residence. Monique dismissed her with a wave of the hand and took mine to pull me into their house, where Jean-Claude showed us his family *blazon*, or crest, with the date of 1649 carved into the stone of the fireplace. He dismissed the question of how many generations had farmed there with a wave of his hand: "Too many to count."

There were three old daguerreotypes of two handsome men on the wall beside the fireplace, along with a photo of a young woman, the parents of Monique and the father of Jean-Claude, though no sign of a photograph of his mother, who was living literally next door. There was also a photo of the La Borie, Monique's parents' farm in Combret, about thirty kilometers from Moussac, which is now owned and farmed by Jean-Claude and his family. An exaggerated frown, shoulders up, shaking head "*J'sais pas*," answered my question about who in the next generation would take over after them.

Monique retired to her kitchen while we followed Jean-Claude, who was still checking on the gathering clouds, and walked down the short gravel drive to the *bergerie*, or sheep barn. A relatively small door led into the near end of a dark, surprisingly cool barn, at least one hundred by sixty feet in size, with a maze of low wooden walls forming large and small straw-filled stalls. Down the middle was a long wooden trough into which a young man, at the far end, was pouring grain from a large bag.

"*Coucou, Raphael, les Californiens!*" Jean-Claude yelled. The man looked up, not missing a pouring beat, smiled, threw back his head in greeting, and went back to dispersing the grain. The straw in the stalls looked clean and there were only a few sheep in the barn, but the smell of accumulated ammonia from several hundred years of sheep *pipi* was overwhelming. Eyes watering, we walked quickly to the far end, where Monique rejoined us and Jean-Claude disappeared, and we heard the rumble of the old motorcycle as it started and moved away up the hill.

We passed through another small door into the milking barn, a stark contrast with the building we were leaving. It was bright and odor-free, the walls, floor, and ceiling all in white tiles, the room about fifty feet by fifty feet, with two rows of metal troughs at each side with about twenty U-shaped openings, all constructed from galvanized steel. Above the troughs was another mysterious mechanism that seemed to have trapdoors directly above the openings in the trough below. In the center of the room, set down about three feet, was a recessed space above which there was a maze of clear plastic tubing with hand-sized metal and rubber tubes on their ends, all suspended on black bungee-like springs. We walked around the end of one of the troughs, staying on the narrow walkway that bypassed the business part of the room.

Suddenly, there was a commotion outside the door on the other side of the room. Monique held us back, like children in the front seat of a car, as the back door opened and forty sheep came running, clip-clopping, slipping, and sliding on the tile floor along the narrow walkway to the edge of the troughs, twenty on each side. Jean-Claude had brought them down, laid his motorcycle on its side, and was heying and hooing them into place. When they were roughly aligned on each side, heads toward the trough, tails toward the recessed space, he clicked a switch and the mysterious mechanism's trapdoors *whapped* open and a cup or so of grain swooshed into the trough before each sheep.

In unison, the sheep put their heads through the slats and a bar clanked down, holding the sheep captive as they munched the grain, oblivious to the action behind them. Florence had slipped in through the side door, and joined Monique in the recessed space behind the sheep, and in unison, reached up and pulled down the vacuum cups and tubing, and quickly attached one to each of the two udders of each sheep. A *jink-jonk* sound of the compressor pulling and releasing the eighty teats in the room was punctuated by the *swish-swish* of the milk sucked into the tubes to be transported to some other mysterious space. In less than a minute, Monique and Florence detached the milking machine cups, another click of a switch made a *clank* as the mechanism released their heads, the two women called "Hey-hoo," and off the sheep went through the other door into the barn, clip-clopping, slipping, and sliding, looking for more grain in the trough that Raphael was filling. Before the last one was through the door, Jean-Claude "hey-hoo'd" forty more clip-clopping, slipping, and sliding sheep into their spaces, *click* went the switch, *whap* went the trap doors, *swoosh* went the grain, *clank* went the bar at their heads, *jink-jonk-swish-swish* went the milking machine, and then *clank*, "hey-hoo," *clip-clop*, slip-slide they went out the door. Ten times the "hey-hoo," the *clip-clop* slip-slide, the *click*, the *whap*, the *swoosh*, the *clank*, the *jink-jonk*, *swish-swish*, *click*, *clank*, "hey-hoo," *clip-clop*, slip-slide. Forty sheep each time. In less than forty-five minutes, they had milked all four hundred head of sheep and washed down the milking barn for the morning. Not bad for a poor, lowly shepherd.

We went back into the house where Beatrice and Sophie had prepared an *apéro*, while Jean-Claude, Monique, and Florence disappeared for about ten minutes. They reappeared together, hair wet from their showers. (Later, on our way home in the car, smelling our own clothes, we knew why.) As they came in, the other two daughters disappeared to go feed the hogs, chickens, and ducks. In fact, they all came and went throughout our visit, maintaining the various demands of animals and plants, each one with her own chores, the comings and goings of real farmers.

And by the way, the stairs on the right as we drove in, where I thought there might be a nice garden? They actually led to the swimming pool, which is elegantly placed in the raised center courtyard surrounded by fir trees and, well, a nice garden. (It seems that if one has a contract with Roquefort, one lives well, since a profit of one thousand to two thousand dollars per sheep is expected. Do the math—four hundred head of sheep and a house that's been paid for at least four hundred years. No wonder they have a vacation house in Sète and another in Spain!)

—*Hugs, Judy*

GOODBYE, FRANCIS

September 1, 1996

JOURNAL ENTRY

Francis stopped by the mill three weeks ago on his way back from the food market in Albi. I heard a car and started out the front door to greet him, wiping tomato-canning juice from my hands, smiling as he walked slowly down the drive. He saw me, but then stopped still, under the grape trellis, out of the sun, and without even the standard three *bisous*, he blurted out that he couldn't go on, Marie-France was angry all the time, she thought all his problems were in his head, and he owed too much money on Les Magnolias to meet the new European Union rules. He was red-eyed and shaking, the gray roots of his dyed hair now almost two inches long.

We had seen very little of him this summer, since on his days off he preferred to stay in the cool protection of their private quarters across the back alley from Les Magnolias, his foot, swollen with gout, on a red damask pillow, his hands shaking from exhaustion.

We had once talked briefly about the coping mechanisms I'd learned—meditation and guided visualization—to try to deal with Mike and Derek's health problems this past winter and spring. At the time, it sounded bizarre and new-agey to Francis, who lived in a fourteenth-century building once owned by the family of the famous poet Paul Valéry. But here Francis stood, eyes searching, for something, anything, more metaphysical: something to quiet the constant internal and external nagging.

He stood rocking heel to toe, with the filtered light of the grape leaves changing the mask of his face. I asked him if he wanted to just sit awhile. He nodded, holding back tears. I turned toward the front door of the mill, pushed aside the hanging rattan fly screen, and led him inside, past the walnut oil press, which he patted gently, through the mill, out the back door, up to the terrace above the dam. I moved two chairs to face the waterfall, and asked him to sit and close his eyes, to breathe deeply, and to walk slowly along a path in his imagination to his favorite place in the woods.

After several minutes, his shoulders began to relax, he uncrossed his arms, and his hands fell to his lap, no longer trembling. Then months, maybe years of tears began to tumble, then stream, down his cheeks, falling unchecked on his chest. He took my proffered bandana and pressed it to his eyes, rocking himself while shocks of sobs poured out, until after about half an hour, he finally fell silent. With his eyes still closed, I asked him to find a safe place in that woods and stay there for a while. After a few quiet moments he opened his eyes, sighed deeply and said, "*Merci*."

He came by every day after that, and we sat quietly above the waterfall while he went back to that place. He sometimes said that while he walked on the path, he would come to a precipice. Then one day I asked him, while his eyes were closed, to envision his heart. After a long pause, he told me he could see it and it was torn in shreds. As he was leaving, I told him I thought his emotional state might be contributing to some of his physical problems, and asked him to promise to go see his doctor the next day. I even said I wouldn't sit with him again until he did.

He has all the symptoms of cardiovascular disease, but his doctor had been telling him it was all in his head, just like his severely depressed mother who ended up committing suicide when he was young. He came back the next day and told me the doctor had taken a blood sample, checked his pulse, and given him some tranquilizers. I asked about a stress test or other cardiovascular exams, but the doctor had told him these weren't necessary—he was only fifty-five. Frustrated, I bit my tongue while we sat up on the terrace, the waterfall crashing below us.

One day after we had sat together, Mike and I talked to Francis and asked him if he had some friends he trusted who could look through his books and help him come up with a plan to present to the bank. We offered to participate if he wanted, adding we are, after all, recovering businesspeople, pretty good with numbers, and that we had a good friend who was a restaurant consultant who said was coming to visit next spring.

Francis said there was one couple, dear friends of his, who were savvy financially and had offered to help before.

We met with them the next day and decided that we four are prepared to do whatever is necessary as long as we can see a reasonable evaluation of the numbers and a general strategy for saving the hotel. We talked through some tough issues, and the general consensus was that Francis needed a board of directors for a while and that the four of us would serve in that capacity. We agreed that we'd communicate after the first of the year and get started then.

The next day, while he and I were sitting above the waterfall, Francis, his head bowed low, told me that Marie-France doesn't agree with our plan, that she thinks Francis could solve the problems of the hotel all on his own if he'd just shape up. Mike and I are leaving in a few weeks, so I asked Francis if there was someplace else he can go to find peace while we're gone. And he said, "Only at the mill."

I will sit with Francis each day until we leave.

September 10, 1996
Dear Linda,

We have just finished with three solid months of guest artists, and I'm out of gas. We've already got three sets of artists lined up for next summer. I hope I'll learn to pace myself better by then. But here and now, fall has rolled in, dragging long shadows behind it, painting the grapes a dusty blue, so it must be time to pack up and leave. This stay at the mill was about healing. Physically, mentally.

We await Steve and Yvette next week and Jenea the week after—then Paris for a bit and on to New York and, finally, San Francisco to see the rest of the kids the 18th of October, so you won't hear much from me until then. God, life is good when we're healthy. I sincerely hope all of you are *en pleine forme.*

—*All our love, Judy*

November 25, 1996
JOURNAL ENTRY
San Francisco

I just got a call from Marie-France, Francis's wife. They had been vacationing in Spain after a tough year when Francis started having severe chest pains. After an angiogram, they were told that he had several severely blocked arteries but they couldn't do surgery because his gout was so bad. They are going to open the most severely blocked vessels now with balloon angioplasty and do bypass surgery after the first of the year when his gout is under better control. I usually like to say "I told you so," but this time I'd like to have been wrong. Marie-France is going to call me from the hospital in January.

January 8, 1997
JOURNAL ENTRY
San Francisco

I'm stunned. Marie-France just called me from the hospital in Toulouse to tell me that Francis is dead. They had performed bypass surgery a few days before, and he seemed to be recovering well. Then, suddenly, his heart stopped and they were not able to bring him back. I guess he just couldn't face the future, the work that would be required to bring his life up to the standards he held for himself. All I can see is that half-smile and the gray roots of his hair.

I'll be in New York visiting Derek on the day of the funeral. I think I'll go to St. Patrick's Cathedral and light a candle at nine in the morning while the rest are at the church in Plaisance. Maybe he'll talk to me, tell me why.

February 12, 1997
JOURNAL ENTRY
San Francisco

Linda is so brave. She's in pain with the contractures in her hand and foot, her bunion surgery hasn't healed well, and she's trying to stay positive for the sake of her children. She says she's humiliated when friends have to add up lunch bills to help her pay. Her losses are very specific—symbol processing and near-term memory—but people tend to treat her as though she's incompetent in general, as in how come she can play cards? She's having some symptoms of further vascular issues, such as cramping of her muscles, but there's nothing that can be done.

March 6, 1997
JOURNAL ENTRY
La Pilande Basse

I arrived back in Plaisance yesterday, and today I went to Les Magnolias to see Marie-France and then to the cemetery to say goodbye to Francis. I climbed up the narrow street from his house behind Les Magnolias, where the two-wheeled hearse would have passed, pulled by the men in the village. The street isn't long, but it's steep, and I could imagine the grunts of the men and the black-veiled whispers of the women. Little Franc would have followed with his mother, and Francis's grown children must not have been far behind them. The octagonal steeple of the church bears witness to its twelfth-century Romanesque roots, more like a fort than a place of worship. The bells in the church tower must have clanged and shook for at least a half hour at the time of his death and before the funeral, to advise everyone of a loss in the village. The church steps are steep, and I knew the cart must have been drawn up to the side entrance so the coffin could be carried inside to be placed on the cold stone floor in front of the sparse altar. Francis didn't often go to Mass, but this time he had to be there for the duration of the service.

Francis now has a place on the top of the cliff overlooking the Rance River, and considering how much grief and pain he had experienced the last two years, I think he may be happier. In the meantime, Marie-France intends to find another chef so she can keep the restaurant open, and we will continue to help her, just as we had promised to help Francis.

DIRTY DAYS AND DORMICE

March 8, 1997

Dear Linda,

Well, I'm here. I left Derek and Kristie in New York, where he's settling into his new job as a graphic artist at an ad agency. Mike's following in a few days, leaving me to warm up these ole walls. As you know, our dear Francis from Les Magnolias died unexpectedly this winter. I lit a candle for him in New York and I visited his grave my first day here. I asked him why he left us, why he quit. I heard his voice telling me quite clearly that he just couldn't go on. He'd been too ostracized in the village for leaving his first wife for his new wife, Marie-France, and then she became hostile and angry about his diminishing health, convinced that it was all in his head. I know you think I'm slightly bonkers when I say I talked to him, but that part of me that knew him spoke quite clearly. He is temporarily in the Parnat family tomb while they await his headstone and a team to jackhammer his grave into the cliff behind the church next to his parents. It's too bad, because Francis couldn't stand Parnat, our local second-hand-goods dealer, and always thought he was waiting for Les Magnolias to fold so he could scoop up pieces to sell. I hope Marie-France doesn't reward Parnat with anything from there to thank him for the temporary housing in the family tomb. It would just kill Francis. Now, that's irony.

I had dinner *chez les Blanc*: pea soup and filet mignon with a walnut tart chaser, leftovers from their family Sunday dinner. Marthe seems a bit better than last year. At least her list of complaints is shorter than usual. The day after that, I began the reentry routine: croissants from the Plaisance *boulangerie*, Odette's for lunch, Saint-Affrique for the license for the car, Géant Casino in Albi for basic supplies.

In California, the seasons slip into spring into summer without much difference. Here, it is still winter, though warming. No leaves, so while driving around on our tiny roads one can see the ruins of abandoned houses that are usually buried in the lush vegetation of summer, their roofs caved in, their stone walls crumbling into the green.

But one can also see all the wrecked cars and construction detritus surreptitiously dumped off the cliffs. But the green—the surrealistic green of the rolling hills that are so much more green without the not-so-green green of summer wheat and hayfields. *Tome fraîche* cheese in the *frigo*—can *aligot* be far behind? (An outrageous dish of mashed potatoes beaten with garlic and that cheese until long strings of goo hang off the spoon. Serving it is a two-person job: one holding the pan and plopping a creamy pile onto the plate, the second with a pair of scissors to cut the strings hanging from the spoon.)

When I arrived at the mill, Germain had already started the furnace, and Natalie had cleaned and put willow cuttings in a vase. It was like I had never left. I opened up the little house today for the first time, terrified at what I might find. What a surprise! Except for a few spider webs— and not many of them—there's nothing. No sign of the critters who usually live here, *les loirs*, no mice, no nada. Not in the big house either, by the way. Last year it was a catastrophe. They had been in my bed, under the cushions, everywhere— especially the dormice.

I've never told you much about them before since I was afraid you might not come if you knew we share our accommodations here with them. They are about the size of a chipmunk, including the bushy tail and big round ears, and I'm sure a dormouse was the model for the first Mickey Mouse. They hibernate in the winter (thus the dormouse sleeping in the teapot at the Mad Hatter's tea party) and have only one litter a year, unlike mice. The first fall we were here, Francis explained their habits, and we even have a picture of him petting the head of one of our fearless tenants. They eat only fruits and nuts, or preferably anything made of corn-based plastic. That would include insulation, plastic lids on turpentine bottles, the caps on Champagne bottles, hooks that hold electrical wiring. Plus of course all our fruits, no matter where they are: on trees, in the garden, or in baskets on the table.

At first we thought they were cute, but when we came back last year and all the electrical lines were hanging about like big black spider webs and the Champagne caps were eaten away, we were less amused. And when I opened my carefully folded plastic tablecloth that I use for big outdoor parties, all the corners had been eaten away, leaving a snowflake-patterned lacy panel of nastiness. That was it. We asked Germain what to do, and he *boff*ed, *"Rien à faire."* I refused to believe nothing could be done, so I consulted Jean-Paul at the hardware store in Coupiac, who sold us a big trap specially designed for them, but he warned us they were smart and not to expect much.

When Berger was staying in the little house last summer, he was overwhelmed. They would crawl out on the exposed beams and shout at him. He swore they threw little pebbles down at him. But he reached his limit when he was peeing one day and one of them jumped down onto the toilet seat. He tried to flush it down the toilet, and when it scrambled out he threw a towel over it and flung it off the balcony. I'm sure it was back up there before we were.

So naturally we set the first trap on the beams of La Ruche. Mike put on my rubber gloves and carefully pierced the plumpest peach we had through the spike at the end of the wire trap. Figuring the smell of humans was what kept them from being easily trapped, he poured boiling water over the entire apparatus including the fruit, to remove any trace of his touch. Throughout last summer he trapped eighteen of them, becoming something of a local hero. At first he released them downstream, but they were back before he was, so he now uses the water chute for execution purposes. We assumed more would move in, but so far, so good.

I spent all day yesterday in the garden, having a very Dirty Day. I found a good landscape designer to help us in the front near the road. (A huge cement culvert was built as a tunnel for the Mousse to pass through after it swishes under our beautiful old bridge. The sides of the slope down to the river are just big chunks of rock, with no dirt and no greenery, which looks quite stark and leaves us visually exposed to the road as well. We've tried planting wildflowers and other normally hearty plants there, to no avail.) His name is Antoine Taillon, and to me is obviously gay. Mike doesn't agree with me though, so we have another thousand-dollar bet going. Antoine has lots of ideas about what we can do to hide the mill and front terrace from the road, and also how we can enrich the soil in the vegetable gardens, and he'll start as soon as Mike arrives. Meanwhile, it feels good to dig in the garden. Berger says it's in our DNA to make things, but society has gotten so specialized that we have to designate people to make art for us—we call them artists. I think it's also baked into our DNA to dig in the dirt, but it seems so childish we call it gardening. Today I'm a gardener, tomorrow maybe I'll call myself an artist. In either case, it'll be another Dirty Day.

—*Hugs, Judy*

GARDEN, STUDIO, FOOD

March 23, 1997
Dear Linda,

Mike's arrived, the garden is half dug up (yours truly is the digger, since Mike's back has conveniently gone out on him), the duck confit is being salted, and the foie gras is being put up in *les bocaux*. I know I said I'd never do it again, but here I am!

I went up to Paris before Mike arrived to see some movies, too many museums, and a lot of bad gallery art. But at an expo at the Beaubourg called "Made in France" had some great old classics too often hidden in dark storage vaults. Giacometti's *Woman Walking Between Two Houses* literally made me cry. I've never seen such an exquisite piece. I came around the corner and there it was, along with several of his larger pieces, but that little bronze box/house on stilts had proportions that were absolutely impeccable. There was such emotion in that little stick figure striding across the internal space. I had just read a short story, "La Petite Place," by Pierre Gascar, about the wife of a *boulanger* in a little village. Several times each day she would walk across the small square in the middle of town, ostensibly to do something important. In reality, she was trying to catch a glimpse of the young blacksmith with whom she shared a mutual infatuation. This apparently innocent commute was noticed by everyone in the village, who oogled and made bets while the woman walked back and forth, zigzagging into a self-destructive affair. Giacometti must have read the same story.

Berger used to tell his students that they will know they've succeeded if a piece evokes the same reaction you have when you see a shoe on the side of the road. I can see Giacometti driving around La Place de la Concorde tossing a slipper here, an oxford there. Everything he did makes me wonder what happened there.

I also saw a rather graphic movie about Verlaine and Rimbaud, which prompted me to find as much of their poetry as possible, and now I am in the midst—in French—with all my dictionaries in bed, trying to make some sense of it. Not only is it in another language but in a late-nineteenth-century context. *Quelle belle époque.* They took their debauchery quite seriously, those two.

I'm trying to get my studio ready for Marianna Goodheart, who teaches at the College of Marin, and Carol Beadle, who is head of the textile department at the California College of Arts and Crafts. They will be here for the month of June to collaborate with each other, something they've wanted to do for years. Berger will be here again for the month of July, and another sculptor, my old nemesis Adrienne, in August. Against all our better judgment, she talked us into letting her come to do a cascading herb garden, which, in theory, will tumble down the terraces, water, plants, and all. Given our experience with her last year, we may live to regret her visit, but the project sounds so interesting.

We will all be exhibited at the Château de Coupiac, Mike and me in one large room with his *Miller's Nightmare* series of runaway gears and pulleys, and my now-growing collection of oversized, abstracted miller's tools. Marianna and Carole are to fill a thirteen-century tower room with something they put together after they arrive. The spaces are nice, but the château organization is sort of "loving-hands-at-home." We don't expect many collectors of fine art, maybe a few local *paysans* sucking their teeth in front of an obtuse contemporary painting, and our group of friends, but I like having this deadline to get work done.

I'm off to dinner at La Chanterelle, a restaurant down by the Tarn River. You probably think that a chanterelle is a mushroom, like it is in English, but in French, one kind of a chanterelle mushroom is called a *girolle*. And a *chanterelle* can also be a bird in a cage that is used as bait for other birds. Aren't you glad you know that?
—*Hugs, Judy*

March 29, 1997
Dear Linda,

Happy Easter. How many eggs did you find? Did you cheat? In France, it's the *cloches*, or church bells that bring Easter eggs. . . . Church bells bringing eggs? It's bad enough to ask a kid to accept a bunny bringing eggs . . . but a church bell? I don't think so.

Mike finally arrived and we had dinner at Les Magnolias. We were pleasantly surprised to see that Francis's widow, Marie-France, had taken every one of our suggestions, persuading her family to come and help her clean the garden and redo a salon for the guests, and they're putting in a garden buffet for the summer. She found a transient chef to help her open and has two permanent possibilities that she's interviewing who come from starred Michelin restaurants. Francis was wiped out during the last two or three years, and the quality of the restaurant had started to suffer. I'm hoping Marie-France has the guts, and now the freedom, to do her own thing (she's a well-trained restaurateur), and the restaurant may even be all the better for it. But I miss Francis enormously.

In the meantime, Mike is in seventh water-borne heaven. He had been doing research on a pump he'd seen as a young lad, called a *bélier hydraulique*, or a ram pump, which he thought would be powerful enough to bring water from the reservoir behind the house, fifty feet up to La Ruche. He finally found one and installed it, and it has been *kachunk*ing along sending water/life up to a horrible bright-blue thousand-liter plastic tank. (Our friends at Moussac had this water tank lying next to the barn, and when we asked him where he got it, Jean-Claude slapped his knees, backed up the tractor, and loaded it onto his animal truck.) Mike has been dancing around, clicking his heels, and patting himself on the back ever since. I'm beginning to feel like some Pagnolian *paysane* who finds herself suddenly water-rich. Before, we could only have our little *potager* behind the house since the upper terrace was so dry. But with a thousand liters dripping down from the tank onto the terrace, there's corn in our future. Maybe even pole beans. We've been cutting the small, scrubby but tenacious chestnut trees that sprout everywhere their hard spiky seeds land, stacking the wood for the wood-burning stove in La Ruche. I even planted some raspberries against the stone wall before the pump was installed. That's how much confidence I have in my miller-Mike-man.

Yves Blanc, Louis Blanc's grandson and one of Germain Blanc's sons, came over on Sunday to help us cultivate the terrace between the barn and the little house. His father had told him we were going to try to do it ourselves, and he rightly told us we had better let him show us how. It had been more than thirty years since anyone had turned the soil, and the ivy, blackberries, and chestnut trees had turned the dirt into a dense, root-bound mass. Yves brought his grandfather's pickaxe with a long point on one end and a sharp hoe on the other to first pierce the soil then turn it to the sun. As we watched in amazement at his strength, we witnessed a changing of the generational guard as he prepared the earth where his grandfather used to plant his potatoes.

Yves is an intense young man, dark and handsome, with the black eyes, moustache, and brows of his father and the thick, curly black hair his mother must have once had. He's the *forgeron* who built the metal sluice gates that control the water flow from the waterfall to the reservoir. He's also building a new turbine that will turn the millstone using the remains of the last metal wheel we found in the mud last year as a model. With each turn of the soil, he bent down, took the exposed, almost cut-through roots, yanked out the clump, shook it loose, and tossed it onto the burn pile in one fluid motion. Poetry. Ballet. Sweat.

The French are serious about their gardens and their *sources*, or springs. (And everyone, even city folk, has a garden somewhere, either in the country where their parents live or on a riverbank in their city. Every riverbank in France is dedicated to gardens, which are sometimes communal, sometimes inherited, and always highly sought after.) Parisians leave the city at Easter to return to their origins in the five corners of France to plant the summer crops. They leave the city with clean shoes and nails and return with splotches of mud and rough cuticles, tomatoes planted, beans in the ground. In the summer, from mid-July to the end of August, they return to water and harvest.

Every house had its own spring right up to the late 1960s, and a good one is still the difference between an acceptable crop or not, since water from the commune is rationed during droughts, and too expensive to satisfy a big garden. We're having a terrible drought right now, and it's the main topic of conversation: "Is yours dry yet?" Now, lucky *nous*, we have a *source* (actually we have several springs that join in a holding tank) that comes out of the cliff on the other side of the Mousse and down across the bridge, its pipe buried in the rock wall and, thanks to Mike, a river that works for us by driving Mike's new pump. *Quelle richesse.* But now we have two projects for Bernard in August, a rock wall to hide the giant blue plastic tank and a real wine *cave*. More later.
—*All my love, Judy*

April 29, 1997
Dear Linda,

Clean Days are getting more and more rare. I get so fundamentally dirty here—dirty like we did as children, and, like then, it's because I don't care, am not conscious of how I look, of what people think. It is just something that happens while going about my business.

But as an adult, getting dirty like that makes going out in public problematic, even to the hardware store for that essential screw that I inevitably can't find. I still go, tool belt fastened to my waist, dust mask on the top of my head, hoping they'll overlook me in the small hardware store, since I'm obviously working, like all the other carpenters, plumbers, and *bricoleurs* standing in line with their tool belts and filthy hands. But it doesn't quite work, since *les dames* don't generally go anywhere in work duds and never go to the hardware store asking for a certain size screw.

Jean-Paul, the proprietor of the hardware store in Coupiac, thoroughly enjoys our transactions, especially when others are waiting. I'm always looking for *un truc*, or a thingamajig, for my art projects that will do this and that—totally unpredictable and always impractical. "I need 104 small clips that will hold a fragile paper panel to a welded frame." I say this glancing at a crowd behind me who are repairing fences and unplugging toilets—real problems. He always finds the solution, digging in his catalogs in the total disarray of the back storage room. He follows the entire process of a project with me, selling me a compressor, an air hammer, stone-cutting tools, and odd fixtures. He's genuinely curious about how I'm making what I'm making, but I don't think he'll go across the street to the château to see the show. Just not his thing.

We went to the director of the Coupiac château, a warm pile of stones being slowly restored by the village, and asked if we could have a small show there sometime, and to our surprise, she asked us if we could put up an exhibition this June! Mike, of course, has lots of paintings, but I'm really just getting started. I have my scissors, a large form in laminated plywood that was inspired by the metal-turning mechanism for millstones, and my Germain hammer, which is starting to take shape. But I'll need at least two more large pieces for an exhibition Mike and I have been asked to do in September in Salles-la-Source at the Musée des Arts et Métiers, where they have a large collection of real millworks. Monsieur Azéma, the president of Des Amis des Moulins de l'Aveyron, asked us to show, thinking the collaboration between contemporary art by almost-real millers would be a good draw for their tenth anniversary celebration.

I expect I'll have the tool obsession out of my system after that. But tools, especially the ones here, still fascinate me since they have such wonderful shapes. The French often try to make the same tool serve more than one function—a table saw turns into a planer, then a router. It takes me back to my fascination for failed tool prototypes. If I start with failed prototypes, overlay them with my fixation on the interface between materials such as stone, wood, and steel, mix it up with things in transition, especially me, I'll end up with interchangeable, unworkable, odd art pieces transitioning toward an uncertain future. Anything that comes out of this line of reasoning is surely a self-portrait.

—*Hugs, Judy*

April 29, 1997

JOURNAL ENTRY

I figured the miller had transitioned into a painter, and so the hammer Germain gave us from his father's toolbox needed to transition into a paintbrush. In the real hammer, there's a square hole in the middle of the hammerhead, which allowed the miller to pop out the metal point to be sharpened, since dressing the millstones damaged them beyond usefulness. So to be true to the interchangeability of the original, and the transitional motif of my work, I need to make at least two more points for the hammer for June. For September maybe I'll make another tool form, equally useless, but one that can use the points from the miller's hammer. The world—at least here in rural France—is transitioning from beautiful old stone and carved wood into cement and plywood, so maybe I'll experiment with those materials. I love black cement; it cures quickly, and I can use Plexiglas forms that leave a smooth, shiny surface on the sides of the points. An eight-foot hammer with a stone head. That's unworkable enough.

I have to do something with the communal braid I put together for Mike's surgery last year, but it's too late to do that for these shows this summer. It's too precious as an object not to do something with, though, so how can I transform it, or make an allusion to it? It has to say something about the artist who is obviously hidden inside every person who gave us a braid.

I'm getting nervous about Adrienne's visit. She sent me a letter saying her daughter was going to join her to help her on the project. First, she didn't ask if her daughter could come, she just told me. Second, there's no place for her daughter in the little house, and that makes for an intimate six weeks in the big house with a total stranger. As I recall, she and her daughter have been estranged for years, so maybe this is to be some sort of reconciliation time.

May 2, 1997
Dear Linda,

Well, another month swirls into history without me having contributed the definitive novel, a lasting work of art, or even a meaningful philosophical query. We're back into our normal rhythm: garden, studio, food, garden, studio, food.

I fixed sushi for a chef from a Michelin two-star restaurant last week. Fabrice is the finalist to be the new chef at Les Magnolias, someone who knew Francis. Marie-France had brought him by, and he asked me about my Swedish smoker I used to smoke sausages and stuffed duck neck for Francis when we still cooked together. He had always wanted to try smoking some fois gras, but he was always too tired when I would ask him over. But he apparently talked to Fabrice about it, who was quite enthusiastic. He told me he would give me the recipe for the preparation of the liver if I would fix him some Japanese food.

While sushi has been popular in San Francisco for years, it's just making its way into Paris and the culinary scene in France. Fabrice had never tasted it! For some strange reason, I had brought some nori, wasabi, and miso soup fixings with me the last time I came from the States, so I could present a reasonably authentic meal. California rolls, and shrimp and smoked salmon sushi with some nori wrapped around a ball of rice with caviar plops were the best I could do. I cobbled together a sliced-cucumber salad with a soy, ginger, and sesame oil vinaigrette sprinkled with toasted sesame seeds and presented it on fresh arugula from the garden and some alfalfa sprouts that cooperated by opening their heads minutes before the meal. I made gingerbread for dessert using fresh ginger, which, while not terribly Japanese, was tasty. And they loved it! I couldn't help noticing Marie-France was quite friendly with Fabrice. That was hard to see.

We have some preparations to get ready for Carole and Marianna, who arrive in two weeks. They both live in rather tony Marin County in California and teach at well-equipped colleges, and I worry that maybe they don't realize we are in the country, and that they have to go to our neighbor's house and admire his garden and frog pond and carry piles of veggies down the hill, that we have critters who join us, usually when we least expect them, that most of the people we know here have Dirty Days every day, that our local grocery store is right out of a Steinbeck novel, with cement floors, three apples, and paper plates sold one by one. I'm worried about what they expect for work accommodations. They're accustomed to art-school workspaces, and my studio is more like Dad's messy garage workshop. I do woodworking on the platform looking down into the hole where our new turbine will be, above the river under the house, and I weld outside. What kind of a serious artist behaves like that? At least their shared studio space in the upper barn is truly wonderful. Mike is working mostly on mill drawings, so he's happy to move out of his studio space for them.

Happily, at least for their sake, we seem to continue to be *bête*-free this year. That is to say, *les loirs* have packed their little bags and moved on. However, now it's *les taupes*, or moles, in the garden. With the drought they've all moved from the dried-up woods into everyone's nicely moist *potagers* for good, juicy worms. And it's war. All the locals have their own methods, explained only after the cocked-head, shoulder-shrugged *bof.* They can't get strychnine anymore. It seems kids and dogs were dying. I tried big cigar-sized sparkler-like things that were supposed to scare/smoke the moles away, to no avail. But the latest trick is to put a rose branch with lots of thorns on it down their hole, since they're supposed to all have hemophilia and will bleed to death if stuck!

The real trick is to get a cat or at least a donkey, like everyone else. We haven't gotten into raising critters ourselves (unless you call dormice "pets"), partly because of our six-month rotation. Many of our city-turned-farmer friends have tried. I have a friend in the Lot region who bought a couple of chickens as an experiment. I told her she was nuts—they're dirty, they eat everything in sight, and you have to put them in the coop each night or the foxes will get them. But buy them she did. When I asked her six months later how it was going, she said, "Well. does it mean anything that I've named them Tandoori and Coq au Vin?"

For Adrienne's seed/spice beds, I've planted seed for at least nine varieties of basil! For Marianna, who used to make her own pastels when she was still a painter, I've got some woad seed sprouting that I hope will transplant into the garden. Woad is a nondescript plant, easily grown, which when planted in the red clay of the region near Toulouse, develops a native rust on the leaves. Those leaves, when dried and ground, make a natural dye, the classic French blue color. It has insect-repellent qualities as well, which is why they once used it on everything—shutters, even animal horns—hence our association with that intense blue and La France. They would harvest the plant, grind the leaves into a paste, and make little golf-ball-sized wads of it called *cocagnes* and put them on racks to dry. Then they would grind the woad balls into a powder using millstones just like ours. The flowers made an acceptable ochre color. It was an expensive process and made many a *seigneur* rich around here. In fact, the entire economy between Toulouse and Albi—sometimes called *"le pays de cocagne"*—in the fourteenth and fifteenth centuries was driven by that little weed.

Then Columbus had to go and discover America, where they had a shrub in the West Indies that could be used to produce indigo. It grew year-round and was much more prolific and hence cheaper than the temperamental woad. Hence, woad is a weed like any other and can only be seen at a tiny museum in a baby château northwest of Toulouse. I'm trying to surprise Mike on his sixtieth birthday on the 27th of July. All the kids, spouses, and one of our two grandchildren are coming over to surprise him. I'm trying to get ready for some serious chaos. If you guys could come, it would be wonderful. I've even got a room reserved for you and Gary at Les Magnolias for the 26th and 27th.

—*Love, Judy*

THE VIPER, THE BEES, THE PIGPEN

May 15, 1997
JOURNAL ENTRY

Last evening I was alone in our bedroom, working on a letter. Mike was up in La Ruche working on his new darkroom. I couldn't stop feeling something was wrong. I went through our French doors into the small den and there, in the middle of the room, staring at me, was a small snake, a viper. He didn't scurry away, he just stared at me. I asked him why he was there, and didn't he know I'd have to kill him? *Call your sister,* he said. I did. She's in the hospital with another heart attack. They're cracking her chest again. Gary sounded tired, but he didn't think I should come home. He reminded me that seeing me would only frighten her as it had the first time, ten years ago. Then, when she was forty-six years old, they said she had such advanced atherosclerosis that she had the arterial profile of a seventy-five-year-old.

May 23, 1997
Dear Linda,

I'm glad you're home and stitched together. You didn't need to have a coronary bypass to get our attention. I was torn, as I told you, about coming back, but I wasn't worried about you. I knew you would be all right. Besides, the last time I jumped on a plane and came back, I scared you into another coronary arrest! Maybe you just need to get your pipes reamed out every ten years?

You asked me to keep my daily activities coming, so here they are. My studio looks like someone took all the tools off the shelves and dumped them in a pile . . . which someone did! Since I'm working in wood and steel and stone, all my metal tools, welder, grinders, and clamps, along with all my woodworking stuff and my stone chisels, are out and scattered, surrounded by bags of cement and sand. A total disaster. And we're trying to control the chaos for Carole and Marianna's arrival.

Last week, a friend of ours came by with his adorable eight-year-old daughter who is quite physically handicapped. Annie wanted to see Mike's studio so she struggled up the stairs and stood in the doorway, where she stopped and looked around the huge space then up at the ceiling, focusing on the sheet-sized webs hanging from the skylights. Without entering at all, she announced, "Looks like you've got some spider work to do." So yesterday a truck pulled in with industrial-sized vacuum cleaners, pails, and ladders, and the magic men started to clean these old stone walls. They started *en haut* in the little house and are working their way down. For one day, at least, there will be no spiders at La Pilande Basse and a little less dust on these old walls.

Richard Berger's coming in July to work on the *porcherie*-about-to-be-Zen-space. He had spent days emptying it, but mysteriously, things crept back in: tools, chairs, odd pieces of iron, and a bunch of firewood hauled in last fall to dry. There is a series of tunnels that brings water under the house to run the main millstones, and one of the exit tunnels curves under the rock and runs under the old pigpen back into the river on the other side. The millstone on which the firewood was stacked was probably used originally to grind grain for animals, and had a turbine below it to make it turn. There was a large hole in the bedrock next to the millstone, over the tunnel, where a porcelain toilet had been used by the previous owners, and Germain's family as well. Enough water flowed through the tunnel to keep the outhouse clean and the river dirty. But now that we have our own septic system and the building is empty, the *porcherie* is about to be transformed into an art space. Another example of art healing old wounds.

—*Hugs, Judy*

June 15, 1997
JOURNAL ENTRY

Linda is healing well, but I'm quite worried about her. She's only fifty-five, and she's had three coronary arrests and two bypass procedures, she's having trouble walking because of bone spurs, and her near-term memory is still deteriorating. She's tired of being dependent on others, but she keeps going. I'll worry in private and keep trying to contribute some pleasure to her life.

Marianna and Carole have been here for two weeks, and watching them work is interesting. Berger is intellectual in his approach to his work. Everything is reasoned; materials are chosen carefully, colors represent something. The esthetics of a piece is last; it's the message that counts.

Marianna is at the other extreme, working almost exclusively at an emotional level with few drawings—just go to the studio and start and something will happen. She used to be a pastel artist and now is working in metal.

Carole is in between Richard and Marianna. She does lots of drawings, primarily of shapes, but works in series and likes to experiment with materials. She's trained in textiles and does interesting three-dimensional shapes using woven material.

They are here to collaborate on a major but still undefined project to be done when they get back to the States, and they are using their time here to develop a collaborative concept, which they'll complete back in California. They have some space in the château in a few weeks if they want to show something in the meantime. Watching and listening, I realized that they weren't collaborating but thinking through pieces that might work together in a joint show. I think it's harder when one isn't used to thinking and planning to do what I consider a true collaboration, which is developing a joint idea into a final work together, without one person's work overpowering the other.

When I, the always too-direct student, asked if what they were doing was really a collaboration, they both looked a little stunned. The next day, they admitted that they hadn't started from scratch together on anything. From that day on, they worked closely together, hours at a time, experimenting with ideas that would leverage both of their talents. They're trying to marry steel and textiles for a piece to put in the tower room in three weeks.

I would love to collaborate with Dan on a project. I hope he can stay well long enough to do it. He has started taking the new enzyme therapy that has helped so many others. I hope this works. He's so talented.

Mike is intent on his project, which is reworking the essentials of the mill so we can say *"Il tourne, le moulin."* He found some experts who have redone other mills, and they are rebuilding the twenty-five-foot axle that connects the metal turbine beneath the house where the river runs through. He's found sluice doors and had Yves Blanc, Germain's son, build the turbine and the metal chute that will open and let the water through with enough force to turn the huge metal wheel. The axle, which rises from the center of the turbine, will turn the top stone of one pair in the house. The bottom one is called *la meule qui dort*, or "the sleeping stone," because it never moves. Like a giant top, the whole affair turns on a tiny point, the tip of which rests on a heavy solid-bronze box that is encased in a huge chestnut beam that lies on the gravel floor of the room below the house, next to the river, where the water runs through the house. For some reason, they call that bronze box the *crapou*, or "little toad." They eventually wear out and have to be replaced. Mike has found three of them, one under the millstones in the *chambre d'eau*, one behind the mill, which is leaning against the millrace, with lacy hydrangea growing through its spokes, and one still half-buried under the walnut mill, which is on the back terrace with ferns growing out of its basin. representing a few hundred years of milling.

June 29, 1997
Dear Linda,

Marianna and Carole pulled out on the train last Wednesday after a three-week visit. They somehow pulled off a full-fledged show at the château, including two huge installation pieces, and finished up by cooking a dinner for forty artist friends where they showed slides of their work with Suzie doing simultaneous translation. I, for one, am toes up on my bed with my computer balanced on my belly.

Both Carole and Marianna have been working artists and professors for over thirty years, Marianna transforming from a pastel artist to a metal sculptor. Carole came to Europe right out of college on a Fulbright scholarship and made interesting loosely woven felts out of raw linen and other unusual materials. Both of them, on their first day at the mill, felt a need to go back and redo some of that history. Marianna took some pastels she had brought for sketching, hung a large piece of kraft paper on the stone wall of the studio, and rubbed the sides of pastels on it, forming colorful lacy patterns of the rough stone beneath. (My attempt to produce woad for her didn't work.) She did a whole series of these wall rubbings.

As for Carole, she wanted to know if I could find any raw linen so she could re-create her old transparent felt. I, of course, called Germain, after some serious dictionary research into "linen, raw linen, felt, loosely woven." He said his sister's son, Gaston, who has a large sheep farm up the hill on the Trébas side, might have some. A few hours later, Germain and Gaston came down with a gunny sack full of cut flax that they claimed was at least sixty years old, having been stored in the far reaches of Gaston's vast barn for just such an occasion. It looked like weeds, nasty ones at that, to me, but Carole knew exactly how these weeds needed to be treated to be turned into fine thread and eventual linen napkins and sheets. But she had other plans. Thanking Germain and Gaston profusely, and promising to bring them an example of her work, she set out to wash, dry, pound, and tease the gnarly mess into loosely structured fabric. It was as if she pulled a cotton ball gently apart, never letting it tear, into a thin sheet, transparent and with a structural integrity helped along with a diluted wood glue. She spread this fabric/felt onto a Plexiglas sheet to dry. The next day, she had a stiff material strong enough to cut and form into small house-like structures, inside of which she put precious objects, like some of the thousands of pottery shards we've found while gardening. She built the forms, Marianna formed some metal bases for them, and suddenly we had art!

Then, in one of our many visits to various hardware stores, they discovered the fifteen-foot rolls of steel wool that woodworkers use while refinishing furniture. Using the same technique as Carole had with the flax, Marianna, the steel person, and Carole, the textile person, tugged and gently pulled these rolls into a single piece of steel fabric, ten feet wide and over thirty feet long. The steel wool was completely transformed into a gossamer sheet of fabric, picky and threatening, with thousands of tiny potential slivers of metal glimmering in the light, but luscious and tempting *en même temps*. They stretched this material high across the vaulted arch of one of the towers in the Coupiac château, attaching it strategically with wire to make it hang in waves, like a passing glistening cloud. They hung Marianna's wall rubbings outside the door, suspended from dowels hanging from the ceiling, which left them free to move with passing air currents. Art in motion.

The only significant nonartistic event while they were here was The Bees. I always take sculptors to the agricultural hardware store, since it's full of odd machinery on a monumental scale: huge tubs and automatic water dispensers for animals, solar lighting schemes, cotter pins (my personal favorite), huge wine barrels called *foudres*, or *fûts*, and beekeeper paraphernalia, including two-foot square sheets of odiferous beeswax used to start hives. (Apparently, swarming bees are looking/smelling their way to form a new hive, and they particularly like the perfume of beeswax.) They're also sometimes used to roll into the world's most expensive candles. But at the farmers' store, they are fifty sheets for ten dollars, and Carole couldn't resist. She didn't know what she'd do with them, but have them she would, and I agreed to split the lot of fifty sheets with her. I intended to roll mine into candles. Carole lugged her half up to La Ruche, where she was staying (Marianna was in the other guest suite in the mill), and I put my beeswax under the house, along with my good intentions, in the *chambre d'eau*, the room where the water passes through the house.

A few weeks later, near the end of their visit, Carole came down from La Ruche saying there were a lot of bees in the skylight and she was worried they would die up there. Mike, who kept bees as a teenager, said not to worry, they'd find their way out. Later that day, I was writing in our bedroom and I kept hearing a strange humming sound somewhat like a large insect, and since we have an occasional *frelon*, a large wasp that finds its way into the house, I walked around and looked near all the windows, their favorite haunt. They have a nasty sting, and I usually just open the window to let them escape. Our bedroom has French doors with gauzy privacy curtains that open into the sitting room next door, where there's a small fireplace, which we rarely use. The sound seemed louder near the doors, and when I opened them I saw thousands of bees coming down the chimney into the little salon.

Of course, I screamed, "*Mike!!!!!*" to which he responded by bounding up the stairs four at a time only to be driven back by the bees. He wasn't as frantic as I was, more worried about them getting established somewhere. While he opened windows— wrong thing to do given the swarm of bees outside trying to get in I called *les pompiers*, the firemen, who are trained to deal with swarms of bees and *frelon* hives. They had lots of questions: How many? How long? Where? And then they promised to show up after work, since bee-rescue is a volunteer activity for them. I asked what to do in the meantime, and they told me to make it as uncomfortable as possible for the bees coming down the chimney by lighting a fire in the fireplace and closing all the windows and doors upstairs to try to contain those inside in one room.

In the meantime, Carole came running down the garden path holding her stack of beeswax in front of her, shouting that bees were coming into the little house in, well, swarms. We'll never know if it was the wax, which we had carelessly left lying around, that had attracted the bees, but we threw all the sweet-smelling waffled sheets of wax out on the bridge and waited, wringing our hands, for the firemen, while Mike lit plastic bottles since there's nothing more obnoxious than the smoke from burning plastic, in the small fireplace, seemingly unfazed by all the thick black smoke and the bees buzzing around him.

Promptly at 6 p.m., *les pompiers* arrived in their little blue truck, with their flashlights and rubber suits, seemingly more curious about these Americans at *le moulin* than concerned about the dwindling swarm of bees. By the time they arrived Mike had driven the majority from the mill with his toxic fire concoction, so the firefighters went straight up to La Ruche, which means "beehive" in French, and which, just then, it was. They checked out the piles of now-dead bees under the skylight and the thousands banging their heads against the glass, and lit off a canister of toxic fumes without asking first, or protecting food, counters, or lungs. Thick smoke filled the twenty-foot-high space, and as we gagged our way out, they closed the door, slapped their hands together, and proclaimed, "*On a le temps pour un pastis.*" (Everyone always seems to have time for a pastis.) We lodged Carole in the big house while we defumigated the fumigation, then swept the piles of dead bees out with a push broom. We decided to let the trapped bees in the salon find their way out the windows since the main swarm had passed.

We have a bit of a breather before Richard Berger arrives next Wednesday for five weeks. He's easy to be around, independent and helpful to me. But we have to clean out the *porcherie* for his installation, and I have to finish my last piece for the real opening next week at the château in Coupiac.

The inspiration for the object I'm doing now came from a visit to a factory in Connecticut where they make rope, mostly for ships. (Remember when I asked everyone to send a braid when Mike was so sick? I love the idea that small threads/ thoughts can produce big results/ropes.) The devices they use to make the ropes continue to fascinate me. They pass thin cord through a huge disk full of holes, and the cord is twisted together by a big machine that moves slowly back from the disk, twisting and pulling, forming the relatively weak individual strands into a thick rope strong enough to anchor a large ship. The big disk is of cast iron and looks like a huge colander. They must use the same kind of machine to make steel cable, so I decided I'd do a prototype of a steel-cable maker, using materials that couldn't possibly work. Out at the end of the bridge, propped up in my sand table is a six-foot-diameter disk of laminated plywood that I've been planing to make it look like a big wooden contact lens. I intend to drill holes an inch wide and pass the unwoven ends of a thick steel braid that I'm going to create using inch-thick steel cable—if I can afford it—*c'est cher*. I'll unwind the unbraided ends after they've passed through the disk so that at the end will be individual strands of wire sticking up in the air working their way back through the strainer to the thick coiled braid, which, I hope, will support the weight of the wooden disk on its edge. I think I'll call it *Steel Strainer*.

I loved the idea that individual well wishes woven together into a larger invocation would be capable of holding Mike safe. But winding steel in the same way, through a wooden structure, just wouldn't work. So is this the anti-safe structure? Who knows?

We had a wonderful dinner on Father's Day *chez les Blanc* with the entire Blanc family, now numbering 28 1/2. It was the occasion to tell Germain and Martou that their family had bought them tickets to go to the United States with us in October. We started plotting the trip the day they asked me if they could go to Toulouse with me to watch the planes take off—they'd never been that close to an airplane. Because of Martou's phobias, we were all concerned she would be too afraid to go. When their oldest granddaughter Émilie read a poem she had written that revealed the plot, Germain burst into tears (he does that a lot—a sentimental sort) and Martou ran out of the room. I looked at Mike. "She doesn't want to go."

The room was totally silent, but she came back five minutes later, red-eyed and shaken, mumbling, "C'est trop. C'est trop," followed quickly by "Can I walk around on the plane? How do I go to the bathroom? What will I wear? Will you go to the Foire de Réquista to help me pick out a dress?" To thank us, they keep dropping off dead chickens and rabbits and piles of Swiss chard because Mike said it was his favorite, but he lied, just to be nice.

The mill-nerd workers have been here getting the millstones ready to turn. Mike's so excited. I hope everything will be ready for his big birthday surprise. (I think he's read my e-mails to the kids, so it won't be a surprise, but he'll never tell me, so I'll never know.) Then we have that museum show to mount the first part of September. Aren't we retired? Bought a drill press for my studio yesterday. Guess it's going to be a holey Dirty Day today!

—Hugs, Judy

June 30, 1997
JOURNAL ENTRY

Things have gone definitely south with Adrienne Mendel. She sent me an e-mail telling me that now her husband is going to show up, and given that they don't even live together I assumed that means another stranger somewhere in the house. I called her two days ago and told her we were concerned about the way things were shaping up, and that I had to think about us and our friends, not just her and her family. She asked me if I were telling her that her daughter and husband couldn't come. I told her that they certainly could come for a few days, but not for the entire visit. She became hysterical, screaming at me, "Do you know who I am? How dare you insult me this way! I've bought my ticket!" I told her to calm down and that I would call her the next day when she had had time to think about our side of the equation.

I couldn't sleep all night, I felt so frustrated and angry at both her and me. I should have known better after her visit here last year. How did I think we would ever be able to have her for a whole month? Finally, at two in the morning, Mike rolled over, patted me on the butt, and told me that she and I were going to part enemies now or at the end of August, and it might as well be now so we can enjoy our August! Today, before I had a chance to call her, she called me and announced huffily that she wasn't coming. And what was I going to do about her ticket? I told her if she sent it to me I'd reimburse her. She was so bitchy, and I'm so happy.

SURPRISES

August 1, 1997
Dear Linda,

The last week of July was Mike's surprise birthday party. I rented a *gîte* (a furnished house with a kitchen, beds, and linens) up in a tiny village perched on a hill called Gaycre and installed all the kids there the day before. I had told Mike we were having a few people over for his birthday and he was to go to Les Magnolias and fetch the food to bring back here. What he didn't know was that the surprise was at Les Magnolias and that there would be about 150 people waiting. But in the meantime, he had set up tables for about twenty around the mill, and I acted like I was preparing for an army.

In the morning, to get away from the Judy-before-party-she-witch, he decided to go out with his huge banquet camera and take some stills of quaint little villages for a photogravure series he was working on. I expect you can guess where he went. He spent all morning in various positions on the hill facing Gaycre, photographing the dramatic profile of the village against the sky, against the green, river behind, river in front. Either he knew they were there or he didn't, I'll never know, but if he did, he later lied.

He took off for Les Magnolias about noon, and I decided to go with him "just in case," I said. When we arrived, him in his dirty-day clothes, screwdriver in his pocket, he saw little Franc running down the stone stairs from the garden to the front door, shouting, "*Il arrive, il arrive!*" ("He's here, he's here!") If he didn't know before, he knew then. He climbed the stairs as all our children and French friends poured through the door to shout, in their best English, "Surprise!"

In the upper garden at Les Magnolias, the place that we had advised Marie-France to turn into a luncheon garden, we spent the afternoon with friends and the friendly ghost of Francis. The Blanc family presented Mike a handcart with heavy wooden handles, wobbly metal wheels, and a curved metal scoop that Germain's father, Louie Blanc, the last *meunier*, used to haul hundred-pound sacks of flour from the front terrace into the mill. They had carefully refinished it and gave it to Mike with many toasts and tears. I gave him a diatonic accordion, which he has always claimed he wanted to learn to play. Again, I think he lied, at least to himself. It's been in the box all week, with not even a wail from its leather lungs.

We had a grand week with all the kids before they split for the four corners of Europe. The family dynamic is always interesting. One thinks that one can avoid the conflicts, *mais non*. When the kids grow up and marry, another dimension is added to an already tipsy structure. But basically everyone is all right. Eileen couldn't come because she's pregnant again. Steve and YaVette were here, and Katie and her fiancé (getting married next summer in Vermont—I hope you can come). Naomi and Tim are making noises also, but we'll see. Derek and Kristie have moved back to San Francisco, and Jenea starts her graduate program this fall at Stanford, having kissed her Cambridge experience goodbye. It's nice to have almost all of them under the same fogbank. Hayden and his bride are separated, which is heartbreaking, with their beautiful baby girl, but he's such a good father, he'll manage it as best as can be.

Richard Berger's visit passed too quickly. He arrived, having taken our fingerprints last year and then having them blown up to about a four-foot diameter. He printed the resulting images on a huge plotter printer with a laser cutter, which allowed him to make stencils of the prints, resulting in large, lacy rolls of paper. When he got here, we went off to Creissels to *chez* Raujole, where they still make tiles by hand, and where one of the owners is a young Beaux-Arts-trained artist and anxious to help us. He had done some glaze experiments on various colors, so Richard had his choice of intense greens, pale sage, intense ochres. He finally chose red and blue, probably to reflect our American connection, not realizing that the French colors are the same. (I'm blue and Mike is red.) Then he had to decide which one would be on top since he's superimposing them—could be a dispute here—but I don't think he'll tell us. We brought back enough tiles to do the whole floor of the *porcherie* and set him up in Mike's studio so he could draw the outlines of the prints here at the mill. After two weeks of tedious hand-drawing

here and enamel painting at Raujole, and after carefully numbering the whole floor on the backside, they fired all the tiles at once.

In the meantime, instead of going to a gym, Mike and I carried firewood—again—out of the *porcherie* and dug and scraped our way to the bare floor, revealing the base of another old millstone—that makes eleven we have found—and an open trench into the tunnel below where another long-gone turbine would have turned to make this mill run. We decided to put a glass opening above the tunnel so we can see the creek pass below. Then we sandblasted the walls and ceiling and had Bernard *pierre* put in beams to properly support the millstone, since it was a bit tipsy. He and Richard laid the tile, speaking Los Angelese/Français the whole time and bumping butts on hands and knees, and then Richard and I did the grouting. The result is a calm, contemplative space, the prints swirling next to the millstone with a slight stream of water coming through below. Our literal prints on La Pilande Basse may well stay beyond us.

Richard was so impressed with Bernard's work of abstract reasoning on laying tile in a difficult space that he invited him to come to San Francisco and give a stone-cutting class at the Toot! Bernard is stunned, frightened, and thrilled. Me, too.

—*Hugs, Judy*

IT TURNS, THE MILL

August 9, 1997

JOURNAL ENTRY

Il tourne, le moulin. While *all* the bits aren't in place, we did see the millstone turn today. We stood on the platform over the horizontal metal paddlewheel in the *chambre d'eau* under the house, and held our breath while Didier the mill expert, above us in the room at the end of the mill near the river, tugged at the long metal bar that reaches down twenty-five feet to open the sluice gate holding back the water from the reservoir behind the house. The loudest, purest, onomatopoetic *clank, clank, clank,* and the small door lifted, the water burst in and slammed and splashed against the cupped spokes of the turbine. It groaned, then turned slowly, then faster and faster, throwing water at us fifteen feet above. The paddle wheel groaned, turned slowly, then faster and faster. The twenty-five-foot oak axle that rises from the middle of the paddle wheel below, then through the ceiling above, began to spin like a graceful giant top. We held our breath, hoping that that enormous toy wouldn't begin to wobble, or turn crazily out of control like some colossal spinning club.

"*Elle tourne, la meule!*" Didier shouted from the floor above us, where he was watching the millstones to be sure they didn't turn too fast or touch, or that the axle was out of alignment. We raced out the arched door of the *chambre d'eau*, up the stairs to the main entry and to the end of the mill, where the slightest *huurgn, huurgn, huurgn* came from the coffers temporarily covering the newly placed stone. I cried, and Mike stood stunned.

"You did it, Mike!" was all I could stammer. "Didier, *félicitations!*"

This coming Sunday, the grain hopper with its little carved horse's head on the front end will be installed, the millstones will be properly dressed, and the whole mechanism will make flour for the first time in thirty years. The grain hopper, or *trémie*, feeds the grain down into the center of the stones, and is knocked gently by the square edges of a wooden shaft at the top of the long shaft from the turbine, much as you would tap the side of a box to get out all the contents. The horse's head is pure folly, as are many frills on tools in rural France, and should be hand carved by the miller himself. But Mike is letting Didier do it since he seems so intent on doing so. We even have the wheat sacks waiting at the end of the long room, gifts from another miller friend. They're stamped "Made in the United States of America." Our friend's father saved them from one of the many post-war relief shipments. Germain and his sons will be there, and I guess there will be a few tears again.

ART AND FLOUR

August 15, 1997
Dear Linda,

Our big news is that after months of work, we are finally made our first batch of flour. We were having trouble finding grain that hadn't been treated with chemicals against weevils, and when Mike mentioned that to Jean-Claude, our Roquefort sheep-farmer friend, while they were standing in line at the *quincaillerie* in Coupiac, he said he'd be happy to bring over some grain that he'd just harvested and hadn't treated yet. The next morning, *beep, beep,* and there was Jean-Claude with his eighteen-wheeler-sized trailer, up to his waist in grain, shovel in hand, asking how much do we need? He would have given us the whole load if we hadn't stopped him after a hundred-pound sack.

But at that time, the mill geeks still needed to finish dressing the millstones before we could actually make the first batch of flour, and we wanted only enough grain to do a trial run or two. By the way, "dressing the stones" refers to the process of making rough grooves in the millstones to allow the grain to be crushed instead of sliding between smooth surfaces, and to be pushed to the edges of the stones into the large wooden box that contains the stones and corrals the flour. When they were used full time, they would have been dressed every few months, but I doubt we'll have to do it but every few years. As the box fills, through centrifugal force and the occasional push of the oak paddle given to us by Germain, the flour finally finds its way down through a hole in the front of the box into a decidedly unlovely plastic crate, a practical

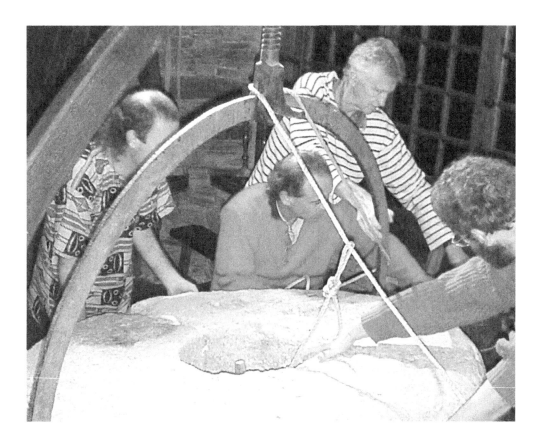

concession to modernity since a wooden box filled with flour would be too heavy for modern millers. Louis Blanc would grind 400 kilos, or over 800 pounds, a day from the same stones, so his crate was a large gunny sack. He moved the sacks of flour around on the handcart that the Blanc family presented to Mike this summer as his sixtieth birthday present.

I'm reading up on my bread recipes, as in really, absolutely freshly ground whole-wheat flour bread recipes. Germain's son-in-law, the baker, says flour has to calm down for at least a few days after it's been ground; it's too "hot" then to make bread and is sticky and unmanageable, and the mix of wheat grains—summer and winter, late harvest and early, hard and soft—has to be just right or the flour will never work, he says. (Sounds like a marriage to me!)

I think a short course for you in getting the grain to the bread might be in order, since I sure didn't know much about it when I started. The grain is harvested when the heads of the wheat are heavy, bent over but not collapsed. (Remember when driving with Mom and Dad and we'd see whole fields destroyed by a violent summer storm?) In today's world, threshing machines separate the grain from the branch, blowing the kernels into some big receptacle on one end and pooping out bales of straw on the other. The grain is delivered to mills, where it's cleaned to remove bits of straw, stones, and other not-so-good bread things, then ground into a powder. That powder includes the outer hull of the grain, or the bran. Then it is sifted with various sizes of screens to remove hunks of bran, and if the sifter is fine enough, almost all of it. (Of course the bran has most of the vitamins, so it's nutritious, but it makes for very heavy cakes!) Enough, you get what we're doing on a very small, very primitive scale.

So yesterday we actually ground our first flour. The gross-motor guys came for the last time and patched up the box around the stones, fitted the big funnel that feeds the grain into the wooden coffers, fixing it on a nice stand that Mike had made, and installed the box with the *tête de cheval* that bounces and feeds grain between the stones. This was after they had tried to dress the stones with the hammer that Germain's father had used. The stones are made of flint, which is hard and dense, and each blow of the hammer threw sparks in all directions and it was obvious it would take hours and hours to finish dressing them. In spite of our collective insistence on wanting to complete every part of the reconstruction of the mill as it would have been done in the old days, we all agreed they should get out the big-guy grinder, à la Bernard *pierre*. Dust, lots of noise, and still more spinning sparks, and then they finished the spaces in between the grooves with Louis Blanc's hammer. They had already installed the controls for the turbine and the positioning of the stone right next to the mill platform. We got our *meunier* and *meunière* crash course on managing the system, and they threw back the obligatory pastis and pulled out, leaving us absolute miller neophytes. There we were, Mike with me coaching and vice versa, playing with one hell of a big toy.

Later, Germain came over to show us how to use the tools he had so proudly presented us with last summer: the flour paddle and Louis Blanc's artist's palette. Germain passed the palette through the flow of the falling flour to take a sample of the white powder. He then showed us how to evaluate whether the bran was coarse enough and the particles of flour were even. He showed us how his father washed the grain, letting it dry a bit before grinding, so the bran wouldn't be crushed in its dry state, making the flour dense and difficult to work. We'll still have to sift the bran out of the flour by hand using a big garden strainer, since getting the *bluterie* to function properly will be even more complicated than the millstones.

But he also brought over a special gift, one we never expected. When the previous owners bought the mill, they didn't do too much damage to the various mill parts except through neglect. The one thing they did do was to remove the wooden doors that encased the giant flour sifter, over twelve feet long, that hangs from the wall in the mill room, and put them out for the garbage man. Apparently, they thought the insides of the sifter, a mysterious turning cage, was more interesting to look at than the solid overhanging doors. Germain, *par hasard*, passed by that morning and saw the doors. As he had already told us, he took them and hid them in his barn for over thirty-five years. And today he brought them back, tears of gratitude spilling over as he thanked us for making *la meule tourne,* and for bringing back the music of the mill.

Before he came over, I had made the first loaf of bread and it rose high and crusty. I broke into the still-steaming loaf to show it to him, and we both took a big bite. He swallowed politely, but I quickly spat it out. He knew immediately that our mill team, in their haste to throw back their pastis, forgot to wash the grit left after they dressed and replaced the stone, so the whole batch of flour was gritty and inedible. So he also showed us how to take off the wooden coffers that contain the flour around the stones, lift the stone, clean out the gritty flour, wash the stone, replace it, and start over again. A good lesson. Number one, I'm sure.

—*Hugs, Judy*

August 20, 1997
Dear Linda,

We're in the small calm before our show at the tool museum. The opening invite is from the minister of culture of the *département d'Aveyron*, and there will even be a press conference. We had a reporter here at the mill for two days taking pictures and interviewing us like we're important. Just shows how exotic we are in rural f'ing France! It's the first time they've had contemporary artists showing at Salles-la-Source, the tool museum north of Rodez in a restored mill building I told you about. We were invited because we have a mill and are working on mill-related themes. It's the tenth anniversary of Le Musée d'Art et Métiers, and they're going all out. There will probably be more mill nerds than art connoisseurs.

Richard helped me with some technical issues on making molds, and I've been making a mill turbine out of cement with saw blades cast into the edges, a play on *sawmills*. Yeah, yeah, I know it's corny but I'm getting desperate to finish another piece. They used to carve the cupped spokes of the horizontal turbines out of wood, and Mike found one at an abandoned mill and he, well, I guess he stole it. I made a mold of that flat, cupped shape and am casting the spoke in black cement, the most illogical material I could think of. Since I have only one mold, I can only make one spoke a day, one a day for twenty days to complete the whole turbine. The flat ends of the cups/spokes should all join together in a circle, but I love the idea of them swirling out of control, so yesterday I splayed them out in the mill end of the house and if I do say so myself, *c'est pas mal.* (Why can't we say "It's great," instead of "Not bad"?)

On the other hand, I've another thing on the sand table that I haven't resolved how to display, how to finish, or even whether I want to use it. It's fashioned after a *martinet*, which is a four-foot-high cast-iron hammerhead that was used in water-driven forging mills until the late nineteenth century. A large (at least ten feet high) vertical wheel with two-foot cogs poking out the side at regular intervals was turned by the action of a waterwheel. As the cogs turned, they would depress a massive, at least fifteen-foot, wooden handle attached to the iron hammerhead, which was balanced on a trestle like a seesaw, depressing the handle, which lifted the hammerhead. As the wheel continued to turn, it would release the handle—like someone jumping off the seesaw—causing the sheer weight of the huge head to slam back to its original position. A piece of copper or heated iron beneath the head would then be flattened smartly.

As the waterwheel turned, the vertical cogged wheel turned, and the handle of the fifteen-foot-long hammer would be depressed, released, depressed, released, allowing for several forging strikes a minute. The *forgeron*, or blacksmith, would stand near the hammerhead and progressively move the metal to form a thinner and thinner sheet. That may not interest you, but I, who love tools, am fascinated with this one, wondering whoever first thought of it, and if they got the idea when someone jumped off a seesaw on them, and how many fingers they smashed while getting it to work, so I am awe-struck when confronted with a working martinet. The sheer scale of it is humbling.

I had in my head a huge hammerhead, four by two feet square, made from laminated plywood. I wanted the cut, formed edges to be in a chevron pattern, so I rough-cut twenty-six 4-by-4-foot sheets of plywood. Bernard *pierre* helped me glue/laminate the plywood sheets together in one fell swoop using his big construction jacks that hold up stone walls during restorations. Bernard, gross-motor movement at its finest, lined up the edges using the wall as a guide, and we quickly glued the surfaces of the plywood with a painter's roller brush, and he wedged the whole thing against the barn beams using thick adjustable masonry supports for leverage instead of my wimpy woodworking clamps. It took us one hour to do what would have taken me three days to do not very well, alone.

The next day, we loaded the now one massive hunk of wood into a wheelbarrow and hauled it down to our neighbor Bernard (*bois*) Guerin's studio, where he passed it through his industrial-sized bandsaw, leaving a tidy edge. A couple of passes through his planer and I was down to finishing work, except, of course, for how I'm going to get it to stand up and what finish to use and why do I seem so paralyzed? Maybe the first part was too easy. I didn't have the thinking time I usually have. I've taken to calling this thing The Monster, probably not a good idea if I'm looking for inanimate karmic cooperation. I was going to glue the two sides together, but I like them several inches apart, as if the hammer struck something that cleaved the head neatly in two parts. But how do I get it to stand on its head, point down, without looking clunky? And what kind of finish?

Since I don't know how to do all that, I've been experimenting with the leftover cement from the molded cement turbine spokes, using a technique that Bernard *pierre* taught me. If you take plumber's packing, which is like unwound rope, but sticky and strong, and wrap it around thin rods of steel, you can use them as internal reinforcement in cement castings and make remarkably thin and strong structures. I've got these figurative lamp-things growing in my head: pigmented cement forms with my hand-cast oriental-paper shades, maybe even lamps. Medieval tool/maiden/knight shapes that light up when approached—maybe one or more secrets that are not evident in the dark? It's not for this show, but at least something is working its way in the dense space of my mind that's not a tool!

I've been going up to *les Blanc* for rudimentary English lessons for their trip to California, which I know they'll never use, but so what. For them this is an unimaginable trip, one they couldn't possibly do without us taking them in tow. But what fun for us, too. It will be like looking at our city and country with fresh enthusiasm. There are three requests from Germain: he wants to see a Buddhist temple, a Protestant church, and eat a real hamburger. I'm trying to put together the ideal itinerary, and because of our rich multicultural city, maybe it will be around churches. In the meantime, Martou and I are going to the Foire de Réquista to buy her a new dress. Want one? Cotton sundresses like Grandma wore when we were kids, with pointy tits and thick-belted waistlines?
—*Hugs, Judy*

September 1, 1997
Dear Linda,

Yesterday, with threatening clouds swirling about, Martou and I risked being blown off the Réquista mesa to go to the farmers' market, the real farmers' market where farmers go to buy their baby ducks and

pieds de tomates. They buy cotter pins for their tractors and pay for salt licks with live chickens. The knife sharpener stand has a queue of *les dames* waiting with carefully wrapped rolls of linen holding their family treasures: cleavers, fillet knives, and oddly shaped scissors. (The smaller ones they themselves scrape across their stone sinks to redo the edge.) They are getting ready to slaughter the winter chickens and they want their ends to come quickly. The *bonhomme* who turns the wheel has black streaks from thousands of swipes of blades on the blue apron stretched across his ample belly. The crowd rumbles with grunts and pleasantries, all in patois.

The ladies then roll their armory in the linen and tuck it in the bottom of their baskets, and go about their business of buying zippered aprons, mucking shoes, and huge pots for the boiling up and down of their charcuterie and the blanching of their beans. There are vegetable stands, some quite handsome in their array, for city folks, but no real farmer's wife leans across the big stall of carrots or onions or bunched baby radishes and stuffs them in plastic sacks to take back to real farm. Only townies and tourists would do that. Instead, they lean forward to suck the air next to the ears of their neighbors, whom they see once a month, the second Thursday, at the Foire de Réquista. The news is passed, mostly about the deaths of neighbors, the often sincere "come and see me's" exchanged. Meanwhile, the husbands having scored their odd bits of hardware and *vracs* of wine, stand gossiping in small groups, berets bobbing, arms crossed against spreading girths, with gapped-tooth grins and hearty laughs from time to time, eyes always searching the crowd. Close to noon, the wives grab their husbands' elbows and stride off, baskets weighing them down, to return to Le Bousquet, La Carrière, Le Carassier. Martou seems to know everyone there and is related to most: "*C'est ma cousine de Villefranche de Panat*" or "*C'est le cousin de Germain d'Aspines.*" She presented me as her neighbor from California, where she's going in October. "*Oui, oui, c'est vrai!*" It is true and nobody can believe it, especially Martou. We visited every truck that had dresses, most of the fabrics in colors of fall: orange, brown, dark greens. When something looked promising, Martou gamely pulled herself up into the back of the truck, jerked shut the sheet hanging from a wire to protect herself from stares, and tried on dozens of dresses. Finally, she found just the right one, a dark green background with small flowers in orange and a bit of blue.

Then we went off looking for shoes to match. It turned out that shoes were easier to find than orange and blue dresses, so we left as the noon crowd was heading home. As we passed Monsieur Serre's meat truck set up in front of the church, Martou poked me in the ribs—actually the hip since she's so short her elbow hits me about there—and jerked her head toward a woman standing waiting to be served. She whispered out of the corner of her mouth, *"C'est elle, la madame de Carassier."* It was the woman she had told me about who had left her abusive husband for another man a few years ago. I somehow expected to see an aging femme fatale, but instead she was a bent-over woman, babushka tied tight against the wind, with tired eyes and twisted knuckles. When she saw Martou, she smiled broadly, her morning croissant tucked in her teeth. Martou hesitated, then in spite of her instinctive reaction to isolate an adulterer, pulled me over by the elbow and introduced me: *"Ma voisine Californienne, Judite. J'y vais en octobre."*

—*Hugs, Judy*

September 5, 1997
Dear Linda,

We mounted the show last week at the tool museum in Salles-la-Source. That is, after we finally got there. We were talking with Jean-Claude while he was shoveling the grain into the burlap sacks that François Castan, another miller in the Aveyron, had given us. Jean-Claude and Monique were going to the United States next month to visit some farms in the Midwest with a group of *agriculteurs*, and he wanted us to come to dinner and talk about what they should expect. It also came up that we had the show at the museum and we needed a truck to haul my oversized tools. He quickly offered his *camion à bestiaux*, or animal-hauling truck, and we quickly accepted.

When Mike drove over the morning of the big haul, a hot end-of-summer day, he found the old blue truck full of straw, sheep shit, and a powerful tear-inducing ammonia smell of urine—remember, Mike can't smell anything, but when his eyes water, he knows there are serious chemicals in the air. Mike thanked Jean-Claude profusely, stuck his head out the window, and drove it back to the mill. He cleaned it out at the end of the bridge as best he could and then announced he was ready to load his paintings. I offered to help since I couldn't load my work until he'd finished. I creaked open the rusty back doors of the truck and almost fainted. We swept it again, we hosed it, we put plastic down, but nothing we did could cover the accumulated odor of sheep, terrified, confused sheep being transported, to be sold, or slaughtered. At that point, we had no choice but to load up, get in, and go.

I climbed up into the cabin and hung onto the makeshift passenger's strap to avoid sliding over onto the engine, which was between us in the front seat, the scalding hot casing leaking diesel fumes into the cabin at an alarming rate. We opened both windows, stuck our heads out, and took off. We bobbled up and up our road that follows the Rance River to the Tarn, then down and down to the road that goes up and up to Réquista, then on up and up to Rodez and further up the Aveyron River to Salles-la-Source. I'm not sure we ever left second gear. I couldn't open my eyes since the truck was wider than road itself, and I was sure we would go into a ditch each time we passed a car—it was that close. We said to ourselves that at least the road that climbs out of the Tarn Valley is wide and reasonably straight, or it was until we hit the *deviation*, or detour, above Cassagnes Bégonhès that took us up onto the tiniest, steepest, most crooked one-lane farm road I've ever been on. I don't know who was more terrified, Mike or me. When we passed a car, the only reason we didn't hit mirrors was because ours was so much higher, high like our center of gravity, which caused us, from the rear, to resemble more a metronome than a *camion*. And from the passenger side, I was sure our right wheels were only half on terra ferma.

By the time we arrived, we were wind-blown and exhausted, and we and our paintings and sculpture smelled like sheep shit. As we pulled into the driveway to unload our work, we were greeted by the minister of culture, the president of Le Musée d'Art et Métiers, and two carpenters who were to help us install the work. The various officials weren't waving little French flags, but they were surely expecting a short ceremony with people a little more elegant than the two bedraggled Americans who piled out of the *camion à bestiaux* in front of them. We collected our dignity, slapped off the straw, and presented ourselves properly. It seemed they were there to explain to us that we were supposed to have our own room but at the last minute they changed their plans and they wanted us to put our stuff in the large mill room. Well, actually, our original room was full of a children's exhibition and the teacher had forgotten to come and take it

away. At first we were worried about competing with the sheer scale of the permanent collection, but once we spent the day nestling our work among many of the pieces that had been the original inspiration for us, we felt quite at home.

The museum houses remnants of old industrial tools and is one of the most artistically stimulating places I've ever been. Form follows function in every exhibition space. The building is an old *filature*, or thread mill. In several different large rooms, waterwheels drove dozens of 200-foot rods, which pulled and wound raw cotton, linen, or wool onto huge spools. The millworks and tooling are long gone, but they've restored the vast rooms and turned them into elegant display spaces for antiquated tools, including one large space dedicated to millworks. At the entry, there's an enormous wooden olive oil press with a 20-foot beam for pressing leverage. To the left is the mill room with an entire 25-foot vertical waterwheel, all its gearing and every type of mechanism that a water mill ever activated: huge forging hammers, 15-foot saw blades, scary points on wool-carding paddles, large vertical stones for grinding walnuts, and other thinner honing blades for sharpening Laguiole knives, and, of course, thick horizontal *meules* for grinding grain. Other ancillary tools, such as various oil presses, cast-iron gears with wooden teeth, and—hanging on the wall—an entire turbine made from wooden spoke/cups, just like mine. Theirs, of course, wasn't cast in cement with saw blades sticking out the sides of the water scoops. I hadn't realized that that very image would be on the posters for this special exhibition in every store, post office, and village bulletin board in the Aveyron.

I had six large tools, the miller's hammer with the stone head, the steel strainer, another exaggeration of the key that turns a millstone, my cast-concrete turbine and The Monster, which gave me fits to the end. I finally finished the cleaved part of the head with pewter metal polish that left a nice contrast with the outside finish, which was a highly polished lacquer that showed off the layers of the laminated plywood. I installed The Monster directly in front of the original *martinet* in the museum, and both he and I were quite content.

Mike, with the help of the two carpenters, hung a dozen elegant large-scale watercolors and several oil paintings in a series that he calls *The Miller's Nightmare*. Whenever we visit a working mill, we run a gauntlet of pulleys and gears operating at high speed, most of them fully exposed and quite dangerous to the uninitiated—not unlike what it must be like to walk inside the workings of a giant clock. Mike, since he's six foot five, always has to duck to avoid being hit by some whirling piece of equipment. In one fifteen-feet-wide-by-three-feet-high painting, he has depicted every imaginable turning mechanism in dense, vivid colors. The other pieces are equally dynamic in their movement, dimensions, and hues.

An art opening, or *vernissage*, is taken very seriously in France. There are speeches by dignitaries and the artists, and our *vernissage* doubled as a kickoff for the tenth anniversary of our mill group headed by Jean-Pierre Azéma. So they had all the various presidents of the Ministre de Culture d'Aveyron and Des Amis des Moulins de l'Aveyron, the press, the mayor, big cheeses everywhere! (We've had three long articles with full-color spreads in the local newspapers on the show.) There were more dignitaries than art connoisseurs, but there were even more mill lovers. After all the speeches and "Oh, shucks," and a naughty song about what millers' wives do when the millers are not looking, the crowd started to circulate a bit. I noticed a tiny, bent-over old man, beret in hand, tapping on the cement turbine. I had displayed it on the floor in the entry to the show, partly in a circle with the last few spokes splaying out down the room with the saw blades reflecting in the spotlights. He finally came over and tapped me on the shoulder, and I bent down to hear his question: "*Pourquoi l'avez-vous faite comme ça avec les lames de scie?*" I was touched that he wanted to know why I'd made the spokes of the paddlewheel in cement, with the saw blades embedded on their leading edge.

I answered the question with a question: "Why do you think I made them like that?"

He hesitated thoughtfully and answered, "*Pour couper le fil d'eau?*" Delivered in his thick patois accent, it took me a minute to realize he saw the blades cutting the threads of water. I found his response infinitely more beautiful than anything I could have said, and gave him my biggest American smile. The minister of culture for the Aveyron, who had been listening while waiting to speak to me, came up and told me he knew why—it was obviously the nuclear family spinning out of control and cutting the threads of civilization! I was glad he was so sure, since I, personally, have no idea, even now, why I made them that way. He did invite us both to apply for a show in Rodez at the cultural center, the Galerie de Sainte-Catherine, for us a great honor, since that public space is usually only open to French artists who live in the Aveyron. Remember, one of our objectives was to live in a foreign country, learn the language, and try to be as involved in the community as we could be. And now we're officially Aveyronnais!
—*Hugs, Judy*

September 15, 1997
Dear Linda,

This has been quite a summer from an art perspective. I can't begin to tell you how much I learned from three totally different professors who came here and one that did not. From Marianna Goodheart: to trust my intuition and go with it; from Richard Berger: how to take an idea and work it into something that transcends itself; from Carol Beadle: to take an experimental approach to materials and form; and from Adrienne Mendel: how not to be in this world.

I also realized that I've learned as much about the process of making things from the Bernards *pierre* and *bois* and the other skilled craftsmen in my life as I have from my professors. In fact, they may be more satisfied with what they're doing, since they're not worried about building a CV, only enjoying the process. And for me, the process is the whole thing: the research, the thinking, the doodling, the making models and prototypes, more doodling, building, solving installation problems, finding cool fixtures, the installation, the panic, the reaction from others, the relief it's over. (There's that Zen thing again . . . being present.) I once asked Berger, right in the middle of a show, why we do this, and he said, "Because you feel better doing it than not."

Mike is taking off for San Francisco next week to get things ready for the Blancs, and I'm going to fly back with them since dealing with gate changes and customs is just too overwhelming for them. I'm trying to avoid too many goodbye dinners, since it usually involves foie gras at this time of year. There is something about fall, long shadows, and foie gras that makes me miss Francis even more. If only I had insisted he see another doctor. Actually, I don't think that would have made a difference. I don't think he had the energy to do what needed doing.

I ground the last batch of grain this morning. I can't tell you how wonderful it is to sift, knead, and bake this freshly ground manna. To *clank, clank, clank* on the sluice gate and watch those huge wheels start to turn and the box on top going *knock, knock, knock* against the little horse's head that gradually feeds in the wheat, and to watch the flour come out in pretty, dusty piles. There is a reason, however, that millers used to wear white. Bernard *bois* is making us some sliding French doors to isolate the mill room mess from our living room, since that fine powder does tend to get everywhere . . . especially when it's the *meunier* and not the *meunière* doing the work! I don't think men see dust, they just see the final result. He's cute, *quand même*. Now we need to get snobby about what kind of flour we want . . . I hear spring red is the best or was it a mix?

Love to you both—

—*See you soon, Judy*

THE BLANCS IN CALIFORNIA

November 12, 1997
San Francisco
Dear Linda,

Here's the letter you asked me to write about our visit with the Blancs. To start: Germain and Martou's grandson, Stéphane, took us to the airport in Toulouse, and I stood on the curb with all my luggage, watching them get out of the car, both clutching their purses, his a typical shoulder-hanging black leather envelope with all his papers, hers a plastic beige affair, the handle of which was worthless as it was almost never used, since she clutched the purse tightly against her bosom during the entire trip. They watched as I talked to the agent at the desk. I showed them the flight and gate information so they would know how to do that on their own on the way back. Going through security should have been simple, but Martou didn't want to give up her purse. Finally she did, then rushed through the detectors and grabbed it as it came out, looking through to be sure nothing was missing. The only time she let go of it was when the plane started down the runway. She clutched my arm and Germain's with her twisted arthritic hands until the wheels cleared the runway. Germain had a silly grin in spite of himself. The flight from Toulouse to Paris was uneventful, Germain staring down from his window, Martou staring straight ahead, her knuckles white against her bag.

In Paris, we were seated in a larger plane in the middle section. I offered to trade my aisle seat but they quickly demurred, then went into the middle and never moved, not once, twelve hours without stretching or peeing. Martou let go of her purse with one hand to eat while Germain sat straight ahead with his hands on his knees until we reached San Francisco. No movie, no magazine, just staring straight ahead. I can't imagine what they were thinking.

Our condominium in San Francisco is small, so their bedroom was our living room and the only time Mike and I had alone together for thirteen days and 4 3/4 hours was in our rather small bedroom. Martou and Germain never left the apartment by themselves, not once.

We took them to Stanford University to show them the campus—Jenea was our guide—and their first Protestant church. The structure is considered the "architectural jewel" of the campus, and is larger than most churches, but Martou exclaimed, "*C'est petit, n'est-ce pas?*" It certainly is small compared to their cathedrals, and when we tried to explain that there are over two hundred churches in San Francisco alone, so no one church is that big, they were sure my French had gone lame. I had to get the yellow pages out and show them all the listings. We then went to the Buddhist zendo at Green Gulch and even attended a gospel church service at Glide Memorial, which is a must for many French people visiting San Francisco. The latter was too much for Martou. When the congregation jumped to their feet and starting singing "Aaaaaamen, aaaaamen, amen, amen," she stayed seated, arms crossed over her purse in disgust. *"Il ne la respecte pas!"* To make any noise in a church was a sign of lack of respect, but dancing and clapping?

That pushed her over the edge. Germain, on the other hand, stood, clapped politely, was thoughtful, and asked lots of questions, little light bulbs going off in that old/young head, remarking that in churches in France everyone is old, here they are all young.

We did Fisherman's Wharf, Alcatraz, a ferry boat to Sausalito, Monterey, the San Joaquin Valley, the giant redwoods, cable cars, Lombard Street, our huge flower market. If it was in the book, it was done. We spent way too much time in Chinatown looking for gifts for their kids, and if you've ever wondered "Who buys those things?" I've got an answer for you: Martou, 28 1/2 of them, one for each child, spouse, and grandchild.

We had decided to vary the food as much as Martou's limited threshold for new things would allow. We had dim sum in Chinatown, good pasta in North Beach, non-spicy Indian, Thai, and Vietnamese. Martou didn't think North Beach pizza was authentic since in Coupiac the *boulanger* makes his base with bread dough topped with tomato paste and ham or smoked salmon and Swiss cheese. The gooey strings on her Italian pizza were just not right, and basil makes the blood pressure go up, don't ya know?

By the time we arrived at the Monterey aquarium (Martou said the one in La Rochelle is much bigger), the only place still open to eat was Bubba Gump's, a chain seafood place with the movie *Forrest Gump* playing on three big screens throughout the restaurant. Dan Pillers—who had graciously agreed to accompany us, giving Mike a break—and I looked at each other and shrugged, "Why not?" We ordered a "Bucket of Boat Trash" for them and one for us. Having dined there before with my granddaughter, I knew what to expect: a large galvanized pail, filled to the brim with French fries and deep-fried fish, lobster tail, and shrimp—all quite tasty and served with ketchup, of course, and enough food for eight. In the defense of the restaurant, they do have forks if one asks for them. The roll of paper towels on the table and the generous basket of packages of hand wipes usually serves most people just fine, since the seafood needs to be dipped by hand and, well, French fries with a fork? Who does that?

Neither Martou nor Germain had ever eaten hot fried shrimp before, had never eaten anything but asparagus with their hands, and certainly never been served from a metal bucket, so they didn't exactly dive in. Dan and I did, licking our fingers and generally being as savage as possible. Germain got into it quickly and polished off a substantial amount before Martou even figured out what to do. She kept saying, "*C'est trop, c'est trop.*" But this time she meant it. There was too much food. We tried to explain our colonial custom of taking leftovers home with us, but that was beyond *trop*. No French person has been able to tell me why, but they would rather die than take something home from a restaurant. It is considered shameful, admitting to poverty maybe, or somehow low class, I'll never know why. But Dan and I were reasonable, finished about half of our portions, and asked for doggy bags. Martou and Germain were still working their way to the bottom of the bucket, which they did finally reach, with Martou keeping pace while still protesting, "*C'est trop. C'est trop.*" The drive back up Highway One, passing thousands of acres of artichokes, evoked Germain's favorite phrase, "*C'est pas possible. Encore? C'est pas possible.*" His fine stand of a dozen plants had been outdone.

At a good hamburger place in Stinson Beach, we decided to give Germain his "real hamburger." They came out of the kitchen piled high on homemade buns with lettuce, pickles, and a few deep-fried onion rings, the mustard and ketchup on the table. In spite of her experience with a bucket of trash, Martou still resisted eating with her fingers. She started to pull her hamburger all apart and I protested, trying to explain that cutting up the meat separately defeated the joy of the bread, the meat, the mustard, and the onion in the same explosion *en bouche*. She protested that it was too big for her mouth, and I lost it. With an insincere smile on my face, I stood up, reached across, and squashed her hamburger with the palm of my hand. "Now, you can." (I was more gentle than it sounds!) Germain, juices dripping from his chin, closed his eyes and smiled.

Marianna and Carole invited us all for dinner, and other friends had us for tea or coffee so our French visitors could see how Americans live. (The open houses for real estate on Sunday was a good way to show them our architectural variety, which is missing in rural France.) So by the time they left, we had sampled food from almost every nationality, tried all our different breads, muffins, the occasional croissant, and, of course, our best California wines. All Martou could remember were the sticky buns and how sweet they were. "*Oh, vous mangez le sucre, vous. Moi, je le crains.*" As she accused us of eating too much sugar, she managed to eat an entire sticky bun using her hands, licking her fingers as she went.

But even with Martou's constant complaining, they were good sports. Their expressed observations were somewhat predictable. "*Tout est en bois!*" I didn't dwell on earthquakes and how wooden houses move, that piles of stone would collapse. "*Mais vos voitures—elles sont enormes.*" I tried to explain our national preoccupation with big cars, safety, and power, even though I don't agree with it, and how moms feel safe driving tanks, that gas costs a dollar and a quarter versus four dollars in France for a gallon, and that our roads are bigger. When they didn't see any guns on the streets, Martou almost stopped hugging her purse to her chest, and she even started to laugh about how everyone had told her it was violent here and to be careful. I tried to explain that while purse-snatching can happen, it's not common, as in parts of Europe. But I didn't tell her that our violence is real, albeit not so much in our part of town.

One night I got up to go to the bathroom, and Martou was standing in her nightie, hugging herself against the cool air and staring at the lights of the Bay Bridge, the view of which fills the front window. I whispered "Are you okay?" to which she responded dreamily, *"C'est un rêve, n'est-ce pas?"* Her exclaiming that the view was a dream was the first sign that perhaps she had enjoyed something new, could be touched. I couldn't help but wonder what in her past had left her doors so shut to most things. And here was a small opening.

My guess is their bottom line to their friends back at Le Bousquet will be: "It was interesting, but I wouldn't want to live there." The same thing we all say at the end of a trip. Guess we are more alike than different.

See you at Christmas,

—*Love, Judy*

March 15, 1998

JOURNAL ENTRY

La Pilande Basse

It takes blue and yellow to make green—a little yellow and a lot of blue is the hillside closest to La Pilande Basse, with a little blue and a lot of yellow on the horizon. And every permutation in between rolls up the face of one hill and down the other. Honeybee sheep swarm, turning in circles in the distance, with heels nipped by barking black spots turning around them. Slowly, they mow from one edge of the field to another, changing it from dark green to yellow as they pass. The hedgerows are purple, since all that's left is red and blue after all that yellow went into making all the green on the fields. The wild plums for next fall's *eau-de-vie* are flowering, but all else is bare. I feel I'm in near time and far time, near time spring with tiny buds and frost-glazed daffodils, and far time with old ruins clinging to the remains of footpaths, hidden in mid-time by leafy shields of scrub oak and alder, the sudden change of pace, the timeless faces, the hunched backs of tiny ladies and gentlemen.

THE LANTERNS

March 16, 1998
Dear Linda,

We arrived Thursday, had dinner with the Blancs, who were full of enthusiasm and fresh asparagus (does one follow the other?). Then we stumbled into the mill, which was all clean with fresh flowers thanks to Natalie. Lots of mysteries, how'd-that-happens, like the sluice gate that appears stuck, the light circuits that pop and go dark, no heat upstairs, primroses on the rock wall, pansies in the flowerpots. Where's that smell coming from? Lots to do, but running on that jet-lag-induced nervous energy that makes one clean out a closet and go through old photos when there are just three dead crackers to eat in the house, shutters on all the windows, and no logs in the fireplace!

In February, Bernard *pierre* came to San Francisco for a workshop in stone-cutting at the San Francisco Art Institute. The school paid him an honorarium and we paid for his ticket, so he felt quite the star. His Gauloise hanging from his lip, brimmed mason's cap pulled low, he sauntered through the class, me translating, him grinning at everything I said and shaking his head when the students responded, like he understood everything I said. Each of the fifteen students who took his workshop adopted him, some fell in love with him, and collectively they took him out to try to find pastis somewhere in North Beach after the class. Afterward, we did much of the same itinerary as we did with the Blancs but we took turns, Mike in Inverness, me in Monterey, Dan and Richard at the Toot, always finishing with pastis all around. He showed up at the airport with one front tooth missing, but the young women found that exotic, and had he stayed longer, I'm sure there would have been cat fights in the halls of the Toot.

But now we're back at the mill, somewhat early since we both have shows in June in Coupiac. Richard Berger's coming back to hang a huge marionette in the *grande salle*, and I'm doing an installation of five large lanterns in the same space I had for my mill tools. Mike is doing an artists' book show, having brought several books from our collection, and Charles Hobson, one of the book artists and a good friend, will be coming for the opening.

My inspiration for the lanterns is quite simple. I believe profoundly that everyone is capable of making wonderful things—witness the spectacular braids that friends produced for Mike's surgery—but they don't necessarily have the motivation, time, or the confidence to continually produce artwork. I have a shy friend whose mother told her, "Don't ever wear a hat that has more character than you do." What kind of an effect would that have on an aspiring young artist? (This same friend says she speaks softly at restaurants so no one will overhear her banal small talk. Does that mean she shouts her profound observations?) But she managed a beautiful braid of shredded photographs—she said they weren't good enough to show.

What do I believe? Basically that everyone, deep inside, is an artist. But we have to take the time to look inside—take the time to investigate, have a reason to make something, have someone give you permission to perform, to light your lamp.

So from that fundamental belief, crossed with the communal braid from Mike's surgery, popped this year's project. Two years ago when he could work in the studio again, Mike made an etching from a photo of the big braid and sent thank-you's to everyone. I was still too shocky to deal with the actual object; I couldn't just throw it away, and it was too awkward to hang on a wall, too fragile to take to France to show, so I stuck it under the desk until I knew what to do. Finally, just before I left, two years later, in some other sort of unknown process, the answer came. Again without thinking why, I took the braid, laid it foot by foot on our scanner, and processed color transparencies of all the sections. I am now in the process of making huge lanterns with separate inner shades lined with those transparencies. The shades will hang freely inside a figurative metal armature that I'm welding from thin stock steel. I am stretching a hand-cast paper skin around the whole structure.

From my prototypes, I'm quite pleased that when the lamp is lighted you can tell there is something colorful and interesting inside, but you can't quite detect what it is. I intend to make five or six 6-foot-high figurative lanterns that will hang in the same room I had last year in Coupiac. There will be a detector system that will make each individual lantern light up from the inside when a person approaches it. The metaphor is perhaps too obvious and maybe even corny—enlightenment, artist-within, take me one-at-a-time, please—but then I've always been completely literal. A basic mistrust of symbols, I guess. Ambiguity and I separate on contact.

I have a real production line working, since I have to make these things with a lot of fancy wiring and complicated internal shades before the first of June. I made 320 linear feet, all about three feet wide, of hand-cast kozo-fiber paper at the beach house and was ready with all the drawings when I arrived so I could hit the ground running. (Kozo is the fiber from which most rice paper is made. I can make it with lots of long, obvious fibers, or short and even ones as in industrial paper.) But since I am electrically impaired, I have a steep learning curve when it comes to the wiring—and in French electrical current and language no less. I have no idea how I'm going to hang them, or even if the whole business will work!

I'll give you a rundown on all the local suspects as soon as I'm *au courant*.

—*Hugs, Judy*

DINNER AT JEAN-CLAUDE'S

March 30, 1998

Dear Linda,

There's a *vent de fou*, or a wind to drive one nuts, up on the high ground so I kept my petite promenade low and snug around the river valleys this morning. Birds singing, buds popping, the occasional little plastic bag in the high brush to remind us of the flood last winter. Mike spent the day yesterday cleaning the riverbed with some other volunteers, but I guess they missed a few.

I promised a rundown on people you've met virtually, so here it is: I haven't seen Anne Charrier, the woman with the difficult, abusive husband, but I heard from Brigitte (our beautiful nurse neighbor, partner of Bernard *bois*) that Christian, who's only six years old, slashed his mother's tires so she couldn't go to work leaving him alone with his father. You are the child psychologist, not me, but that's about the loudest scream for help I can think of short of attempted suicide. I have horrid images of this little boy with a big knife at dawn on his knees, desperate, sobbing and stabbing.

And Odette Soulier, who has changed her name back to Ravel, has left our green hills for Montpellier to recover from the horrid end to a difficult marriage. Her former husband, Jacques, doctor-turned-pig-farmer, has bought a sailboat and is going around the world with a very young woman who fell for his considerable charm. After years of infidelity and general philandering, he's sailing into the sunset in total disrepute.

And more bad news, Christelle told me that Maran has slipped back into his old ways: tight with their money and scolding her when she washes the linens, but the worst is he isn't bathing again. She is exhausted, trying to make a few sous to send to her children in Madagascar, but she's fed up with him. They were married in a civil ceremony in Paris when she arrived but never at the church in Plaisance, which Maran would like to do. I suggested she agree to the wedding, but only after he pledges, in front of the mayor and the priest, to agree to those demands on the list she made two years ago, but that she had to be ready to leave for Madagascar if he didn't agree or didn't change. She seems quite committed to following through this time. We'll see.

Marie-France, Francis's widow, and Fabrice, who are now a couple, are opening

Les Magnolias again this weekend. The dilemma she faces is that half of Les Magnolias now belongs to Francis's adult children, and while they're not demanding or even around, she feels like she's working to build a business for herself and little Franc but that they will only see half of the rewards. My guess is she'll sell the restaurant and leave. We'll see.

Germain stopped by yesterday to ask me a favor. He had seen the feathers that I had put in the cement potato, and was embarrassed by their lack of grace. He knew I told everyone the story of him painting his room as a lad, and he wanted the plumes I showed to be at least pretty. Without waiting for an answer he pulled some new black-and-white-spotted guinea hen feathers from a plastic bag to replace his former sparse offering, then a *bisou* on the cheek and he was gone.

We had dinner this Sunday with Jean-Claude and Monique Fabre at Moussac. (Since we're in Roquefort cheese country and all our neighbors have profitable contracts with the Roquefort cheese cooperatives, I know more about sheep than I care to admit: when they breed, when the lambs come, how they are milked, and how the cheese is made and stored in the caves in Roquefort. But then, there are also all the custards and cookies made from the *recuit*, or whey. And as you know, I've even participated in the slaughter of sheep. I've searched for the socially redeeming feature of that knowledge base to no avail.)

We were to have eaten lunch with the Fabres, but they called to ask if they could change it to dinner since the weather was threatening to ruin the hay they had cut over the previous four days and they needed to get it all in *tout de suite*. When we arrived at 8 p.m., Monique pulled us into the family kitchen with a table that seats ten and sat us down saying that Jean-Claude was late and Florence was cleaning out the milking barn and Raphael was doing something, as was his wife, and Patrick, Florence's boyfriend, now the father of Angel, their two-year-old, was filling the grain trough, and, well, I lost track of who all those people were and what they were doing.

When we later moved into the dining room, the table was set for twelve, and everyone was someone who worked at the farm or their children. When I asked Monique if she does three meals every day for twelve, she pooh-poohed me, saying she makes enough at dinner for lunch the next day and that the *petit déjeuner* is simple, but she showed me her hands, saying that she also plants, weeds, grows, and cans enough vegetables for twelve people to eat 365 days a year.

Jean-Claude came through the back door from the summer kitchen into the family kitchen, where we were sitting waiting to go into the dining room. He was covered with hay droppings stuck to his honest sweat, and his teeth showed through the straw with the same silly grin on his face as usual. When I jumped up to give him a *bisou*, Monique protested that he was too filthy but he didn't seem to care, nor did we. He disappeared for his shower, reappearing in a bright blue and green striped bathrobe and slippers, his hair in a wet punk do arranged by the towel. He didn't want to miss anything, so he just didn't leave again, finishing his dinner in the dining room in his bathrobe. Near the end of the meal, Monique laughed and pointed out that he still had it on and that it wasn't polite. But he didn't care, nor did we or she, really.

Dinner there follows a delightfully fun and crazy pattern. Everyone shows up more or less at the same time, all fresh from their showers. Sunday, after fifteen hours of pitching and stacking hay bales in sticky ninety-degree weather, they were also exhausted and thirsty. Jean-Claude says he doesn't drink alcohol, but they always prepare an *apéro* for guests and the itinerant workers staying with them. There are always several bottles of *vin de noix*, a sweet wine that nobody seems to want. Those bottles get pushed aside, the pastis comes out for the workers, and then Jean-Claude always admits he likes a sweet wine as an *apéro* or for dessert. I join him, as I actually like *vin de noix*, then Monique remembers she forgot the sliced sausage, in this case homemade, and everyone says they shouldn't and they do because it is so good, smoky, and sweet. Then Monique slaps her knee and remembers to dig out the two cloth napkins from the buffet, one for Mike and one for me. One of the kids always says, "I want one, too!" "Okay, you're a special guest. The rest of you, too bad." When there are no guests, fingers and plates are kept clean by an omnipresent hunk of bread, which is placed directly on the table to the left side of the plate.

Two huge platters of *crudités* come from the summer kitchen, even in the winter, one on each end of the long, wide dining room table that seats sixteen with ease and plenty of room for the food in the middle. Sunday's veggies were shredded carrots and crunchy cauliflower from Monique's garden with a creamy vinaigrette, one with herbs and one without, since Jean-Claude likes everything *nature* and the younger generation wants to try new things. When everyone has mopped their plates with their bread, Monique disappears for a few minutes, then bumps open the swinging kitchen door with her butt, turning to show off the hot vegetables coming out of the mysterious summer kitchen. Sunday's offering, two huge platters of *cèpes*, or porcini mushrooms, sautéed to a dark golden brown in butter and garlic with a sprinkling of parsley, was passed at each end of the table. The meat course is always farm-raised something; this time Monique groaned under a steaming platter of lamb studded with garlic and finished with a crunch of *fleur de sel*. She left and reappeared with a salad bowl piled high with a purée of last year's potatoes. But Jean-Claude, like many traditional *paysans*, doesn't put meat on the same plate as any vegetable, so he finishes mopping up the juices of the mushrooms while everyone else digs into both at the same time. From somewhere, a bottle of *vin ordinaire* appears, which, even with ten adults, even with us there, is never finished.

The cheese course is never omitted. (After the normal milking period, from November to the end of June, Roquefort sheep farmers stop delivering milk since the cooperative at the caves won't take any more. The sheep don't understand and can't stop their milk promptly on June 30, so the farmers wean them slowly, using the milk to make their own fresh and hard cheeses, perfect in their imperfections.) I prefer the Fabres' own cheese, but there's always a significant chunk of Roquefort circulating at the same time. Then the dessert, either several fruit tarts or on Sunday an apple crumble, pronounced "crewmbell," made for their special English-speaking guests, drizzled with caramel syrup and melting homemade ice cream. And then, pretending he almost forgot, Jean-Claude always remembers to bring out the special slightly sweet wine, this time the Cramphil from Madiran, that we always bring, because we know he loves it. Then all the rest, even those who haven't touched a drop of red, push their glasses to the center of the table and we finish that bottle.

This meal for twelve always looks so easy, is always delicious, and somehow just appears from behind the door from that summer kitchen into the family kitchen, where it's staged for the table, and then into the dining room. Monique is never stressed (she once forgot to put the meat in the oven, and we all laughed and waited), enjoys the evening with the rest of us, and is off to bed at the stroke of ten since tomorrow starts at five all over again. *Bonne nuit.*

—*Hugs, Judy*

LANTERNS AND MILL NERDS

April 27, 1998

JOURNAL ENTRY

We met last week with the new "commission" for the Château de Coupiac, of which we are charter members. It's a group of local artists who will choose the artists for the exhibitions with the intention of getting the quality and consistency up, the publicity out, and the government grants in. Somehow, we managed to fool them into thinking that the "California" connection was good for the place, so they want us to continue to show our work and our guest artists' work. There are eleven people, all local and all serious working artists. They are all enthusiastic about our show this summer, and we committed to start planning for next year's show *tout de suite*.

In the meantime, my project progresses. I'm a little worried that I'm not more worried at this stage. That usually means that I haven't thought about something important. Berger always talks about the "equation" in art, that there has to be a balance between opposites for a piece to work: the message and the medium, masculine versus feminine, hard versus soft. With my lanterns, it's light versus dark, but I'm abstracting the lanterns into ladies and guys. The feminine side is easy, since even with abstractions, I understand where to round a form off, but I don't do abstractions of guys well and I'm still cutting and welding important parts in a vain attempt to be less literal.

For the masculine form, I'm trying to roughen the edges by mounting the paper along the welded form with the seam sides out . . . like a nouveau Gap sweatshirt. The modern man can have soul, too. I'm having significant technical problems doing that since I don't want to sew the pieces together, and most glues stain the paper. The best adhesive is good old cellulose, wallpaper paste. But even if I can get the inside-out seams to hold, I'm worried about transporting it since it seems so fragile. Ironically, the feminine form, with the edges firmly glued to the frame, is much less delicate, and I can easily roll it around without tearing the paper. I've decided to hang them from the ceiling, which makes the detector system easier to mount and it looks more ethereal in my mind's eye. (Where is that eye, anyway, and how come it can't see things the way they actually will be?)

April 28, 1998
Dear Linda,

For a break, we packed up last Thursday and went off to Bordeaux for a weekend with the national organization Des Amis des Moulins, or Friends of Mills. This annual meeting is a good chance for us to meet people from all over France with a shared interest and open invitations to visit members' homes, which are converted mills. There were about 150 mill nerds, all French except us, all completely obsessed, as we are, with the workings of old mills. We saw windmills turning and stone quarries where they cut millstones in the fourteenth century.

Hours of esoterica about water rights and electrical turbine manufacturers and then hours of bus rides to old mills—some from the fourteenth century, fortified with drawbridges against either the French or the English, depending on who had just won what the last go-round. Since the region is at the lowest point of a complex river delta, right next to the Atlantic, most of these old buildings were built smack in the middle of the riverbed to maximize the water flow against their waterwheels. Wide, flat rivers joining seas, like our Mississippi, flood often, and I can only imagine the terror those millers must have experienced watching the river rise through the floorboards in the inevitable flood stages of the rivers. Fortunately, our little mill is built on the side of a cliff well above the river, and the water, to our knowledge, has never come up into the house. When we left, the creek was *en crue*, which is flood stage. One meaning of *crue* is raw, harsh, brutal, or as Germain says, "angry," all of which the Mousse can be when its banks try to contain the torrents careening down the canyon. The first time that happened we were terrified, even canceled a trip to Paris. Now, after at least two flash floods each year, we're quite blasé. Don't get me wrong, it's very exciting, but no longer terrifying.

Many of the people at the meeting only dream of owning a mill and restoring the waterworks, but mostly so they can generate electricity. When we talked to them about the last four years of getting our millstones to turn again, and how we make our own flour and bread, they were truly enchanted. But when we said we sift the flour by hand and we don't make our own electricity, we exhibited some sort of character weakness, I guess, at least by the reaction of those in the do-not-do-but-would-do-differently crowd. Given there were thirty-six thousand working flour mills in France a century ago and now there are fewer than one hundred that turn, almost all in order to generate electricity, we should be congratulating ourselves, but Mike spent the whole trip back on the train reading esoteric manuals on do-it-yourself electrical turbines. So now I've got this light and sound show fantasy working for our back terraces—lighted by our own electricity from the Mousse.

But, back to work. I've male parts to modify.

—*Hugs, Judy*

HEART PROBLEMS

July 1, 1998

Dear Linda,

It's been a difficult month. I know I told you on the phone, but I'm writing this all down for you to read to Gary. As you know, just before we were to leave for Katie's wedding in Vermont, Richard Berger and Mike left to ride their bikes and Mike came back five minutes later, ashen, trying not to alarm me or him. "It just felt funny, different, like nothing I've ever felt. Tight, right here," he said, thumping his left breast with his fist.

It was as if everything I learned after Mike's serum cholesterol level was tested at 340 years ago clicked into place. This was it. I tried to be nonchalant, suggesting he call, no, go see the doctor in Trébas. I'd go with him. Silence in the car, "Do we need bread?" I asked, trying not to sound terrified.

Dr. Vianez said we should go see a cardiologist in Albi, nothing too serious, but there was an anomaly in the EKG. He'd call, we'd go there by car.

The cardiologist agreed. "You should probably have an angiogram some day, but there's no rush," he said. We were quite relieved, especially when he said, "Have a good time at your daughter's wedding. Here's some nitroglycerin pills for you just in case the pain is bad."

So we went. When we came back, right after the wedding, we decided to go back to San Francisco to have Mike's health checked out, see the other kids, slow down a bit. We had our tickets, the EKGs from Trébas and Albi, everything worked out. Richard was going to stay at the mill until we returned in a few weeks. Then Brigitte's cousin, a Canadian cardiologist, came over the night before we were to leave, probably at Brigitte's suggestion. He took one look at the EKGs and said bluntly, "You cannot get on an airplane with this pattern. You MUST go to Albi, tonight."

First, Mike is fine. He is probably in better shape than he was two months ago, when he was complaining of being tired sometimes. But it took a blunt assessment of his chest pains, EKGs, and a serious dose of panic before we got to Toulouse by ambulance for his angiogram, balloon angioplasty, and the placement of two stents. The good news is he didn't have a true infarct so he had no loss of muscle tissue, just his sense of immortality shaken to the core. Two of his three coronary arteries were seriously occluded, however, one over 95 percent! He's now home at the mill, doing great, gently tending his garden, breathing deeply, metaphorically smelling the roses (since he can't actually smell after his surgery).

The other good news is that we were not in a third-world country, and the quality of care was excellent. The hospital was a private cardiovascular clinic where they do over a thousand angioplasties a year with an excellent record. In fact, the surgeon who operated on Mike actually invented the stent and had inserted the first ones, way before the surgeons at Stanford. But the cardiologist in Albi was much too circumspect with us, not telling us everything, just what he thought we should know, and I let him know that if there was a next time, he was to pull no punches. (I didn't say that in French, fearful he might sock Mike in the nose.)

Now, it's the aftershock. The realization that life must change fundamentally from now on; that indeed Mike has atherosclerosis, not just the risk because of his high cholesterol. Of the five big risk factors—being a man, genetics, high cholesterol, smoking, and overweight—he had only two, but he has serious sleep apnea, now considered an important cardiac risk factor, and the chronic problem in his sinuses before his big surgery two years ago probably contributed to the inflammation in his coronary arteries.

We've always tried to eat "light and low fat," but we were definitely overdoing the past two years, celebrating the tumor bullet he'd dodged. So, with enthusiasm, Mike's decided to do the Dean Ornish diet: vegetarian, no fat, not even veggie fat, with lots of exercise and meditation. He's signed up for a class this fall, and in the meantime our plan is to continue life as normal with those changes . . . maybe a little calmer, with less

entertaining, more boredom. That's my goal after last week. A whole month of total, complete boredom. In the meantime, I just stand around and watch him breathe and try to make soy paste into foie gras. I'm getting close. Any good sawdust recipes?
—*Love, Judy*

July 29, 1998
Dear Linda,

After all you've been through, I almost hesitate to tell you about all the heart problems Mike's been having, and since at this point I don't know what I've told you about which coming and going, please excuse any redundancies. After the initial shock of his new stents, we were almost back to non-shaking status, when off we went again. When Mike says he has additional "pressure" I believe him, even at 11 p.m. Sheer terror. We are only five minutes from Dr. Vianez in Trébas, and this time he decided it was faster if I took Mike to the emergency room and not wait for the ambulance, in other words, get him there now, so off I went on a midnight drive to Albi with a time-bomb beside me. "Got your nitro, sweetie?" I said nonchalantly. There is a significant risk of blockage with stents, so we were very vigilant.

We had made three emergency trips and one "not urgent—just chest pressure" since the 16th of June—the latest this past Sunday. Even after having the two arteries opened with two stents in mid-June, Mike continued to feel "pressure" in his chest, albeit less than the first time. The docs here, I think, were starting to believe it was all in his head, since one month is way too early for a stent to close.

After three days in intensive care, a week of hellacious medicines and shots morning and night, they did a nuclear scan last week that was *pas normal* but not *grave*. Easy for them to say. I finally got aggressive, reminded the cardiologist that Mike was feeling this pressure just lying in bed without exercise, in other words, unstable angina, the most unpredictable kind. I don't know if it was the information or my litigious tone of voice, but that kicked him over the line. He called the cardiovascular surgeon, who made an immediate hospital entry appointment for a look-see. Even the night before, the surgeon said he didn't think he would see anything, but "we" needed to be reassured that the two stents were functioning well.

After the first procedure last month, the doctor had said that one of Mike's arteries was 95 percent blocked, another over 70 percent, and that the remaining third artery was narrowing—about 30 percent—but that it wasn't enough to justify a dilatation, so they did just the two. I know it sounds odd, but we both felt something else was profoundly wrong and were jumpy. And when they went back in this time, that third one had mysteriously moved from 30 to 80 percent blocked, so the surgeon put in another stent. He was stumped: either he underestimated the first time, the artery had closed rapidly, or some combination of the two, and we'll probably never know which exactly. In spite of all that, I do have confidence in this guy and I think he was genuinely perplexed. This is not, after all, an exact science. We still have to be vigilant in case those stents block, but at least the problem was found. Sounds even better in French, I might add: "*Ça y est!*" Whew, that's that!"

They will give him a couple of treadmill tests before we leave France. But, frankly I wish we could stay here the whole crucial six-month time window and not climb on the airplane for Naomi's wedding, yet the doctors don't seem too concerned, either the French or the American ones (his doctor at Kaiser has been following all of this online, and since you asked, our insurance covers all emergency treatments, and these interventions were that).

Now he's back at the mill and gets to have Brigitte rub his belly and give him shots twice a day. Damn, she's gorgeous. By the way, although his surgeon spoke perfect English, we still did this all in another language (is that the same as the Ginger Rogers routine, "backward and in high heels"?), and we have another new medical section in our French vocabulary. And my Mike? He's lost his sense of taste, he's mostly deaf, he can't eat anything but turnips and tofu, and he can't walk up a hill without nitroglycerine in his pocket. Enough.

Trying to make some contribution to the healing process, I've been on a cooking binge, rereading all my old cookbooks, taking out the fat and trying all sorts of weird combinations, making chapattis, pita, corn flour crêpes, wannabe tortillas, chili with soybean grains. I smoked some old dried chilies I had in the pantry, ground them up in an old coffee grinder, roasted some cumin seed, chopped up some fresh oregano, and threw it all in with fresh-cooked red beans and tomatoes from the garden.

I have some weird Tibetan mushrooms that are used to make kefir from milk, and when I put them into soy milk, the only fat Mike is allowed, they turn it into a delicious, thick fresh cheese. A little salt and herbs, and we can't tell the difference. Can Roquefort be far behind?

Now I will confess: when we were in Toulouse this past week for the last roto-rooter, I went directly to MacDonald's for a big ole hamburger. I also fried up the last hunk of meat in the freezer. Couldn't throw it out: starving kids somewhere and all.

As I'm sitting here, it's pissing rain, big lightning and thunder stuff, which is a good excuse to do nothing . . . not that I need much of an excuse. I'm genuinely, sincerely yours, exhausted.

—*Love, Judy*

July 31, 1998
JOURNAL ENTRY

Entering the courtyard at the Château de Coupiac requires total concentration to keep from tumbling on the *calade,* the small river stones laid edgewise, that fills the uneven parts of the bare rock on which the building rests, forming a rough but passable walkway. On the left is an unfinished garden, piles of rock waiting for volunteering hands to crack and stack. A tarp over the bags of cement breathes with the wind. Up, sigh, down, sigh, up, sigh, down. To the right, the step down into the vaulted entry is higher than it should be. Too high for one step, too low for two. But once inside, the warm colors of the stone lighten the windowless space. Past the kitchen with its walk-in fireplace, not ornately carved like those in many later castles, and a circular stone stairway tucked into the northeast tower.

Halfway up the stairs, directly off from the steps, is the entry to the only finished space on the second floor. The floor appears at eye level before you get high enough to actually step into the room. As soon as a head bobs up the stairs, a six-foot paper lantern at the far end of the room lights up, showing a vaguely colored interior. When you enter the room, another lantern, the second to the right, illuminates, then the one on the left as the end lantern goes dark, the one on the far left blinks on, then the right while the second blinks off. If you walk quickly while waving in different directions, performing a silly ballet, they will all turn on, but not for long. The stained-glass window isn't one at all, just a Plexiglas sandwich of confusing colored transparencies, similar but different to the images inside the lanterns. In the corner of the room, a woman observes the reaction of the people entering, finding the right spot, waving, dancing. Sometimes she helps by a slight wave of her hand, but mostly she just watches. Probably the artist. She seems content with the results of her work.

TIBETAN-MUSHROOM CHEESE

August 15, 1998
Dear Linda,

I've been holding my breath since Mike stopped his heparin shots, which keep his blood from clotting, waiting for more weirdness. And, on cue, it arrived. He went for another nuclear scan, and the technician thought he should go see the cardiologist since there was another anomaly. His regular cardiologist is on vacation, and the associate brushed it off: "*C'est pas grave.*" The Stateside doc read the scan we express-mailed to him, said there are certainly some smaller vessels that are still pretty clogged up, and that they will show up as weirdness and that Mike probably will experience angina for at least a little while. Evidently, once the major vessels are blown out the little guys regroup and can revascularize, but it takes time. In the meantime, Mike has twinges and other scary stuff that fortunately respond well to the nitro. He's started riding his bike again, gently, I hope. Suzie's husband, François, who has already had his carotid arteries reamed out once, decided he might start biking again with Mike. François can barely walk up a flight of stairs, so I'm not too worried about them doing too much.

But it's hard to keep the old man down, even on beta-blockers. I keep telling him that this is easy for him, he gets drugs! I'm running, making Mike play dominoes with me to relax, napping in the afternoon, sipping the occasional glass of wine, and talking to myself a lot. That seems to help— except when I answer. Over a million families in the U.S. alone get used to this each year, so I guess I will, too. Mike is taking this, even the new diet, in stride . . . even the ground garbanzos. Me, I'm ready to eat a little meat. Actually, I'm ready to KILL something. Songbirds are not even safe right now in my proximity!

Meanwhile, I cook. I mean literally all day. One doesn't dash into Whole Foods and grab whole grains and tofu hot dogs here. I have to sprout my own sprouts, clot my fake cheese, knead my bread, cut, and chop. Secretly, I'm having a great time. It makes me feel like I'm doing something, or maybe everything, that I can possibly do.

After a few weeks on no fat and no meat, the thing Mike missed the most was his Roquefort cheese. So after much experimentation, and I have succeeded in making an outstanding almost-Roquefort using soy milk clotted with that Tibetan mushroom I mentioned. The mushroom turns it into a yogurt, and then I drain that to make a thick cream cheese that is delicious all by itself. I can use it to make hummus, and some great sauces, and salad dressings. One day when I was cleaning out the fridge I saw an old chunk of Roquefort left at the bottom, which was mostly mold after who knows how long. I thought, "Why not?" I carefully scraped off the mold from the little holes in the Roquefort, sprinkled it over the cream cheese, made a round, put a thick layer of rock salt on it, wrapped it in a clean napkin, and stuck it back in the fridge. Bingo, two weeks later, not just a respectable imitation, but a rich, creamy blue cheese with impressive veins of real Roquefort mold growing inside! Jean-Claude, who thought my cheese was delicious, has even brought me some real Roquefort mold so I can make Mike his Roquefort cheese without scraping old cheese.

I won't go into the details of my failures at duplicating foie gras from wheat gluten or my disgusting attempts at desserts. Mike's diet is completely nonfat, so instead of oil I use applesauce or puréed prunes for moisture in sweets, and roasted onions whizzed up in the Cuisinart in savory dishes. Whizzed cukes do well also, especially in vinaigrettes as well as in puréed veggie soups.

After the stress of this summer, I've settled into a comforting routine: coffee while I rinse all the sprouts and feed the mushrooms; start the bread onto its first rise; clean out the studio; punch down the bread; rearrange the studio; punch the bread down again. I think the secret to cooking with beans, rice, and tofu is to make tomorrow's dinner today since it's all so much better after it sits. And good sauces. I now have a refrigerator full of Indian curry–style fixings, miso-honey Asian, and salsas. I grab some veggies, steam some couscous, and it's on the table. (I confess to having dreams about spareribs and sirloin steaks.)

Sunday was tough, since we went up to Le Moussac for a wedding meal from midday to about 7 p.m. with over 120 of their friends and neighbors. Jean-Claude's gorgeous three daughters and their husbands/boyfriends tended the lamb on the spit, while other friends and relatives rolled out the food. No buffets here. Everyone is served at the table, and not by caterers either. They obviously do this often and thoroughly enjoy themselves in the process.

The pine trees that surround their swimming pool were almost enough shade for everyone seated at the banquet tables. They had put all the drinks and fresh food into an enormous industrial refrigerator, which they rolled out onto the lawn with the first course: slices of farm-raised ham with the sweetest, coldest melons I've ever eaten. The younger kids circulated and put hunks of bread in the middle of the table next to the water pitchers dripping with condensation. Then the salad course: huge bowls of chilled lettuce were passed, everyone serving themselves with their hands to plop a pile on their plate. Next, big bowls of hot sliced *confit de gésiers*—preserved duck gizzards— were circulated to dress the lettuce, followed by cool slices of smoked *magret,* or duck breast, with pitchers of vinaigrette passed around to be swirled over the lot.

We had already decided that Mike would have a little dab of something, and he carefully removed the two inches of fat from around his tiny slice of ham and refused the duck breast, but I watched the farmers around me, their Laguiole knives in their right hand, and the fat was the first thing in their mouths, especially with the skinny old guys —the French paradox at work. As for me, I hadn't had meat in so long I was practically shaking with pleasure. I ate it all, fat, seconds, thirds of the *gésiers*. Not too fat, those.

That just greased the skids for a slab of hot spit-roasted lamb served from a huge tub by the sons-in-law, rugby players all, grunting as they passed the meat sloshing in its juice and the fat floating on top. Mopped it up, I did, from my plate, that is. The lamb was stuffed with couscous, which was plumped up with all those smoky juices. Two-foot-long forks and ladles brought it, none too neatly, to the plate. Then came the flageolets: beans baked with hunks of ham and roasted onions. I self-righteously passed on the cheese and took only one slice of apricot tart before I saw the *gâteau brioche*. That's a cake made by turning a rod on a spit in front of an open fire while drizzling a rich cake batter over and over it until it forms a falafel-shaped cone—dense, and sweetened with nuts and honey. What could I do? I was completely out of control, and Mike was on his own. (He was remarkably good.)

Did you notice how many times I said *cold, cool, shade, chilled*? It has been 104 degrees in the shade all week, and yesterday was no exception. All those young rugby bodies were in bathing suits, and the kids were encouraged to splash everyone. By the end of the meal, everyone had found some excuse to go in the big house to cool down a bit. It was wonderful to get back to the mill, where it is always at least ten degrees cooler than up on the mesa. It was a mild ninety-something, but inside our thick stone and mud walls we are truly cool, man.

This is the time of the year that you get up at 6 a.m., do anything that needs doing outside until 10, close the shutters and windows and retire to inside activities until about 4. We are lucky that we have our little river right next to us. Even the sound of the waterfall helps keep us relatively cool, plus the fall itself provides a place to wet down our T-shirts and keeps fresh air blowing through the terraces. (We have five different ones now, one for cool-weather lunches, one for hot weather, another for unbearable heat, one to contemplate the waterfall, and another for our guests to hide out on. We're truly terrace-endowed.) Even Mike has started to take Mediterranean-style naps when the heat's this unbearable. But then we work until 7 or 8 in the evening, eat outside at 9, and sip tea by candlelight until 11.

It's also the time for all the village festivals, which we used to religiously attend. The first few years the fêtes were exotic, or we were still romantic, but after a few years, when well-meaning friends would bring along their English-speaking-only friends, most of whom got drunk on the cheap wine, we begged off. But I have to admit I don't miss the insufferable meal, the dry inedible ham, the sticky paella, more cheese, and packaged ice cream, all of which takes seven hours to serve. A paper tub of melting ice cream at two in the morning just isn't worth staying up for—no matter how great the company is. And since we're in the center of four different villages, Plaisance, Solage, Coupiac, and Trébas, we were stuck with four evenings like that. Using Mike's special diet as an excuse, we just leave after the aperitif, which allows us the time to circulate without the table time. I think they forgive us, since we know not what we do.

It's also time for the garden. We can't get sweet corn here, even the seeds, so we bring them from the States and Germain plants it for us in his way-too-big garden. He loves eating it off the cob with butter running down his chin, but Martou won't touch it, so we go up and bring heaping baskets down, and have just corn. Well, a hunk of our bread, on which I put a big knob of butter to roll the corn in (no butter for Mike). Best bread ever. And we now grow our own potatoes, which I thought wouldn't be worth it until I tasted them freshly dug from the ground. First, it's an egg hunt with the thrill of finding them, then I roast them with garlic and rosemary. They're like little butter chunks, with no skin at all. The other essentials are zucchini flowers, basil, arugula, cilantro, fresh onions, cucumbers, and eggplants. The latter just because they are so beautiful, and how else can you make ratatouille and say it's all fresh from the garden without them?

It was nice to talk to Gary yesterday. He loves to tease me about my la-dee-da letters to you. I'm working on my dark-and-stormy side, but somehow it always comes out somewhere between *Days of Our Lives* and du Maurier's *Rebecca*. We're leaving here the fourth of September, and as usual, the biggest problem with our lifestyle is the countdown, last meals with friends, not enough time to start a real project, too early to pack, eating all the food in the refrigerator, vitamin packs to refill before San Francisco. Off to punch it down. The bread, that is.

—*Hugs, Judy*

THE CAVE

September 2, 1998
Dear Linda,

Bam—it's fall. No warning, just oppressive heat and a huge storm, followed by long shadows and cool evenings.

I've been so obsessed with Mike's health that I forgot to give you the rest of the rundown on our friends and acquaintances. First, Les Magnolias stayed open all summer but Marie-France has put it on the market and is hoping to sell out before next season. She's quite frustrated with the new EU regulations, which will take more money than she can justify, and she still would have to deal with Francis's adult children who would share in the benefits and not the work. She appears quite happy with Fabrice, so I doubt we will see her again.

And Christelle got married last week—church, dress, veil, cake, Champagne. Apparently her sit-down with the mayor and the priest worked, Maran cleaned up, and she agreed to the church wedding. The whole village turned out to climb up the hill then the steep stairs leading into the twelfth-century chapel. The Mass was short, since the *curé* is old and can't stand too long. Christelle stood, almost smiling, her back stiff, with Maran at her side, staring up at her, his eyes misty with joy. There was a glass of Champagne in the *cave* under the *curé*'s house, but no cake cutting or big meal since they can't afford it and I don't think Christelle wanted to pretend that long.

So now she's got herself a husband she doesn't love, who has, for most of the last four years, actually disgusted her. But she's sending money to her children, which has allowed them to open a little store in Madagascar, and Maran is trying to learn how to treat a woman with respect after his own miserable childhood of abuse. Is she better or worse off than what percentage of women in how many marriages?

And Bernard *pierre*? He's here most weekends building and repairing, since it seems as we rebuild one wall another falls down. Then in August we decided to build a real wine *cave* under the mill where there was an opening of sorts leading only to dirt and rock, possibly filled in by Louis Blanc as he dug out the millrace tunnels each year. We were tired of our *vrac* wine, as either you buy wine in France to be "put up" in a wine *cave* to age or you pay a fortune for a decent bottle. And every house has one, including people in Paris who rent spaces for their stock. Affordable wine is quite undrinkable,

and drinkable wine is unaffordable, hence *les caves*, dark, mysterious, cool, slightly scary places to put up wine, cheeses to age, potatoes dug from the garden, and *bocaux* of tomatoes, green beans, and pâté. (In Martou's *cave*, many of the preserves are as old as the wine next to them.) A good *cave* is about sixty constant degrees, humid enough to keep the corks from drying out but not so dank that the labels slide off.

Pail by pail, we dug out that space until we had a real *cave*, about 15 by 20 feet, the back wall formed by the reservoir behind the house. To our surprise, we discovered a rock tunnel under all the dirt, which corresponded to the placement of the turbine for the oil mill that sits on the back terrace just outside the back door. What is left of that millworks consists of a stone basin about 4 feet in diameter, the wall about 2 feet high. The thin wall of the basin had been broken and repaired in several places, then abandoned. The former owners had filled it with dirt, and an extraordinary display of volunteer ferns, primulas, and stinging nettles had quickly settled in. Germain said his grandfather stopped milling oil right after World War I.

Since we found the tunnel, Mike has put the oil mill next on the list of follies to be renovated. La Pilande Basse appears to be built on solid earth like any other house, but if one could see a cross-section, there would be a gigantic ant farm of tunnels, some above ground, most below, starting near the waterfall through the various sluice gates, through the rock, into the chute, over another waterfall, into the reservoir, through more sluice gates, under the house, then into more tunnels that finally rejoin the river, just under the bridge.

The water for this tunnel running through our wine *cave* would have come through the waterfall sluice gate, down the main water chute, then diverted to a horizontal paddle wheel under our back-door terrace, rushing into the spokes of the turbine, which, in turn, would have turned the millstone above it, which rests on its side so it could roll over thirty pounds of shelled nuts, forming a paste—a lot of nut butter! That paste was then heated in a large skillet in our fireplace to release the oil, then dumped into an iron basin lined with a coarse linen cloth in the huge oil press that divides our living room and dining room. A solid oak and metal plug, the same size as the press basin, would have been placed on top of the soupy nut paste, and been compressed against it by the 3-foot beam forced down by the action of a 10-inch metal screw cranked tight by a 4-foot handle. The oil would have been forced out a small hole on the side of the press into a series of sieves, leaving a clear golden liquid. The smell must have been divine: fresh, warm walnut oil. (The dormice must have put on their bibs and sat on the edge of the stone basin, knife and fork ready for the *meunier* to quit work for the evening.) The water then would have continued under the house through the tunnel we just uncovered, then off through that long-unused section of the tunnel that runs under the *porcherie*, back into the river. In the meantime, the pigs in the *porcherie* would have been enjoying the solid block of nut fibers left in the linen cloth at the bottom of the press basin. So how many people do you know who have a wine cellar with a river running through it?

To build the wine racks, I decided to go to the building supply store in Réquista and look at chimney tiles to see if we could stack and use them instead of building expensive wooden racks to store wine and canned vegetables from the garden. As I stood in the outdoor storage yard and gazed at the surprising variety of sizes and shapes in clay and cement, a young employee asked me if he could help me. I was contemplating a twenty-four-inch chimney tile and asked him, expecting to surprise him, "How many bottles of wine would fit in that tile, monsieur?" Without missing a beat he responded, "*Ça dépend, madame, si c'est du Bourgogne ou du Bordeaux.*" So I wasn't so clever after all. Clearly others had asked him the same question, and he could actually tell me depending on whether we preferred Burgundy or Bordeaux wines. Bernard *pierre* has cut and stacked my selection, so now we have a lovely new wine cellar with a tiny stream running through it, and 160 square chimney tiles that will hold each at least a case of wine each, and our four lonely bottles.

It's been a difficult summer, full of anxiety, and we're not past the danger point for Mike yet, but we're packing our bags (we used to call them body bags, but it's not funny this year) for the winter, ready to go home to Naomi's wedding. See you there!

—*Love, Judy*

September 5, 1998
Dear Linda,

Okay, one more letter. You haven't heard much lately about Monsieur Parnat, the local *brocanteur,* since we work hard to avoid him, but one more time this week, he showed his true colors to us: yellow on yellow. We have a huge grapevine trellis in front of the house that is beautiful, prolific, and provides the only shade in front of the mill on hot summer days. The only problem is, no one wants the grapes: they're too sour to eat and they make bad wine, so we try to get someone who likes bad wine to take them. Monsieur Parnat volunteered to come with his brother and pick them on Sunday. The day before, at the *brocante* in Albi I had found a beautiful porcelain bell, called a *clochette,* about the size of an inverted teacup, that was used to protect a gas lantern from the weather. I had paid too much for the *clochette* and stupidly had hung it on a metal rod sticking out under the grape trellis, admittedly a hazard, waiting to take it up to La Ruche to hang it for decoration on the porch light that I had bought from Monsieur Parnat, also for too much.

So Sunday morning, Monsieur Parnat and his brother backed up a truck under the trellis and started to pick the grapes. We had to leave before they were done, and when we came back two hours later, I saw my beautiful bell in shards on the millstone below where it had been hanging. I assumed that Monsieur Parnat had knocked it down, my fault, really, for leaving it in such a precarious place. I decided to go into Plaisance to his little *brocante* and see if he had another.

It never occurred to me that he wouldn't tell me what had happened when I arrived, the shards in my pocket. But I could see the wheels turning in his head as I came down the asphalt drive. His lips moved back and forth over his tiny worn-down teeth, and he lifted his beret in front, holding it in his thumb and forefinger as he scratched his head with the other three fingers, trying to figure out what to say. Since I didn't jump in with the topic, he decided to dodge it and just said, *"Bonjour."* I chatted a bit, watching him squirm, but when it became apparent that he had no intention of saying anything, I got a little peeved. When I asked him if he had *quelque chose comme ça,* as I pulled the pieces from my pocket, he got quite agitated and lied, *"Non, non, c'est rare, une clochette comme ça."* The wheels kept spinning, the lips twitching, head scratching, and finally, mostly because he couldn't think of any way out of the trap, he admitted that they had banged it, well, his brother did, anyway. His brother is mentally retarded, and certainly I couldn't be angry with a handicapped person. I looked around and saw another Plaisance cast-iron porch light leaning against the wall. I walked over, picked it up, and started up the sticky asphalt drive saying over my shoulder, *"Quand vous aurez trouvé une clochette, je reviendrai pour vous payer. C'était à peu près le même prix.*" ("When you've found another bell, I'll come back and pay you. It's about the same price.") Or that's what I wanted to say in my best French, using the future perfect, simple future, and imperfect without even thinking about it, but I'm sure he got the drift in my simplistic chopped-up, very angry words. In any event, I strode off with style. You'd have been proud.

—*Hugs, Judy*

September 5, 1998
JOURNAL ENTRY

An American friend married to a Frenchman told me once that it took her five years to be able to speak enough French to be herself, to use a normal tone of voice, to argue, tell a joke, be truly understood. We're here only six months of the year, so do I have five more to go? I so wanted to tell Parnat, with some dignity, what a jerk I think he is. *Connard? Con?* It is so frustrating to be so limited, even after five years. I want to go home.

September 6, 1998
JOURNAL ENTRY

The path leading from the front door of the mill down to the river starts with four flat rock steps that lead to a landing of solid stone, which probably is the bedrock sticking through the thin soil. To the left, the path becomes a *calade*, small flat river stones set on edge over a hundred years ago, tedious work but effective in forming a solid nonslip surface. It runs down into the *porcherie*, which is below the front terrace, its feet in the river. To the right of the landing are five more wide flat stones/steps that lead to the low door of the new *cave*. Mike built the door from old boards, and its cracking gray surface is hot in the full sun. I had to pull outward on the door handle to release the top bolt that holds the door tight against the heat. The trapdoor spider sits quietly in the hole in the center of her web, in the upper right hand corner of the doorframe. A flick on the web sends her deeper into her trap, and then the race starts to keep the cool air from escaping and to find the light switch before the spiderwebs suspended from the ceiling slap me in the face. The crunchy new gravel shines white in the dim light. The little canal lined with flat river rocks is still damp with trickles from leaks in the reservoir, and the rusty brown and blue schist walls are witness to the last tomatoes of the summer. Their bright red through the clear glass jars is a colorful contrast to the yellow/green chutneys and fig jams, each tucked into their own gray cubicles on the far right side of the cave. As I closed the door behind me, I whispered: "See you next spring."

We were late in arriving at La Pilande Basse this year, and we were sure that the garden wouldn't have been touched since September. But Maran had come with the *débrousailleuse* and whacked away the major green dragons so we could get to the front door. And Germain had rototilled our little *potager* and even hauled in some manure for me to spread. (He and Martou are in Italy with a group of third-agers, so we haven't had our *bisous* from that front yet.) Thanks to Natalie, the house was mostly clean, the sheets off the furniture, the mice sent to their rooms for the summer. We don't have much of a problem anymore with critters like we did the first few years, but I'm convinced that they just know when to come and go and that they're never far away.

There were a few more births in the village than deaths this winter, which is a significant change for the better since the countryside has been decreasing in population since the war. Les Magnolias has been sold to a German, and supposedly he's going to restore it and reopen next year. This winter by phone we did a deal with Marie-France and bought the wine cellar from the restaurant, and thanks again to Germain and Bernard *bois*, our new *cave* was quickly filled with some nice old wines. As Churchill said, "So much to drink . . . so little time."

We lost a neighbor, Monsieur Gissac, eighty-two years old, who died this winter from a broken heart. They say it was his wife of fifty-two years who left him two years ago to live with a long-time lover, a nineteen-year affair, that caused his quick demise. That was the woman I met with Martou last year at the Foire de Réquista. When she left, no one blamed her, as the old man was a drunk and he was probably at least verbally abusive, but somehow now it's her fault he's dead and she's gone from being a victim to a mean *salope*, or bitch, with his passing.

Their farm, Le Carassier, is just down the road from La Pilande Haute. (Germain thinks someone many generations ago came down from there to marry someone at the mill, so they renamed the mill La Pilande Basse, or lower mill, and the former La Pilande Haute.) La Pilande Haute is just up the hill from Lespinaudie la Creste, a large, classic Roquefort farm, where a handsome man of forty-five named Christophe Berlan lives all alone. His farm has about three hundred head of sheep, and he grows grain for his animals and tobacco for the government. As I drive to Coupiac, I look down on his tidy fields and immaculate stone courtyard and wonder what he does when he leaves *la bergerie* and enters his imposing stone house at night alone.

According to Germain, when Christophe was in his early twenties he was in love with Mélie, who lived with her parents at La Pilande Haute. But the parents of Christophe and those of Mélie had been feuding for many years, no one remembers why, and they refused to let them marry. The idea of the two farms being joined was too much for them to contemplate. So Mélie went off to school in Bordeaux, married a young coast guard officer, and had a baby girl. The husband was killed in a boating accident off the coast of Biarritz shortly after the baby was born. Christophe and Mélie never saw each other again after the last funeral of Mélie's parents. No one knows what's happened to her since, and Christophe climbs the stone steps to his house each evening, knocks the mud off his boots on the stoop, and pulls the door closed behind him.

And the inevitable happened over the winter. No one was there to watch, but the fragile form of Dan's grapevine man slid lower and lower down the rail, the last molecule of the wire holding him to the balustrade oxidized into red powder, and he fell onto the stone terrace. I stood in mourning above him trying to decide what I should do. I've never contemplated a proper burial for a work of art. I burned the chairs, but that was part of the work. What to do? I finally decided I'd best ask the artist. But fate stepped into the vacuum. Christelle, who had been working all day to help us with the spring cleaning, went up to La Ruche to prepare for Richard Berger's visit next week. When she saw the fallen form she tried, unsuccessfully, to right him. I wasn't there, but I can imagine an Abbot and Costello routine with an arm around a floppy leg breaking off in her hand. In any event, he's but a stack of sticks at this point. At least she was sensitive enough to not just toss him off the terrace cliff. I'm going to suggest to Dan that we let him free fall from the top of the waterfall, slip down Le Mousse, join the Rance, the Tarn, the Garonne, and the Atlantic, yelling "Wheeeeeee" all the way home.
—*Love to all, Judy*

May 21, 1999
Dear Linda,

We had sixty-three people for lunch yesterday—all mill wonks anxious to see a working mill, since there aren't many left in France. We had worked hard, and the garden, the millraces, and the *chambre d'eau* were as clean as they get, and the barn-turned-Mike's-studio was set up with chairs and benches for the business meeting, ready for a quick conversion into a dining room. We had planned tables outside—the Ping Pong table will seat sixteen under the grape trellis, then six more scattered on various terraces—but the weather was too threatening so we decided to squinch the tables into the barn.

By the end of the event, I had learned several things the hard way. First, Murphy's law applies even in rural f'in' France. At 2 a.m. the night before the big affair we had a real *crue*, a flash flood. A wall of mud with trees and rocks came down the river, smashing against the three-foot-thick walls of the house hard enough to wake us forty feet above in the *grenier* turned bedroom. There's nothing one can do when the river is so angry, except wait, wide-eyed, for the early-morning light to see the waterfall gone red, with mists of rushing water filling the air. We have much less trash coming down during floods these days with the abandonment of the garbage dump upstream, but there was still enough to temporarily block the grate that protects the entry to the main water chute that fills the reservoir behind the house. Hanging tightly to the guardrail we'd just installed, Mike pulled himself along the slippery wall twenty feet above the rocks below the dam and stood in the rushing water at six in the morning to pry the debris from the grate. I stood guard, praying that the big logs that can fly into the air over the dam propelled by the force of the river *en colère*, or when it's angry, had already passed on their way to the Atlantic.

Another lesson: sixty-three Frenchmen can sit stuffed into a small barn for a business meeting for three hours without one of them having to leave to pee. Secondly, the air in a small barn can get stuffy after sixty-three Frenchmen spend three hours there in a business meeting, so, without hardly asking, in a few minutes, the weather now permitting, the tables were moved outside (the Ping Pong table under the trellis, three tables for six on the bridge, and the other three on the front terrace) and set, the buffet was in place, and lunch was served—catered by the chef who had helped Marie-France at Les Magnolias the first year after Francis died, and is now in Coupiac at the

Hôtelerie, Lynne and Robert having been successfully shooed out of town by the mayor.

The mill turned, the flour was ground, the mill nerds were happy. The only significant event was a wasp sting on the ass of Madame la Secretaire des Amis des Moulins. Her dignity abandoned, she ran out the door, dropped trou, and asked me to help. (There is a new market for Sting-Ease in rural France.) It was a great day.

—*Hugs, Judy*

HOUSE OF CARDS

June 15, 1999

Dear Linda,

How am I, you ask? In general, I'm just paddling through life, avoiding most of the big stumps, taking an occasional risky ride through some whitewater, but mostly letting the current take me wherever. In case you wonder from whence cometh that ridiculous metaphor, a group of kayakers actually came down our river last week. They did ford the twenty-foot waterfall, but the lower one they just "wheeeeeed" on through. I pick my way along the river rocks with a long pointed walking stick from time to time, but I confess I'm afraid to take those kinds of risks.

The river can be a sweet babbling brook or a raging torrent, and the sound, *le bruit du ruisseau,* absolutely permeates our life. The first thing in the morning, out my bedroom window, I look to see how much water's coming over the fall. My bath in the clawfoot tub is accompanied with the sound of the little waterfall just outside, seeping through the open window over the low, flat rock sink. My garden is watered from the chute running through the backyard, by scoops of my green plastic watering can (my initials, JOS, in black indelible ink so Mike can't steal it) as I try to dodge the frogs who plop into the water from the weeds under my feet and the little fish who make their way from the river through the sluice gate grate and tunnel into the chute. (A visitor was startled to have a fish jump out on her feet as she stood on the back terrace admiring the garden.)

As for art, stress is building for me with an ambitious installation at the Château de Coupiac. You asked about the process I go through for my installations, which is easier to describe afterward than before, but I'll try. I seem to be most comfortable starting with the space where I'm to exhibit and designing something that speaks to it. I research it, spend time just sitting there until a usually clear image comes to me. I don't draw or doodle until it's time to build maquettes and actual objects. Others tend to build something and then look for an exhibition space, which is frankly more intelligent. That way if something doesn't work well, one can always pull something else out of storage. But I seem to need to have a dialogue with the space and the viewers.

The château belongs to La Route des Seigneurs, a group of châteaux that all display a twelve-foot banner with a foreboding black and red crest representing their association. They publish maps showing tourists how to pretend they're noblemen, moving from house to house. (The irony is that if the châteaux had actually belonged to the counts of Toulouse or Rodez, they would have been destroyed during the French Revolution. Since they belonged to lowly bourgeoisies instead, they were spared.) When I saw the banner unfurled from the one-hundred-foot-high roof of the Château de Coupiac for the first time, with much ceremony, I couldn't help wondering what the original *blason*, or crest, of the *seigneur* looked like. And would there be anything left of the cloth after eight hundred years? Did they wash it? I kept thinking that the whole feudal system was just a house of cards waiting to collapse. When I asked Germain what the French call "a house of cards" he said, "*un château de cartes*," and while the Coupiac château didn't fall down with the rest of them during the French Revolution, I kept envisioning a joker dangling up there instead of the impressive *blason*.

I went back later to sit alone in the courtyard (Marie-Hélène had given me the ten-inch key ring with several rusty tumble-lock keys to open the big gate). As I waited for some ghosts to speak to me, I noticed out of the corner of my eye that the tarp that covered some still-to-be-stacked stones seemed to lift and sigh back down in the slight breeze. Lift and sigh. The stones seemed to be breathing. I walked up the circular staircase, past the exhibition space where I installed the braid lanterns last year, into the *grande salle*, which is about 30 feet wide and 100 feet long. The floor is the original wooden planking, rough and patched, and the walls are peeling plaster that hasn't been touched for at least three hundred years. The sheer size of the space overwhelmed me. To own the room I figured I'd need to fill at least the middle third of it. I paced that off and it came out to about 9 by 6 yards. Hum, nine times six makes fifty-four, a deck of cards with two jokers.

That was it. I could see fifty-four pale banners, all about twelve feet long, frayed, holey, with the slightest trace of the marks of cards, like watermarks in paper, suspended above from the twenty-foot ceiling like laundry on clotheslines, brushing the shoulders of people passing through. In my head they're some conglomeration of flags of the counts of yesteryear, and the house-of-cards of all social structures, and last century's laundry hung to dry and then forgotten.

I make large-scale hand-cast paper, but that's a lot of mulberry fiber, and because of waste due to tearing during production, I need to make two to net one when I'm on the learning curve for a project. That means at least one hundred sheets. But the image of those banner ghosts hanging in that huge space is so strong I know I'll do it. I see them sighing, dancing, moving when someone enters the room. I won't know until they're up, but I think a row of fans on motion detectors will push enough air down the length of the room to make them dance.

My technical problems are significant because of the ceiling height. And I need to be able to easily raise the banners high enough that the château association can have their annual fund-raising medieval dinner beneath them and then lower them again the next day. I saw an ingenious system in Paris for hanging laundry in apartments, a horizontal frame with clotheslines stretched between the sides. The whole business can be hauled up and down through pulleys mounted in the ceiling. I'm into plagiarism: a twenty-by-thirty-foot steel frame suspended by pulleys, with steel clotheslines on which I'll hang the laundry/deck of cards/banners. I want to be able to lower the rods to the floor, clip on the banners, and haul the whole affair up to the desired height. That means there must be counterweights to balance the minimal weight of the banners and keep the rods from pulling inward, in other words, something to keep the *château de cartes* standing. How I do that is still a mystery.

I can only make five banners a day because I have to cook, soak, and beat all of the fiber, and my cooking pot can't hold more. I also don't have enough hanging space, or even hours in the day. Given that, I think I need to make ten banners to have five good ones come out, and since I have only thirty days to finish this, I can't miss a production day. I deal myself a poker hand with a deck of cards, five at a time. I retire the dealt cards when I'm successful in making that card. I take two bundles of mulberry fiber, which is the basis of kozo, or rice paper, and stick them in a big bucket to soak, taking out the two from the day before and putting them in a large canning pail with lots of soda ash, which I get in ten-pound sacks from Jean-Paul at the *quincaillerie* in Coupiac. (I bring the fiber from my studio in California, where I have a stash that I imported from Japan a few years ago. I'm glad my friend at the customs desk in Toulouse didn't look in that suitcase!)

I fire up a huge propane cooking ring like the one Martou uses to make her jams, and cook the fiber for about six hours. I put the cooked fiber from the day before into a large pail and let water from our springs rinse the ash and nonfibrous material off downstream. (It's quite handy to have a river running through your house with a water-driven process like paper-making.) I take the fiber that's been rinsing since the day before off to the end of our bridge to the Richard Berger Memorial Sand Table. I have a work surface on it that serves as a beating base for the fibers. I chant and grunt while I beat the cooked, rinsed fibers with two large oak paddles until the fibers are short enough to put into a solution. (Richard came out one day and took over the beating process. That lasted about five minutes and he handed them back to me, with a better appreciation for the physical labor involved.) After forty-five minutes of arm-numbing pounding, I take the smunched pulp to a large vat and soak it in lots of fresh, cool water. (I have this vision of those poor fibers curling their backs against the flow, sighing, "Yes, that feels good. I'm glad she finally quit.")

I love the process, the feel of the fibers as they soak and give up their bits of bark. The fibers swirl in the water and form a sensuous, creamy mixture. I love the surprise when I pull the dried fibers from their couching sheets. The paper is so translucent, so elegant, so strong. I taught myself to make paper, instruction book in one hand, beating paddles in the other. I'm sure any Japanese papermaker would cringe at what I make, but I want the paper irregular, with small holes and jagged edges: ghosts of cards.

I'm working in a makeshift studio at the end of our bridge, a garden tent that keeps the rain/sun from interrupting my workday. I measure the pulp and the gluey substance called formation aid, used in oriental papers to keep the fibers in suspension, into five buckets and add water from another spring to make enough pulp to form ten large banners. The fibers need some time to plump up with the water and formation aid, so I go down under the mill into the *chambre d'eau* to take down the dried paper from the day before, my favorite part, pulling away the couching sheets (special fabric, a felted material like the interfacing used to make collars stiff, only thicker, that lets water drain quickly without deforming) to see how much gossamer paper I can retrieve.

The top couching sheet comes off easily, but the paper is gently stuck to the bottom since the initial fibers find their way into the interstices of the couching fabric. Starting at one corner, I pull the newly formed paper from its protective sheet, little by little. I pass my left hand under the paper while I tug gently with the right. When I come to a particularly thin section, I start from another corner, hoping to be able to lift the entire twelve-foot sheet in one piece. But sometimes, well, half the time, almost near the end of the removal the whole sheet just rips, tearing my patience as well. I have to leave and have a cup of tea. (The ten of clubs, for some reason, refuses to be formed, so I put him in the bottom of the deck for when I might be more proficient and he might be less recalcitrant.) From ten formed sheets I'm now getting about three that are strong enough to hang and blow but thin enough, with a few rag-like holes, to let an air current tease them into a dance with their partners. I learn something each day, and I keep copious notes in my studio journal. I recycle the failed cards, or keep the sections that are good for other projects.

I then roll up the couching sheets and take them out to the tent to soak in a large vat. I roll out several membranes of more couching material on a 13-foot table, soak them by pouring buckets of water on them and me until the water runs through easily, down the overhanging sides into my green rubber gardening shoes. (My feet are puckered gray by the end of the day.) Now, two hours later, I can start to cast the paper. I made a 12-foot-by-30-inch wooden frame, which I manhandle into place on top of the couching materials, weigh it down with scrubbed river rocks, and start casting pulp inside its borders. The paper emulsion must be just so, the water the right temperature, the fabric stretched tight and wet. Before I dip into the pulp, I agitate the liquid with my whole arm up to the shoulder. By this time, I'm soaked along with all the materials. (I love the combination of that child-like seriousness coupled with the total mess that is required to do this Clean/Dirty Day activity.)

Using a large ladle and dipping back and forth in the vat of pulp, I lay down several overlapping layers of fibers, letting most of the water drain through before the next *couche*. If I cast the next layer too quickly I blow a hole in the fibers below, so it's slow, deliberate work. Then I take the cookie-cutter card image—a stylized heart, diamond, spade, or fleur-de-lis, for one of the five cards I've been dealt that day, the ten of clubs for example, and place it appropriately on the sheet of paper and cast more

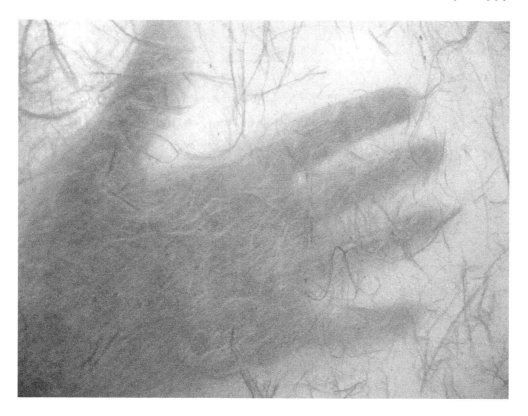

paper pulp around it so that when dry, the part inside the stencil walls is thinner, a literal watermark. (I'm quite pleased with the subtlety of the images that show through with light behind them, which almost justifies the ridiculous amount of time it takes to make them.) It's difficult to see the thickness of the fibers while I'm casting them, so I count on subtle differences and the quantity of fiber I put down to tell me when to stop.

When I think the paper is as formed as I want, thin but not too thin, no big holes but some holes, I roll out another layer of the couching fabric so I have a sandwich: couching material, paper fibers, couching material. I continue forming like that, one on top of another, until I have ten sandwiches. By the end of the stack, the water drains differently than the first, so I can't let myself mentally wander too far or be diverted by much more than music from my little radio.

Each banner, a thin sheet of paper that can't weigh more than a few ounces, requires about twenty gallons of pulp and water to be lifted and poured, 160 pounds per sheet. Ten sheets and about three hours later—which is all the couching material I have, and all the weight my back and arms can lift—I stagger back to the mill and collapse.

(Add the beating and lifting of gallons of water for the cooking and rinsing of the fibers, and you've got a full-body workout!) But I'm not done, since the stack has to be hung to dry. It drains on the table for at least an hour while I fix dinner, then I fold the stack back over an eight-inch-thick PVC tube with a rope through the middle. It is all Mike and I together can do to lift the roller with the twenty couching sheets and hang it on the iron railing of the bridge gates for a few hours to let the bulk of the water drain out. After dinner, it still takes two to carry the load to the *chambre d'eau*, where I have clotheslines strung to hang the paper sandwiched between its couching sheets to dry slowly overnight. I start over again the next morning.

I love the rhythm of these long days. I am completely immersed in the sound and feel of water everywhere. On the bridge, the sound of the river, rushing over the rocks below, rises like an audible mirage against the roar of the three waterfalls in the background. Even in the room under the mill, the *chambre d'eau*, even when the sluice doors are shut tight, water leaks around the *vannes* from the reservoir behind the house and tings against the metal scoops, the echo of the falls muffled by the thick walls. I'm always soaked to the skin and don't care since it's so warm, the roadbed of the bridge is swamped with runoff from the couching sheets, and the springs that pop out of the cliff at the end of the bridge are all either rinsing or soaking something. Time flies by in the soggy here-and-now!

The show goes up the 25th of July and I'm down to mass banner production and mechanical problem solving. The solving of installation dilemmas adds layers of complexity that only I can enjoy, but nonetheless it triples the pleasure and the confidence with which I present the work. I always enjoy this part because I try to resolve problems based on the original symbolism of the whole piece. For example, what do I use to provide the counterweight to keep the banners in the air? The easy answer was cleats on the floor, but when one starts to speculate on exactly what it is that holds up our personal house of cards, things get interesting. In my head right now I've got four to six galvanized pails hanging from the rods, but off the ground with enough of "something" inside to keep the whole thing from crashing down. I've been surveying friends and family on what holds up their personal *château de cartes*. So far, from over fifteen people I've gotten virtually the same response: family, health, friends, integrity, meaningful work, faith in the future, the arts.

Today, the whole project is at the point where I don't know how in the world I ever thought something as stupid as this would ever be considered worthy of hanging in the first place. So I must be close to being done!

—*Hugs, Judy*

June 25, 1999
Dear Linda,

I dropped Richard Berger off in Toulouse last Tuesday, picked up some short-timers the same day, took them back on Saturday, and picked up Kay Bradner (painter and photogravurist) the same hour. We've had too much peripheral company this year, some invited, others not. If you are talking to someone about going to Chicago, and they say, "Oh, I have a friend there, you should look her up. You'd love her," you'd nod and change the subject. Right? But when someone we barely know is talking to someone we don't know at all, they feel free to say, "Oh, you're going to France. You should go see some friends of ours, they live in the south of France somewhere, I'll give you the address," thinking, "Oh well, they'll never call anyway. I never do." Not only do people take the address, they sometimes plan their trip accordingly!

Occasionally, the friend will tell us they gave someone our phone number, hope you don't mind, etc., they'll never call. Wrong, we get people dropping in, usually at mealtime, whom we've never met and whom we'd never want to meet, and we then spend a week in an afternoon trying to be polite for the sake of our "friend." And too often people whom we don't know well or whom I wouldn't be able to tolerate for more than a dinner out somewhere will invite themselves: "I'll be in France this summer, I'd love to see your place. We could sandwich it in the week before we go to blah, blah, blah." I usually back away saying, "Yes, let's talk." Or I ask the dates and say, "What a shame, we'll be hiking in the Pyrenees that week," whether we are or not.

If I'm sounding inhospitable, I am: we often have three artists a summer, each staying for a month at a time, interspersed with a week of invited friends here and there, and we love it, if we know them and have invited them. But we also cherish our time alone together, needing to recharge, to spend more time with French friends and each other before we then go full force into another long visit.

A particularly prickly acquaintance (from whom I had backed away when he offered to come and stay with us) sent me an e-mail last month, asking us to invite a couple of young artists he knows who are studying in Bordeaux for the summer for a long weekend "so they can relax!" Does that seem cheeky or am I just on my progesterone cycle? I sent him our schedule for June and July and said more politely then I felt, "I hope you can understand why we don't entertain people we don't even know!" I never heard from him after that. But you, you are always invited.

Back to work.

—*Hugs, Judy*

July 26, 1999
Dear Linda,

I hung the banners last Saturday with Bernard *pierre*, which is always a mixed experience. We've worked together now for six years on many complicated projects, so he's like an old dance partner. It takes a while to learn the new steps, but we usually hit a rhythm and relax and enjoy the process. He climbed around the rafters hanging hooks and stringing pulleys, talking to himself, the ladder, the pulleys, the drill: "*Putain, la vache*"—literally, "You whore and cow," but in the vernacular they're the equivalent of the "*f*" and "*s*" words. And Bernard takes them to new heights of meaning, depending on the tone of voice, sometimes sweet and persuading and other times full of threat and violence as he slams the offender to the floor. Saturday, given that he was twenty feet in the air, he didn't resort to throwing, just more and more subtle tonalities, adding a few *merdes* from time to time. Meanwhile, I crawled on my hands and knees through literal pigeon shit on the floor (there are huge holes in the ceiling and no windows in the top floor or the belfry), marking cables and screwing cable clamps to the side poles.

I had had Pierre, our metal-working neighbor, cut four 15-foot lengths of 1 1/2-inch steel rod for the side bars, calculating that we would not be able to walk them up the narrow circular staircase but that we could pass them up through the six-foot paned window from the courtyard below. The long, rusting fastener on that window is original, the handle a locking, turning bolt structure forged at least five hundred years ago. What I didn't know was the fasteners haven't worked for five hundred years either, and the windows wouldn't open. Now it was my turn with the *putains* and *la vaches*. (It's funny how vulgar words in a foreign language are not shocking to the nonnative speaker. I have, by accident or on purpose, interjected several in polite conversation.

Depending on the listener, I either got a hysterical knee-slapping laugh, or a shocked look and a wagging finger. I guess we never had the look of horror from our mother that would have burned those words onto the no-no list.)

Fortunately, when Bernard isn't mad at himself for problems, he's incredibly patient. He got on the ladder and jimmied the fastener ever so gently until the layers of rust finally gave way, the window sighed open, and the rods passed through. We left the window open while I connected the rods with some couplers to make the resulting side bars each thirty feet long. After I had attached the fasteners on the rods and the hooks for hanging the banner/clothes lines, we passed the cords through the pulleys and attached the rods. We hoisted up the hanging structure without the banners first to make sure it worked, then after much measuring, marking, grunting and nose-to-nose discussion (we always have at least one disagreement, which in the telling leaves Mike slapping his knee in glee over our ritual pastis back at the mill), we attached the banners—all fifty-four of them, six in a row, nine rows three feet apart with little metal clips by the top two corners. We hauled it up slowly and tied the whole *Château de cartes* up in the air awaiting its counterweights the next day. It is stunning, if I do say so myself. Fifty-four 12-foot cards/banners, or 648 feet of thin hand-cast paper with odd watermarks on each, some slightly frayed, some with slight tears, swaying in the wind from the open window.

The next day, I hung the galvanized pails, four on each side, to the lines coming out of the pulleys in the ceiling, the other ends of which are attached to the bar. I put enough sand in the buckets on one side and salt on the other to actually balance the weight of the two 30-foot steel rods, the steel cable/clothes line, and the fifty-four cards. The lower ends of the banners are about shoulder height, and to get to the other end of the room, one must walk through them, brushing against the wispy pointed ends of the banners. The pails hang below, about three feet off the splintering wood floor. I was surprised by how little weight it took to keep the whole business high in the air, less than two pounds of either salt or sand, fundamentals of life, in each pail, a total of only sixteen pounds in all.

Bernard went back up the twenty-foot ladder and put stops on the pulley lines so no one could bring the structure down, but I could still pull on the buckets and raise the banners above the tables for the medieval dinner planned for the end of the month. We darkened the windows and put five large spots shining from below. I then put three

fans on the floor of the entry side of the room, pointed low toward the floor. I put them and the lights on motion detectors so that when someone enters the room, the lights go on and the fans start to push the air down the long room against the back wall. It takes about fifteen seconds for the draft to hit the far wall and ricochet back against the hanging panels of thin paper. The banners all begin to move slowly forward together in that first gesture of a waltz. When the viewer moves into the wind of the fans, the air is deflected and each banner starts a slightly different slow dance, moving to the whim of its own breeze.

The opening, or *vernissage*, was yesterday and I'm still recovering. In the true French fashion of an art opening, first the mayor of Coupiac spoke, then the head of the department of culture for the Aveyron, and then I gave a short presentation about the piece. Need I say this was all in French? The mayor's comments were predictably kind, and the president of the Ministre de Culture d'Aveyron gave me a nice, warm critique and invited me, again, to show at the exhibition space in Rodez. There was a woman from Cahors who has a gallery, and she asked me to show there next year. I told her I would get back to her next month. I'm not sure galleries are the right place for me. They're a little too neat for my projects, and they actually expect to sell something. Since my projects are more about the space and too large to be collected, I tend to prefer dilapidated exhibition places. And I care more about the reaction of ordinary people than those accustomed to "art speak," which I find not only inane, but frustrating. I like to stand in the corner and observe as people enter the room, never thinking about buying or owning anything.

So net/net, I feel quite satisfied with the whole thing. It profoundly changed the room, it makes everyone stop and wonder why the hell someone would bother to do that, and it gave me some confidence that I can do a rather monumental project. It's still a little on the pretty side . . . but I'm workin' on getting ugly . . . trust me.

—*Hugs, more later, Judy*

July 27, 1999

JOURNAL ENTRY

The lights stay on for about three minutes if there's no movement in the *grande salle*. The fans stop, and the long, thin slips of paper sag into their patient hang. The holes in the ceiling above are dark, and the plaster that's left on the back wall looks even more decrepit in the dim light from the hall through the open door. Sounds echo up the circular staircase as groups of tourists stomp up the stone steps into the entry hall. They are coaxed into the dark room by the guide, who stands smiling, waiting for their reaction as the lights flash on, the air begins to dance, and the surprised guests respond: "*Ohhh. Quelle beauté! Elles bougent!*" Someone, me again, is standing in the corner, arms crossed, just observing. I had added a sign that said "*Touchez-les, s'il vous plaît*," ("Touch them, please"); if not, no one would have dared stroke the banners as they passed through them to the end of the room to finish their tour of the château.

SUMMER'S END

August 29, 1999
Dear Linda,

I reluctantly took Kay Bradner back to the airport after a month's stay in La Ruche. She's been a professor for years, had her own fine-print shop, and is now in high demand by some big-name artists to help them with their printmaking. But mostly she's a painter, a wonderful craftsman, but also a sensitive and emotive renderer of everyday things/people/life.

Having serious artists working on projects is energizing, instructive, and intimidating. But Kay was pure inspiration. She was up painting at seven in the morning, and the last cap went on the tubes after 11 p.m. She was fascinated by the openings in old walls, windows, doors, and abandoned frames, the light cast by the shadows of the thick walls, the play of shadow in the dark spaces. She loved my small tool collection and drew and photographed it in every possible light. She painted the water in the stream and the changes in the waterfall when we opened the *vannes*. She wanted to make bread from our flour, to drive off in the Twingo and get lost for hours. (She often ended up in some farmer's kitchen snapping beans with madame, carrying on perfectly with her two-month-old French vocabulary.) She rolled around in the pigeon shit on the château floor with me, taking pictures of the banners from below and above. She coached Mike through some blockages in his painting and offered well-developed critiques when asked. She will be missed.

We spent the week with Bernard *pierre* putting more money into *la cave maudite*. I call it accursed, since everything we do to make it better for the wine seems to make it worse. As you remember, we started out by digging out an old cellar under the main part of the house, through which passes a water tunnel. Even with the chute closed, a small amount of water trickles through, and after a year, we realized it was too humid to keep the labels from sliding off our ever-increasing supply of wine. With the bounty from Les Magnolias, we have a substantial investment to protect, so we've been putting in drains, false walls, and then . . . yes . . . an air conditioner. I thought we needed a dehumidifier, but the monsieur at the plumbing and heating said, "*La clim, c'est la meme chose*." But an air conditioner isn't the same as a dehumidifier, I don't care what Mike says. And isn't a cave supposed to keep things cool?

By now the lovely stone walls are hidden behind stuccoed bricks since we had to put in a French drain, the little stream runs under heavy stone pavers, the ceiling has a layer of blue Styrofoam since the in-the-floor furnace above was heating the wine cave below, and a compressor howls every few minutes to keep the temperature below boiling as the summer sun hits the face of the mill with blinding heat. Each bottle will have cost us a fortune by the time we're through. I told Mike the best solution was to get all our wino friends over and get into some serious drinking.

As I write, Bernard *pierre* and his wife's son, Titi, are crashing around downstairs trying to block the biggest holes in these old walls against *les loirs*, since the cute little guys have moved back in after a few years hiatus. A few minutes ago. Bernard took Mike's six-foot millworks painting down to slop some mortar in the holes to the attic, and he woke up one of those cutie-pies who had built a huge nest behind the painting. The terrified dormouse was running around the edge of the painting trying to find a safe exit, while Bernard kept turning it from side to side to keep him from jumping while he shouted at Titi, "*Tue-le, tue-le!*" Bernard was pointing with his head toward the broom leaning against the wall, demanding that Titi kill the round-eared creature. At the same time, Titi was shouting, "*J'peux pas, j'peux pas!*" as he couldn't bring himself to smash that adorable little animal.

Meanwhile, I ran down the stairs to see what was going on, and Bernard, now in the middle of the living room, still turning the painting around and around with the terrified *loir* racing on it from end to end, turned to me: "*Tue-le, Judite, tue-le!*"

"*J'peux pas, non plus!*" I couldn't do it either, so I opened the door to the front terrace. Bernard, disgusted with us both, charged out the door to the edge of the terrace near the river, held the painting up high with the *loir* clinging to the top, and flipped the frame as hard as he could, sending the dormouse, fluffy tail and all, twenty feet into the air. With a tiny plop he dropped into the river and disappeared downstream, probably to resurface *chez* Brigitte. With Bernard *bof, bof, boff*ing his disgust at us both, Titi went back to work and I ran up the stairs, heart pounding, to finish this letter. *La fin.*
—Bises, Judy

September 18, 1999
Dear Linda,

We just arrived back at the mill after five days with friends in Venice and eight days hiking in the Swiss Alps. Venice was Venice: unbelievably, outrageously, baroquely, extravagantly beautiful. We did the Biennale and more damn churches and saw lots of nice, safe contemporary art followed by stunning Bellinis, gigantic Titians, Tiepolos, the whole, well, Venetian school. We've been going every two years for the Biennale, and this time we ran into some nasty people. A man followed Marianna (yes, the same from the Marianna and Carole collaboration) and me around the park among the works, hassling us in broken English about how arrogant Americans are and how we shouldn't be allowed to be there. Either the anti-American thing has taken on more momentum or we were just in the wrong place at the wrong time, but in any event we were frightened enough to get the hell out of there. I know it exists in France, and the better our French the more aware we are, but our friends either don't talk about it, or think we're just different.

Mike, whom I've never seen even cross with anybody, almost got into a fistfight at the local market when the vendor accused us of touching the mushrooms, being ugly Americans, etc. The man was so angry he knocked over his own mushroom stand, and a few people started to help by picking them up. I think Mike shouldn't have pointed out, somewhat sarcastically, that people were touching the mushrooms and the vendor wasn't yelling at them. In any event, we took off before it came to blows. Everyone needs to see Venice once—four days is just right, but wear bad shoes and too much makeup and speak Spanish, or anything but American English. I've never experienced anything like that kind of hostility, ever, in France, or in any other part of Italy for that matter.

We then went off for eight days of four- to six-hour hikes in the Engadine Valley in the Swiss Alps. Because of the potential for vertical climbs, hikes are mapped by time, not distance, as it can take two hours to go only a little way. We started out on the last day with a "cakewalk" of two hours and only a three-hundred-foot climb, or so we thought. Somehow we zigged when we should have zagged and ended up going two thousand feet straight up and around a promontory that, when I saw it again from below, I thought was impossible. Good thing I didn't know and just kept putting one foot in front of the other. I've learned one thing: I can do just about anything if I do it slowly enough. We didn't do any steep rock-climbing alpine trails, mostly because I'm chicken and "Mike's been sick, you know." He did get light-headed on one trail, but I think it was low blood sugar. We took a couple of days to adjust before we headed out just to be sure, and he felt great the whole time.

I met with Noémie Delorge, the Cahors gallery owner yesterday. She has a rather small gallery in a vaulted room under her nice, high-quality bookstore called Calligramme; the name comes from a collection of poems by Apollinaire, the Surrealist poet. The typography of his poetry often takes on an image mirrored in the poetry. Words become image. As you know, I like that transformation stuff, and almost everything I've done at some level is about transformation: millers' tools to artists' devices, plain lamps to animated artists' works, medieval banners to a deck of cards. The month of sightseeing and hiking was leading me away from any more "pretty" paper stuff, but when confronted with a vaulted gallery space underneath an elegant bookstore, what's a girl to do?

So I experimented with some poems in actual paper fibers on top of a partially formed sheet, still twelve feet long, and cast more pulp on top. The words distort a bit and become an integral part of the finished paper, and are even slightly legible if done just right! Unfortunately, they're still pretty. I thought maybe I could make some panels, like vertical venetian blinds, that would slowly separate and come together (with a little motion-detector rig) so that each panel would be its own thing but form a larger poem when lined up together. You know, words become paper become image and back? And were I to make more large lamps with lettered pages, would they be reading lamps?

We met with the "art commission" of the château in Coupiac and decided that for next summer, 2000, we are going to invite all the people who have ever had a show there to make a site-specific piece for a summer-long exhibition. As for us, the studios are packed up and we're on our way home for the winter.

—*Hugs, Judy*

February 25, 2000
JOURNAL ENTRY

Photos of the valley surrounding La Pilande Basse have to be corrected to lessen the green or nobody would believe them. The shadows of the trees, still long, point down the hills in the morning, and the green in their puddled shapes is a dark forest/kelly wash, while the tops of the hills are yellow/chartreuse. At noon, the shadows at their feet are fuzzy and bunched, as if the trees had stepped out of their half-slips, the better to present their naked forms to the rays of the early setting sun. And why are the borders around the fields and the leafless trees and shrubs purple? If there were a bit more yellow in them they would be brown, like they should be. I used to think the yellow had been used up by the chartreuse tinge outlining the hills, but now I think there's a competition between the fields and the trees: Who can present the most outrageous color?

The new front door (Bernard *bois* built a French door to let more light in on the dark contours of the chestnut-wood oil press) opens easily into the dark mill room, and the mixed smells of closed-up fireplaces and musty dried spices still hanging from the beams creeps into jet-lag-tired brain cells, sparking memories. After seven years, the mill just smiles at our efforts to push nature back from its stones, to reclaim its paths, to reopen the millrace, to shoo out the spiders sleeping in dusty, sagging webs in the windows. Having cranked open the main gate, Mike stands, arms crossed, while the water slides down the chute, hits the end, sends a small wave back toward the middle, fills to the edge, hesitates, and then jumps/flows down into the reservoir below. The water is clear from the cold winter rains, misting the air for last year's vegetables still poking through the weeds in the garden. Elsewhere, primulas and daffodils, unafraid of frost and foggy mornings, are pushing their way through the dense soil. We're back.

March 14, 2000
Dear Linda,

The weather has been gorgeous . . . almost too gorgeous. The fruit trees are starting to bloom, and it's at least six weeks too early, which means they will undoubtedly get hit by a frost. *"C'est pas normal."* Have you noticed that the weather's never "normal"?

Les Magnolias is still closed, and according to Bernard *bois*, who is doing some windows for the new German owner, Karl, they are doing a decent job of restoring the building. Unfortunately, Karl speaks no French and has no intention of learning, counting on his harem of three girlfriends to run the place. Apparently, they all live together, or at least the locals would like them to just for a few vicarious thrills. (Since the woman from Le Carassier left her husband and then he died, there haven't been too many exciting extramarital affairs, or much excitement in general.) According to Suzie, who's not prone to gossip, Karl is very handsome, smokes huge cigars, and likes the ladies very much. I don't care, just so he does a good job on Les Magnolias.

We had dinner with the Blancs last night, and Martou made her first relatively low-fat dinner for Mike: noodle soup with beef broth, cabbage, rice, and tomatoes; monkfish in parchment with lemon, onions, and white wine; and a *clafoutis* with just a few eggs. This was a huge effort for her, given the menu two years ago was pâté, sausage-stuffed potatoes, duck legs, cheese, and apple tart. Germain's hearing is getting so bad he turns to me when Mike speaks—I guess I shout louder. Martou, still a hypochondriac, now at least stops when she loses her audience, which is quickly. I do need to learn not to say, *"Comment tu vas?"* We toddled down the hill afterward, arms full of *pastèques*, whatever that is. The dictionary says watermelon, the skin on it says watermelon, but the flesh thereof is yellow and inedible. I'm supposed to make *confiture* or some preserved thing. Remember Grandma's watermelon rind pickles? They were awful, weren't they? I expect this/these will end up in our compost along with the chard.

My other news is that I'm going to Morocco tomorrow for ten days! Two days ago, I went up to Cahors to revisit the gallery where I have a show in June, and while I was there Noémie Delorge, the woman who runs the gallery, asked me if I thought she was crazy to drive to Marrakech and back by herself. I told her, "Yes, I do think you're crazy, but I'll go with you!" That came out of my mouth with no thought whatsoever.

"Super!" she shouted. We are going to be hosted by a couple, she French, he

Moroccan, in his natal village to celebrate the Eid al-Fitr, whatever that is. The French wife wants her son, Pierre (what else?), to go to school in France, and since she's from Cahors, where Noémie lives, Noémie will sponsor him. Mike reminds me that I don't know Noémie at all, that two women alone in a Muslim country isn't smart, and that we don't have enough time to do our homework. We have no idea what the festival is, or even how far we have to drive. Sounds like a good time!

—*Bisous, Judy*

JUDY AND NOÉMIE VISIT MOROCCO

March 30, 2000
Dear Linda,

I'm still trying to distill all the input from a ten-day whirlwind trip to Morocco. So, here it is . . . stream of consciousness. As you know I decided at the last minute to drive there with a woman I had just met, but after eight thousand kilometers in a car in ten days, I do now: Noémie, a dark-haired, elegant, stubborn French-trim woman in her early fifties. She had been invited by a French/Moroccan couple, Dram and Anne-Marie, to stay in the tiny mountain village where Dram was born to participate in some festival, and then she wanted to visit some artists' studios for potential shows in her gallery.

With only three days' notice, we left Cahors at five in the morning, after a strong coffee and one last good croissant, and drove straight through to Granada, Spain, in sixteen hours. We talked about art, government financing of exhibitions, French literature, families, makeup, and diet—normal stuff. (Since Morocco was a French protectorate, and higher education was always in French, nobody spoke English, so *on n'a parlé que français* the entire trip.) The next morning, we caught the first ferry across the Strait of Gibraltar, intending to arrive in Tangiers about nine in the morning. The ferry, which normally holds two or three hundred cars and trucks and has banks and restaurants, was almost completely empty. There were three cars and two trucks, and no food, no money exchange, no one to explain to us what festival was happening. When we arrived in Tangiers, the normally crowded port was empty, and the customs officer, a scar-faced man with a snarly half-grin, took Noémie into the building with her car's papers, leaving me to guard the luggage from the few odd men who were wandering the docks. I locked the doors when the first dirty face pressed up against the window, showing missing teeth in slightly deranged smile. To avoid looking frightened, I was reading a guide book on the importance of women not being alone in Morocco except at markets, and how one needed to pay a "guardian" to watch your car so it wouldn't be vandalized by the guardian. In other words, extortion.

Noémie had been gone quite a while, and I was starting to panic. Do I stay with the car or do I try to find her? Finally, after forty-five minutes, she ran to the car, quite flustered, jumped into the driver's seat, and took off across the empty parking lot of the port. She had bribed the customs official, but she wasn't sure it was enough!

"Look up *pot-de-vin* in the guide book," she said.

We were, of course, speaking French, and while my vocabulary has greatly improved in the past seven years, I didn't know what the hell she was saying. Noémie, it turns out, is a shouter, so louder and louder she cried, "*Regarde pour l'extorsion!*" Finally we both burst out laughing at the absurdity of the situation: reading the instruction manual on how to bribe someone.

Still giggling, we pulled out of the docks onto the main streets of Tangiers, which were strangely deserted. Just when we thought there was no one there, we spotted several men, covered with blood, with huge butcher knives in their hands, wandering through the dusty streets. Terrified, we imagined the worst: civil war, ethnic cleansing, mass murder? We rushed through the deserted streets, desperately trying to find the road to the coast. Then, on the outskirts of the city, we drove into a cloud of smoke, and the smell of burning hair filling the car. Then, through the haze, on the sidewalk, we saw a huge pile of sheep heads, the feet roasting nearby on rusty barbecues. More men, also clad in blood-covered white robes, waved their butcher knives at us with tooth-gapped smiles. All of my worst nightmares about Tangiers had been completely surpassed.

We decided to take the autoroute in spite of not having any money in dirhams. Nothing was open, not banks or even hotels, but we figured they'd have to let us pay somehow. The road was four divided lanes, smooth and well marked, the white beaches of the Atlantic on the right with an occasional camel sauntering through the sand, and white/red hills with a border of cork trees on the left. The road was lined with fences like one might see between San Francisco and Sacramento, except the fencing was to keep the sheep, men, and goats that lined the road from entering the forests that stretched for miles. Every big rock had a child sitting on it, staring without expression at the occasional car that passed.

Already shaken by bloody knives in Tangiers, we read the part of the guide book that warned visitors about armed youths forcing traffic stops and stealthily dropping hashish into cars in order to turn you in to the police (who then demand you pay them, and they in return reward the hoodlums), so we refused to stop for anything. We couldn't even stop to *faire pipi* since there was always a man every hundred yards or so the entire length of the trip, usually alone, watching the cars on one side and the sheep on the other. And when we tried to stop to take a picture of the Atlantic beaches with their camels, a dozen boys appeared from nowhere, pulling on the camera strap and frightening us back into the car. Donkeys with huge double baskets overloaded with hay, water, or babies, and someone riding sideways and kicking with each step, were everywhere.

For the next twelve hours, we drove down the spine of Morocco talking about cultural differences, art and its role in international understanding, skin care products, my upcoming show, anything to make the time pass. We did not know that Eid al-Fitr was one of the biggest festivals of the year, where every family returns to their place of birth, breaks a long fast by the men slaughtering a sheep, and the family gorges themselves until the sheep is gone.

Following our map, after hours on the road we pulled off the main highway onto a dusty dirt road that began to climb, bump, and narrow into the foothills of the Atlas Mountains. At 10:30 p.m., we finally pulled up to the entrance of the village, its red adobe walls reflecting in the headlights. With our tires banging against the deep ruts in the road/path, we congratulated ourselves on surviving two thousand miles in two days.

Dram, the Moroccan half of the couple, was there with his son to meet us, along with the entire village of three hundred people. Inside the village walls, they had been celebrating in the square with performances by the returning university students satirizing the fundamentalist extremists who didn't agree with not letting thirteen-year-old girls be forced into marriage. They finished just as we stepped through the village gate, and their strange, primitive Berber cries cut through the night, and then, slowly, the people turned from the stage toward us, still applauding and ululating. Dram stepped forward, applauding and laughing at the terrified look in our eyes.

Dram explained the performance to us later, as we sipped tea and nursed our clattering nerves. He told us about the Festival of the Sheep: the symbolic slaughtering of a lamb, which dates back to Abraham and is the equivalent in importance to Muslims as Christmas is to Christians. Every family kills at least one sheep, hangs it in their courtyard, and eats it in every imaginable way for four or five days until it disappears, hence the *Slaughterhouse Five* scenes in Tangiers. While I've actually participated in slaughtering a sheep (as you know), I've never slept with the carcass and watched it get hacked apart slowly until the immaculate white cloth that protected it from dust (NO flies to be seen) hung loosely over nothingness. (There's a metaphor in there somewhere.)

Dram was born in this village, Lalla Takerkoust, thirty kilometers south of Marrakech, and still maintains his family home, which is the only one with electricity and running water (I didn't say *hot* running water). His father died in an electrical accident when Dram was young, but his mother made sure he went through engineering school, which he did, becoming an expert in the transportation of explosives. His mother had expanded their household by taking in women who would otherwise have been abandoned in their culture when their husbands threw them out. While his mother died, there were still two women living there whom he called his aunts, Mahjouba and Jima.

Dram continued to support them financially, and their gratitude expanded to include us, his mysterious friends. Their henna-stained hands prepared breakfast, lunch, and dinner from lamb carved from the carcass hanging on the terrace. The first thing in the morning, Mahjouba, with a big tub of fresh soapy water, scrubbed out the accumulated dust (did I mention it was dry there?), and Jima threw buckets of rinse water, whisking the water out the door, the terrace drying in seconds. Then Jima would go off to their little garden to pick olives to add to the brining pot, and the mint and other greens that were served fresh with every meal. In the house, the women wore only a scarf over their hair, with elaborate silver pins to hold the scarf in place, and a long skirt and long-sleeved blouse, but in the streets another layer went on to cover everything, their black eyes shining above their hijab. They would smile sweetly when they saw me sketching, but language barriers were too great to communicate in words.

They started cooking at daybreak and didn't stop until well after the last mint tea was consumed at midnight. The kitchen was a tiny room for storing utensils, and all the chopping and cooking was done outside on the central terrace right next to the diminishing lamb. The meat was cooked over a ceramic pot with holes on the side to add charcoal. There was always a tajine simmering on that pot, and slight poofs of cinnamon and coriander mixed with slow-roasting meat escaped when the top was lifted to push meat into the accumulated juices. The women moved a small, low table from side to side in the court, depending on where the sun was, and squatted on low stools to prepare the food. The food was served on a huge platter, with the bread and fruit in bowls, and that was it. No plates to wash, no silverware to deal with, and the bread served both as napkin and serving implement.

Brochettes of barbecued lamb, warm pita bread drizzled with butter, honey, nuts, fresh-squeezed orange juice, coffee, mint tea—it just never stopped. If someone came by to visit, which they did every half hour, it started all over again. This time a cilantro/tomato salad, steamed lamb stuffed in bread pockets, a big bowl of fruit with several steak knives sticking out. Then curried lamb with carrots caramelized in a delicious sticky sauce, then a tajine of lamb, prunes, and roasted almonds, sweet with honey and bread from the same dough, only fresh from the village bread oven. Did you ever wonder what would happen if you ate nothing but lamb for three days, breakfast, lunch, and dinner? Sometime I'll tell you . . . but up close and personal. I picked some mint and even it smelled like lamb.

Noémie and I had our own small room, with a comfortable mattress on a simple frame. There was a small bathroom with a toilet in the middle of the room under a lamp bulb hanging from a wire from the ceiling. A tiny corner sink dribbled enough cold water for brushing teeth and a simple wash-up, but serious bathing was done in the village hamman, which we were not invited to see. The water came from a cistern on the roof, and was used sparingly.

In the afternoon we toured the tiny village, which consisted of about forty houses, most with simple cement floors, a courtyard, and for this weekend, a dead lamb hanging in the middle of it. We went into the community bread oven building with Dram's aunt, who had been carrying a large wicker basket as she led us around. When we entered, the heat from the open wood-fired stove was a welcome relief from the chilly March air. The walls were lined with baskets similar to Dram's aunt's, and every few minutes the baker would reach up with his long wooden paddle and bring one down, flip a large wad of dough onto the paddle, and toss it into the oven, then return the empty basket to its place on the shelves, all in one smooth gesture. He paused to smile shyly at us, covering his tooth-gapped grin with his hand. He bent over slightly and touched his hand to his head, then reached for another basket, this time tossing a freshly baked loaf into it.

We did the whole tour of the village in twenty minutes, stopping to admire the lush winter gardens of fresh mint and the lemons hanging low on small trees. There was a ditch with water running through it, which was communal, coming from a reservoir about twenty kilometers in the hills, presumably used to water the small garden plots around the houses.

While we found the village hospitable, we were anxious to get into a city, and fortunately, we had Dram to take us to the souk in Marrakech. Noémie and I walked huddled together, Dram close behind, as we entered the vast, dimly lit market with its miles of small, dark alleys lined with tiny stalls full to the canvas roof with spices, sandalwood carvings, and leather everything, including babouches, or pointy little house slippers. There were blacksmiths next to spice grinders, their smoke and perfume hanging low over the market. Dram, just to prove his value, would drop behind us from time to time, leaving us two women alone, then heroically reappear to chase away the aggressive vendors pulling on our sleeves and the kids hawking their wares.

As we two women walked arm-in-arm through the maze, trying to look casual, we had the sensation of getting smaller and smaller, pulling toward each other for protection. Noémie said she felt like she was looking through a fish-eye lens, the swarthy, often scarred faces of the vendors seeming bigger than they were, and the mountains of merchandise seeming poised to tumble at once from high shelves, creating an avalanche of ceramic barbecues, cone-shaped tajine pots, brass and copper plates, teapots, swords, exotic medicines, and metal brochettes creating clouds of orange-red paprika and tarnished-yellow turmeric and waves of green and black olives.

We were relieved to find ourselves back at the edge of the market, where snake charmers and henna artists were set up on woven mats. I started to take a picture of a beautiful young woman with lacy patterns of burnt sienna covering her entire face when Dram reached over and took my camera, just as the seemingly tranquil lady jumped to her feet snarling and trying to do the same. Dram gave her a dirham and pulled me toward the car, explaining the importance of asking and paying for an artist's work. I've often felt like a stranger in France, but never have I witnessed there the hatred in that woman's eyes, not because I was an American, but because I didn't understand.

We spent a few days in Agadir on the Atlantic coast, where Dram and Anne-Marie live and work. It's a large, relatively modern, industrial city, without much architectural charm, but the vast beaches, with loaded camels lurching back and forth on the sand, lent an otherworldliness to the otherwise dull buildings. Dram and Anne-Marie had arranged for us to stay in a friend's apartment, not far from their house and very close to the beaches. While Anne-Marie went off to the French school she runs and Dram went off to dynamite something, Noémie and I did some serious souking.

We went with Fatima (what else?), their housekeeper, who helped us negotiate the alleys through tons of spices, olives, pots, pans, clothing, metalworkers, letter writers, and snake charmers. She helped us buy an overabundance of spices, putting handfuls in small plastic bags and telling us to mix them together back home, then roast them, grind them, and toast them in oil in the pan before we add the vegetables or whatever. She wasn't sure I knew what the patterns for henna tattoos really were, but helped me negotiate ten sheets down to about a dime. And we finally found the large, flat ceramic plates that Mahjouba had used to make bread. We also visited several artists' studios and found some interesting work for Noémie to show in the future.

Dram picked us up for lunch the first day and took us to an open-air restaurant on the beach for some more real Moroccan food. *Open-air* means a large terrace on stilts with a palm roof, next to a cement block building with no windows, just a large chimney in the middle, which was belching sweet-smelling *je ne sais quoi*'s. Other than the parked cars, there was no sign from the front that it was a restaurant.

We entered the cement building directly into a large kitchen with a six-by-five-foot fire pit in the middle of the space, mostly contained by three brick waist-high walls. Most of the smoke was going out the chimney above, but some of it filled the rest of the space so that it was hard to see what was happening. The grates over the fire held about fifteen tajines, their contents hidden by their cone-shaped lids. There was also a variety of meats and vegetables cooking directly over the fire, and a large pot for cooking couscous. A shy woman shuffled over, and Dram talked to her quietly in Arabic. She led us to the fire pit and, with the edge of her apron, one at a time lifted off the lids of three of the tajines. The smells of roasted chicken, lamb, dates, and peppers with cinnamon, cardamom, turmeric, and coriander all burst out together.

In response to our *ahhh*'s, Dram picked up a piece of chalk from the edge of the brick wall and chalked a distinct mark on the side of the tajines, making sure it went from both the top and the bottom. We then went into a dark corner of the kitchen where another small, igloo-shaped oven, its opening at floor level, was glowing and smoking. An old woman sitting on the cement floor kneading dough smiled in recognition when she saw Dram. He gave her two French-style *bisous* and held up his thumb and two fingers, again French style, to order three of whatever she was making. She reached over to a large flat basket covered with a strikingly clean cloth, pulled back the linen, and pinched off a large hunk of dough, deftly shaped three fist-sized balls, flattened them on a large wooden paddle, and tossed them on the loose flat stones on the bottom of the oven.

I wanted to stay and watch, but Dram herded us out the back door, into the fresh sea air, and up the stairs to a table on the raised deck. A waiter scurried over with a water pitcher and some paper towels for napkins. Dram waved his finger no, and in a few minutes the waiter reappeared with a water bottle, which Dram insisted on opening, after inspecting the cap's screw top. When our tajine arrived, he likewise inspected them, then turned to show us the chalk marks. "How else do you know you'll get what you ordered?" The flatbreads arrived shortly after, which were to serve as our utensils as well as our napkins. But before we could rip and dip, Dram turned each loaf over and inspected the slightly charred bottom. "Ah ha," he exclaimed as he pulled off one of the flat oven stones stuck to the crust, "at least they're sterile."

The food was spiced to perfection, enhanced by the smoky crust of the bread, and the sea breezes salted the conversation, which mostly focused on the sorry plight of the women in the kitchen below. Dram obviously felt ashamed of a culture that relegates divorced or widowed women to the most menial jobs, or worse, prostitution. He explained that he and Anne-Marie had helped to start a women's cooperative, where they gather argan nuts and make an expensive cooking oil exported mostly to France. Anne-Marie was to take us there the next day. When he said this, I noticed an odd eye exchange between Noémie and Dram, which set my feminine radar spinning rapidly. Later that night, back in our private apartment, I quizzed Noémie about Dram and why we hadn't seen much of Anne-Marie, and she told me that they were separated. And while she and Anne-Marie had been friends and colleagues in Cahors before Anne-Marie married Dram, Noémie admitted that she couldn't help it: she had a *faiblesse* for him. *"Qu'est-ce qu'on fait?"* ("Whatta ya gonna do? A crush is a crush.")

We did go inland the next day with Anne-Marie, driving through the rugged desert up into the foothills. We passed wind-sculpted adobe houses, children sitting on rocks watching the road and a few goats, some of which were up in the branches of the few scrubby trees, eating the only green foliage to be seen. We also passed tacked-together shacks of corrugated metal, with plastic bags flapping over parched gardens, which Anne-Marie called *les bidonvilles* after the French word for a metal drum, often used as a building material in these shantytowns.

We finally pulled into a whitewashed brick compound, with a bright blue wooden gate that opened into a courtyard, its dry soil splashed with potted flowers. She led us through a door into a thirty-foot-square room ringed with women, all sitting on the floor with their long robes scrunched up around them and cradling a flat basketball-sized rock between their crossed legs. Each had two baskets at her knees, one filled with walnut-sized smooth nuts, the other filled with their kernels, with a flat stone and a pile of cracked shells in front. The women barely looked up as they pulled a nut from the basket and placed it on the flat stone, then smacked the nut sharply with a fist-sized rock. Most had at least one finger bandaged in white cloth from unexpected slips of the rock or nut. In a Western country, this would have been considered sweat-shop conditions, unbearable to watch, but Marie-Anne went around the room, telling us which had been saved from begging, thieving, or prostitution. We bought a lifetime supply of argan oil from the small bottling room next to the production space. The little mill that crushed the nuts and the press that extracted the oil were modern stainless-steel, in sharp contrast to the room next door.

Our last night in Agadir, Anne-Marie insisted that we all go out to eat at a proper French restaurant, also on the beach, not far from our apartment. Dram drove over to guide Noémie and me there in our car, and we parked in the only spot in the back parking lot while he parked on the street. Anne-Marie appeared after we had arrived. We had an uneventful meal, and I think everyone was anxious to get back to their respective places, since by now it was openly acknowledged that Anne-Marie and Dram were separated, as they discussed how their son would split his vacation time from school, first with her, then with him.

We left the restaurant together and stepped into the now-dark night to go to our cars. Thinking that by this time we could make our way on our own, Noémie and I decided to drive back to our apartment without Dram as a guide, over his objections. We walked behind the restaurant to our parked car, got in, and were backing out when a man stepped in front of the headlights and held up his hand, signaling "Stop." He was covered in blood, with cuts on his face and his hand literally dripping. He ran over to Noémie's window and started banging a bloody fist. We couldn't drive off without hurting him, and we were frozen with fear. Then, out of the shadows behind the restaurant stepped Dram. He strolled over, paid our "guardian" off, smiled and waved, and slipped back into the shadows. One needs an angel every now and then in Morocco.

Dram told us the next day that fighting, especially with knives, is a recreational pastime in Morocco, and cuts and scars are to be appreciated. Apparently, our bloody monster was just a guy who had decided to protect our car and felt that we were leaving without paying him. A serious no-no.

Finally, after a good education in what to do and not to do, Noémie and I drove off, alone, north along the coast for our return to Tangiers. We stayed one night in a whitewashed medieval fishing village called Essaouira, its blue shutters mirroring the sea to the west and holding back the desert to the east. Black silhouettes moved slowly along the cobbled streets, their elegant silk burqas billowing in the sea breeze, the veils protecting eyes and noses from the blowing sand. We even ventured into the medina, the old cobblestoned part of this medieval site. The people here were used to tourists, and as long as we weren't out after dark, we'd been told, we would not be hassled too much, which proved to be the case.

The next morning we pulled out early, determined to reach Tangiers that evening. For twelve straight hours, Noémie and I talked about our collective cultural ignorance, our religious intolerance, our husbands, children, French literature, American ingenuity, makeup, poverty, and diet, in no particular order. We finally arrived in Tangiers at eleven at night, and since only prostitutes are generally out after dusk, by now we knew that we had to be careful. I won't go into the beggars scratching at the windows, the men jumping in front of the car trying to stop us as we drove through the narrow streets of the medina.

Noémie was a literature professor before she became a gallery owner and was extremely taken with the romantic notion of staying at the hotel in the center of the city where Paul Bowles had lived and received like-minded literary drug users. We relaxed our knuckles as the gate of the Grand Hôtel Villa de France clanked behind us and nonchalantly paid our new "guardian" to watch our car, hardly noticing the Z-shaped scar running from his forehead to his chin. We entered the hotel stepping over a grungy dog, who gave a us a perfunctory growl and put his head back on his outstretched paws. There was one bare light bulb hanging over the reception desk, creating eerie shadows on the sagging face of the desk clerk. He wiped his flabby lips with the back of his hand, brushed the crumbs off the top of his bulging belly, and smiled a black-toothed sneering grin as his front gold cap blinked in the light. No, I'm not making this up.

"What can I do for you luscious ladies?" he said as he rubbed his chubby palms together.

My most basic instinct for survival kicked in and I nudged Noémie, "*Je ne reste pas ici, moi*." I wasn't sure where we'd go, but I wasn't going to stay there, Paul Bowles be damned.

Round-eyed, Noémie whisper/hissed, "*Mais, qu'est-ce qu'on fait maintenant?*"

I didn't know for sure what we were going to do, but I spoke out the side of my fake smile, "We're going to back out smiling, repay our guardian, and get out of here! You're going to drive us out of the medina, slowly, but we'll hit someone if we have to, then drive around until we find a taxi, I'll jump out and ask him to take me to a decent hotel, and you'll follow us!" It sounded easy.

We raced out of the hotel dragging our luggage behind us, bumping down the stairs, now in the dark. Noémie nudged me with her finger against her lips: "Those men have knives!" The scar-faced guardian, who had taken our money, was circling another man sumo style, both with knives drawn. We hurried toward our car, now parked close to the gate, and tossed in our bags. The desk clerk came out the front door and began yelling and shaking his fist at the two men in the parking lot. Using the commotion as cover, I sneaked over and opened the gate while Noémie slid the car behind a hedge, and we made our escape—back into the narrow streets of the medina, barely wide enough for one car to pass, pushing the crowd of night revelers aside. Fear straightened our backs and we refused to look at the sneering male faces and hands at the windows. We finally blasted out of the medina onto the wider streets of the modern city, still bustling with men. We drove around the main square until a taxi pulled beside us at a light. I jumped out, flagged him down, and asked him to take me to a tourist hotel. He asked me what we were doing out alone, and I was forced to explain our plight. He stared at me with a slight scowl and finally grunted, "Get back in the car with your friend and follow me."

We had no other choice but to trust him, so follow him we did, beyond the lights of the central city, down by the dimly lit wharfs, several miles along the beaches of North Africa. We were starting to get nervous when suddenly he turned right into the circular drive of the Atlas Rif Hotel and the welcoming bow and heel-click of a white-suited bellhop. Fifty-three dollars and a clean bed. When I tried to pay the taxi driver, he refused, saying he couldn't accept money from two women in distress. "Just don't go out alone again, hear?"

In the sixteen hours in the car from Tangiers to La Pilande Basse, Noémie and I talked about love and deception, incest and rape, fear for our daughters, how to tie scarves, and how to pronounce *frog* in French. Never have I spent ten days without speaking one word of English, and never will I be able to say *frog* in French correctly!

To summarize: spectacular countryside, unbelievable squalor around the big cities, warm, welcoming people in the mountain villages, strange and exotic markets, smells, and colors, scary men with lewd intentions. Sounds like everyone else's experience in Morocco, doesn't it? Did I mention the lamb?

—*Hugs, Judy*

CALLIGRAMME

March 31, 2000

JOURNAL ENTRY

I MUST focus on the show at Noémie's gallery. She was a literature professor before becoming a bookstore owner with an art gallery in the vaulted cave below. She is known for her literary excellence and her vast collection of art books, including biographies, photography, and essays, many quite esoteric.

So even though I am sick of making paper at this point, the place is, above all, a bookstore, so it is just logical to write a book and display it with the other books. If I were to make huge sheets of paper I could write something on them with the paper pulp, not so they can truly be read, but as wisps of thoughts, suggestions of profound thinking but not saying anything. And then I can make the paper into large lamps, reading lamps for a bookstore. Oh, this is the fun part. First, I have to prove I can actually write with the pulp, then find something worthwhile to NOT say!

April 15, 2000
Dear Linda,

I'm agonizing over the show at Noémie's that I have to hang in six weeks. *Panicking* is a better word. I was well into the project and not sleeping at all, which usually means it sucks. I got up this morning and threw out all the work I had done and started over.

I've found that I can take the cooked fibers that I would ordinarily beat into paper pulp, tear them finely, and write with them on a partially formed sheet of paper while it is still wet, then add a bit more paper slurry to the sheet to hold the words in place. The pressure from the drying process moves the word fibers around a bit, but in a natural way that makes the words slightly obscure and mysterious, the words almost becoming the page. I was welding together some predictable lampshades with the mysterious words on them—okay, hokey "reading lamps"—in a vain attempt to make something that someone might actually buy since I now know Noémie's gallery is in trouble. But I was letting our friendship, and my wish to make something that would sell well for her, get in the way of the creative process. Everything was wrong: the scale was wrong for the space, wrong for my pulp writing style, mostly wrong for my own stated values. In my original art school "manifesto," I said, first off, that I would not sell what I do. Noémie wants one of my installations, not because they're predictable and the components will sell, but because they are unpredictable, out of scale, and awkward to display in most homes, so I was letting her down as well as compromising my own manifesto! *À la poubelle*, into the trash it all went.

I started over, staying with the concept of an art book among art books, but decided I needed to write the book first, especially since every page takes two days to make and one to dry. I started with the place. The word *calligramme*, which Noémie has had made into a sign for the bookstore/gallery in scripted blue neon, comes from Apollinaire. (I had to memorize some of his poems in my French class, and only after copying and recopying them could I partly decipher their meaning. Even my professor, Paul Fournel, a relatively well-known French poet, called them dark, dense, and impenetrable.)

Apollinaire was one of the few of his generation who survived World War I, and he wrote thousands of these difficult pieces, each dedicated to yet another friend who didn't make it, works describing bodies with unseeing eyes, purple skin and no arms, images of gun smoke tamped down by streaks of rain, skies backlit with red from missile fire. He twirled the words into familiar forms, satirizing the content with civilian objects like pocket watches and neckties. I suppose I could rewrite his poetry in my fiber script, but that feels hollow and facile. How can I even pretend to feel what he felt? Mike and I often talk about great artists who struggled with their demons and wonder if we're not too happy to be artists. Maybe I'm just a spoiled brat who should be doing something else. Oh, the doubts are moving in. Must be time to get into the studio again.

—*Hugs, Judy*

April 30, 2000
Dear Linda,

Two new babies coming this summer, one in August and one in September. Mike will be going back early, and I'll follow after I take down three shows, including his.

I like this part of the project. Too late to rethink and second-guess. Not even enough time to do what I should be doing, but at this point, I can't do anything else except what I'm already doing. There will be a point where I call it "art."

I told you I threw out the precious little reading lamps and have settled into lamps so large they need at least two bases to hold the shades. One piece is more than 12 by 9 by 4 feet. Noémie saw the work in process last week and is thrilled. So I'm at least not totally panicked. She explained that she's actually curating the ancillary exhibitions associated with the international photography show, and they expect over a hundred thousand people to pass through the city in June. The whole place will be turned into installation/gallery spaces with light shows in the evening where they project modern buildings and images onto the old churches and châteaux. I think she came to see me to make sure I wouldn't embarrass her.

For the book among the books, I finally decided to rewrite my manifesto (the document one is required to write in art school that reflects your artistic values), only this time publish it in a huge format as a deconstructed book turned reading lamps, lamps to read, not read by. At the Toot I took the text and edited it into one-liners— some would say poetry—and printed each line on separate thin sheets so that when the stack was pressed flat you could read the whole poem, but when leafing through the bound document one page at a time, one phrase would be read alone, out of context, sometimes suggesting the opposite of the sense of the complete work. Kind of like everything I do.

So, I've rewritten that manifesto, in French, and am publishing it in this wandering three-dimensional book in a gallery in a bookstore. I am putting poeticized sections on the various free-floating pages, all, of course paraphrased, pounded into abstraction into the paper, the pages layered where appropriate. Apollinaire hid his blood and guts behind watch forms and smoking cigarettes, and I'm hiding mine inside the paper turned lamps, banners, and other pretty things. The only truly legible thing will be the preface to my manifesto, a quote by T. S. Eliot: "The chief use of the 'meaning' of a poem . . . may be . . . to satisfy one habit of the reader, to keep his mind diverted and quiet, while the poem does its work upon him: much as the imaginary burglar is always provided with a bit of nice meat for the house-dog so the burglar can go about his business." I love the concept of keeping the viewer occupied while I go about my business. Such a business!!

—*Hugs to you both, Judy*

June 15, 2000

JOURNAL ENTRY

In the front window, a 4-by-3-foot coarse-fibered object glowed in contrast to the somber bookstore behind. It could have been an old manuscript cover, but it was much too large. It stood on two separate lamp bases, which explained the glow, but not its presence. As one walked down the steps from the main level of the bookstore, the vaulted space radiated with a warm light. In the center of the space was a structure composed of three 12-foot lamps, each with a narrow rice-paper lampshade running from just above the cast cement base to the top. There were five soft bulbs inside each, which illuminated the room and ten 12-by-3-foot sheets of thin hand-cast paper, five on each long side of the 9-by-5-foot rectangle formed by this large piece. The pages were suspended like banners, with a swivel in the middle of the top edge that turned the thin sheets with the slightest current of air.

The rough text formed by fibers cast into the pages lent different meanings in motion, as the words were either backward or out of alignment with the nearest page. When still, the pages formed a solid surface with semi-legible writing, some clues

perhaps, to the entire piece. T. S. Eliot's comments on providing the reader enough information to bring him or her into a poem, like a burglar enticing the dog with a piece of meat, were the text. On the perimeter of the room, against the side walls, were more lamps with elongated shades with mysterious isolated words resembling giant books. They were all animated by motion detectors, which made them light up when approached and go dark when no audience was present. The large center piece with the pages that turned filled the vaulted space with a luminescent silence.

Noémie was pleased to leave the art books among the reading lamps/book, something to almost read surrounded by real books, each increasing the importance of the other. Claude, her husband and bookstore manager, said it was the best show they'd ever had. Noémie had arranged for the press to interview me, the museum director to give a special tour. Most artists are much better than I at explaining why they do what they do. I don't always seem to know until after I've made something exactly why I did it and have a hard time imagining that anyone would seriously care about the piece, so I stay silent, too, hoping I can replicate the quiet presence of the T. S. Eliot quote with the turning pages.

LIGHT WELL

June 15, 2000
Dear Linda,

I must be important, since I have three shows this year: Noémie's, a group show at the château in Coupiac (which Mike and I are curating with Jean-Michel), and I've been invited by the minister of culture for the Aveyron to show with twenty Aveyronnais artists, theoretically the *crème de la crème* as we say in English. I was stunned to be invited, since there are some sensational artists here. There will be a contemporary art conference at the Abbaye de Sylvanès, where important French art critics and all public officials involved in managing exhibition sites will be invited first for panel discussions, and then to see and comment on the work.

But while our art reputation grows bit by bit, our ability to show in our local château is all but kaput. Thanks to Julien. That's his name, just Julien, the new director at the Château de Coupiac. Or should I say "Sir Julien, *châtelain du Château de Coupiac*"? With his natty silk scarf wound around his neck, his slicked-down David Niven hair and mustache, he plays the role of the *seigneur*. He's working on a "new look" for the building by covering thirteenth-century scars with bits of twentieth-century fabric borrowed from Madame Creste, the sexy wife of the serious furniture maker in Coupiac, serious if you like oversized fake Mediterranean darkly stained wood with faux worm holes. Sadly for the village, the furniture factory is slowly going out of business, due to being completely clueless. Madame has graciously consented to put part of their showroom in the château, giving the company unlimited access to the three thousand visitors that pass through each year. Since she is on the board of directors and employs around thirty people from the village, nobody dares contradict her, and Sir Julien seems to have free rein. I wonder what else she's lending him?

Julien decided that tourists want to see a medieval building and not the "ridiculous" contemporary art shows that the château has been sponsoring for the last ten years, and is making it difficult for us to get our show hung. He refuses to take out the bales of straw that he dumped in the *grande salle* before setting up a preposterous long table using plywood and sawhorses covered by more of Madame Creste's textiles. He's presumably reenacting some anachronistic animal/human habitation or *chevalier* food-fighting arena. But it's painful to see the Bel furniture fabric samples covering lovely old wavy-glass windows, and fake Louis IV furniture in front of a fine plaster fireplace. There are loving-hands-at-home mannequins frozen in awkward gestures like scarecrows, with homemade medieval costumes draped on them, and glazed, wide-eyed looks on their faces. Julien even hung flowerpots out the tower windows. The château looks like someone's dignified grandmother who got painted up like a hooker while she was sleeping.

Since the building is only open to the public three months of the year, finding a full-time employee is difficult, and most of the work is done by the board of directors or volunteers like us or a young person right out of school who won't stay long. We can only hope Julien will follow the rest as quickly. Frankly, I can't imagine how he was hired in the first place. He's in his thirties and must have been quite desperate to accept a position in a tiny village in *la France profonde*. His wife, having seen the living conditions in the employee quarters in the attic of the château, pigeons and all, decided to stay in Lyon.

It's taking us twice as long to get the show together because of Julien, and in the meantime I've got to build something for my own entry, with two weeks to go. For the year 2000, our art commission at the château decided to invite every artist who had ever showed there to choose a spot in the building and make an *œuvre* for it. Since I'm on the commission, I decided to wait until everyone else had chosen their spot, and then I would take what was left over. I was shocked to learn that somebody else wanted the latrine tower, and every obvious wall or floor space was spoken for, so I needed to find a more obscure corner of the building.

I had often climbed up the circular stone stairs into the clock tower to stand dwarfed by the enormous mechanism that hisses and clinks the gears of the big white clock stuck unceremoniously and anachronistically in the late nineteenth century under the pointy roof of the tower. But the stairway going down had always been blocked by a flimsy rope with a red flag, so I decided to crawl under the line and go down, flashlight in hand, to see what might be below. The château, a fourteenth-century original, still has two of its four towers and the walls are intact, but the flooring and plaster haven't been touched in several centuries, a perfect backdrop for art. The stone treads on the staircase leading down the south tower are scuffed into concave scoops from thousands of wooden shoes clopping up and down from the cellar door that leads to the servants' entrance below and, I presumed, to the dungeons.

In the eerie spot of the flashlight, I saw a small hallway leading off to the left, directly below the small room above where Jean-Michel is going to put his ceramic shields. There was a wooden walkway with a waist-high wooden wall on both sides. As I reached the end of the walkway, I flashed the light into the 40-by-40-foot space and saw neither a floor nor a ceiling until I leaned over and shined the circle onto the rubble twenty feet below. The floor and ceiling had collapsed into a steep and unstable bank of dirt and stone. A dank, cold wind wafted up, bringing unpleasant odoriferous reminders of what must have happened in the *oubliette*, the dungeon, where they put people and forgot them until they died of starvation or thirst. I was disappointed, since the space was obviously unsafe, but as I backed away, my eyes now accustomed to the dark, I realized there was another excavation to the left, which I hadn't seen at first. As I leaned over the wooden barrier, my light showed the opening of another *oubliette*, smaller than the other: it was only about 5 by 5 feet but equally deep, at least 20 feet

straight down. It was an impressively nasty round vertical shaft with nothing apparent on the bottom but cigarette butts and soda pop cans. Perfect.

There are two long, narrow tunnels that I have to drive through when I go to the market in Albi, both built after World War I by German prisoners of war. They're a slightly horseshoe shape inside, allowing for the sway of a train on top, but leave no room for error at the base where two cars must slow to a crawl to avoid clacking side mirrors in the center and scraping the stone walls on the sides. They were supposed to be for a rail line between villages, but they became integrated into the road system and now form a foreboding gauntlet to anybody with a big-ass car. One of the tunnels is straight and over a mile long, lit every fifty feet or so by small lights that create the false perspective of seeming to be closer together the farther away they are. I can make myself feel like I'm falling straight down a shaft there, not proceeding straight ahead. I've counted the lights many times, trying to see how many it takes to form the sense of distance . . . and it's only three, but the more the better. Combine this fascination with perspective overlaid with the Alice in Wonderland horror of falling into a rabbit hole, and you've got the gist of my project.

I'm going to put a squarish framework, twenty feet deep and roughly five feet wide, down into that hole, attach thirteen descending layers of paper or fabric with a large hole in the top layer and more holes that get progressively smaller on the deeper layers, decreasing the distance between them, and then light the layers from the side so that, I hope, I'll get an illusion of infinity. How exactly I'm going to do this is unclear, but Bernard *pierre* assures me that I shouldn't worry about the installation, just build the frame so it can be reconstructed from the bottom of the hole. I'm not sure I would be doing this without him since he doesn't mind climbing down there, while I shudder to even contemplate slipping into that pit.

I don't really have the time, but we're off to Rodez for a weekend of poetry and film, which will be tough slogging in French, but then sometimes it's tough slogging in English, too.

—Hugs, Judy

July 1, 2000
Dear Linda,

I'm alive, but barely. I hung my through-the-looking-glass-look-down-the-well piece this weekend, or I should say, Bernard hung my very-difficult-impossible-to-take-apart-and-get-through-the-narrow-passage-and-slip-into-the-hole piece. In all fairness to me, I had taken him to the château to see the space and he *pas de problème*'d it, saying, "Just build the frame and I'll get it down into that hole." I usually sweat over installation details, and having worked with Bernard now for several years, he's always been complimentary about my compulsive organization. Up until now he only had one rule I had to follow: "*Il faut pas pèse plus de cinquante kilos.*" He doesn't want any component that weighs more than one hundred pounds, since he can throw that much on his shoulder and climb three flights of stairs, *pas de problème.*

I used copper left over from my reading lamps, since it's lightweight and I could assemble it in the studio, drill holes in the pipe, and using cotter pins at the connections, take it apart to be reassembled later yet still have a fairly sturdy framework. (I love cotter pins. They look like bobby pins for giants.) I wasn't sure about the exact dimensions on the bottom of the pit, but Bernard said not to worry since he'd adjust the piece when he got down there. This meant, however, that the layers of paper needed flexible dimensions also. I knew roughly how big they needed to be, but decided to use eyelets with large rubber bands to attach them to the frame with small clips, so Bernard could adjust everything as we went. Everything worked well in my studio: the frame on its side, of course, and all the layers of paper being accessible. It dismantled easily, collapsing into three tidy bundles: a roll of paper layers, another with the copper pipes strapped together, and the lights. But then we got to the château.

As soon as we walked onto the narrow wooden walkway passage with the low ceiling, it was obvious that our long ladder couldn't turn the corner and go down into the hole, and Bernard, usually unflappable, started lighting one Gauloise from another, muttering, "*C'était toujours si petit?*" He had remembered it being bigger, wider. He then spied an O-ring cemented into the ceiling above the pit, tested it for strength, and ran out the door shouting, "*Ne bouge pas, j'arrive!*"

When he reappeared, he was dragging a stout rope and a canvas belt like a cross between a straightjacket and a surgical truss, with several rings attached. I recognized it as the security belt he was supposed to have worn for the tricky parts of building our chimneys and roofs, except that he had never taken it out of the box. Now, he jerry-rigged a second attachment around the wooden railing, strapped on the safety belt, and began hoisting himself up and over the railing and down into the hole.

"But you weigh more than fifty kilos," I shouted after him, wondering how he could lift his own weight out of that hole. In the meantime, I had found a shorter ladder that reached only partway up the pit, but he seemed confident that between the ladder at the bottom and his improvised bosun's chair without a chair he could get the frame put together, attach the bottom layers of paper, pull the ladder out when he was about halfway up, and finish by using only the safety belt. He dangled in a Peter Pan flying position over the dark hole as he explained the plan, while I frowned in fear.

I lowered frame parts and bags of cotter pins, delivered with an abundance of compliments and encouragements like "*Merci bien*" and "*Tu es ingénieux,*" while trying to ignore the "*merdes*" that were now every other word. He installed the lights as I fed them down the ladder, me hoping the fragile bulbs could withstand the virtual onslaught of epithets exploding from below: "*Merde, putain, con.*" It seems my ingenious system of holes and cotter pins worked well in my studio, but lining up the holes once disassembled was way beyond problematic in a cold, damp, earthen pit with the only light the flashlight in Bernard's teeth.

By noon, he'd reached the top of the ladder, and I reluctantly raised it out of the pit with the auxiliary line. He had attached the lower layers of paper, leaving on the dirt floor in the center of the descending holes the largest stone he could find. Even with only six layers of perspective, the progressively larger holes left the illusion that the rock was much bigger than it was.

Bernard spent the entire afternoon suspended from that belt, bouncing off the four walls above the layers of paper below, lining up the descending holes as carefully as possible. In the meantime, I installed motion detectors to the string of patio lights hidden beneath each layer of paper and placed a lighting system on the stairs and the walkway. I wanted the hole to be completely dark, with the startling illumination a complete and disorienting surprise when, or if, a spectator dared to lean over the railing and peer into the pit. I didn't want any warning or sign, leaving the discovery to the individual. Bernard complained less and less as the air was squeezed out of him and the sheer beauty of the illuminated hole became evident. By the time he hauled himself over the railing after installing the last layer, even he seemed pleased with the result. The successively smaller holes with the rock placed in the bottom did distort the space and give the illusion of a much, much deeper pit.

He attached thirteen layers of paper, which might have been prophetic of what was to come. It was already six o'clock, and just as we were packing up our tools, anticipating the pastis waiting for us at the mill, there was a soft *boing* and *swish*. When we looked over the railing into the dark hole, the lights came on as planned, revealing a detached layer near the bottom, its edge folded over and blocking the whole illusion. We couldn't reach it, couldn't leave it, and couldn't imagine undoing the whole thing. I confess I sat down on the wooden passageway and started to tear up. Bernard, who would probably have liked to strangle me, instead sucked his teeth, told me he'd be right back, and again he went out to his truck stuffed with mason's tools.

When he came back, with a huge crowbar over his shoulder, he told me to go up to the only entrance to the stairway and not to let anyone come down, and not to say a word, especially not to Sir Julien, who was making things difficult in every corner of the château, until Bernard hollered to me. At that point, maybe for the first time in our seven years of working together, I asked no questions and did what I was told.

Jean-Michel had been helping other artists put up their work, and since everyone else was gone or leaving, he came over to see what he could do to help us finish up. I not-too-casually blocked the door and sighed, "Oh, nothing," hoping he'd just back off. But he pushed by me saying, "*Au moins je veux voir çe que vous avez fait.*" He just wanted to see what we had done.

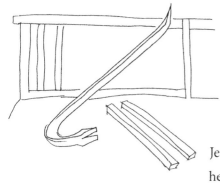

Running down the stairs after him, talking loudly to warn Bernard, I was terrified as to what we'd both find. As Jean-Michel bent down to go through the low door to the *oubliette* I saw Bernard, standing on the wooden passage, turn quickly, and hide the crowbar behind him, adopting a gap-toothed Cheshire smile. Jean-Michel bent over the railing, the light went on, and he gasped, "*Comme c'est beau!*"

I looked at Bernard quizzically and then leaned over as well. It *was* beautiful. The decreasing progression of holes were perfectly lined up, every layer in order, the round rock at the bottom, the warm light making the whole space glow. Bernard's tools were in a tidy pile, and he asked Jean-Michel if he wouldn't mind helping us carry them out to the truck.

Stammering after them, I *bisou*'d a goodbye to Jean-Michel and asked Bernard what he'd done. "Simple. I jimmied out the wooden passage with the crowbar and lowered myself down the part of the pit covered by the walkway, fixed the sprung layer, tested the others, came back out, and rebuilt the passage." All in an hour and a half. My hero. "But now I have another rule," he said, finger wagging in my face, "*Désormais, il faut être pratique.*" I promised that from now on, everything would be practical.

I, of course, have total confidence in Bernard; he is, after all, an experienced construction mason. But I can't even imagine what Les Architects de France would think if they knew he'd torn out and rebuilt a passageway in a *monument historique*!
—Hugs, Judy

July 3, 2000
JOURNAL ENTRY

I got the keys for the château from Marie-Helene at the pharmacy in Coupiac. While

I felt privileged to hold the five heavy hand-forged keys, anyone with a reason, including just curiosity, can borrow them to get into the building. It now belongs to the village and, with the help of Les Architects de France, is being slowly restored. As per instructions, I tugged the handle on the main gate, jostling the key until I felt the tumblers inside engage a full three turns to the right, and the gate creaked open. The bright blue tarp covering a pile of good intentions was still in the corner of the courtyard, still breathing with the slight breeze. The sigh of that tarp had inspired me to make the banners for the *Château de cartes* installation I did last year, and reminded me that the château has its own life and that it would remain long after us. Long after Julien. The upended pavers funneled the light rain out under the gate. The main door to the building required more fumbling, shaking the door at each turn until the two-inch hand-wrought teeth at the end of the eight-inch key caught the mechanism inside the thick door.

I walked up the circular stone staircase to the second level, across the *grande salle* where the banners had been, to the low door that led down to *les oubliettes*. The bare light bulb above the steps did little to chase the shadows from the edges of the stairs. I hesitated at the dark entry of the wooden walkway with no light at the end of the passage. When I approached the first pit to the left, I leaned over, trying to pretend I didn't know what was there. A soft click, and the rabbit-warren tunnel shone softly. It worked. Noémie came all the way from Cahors to see our show. She came running up to tell me how fantastic my *oubliette* piece was, calling it *Le puits de lumière,* or *Light Well.* Perfect. She was upset that I didn't have signage so that people could find it. I couldn't make her understand that it was the surprise I was after.

The *vernissage* was an artists' reunion, bringing twenty artists back for the grand event. The minister of culture for the Aveyron department came and gave his usual flowery introduction, mixing art speak with political nonsense. One of the nationally known artists stood up and asked when the department was going to start providing some significant money to the château now that we had established its reputation as a serious art center. The minister promised the check was in the mail; we just need to write the grant.

SUMMER KITCHEN

July 15, 2000
Dear Linda,

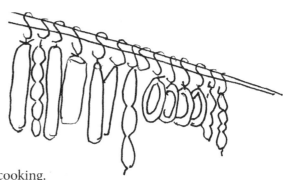

It's hot. I mean *hot*. I went out early this morning to Moussac to see Monique and maybe bring back a couple of pails of manure for my compost, just to get it cooking.

When I arrived, Jean-Claude yelled from the hay barn that she was in the kitchen and I should just go on in. I opened the kitchen door, to a tidy array of plates ready to be put in place for their lunch, but no Monique. Jean-Claude came in and pushed me toward the summer kitchen, behind the mysterious door that Monique slams shut whenever I come into her brightly lit, Formica-countered kitchen.

The dark room was almost surreal in its juxtaposition to the bright, shiny one I'd passed through to go into another world, another century. The worn stones that formed the floor were uneven and stained dark with several hundred years of serious cooking, not the everyday (for her) fry-up-a-couple-of-ducks-for-twelve-people kind of cooking, but the mass processing of thousands of mason jars of beans, tomatoes, and pâté, the butcher-block counter worn down in the middle from chopping up halves of lambs, ducks, chicken, and pigs. Bunches of mint, lemon verbena, rosemary, and sage hung at the far end of the room, and thick braided ropes of sweet onions covered one wall. A cauldron, large enough to hold about two dozen quart jars, balanced on a cast-iron gas burner at the other end of the room. There were two rubber hoses, one leading to the propane tank in the corner, the other outside to the spring water used to fill the cauldron. I could see where overflow water was running out of the room through a drain hole in the thick stone wall, its plug a cone-shaped stone off to the side. Dark, dripping ropes of freshly stuffed sausage hung from the ceiling, today's chore. Empty sausage casings were hanging from a hook, ingeniously feeding into the hand-cranked stuffing mechanism clamped to the worn oak table, where Monique was maneuvering the casings with her right hand as she stuffed the chunks of seasoned pork with the other, her back to the door, twisting the gut every two feet or so. Without looking, she asked Jean-Claude to turn the huge fresh leg of the pig on the butcher table, one side crusted with rock salt and herbs. The leg/soon-to-be ham must have weighed eighty pounds, the largest I'd ever seen.

Jean-Claude laughed and said, "*Non, non, Judy va le faire.*" When she turned and saw me, she blushed with embarrassment. She had never offered to show me this space, thinking I wouldn't understand, but after my own confit and pâté experiences I was taking notes on how I might create a clean/dirty place to deal with the abundance of the garden and generosity of friends. I ran over to ask her to show me the contraption she was using for stuffing and to ask where had they hidden such huge pigs?

She shrugged toward the outside door as Jean-Claude pulled me to a stable at the end of the large barn that houses the tractors, various trucks, and scary pointed farm machinery attachments. As we entered, I heard grunts and banging against a wooden wall, barely containing two enormous pigs, with an empty space for the one that was now in bits and pieces in the summer kitchen. The pigs rushed to the trough under the wall, their portly snouts quivering for food. Coincidently, Agace and Angel, the Fabres' five- and three-year-old grandchildren, already performing their chores, came through the door, struggling under the weight of two huge pails of slop for the pigs. They were completely comfortable with the wall-shaking and exuberant vocalizing of the hogs. Jean-Claude explained that he buys pigs at the weight most farmers sell them, and then he fattens them even more to get the huge hams that they salt, smoke in their wood-burning furnace room, and then pack in cinders in their attic for a few years.

He smacked his lips in anticipation, "*Y'a rien de meilleur.*" I've tasted that ham. He's right: there's nothing better.

As I drove off with a freshly skinned rabbit by my side, along with a large wheel of Jean-Claude's homemade sheep cheese, I wondered if I will ever get used to preparing an animal with its head still on, especially a rabbit, its eyeballs bulging and buckteeth clenched in a death grip. But red wine, bay leaves, juniper berries, garlic, and a sharp cleaver can make up for a lot.

—*Hugs, Judy*

THE ABBAYE DE SYLVANÈS

August 1, 2000

Dear Linda,

I gave you a one-liner about being invited to show at a conference this fall with twenty other Aveyronnais artists, quite an admirable list of people, some of whom have international recognition. Apparently, there will be a group show spread out among two châteaux and the Abbaye de Sylvanès, a handsome set of buildings including a still-consecrated church, though the monastery buildings now house a cultural center specializing in liturgical music. It's located about an hour from the mill, and we often drive over in the summer for an outdoor concert. They are trying to develop a year-round center with a broader focus than music and dance, hence the conference on contemporary art in November.

I assumed that I was invited because I'm the only one doing installation art in our department, and since that is the state of the art in art, I was a shoe-in. Besides, I'm their token woman and foreigner. They have invited every serious art critic, the media, and every bureaucrat who organizes shows in every public venue in France. I didn't realize that being one of the chosen twenty was such a big deal until I started to hear about other artists who were seriously upset that they hadn't been invited and were wondering just who decides what important contemporary art is, anyway?

Many of our artist friends are serious anarchists, and even those who were invited were horrified at the thought of the secular government organizing a potentially important show in a religious setting. (Those that weren't invited all exclaimed, "No way would I show at a church.") I don't have enough time to build something new, so I'll probably show my manifesto book/lamps and while I, personally, like the idea of a big book in a church, I've asked for the attic at the château in Fayet because I like unfinished spaces much more than elegant, freshly plastered ones. The juxtaposition of the oriental paper of the banners would show better, too. Besides, I knew the other artists would want the spaces nearer the conference. The conference and show will be in November, so I'll have to come back over to participate.

Mike is hanging another show next week in another museum near us. It's a nice old mill that has been destroyed and turned into a moooodern glass and plastic building in the middle of nowhere. The mayor of the village is the consul general for the region, meaning he's in the national legislature, and the museum is his little pork barrel project from the French government. But there is a nice display area, and Mike's work will fit well with the remains of the millworks.

I'm girding myself for the onslaught of guests this month. Everyone comes at once, French and American, and I just cook, sigh, and smile while Mike disappears into his studio/barn. We're getting better at dodging people who just come because they're here and we're here. The friends we invite are usually great, and those who are passing because a friend of a friend gave them our address are usually confused by what we're doing and it's too hard to explain, so we start with the art speak, like "We're working on the transcendental interpretation of the effects of wind and water on the aftermath of the subsistence agricultural cultural landscape," whatever the hell that means. No one can understand what we're saying, nor can we, and I'm sure as they drive away they're asking each other, "What was that?" But if I'm going to have to talk to a bunch of art critics I better get my art speak down. I do it badly in English, and in French I still sound like a Valley girl due to my adolescent level of vocabulary.

We went to a Gypsy music concert last night at the Abbaye de Sylvanès to check out the spaces and the last of summer's warm evenings. I am still stunned at the beauty and primordial resonance of the music bouncing off the exterior walls of the cavernous church. Twenty years ago a young priest, Père Gouze, was sent by the Cistercians to take over the church next to the ruins of this abbey in the middle of nowhere. His only company was a few suspicious *paysans* and a donkey that he used to clear the stones out of cloister. He would sit at mealtime next to the donkey's stall to fend off the loneliness, singing to him with the donkey braying in accompaniment.

But little by little, the local people began to have confidence in him, his parish grew, and the volunteers showed up to restore the church and eventually rebuild the monastery. Père Gouze loves music and began inviting other religious groups to come and perform. Gradually, the reputation of the Abbaye de Sylvanès grew to the extent that over 150,000 people visit this isolated valley each year. The scope of the music has broadened, and with a professional staff, so has their cultural mission.

Seeing the Gypsy performers on an outdoor stage on a warm summer night, their backs against the warm limestone, was transporting. There was a joy that one doesn't often find in contemporary music, and certainly not in classical music or even contemporary jazz. The French call Gypsies *tziganes* or *gitans*. They are not allowed to form camps here except in limited areas, and then they are guarded by the gendarmes as if they were lepers. The leader gently, but effectively, chided and educated the organizers and the audience. He said it was okay to say *tzigane* music, but "Don't call me a *tzigane*. I'm a Romani, and I've been in Europe as long as you have." As we were leaving, close to 1 a.m. he said, again gently, "Have a safe trip home. Remember you can always stop by the side of the road to rest. Funny, isn't it? You, who have a permanent home, have the right to stop, and we, who have no permanent home, have no right to rest." I will look differently at these camps from now on.

—*Love Judy*

August 20, 2000
Dear Linda,

Mike's in San Francisco to welcome another new grandbaby. This makes number five and counting! I'm on my way home for a few months, too, but I had to tell you about a rather ridiculous experience I had this week. It's been quite warm here and I've been sleeping with all the windows open, with just a sheet to cover my bare, sweaty skin. The other night, about 1 a.m., I was sleeping none too soundly when I heard something moving across the gravel on the front drive. We have a motion detector light that goes on if someone or something passes the barn stairs, but at this time of year, the vines have overgrown the wine trellis and have blocked the detector until they're trimmed back next spring. It's just as well, since we have a badger that comes every night and I don't get to see him often, so that night I tiptoed to the window and stared out, trying to get my eyes accustomed to the darkness. I couldn't detect any movement, but as I turned to go back to bed I smelled cigarette smoke coming from below. I squinted my eyes and, sure enough, I saw the red glow of a cigarette below on the terrace and I could make out the outline of a man in a sport coat sitting on the stone wall along by the front door, ten feet below me.

I instinctively shouted, "*Qu'est-ce que vous foutez là?*" The French verb *foutre* has many meanings, but in this context, what I said roughly translates to "What the fuck are you doing out there?"

A deep voice mumbled something indecipherable, so I said it again, in English, using the *f* word, hoping to show him I wasn't a sweet, shy thing to be messed with. Again, a stammering response, but all I could understand was, "No English."

Not knowing what to do, I told him I would call the gendarmes if he didn't leave immediately. He shouted something that ended in "*chez Bodt*." The Bodts are a Dutch couple who live directly above us on the high ridge of the valley, less than a thousand feet from us as the crow flies, but at least three miles by the road. I told him how to get there, in both languages he didn't understand, and waited with the phone in my hand until he walked back to his car parked out by the road. I then did the most irrational thing: I called Mike in San Francisco. "Just what do you want me to do?" he asked logically.

I called *chez les Bodt*, as Mike suggested, and told them there was a stranger looking for them. The wife explained that her brother-in-law had left Amsterdam that morning and was navigating with his GPS, which apparently can't distinguish between the top and the bottom of a hill, so he must have thought he'd arrived at their farm. He was probably smoking his last cigarette before entering the house and waking everyone, which would have been me, all alone. That's the last time I leave the front door unlocked.

Well, back to work for me.

—*Hugs, Judy*

October 31, 2000
Dear Linda,

Sorry I didn't get a chance to call just before I left San Francisco to come back to the mill. Having two new grandbabies, setting up a new studio with Dan Pillers, and getting ready for this exhibition just confused the hell out of me.

But I'm here, and the show is up and *vernissage*'d. Next week, the *critiques d'art* arrive and the show goes on. Those who were not invited to show are boycotting and having their own shows (I guess that's happened before). Those who were invited are shrugging their shoulders and hoping for the best. I must say that the work that I've seen so far is good. My stuff is different from the rest, but altogether the work at the two châteaux is interesting and diverse. I hung the banners in the attic of the château in Fayet, and put a few of the larger book lamps with them, for light and levity. The ceilings are much lower than in Coupiac, and the bottoms of the banners sweep the rough wooden floor. They're more dense, less penetrable. For me, the best thing is that I've finally met twenty of the most mature artists in our region, and maybe by inference, I'm considered one of them. We shall see.

Jean-Claude Leroux, a painter friend from Rodez, asked me to have a show with him next year at Cordes-sur-Ciel in a new exhibition space, which is exciting and technically scary for me. It's a closed courtyard covered with a glass roof that creates a space begging to be hung with something from a skylight more than sixty feet in the air. Jean-Claude is hanging some architectural paintings below, so I'd like to "reflect" that somehow, dance with him, again in high heels and backward. More later.

—*Hugs, Judy*

November 12, 2000

Dear Linda,

Okay, I voted, by mail, but unfortunately not in Florida. I won't bore you with the French reaction to all our election gymnastics. It's too painful.

Being here alone without Mike for a month changes my perspective for some reason. Maybe because I've spent every day with only French artists, speaking nothing but French, I seem to be seeing the duality of life here more clearly. There's the *National Geographic* version: the incredible beauty of the French countryside in the fall, the orange vines cloaked in long shadows; the invitation to exhibit at a seventeenth-century château; the *châtelain* who kisses my hand when I enter his palace and showers me with flowery exuberances; the pompous French celebrations of all sorts of things, especially art, with the *fonctionaires*, or bureaucrats, giving speeches, relating all activities to either Napoleon or Louis XIV, depending on their political party.

Then there's the world that one discovers, with time and language, that can't be experienced otherwise . . . the world that doesn't sell magazines or make Americans particularly happy. We want our foreigners to be exotic and, above all, content. We are accustomed to have our adventures edited, packaged, and well photographed. So, I won't tell you about the two inches of pigeon shit that covered the floor of the château where my work is being shown because that pompous *châtelain* can't afford to have the place cleaned. I won't tell you about the *apéritif* he gave me, hoping (since I'm an

American and therefore must be rich) that I can help him keep the place open. And I certainly won't tell you about the politics of the art world here, which has divided our Aveyronnais group of artists into "dids" and "did nots" around this show, which has become increasingly important, at least in the eyes of the did-not-get-inviteds.

And I don't want to tell you about a story that Shirley told me about Germain and his sons, all of whom have worked with us on the mill and seem so stereotypically and ideally, well, French. It seems that Alain, Germain's oldest son and a well-respected contractor who lives above Plaisance, did a rather difficult project for Shirley and Berteau at their farm-turned-contemporary-art-project. He put in a complicated tile floor that he had warned them he didn't know how to do, and when it turned out to not drain properly, they started to dispute his fee. The discussion got quite heated, and they parted on bad terms. At the fête de Truel, one of their local villages, Germain, Alain, and the other Blanc sons saw Berteau and Shirley and ran after them, threatening them if they ever came near *la famille Blanc* again! I'm sure there's another side to this story. At least I want there to be one. Aren't you glad I didn't tell you?

But I will tell you about the village fête at Plaisance last night, with everyone within hearing of the church bells. Mike and I have a rib-poking signal that means, "What century is it?" when we see a particularly timeless chin-to-nose or sun-creased face. And in the last of the November light, as I stood by the river watching people bundled up against the cold in hoods and long coats, walking slowly down from several paths between the walls of the houses, their flashlights blinking against the gravel and the backs of their neighbors, I had to wonder: For how many centuries had people performed this autumn ritual?

They had set up a big tent with a heater, and the school kids were enlisted to help serve a full-fledged Aveyronnais meal, which takes days from beginning to end, first to prepare, second to serve, then to digest. They started with cold slabs of pâté from Monsieur Serre, served up on floppy paper plates, then *soupe au fromage* in sturdier plastic bowls, followed by sautéed potatoes with bacon, duck in wild mushroom sauce, Roquefort cheese, and the best apple tart I've ever had—and at a fête! (I ate the whole thing.) Then, in five minutes, the tables for three hundred disappeared, stacked against the flood wall next to the river, and the band started: waltzes and polkas for the old folks, "La Bamba" for us middle-agers, and techno for Generation X. The music was mixed together, and everyone waited their turn, giggling at the young/old dancers not

of their generation. It was great fun, but too much food. (In France, that's redundant.)
—*Big hugs, Judy*

November 15, 2000

JOURNAL ENTRY

Of all subjects, racism is the one that rankles me the most. I hate it in our Southern culture and in our lingering discrimination in housing and hiring. The French tend to believe they're not prejudiced at all—after all, Josephine Baker and many black musicians chose to live here instead of in the States. When pressed further, they explain, "Why, we don't even keep statistics on race, since that would be racist."

At dinner with Jules and Sabine Jémy's last night, I lost it. They're a Parisian couple who bought a farm complex above Saint-Sernin-sur-Rance called La Gordette and have mostly restored it with fastidious care. Sabine can't be five feet tall, has the reddest hair possible, courtesy of L'Oréal, and is living her retirement fantasies: learning to play the piano, painting, drawing, making dolls, and learning the hurdy-gurdy, a wind-up musical instrument that gives medieval music the hair-pulling whine that helped to bring on the Renaissance. (When asked if we'd like to hear a little concert, we have lapses in our French and change the subject.) Jules is an intense former businessman who compulsively organizes every newspaper clipping about the United States and pulls them out when we dine at their house.

Shirley's theory of why people move to R.F.F. must apply to this couple, but they refuse to talk about their life in Paris, claim to have no friends there, and are not interested in going there ever again. They both have stiff backs and bourgeois tastes, which means they don't mix well with our artist friends, so we used to limit their exposure at our art events at the mill but in a small, rural community, one has to make compromises. No more.

I don't remember why, but the topic of affirmative action in the States and its effect on hiring practices, university entry, and housing came up. They found the idea of the practice despicable, stating it wasn't necessary in France as it is in the States. When I asked them why Belleville, a large neighborhood encompassing parts of Paris's 10th, 11th, 19th, and 20th *arrondissements,* is so predominantly black, with so many idle people on the streets, they had no idea—they've never been there. When I asked about youth unemployment among blacks and North African immigrants, they were clueless. "It's high among all young people. They just don't want to work, those people."

When I pressed them into being more specific, Jules became more and more animated: "The Arabs just don't want to integrate into our culture."

"So it's the Arabs that are the problem in France? You say you're not prejudiced against blacks, but isn't what you just said a bit racist?" The irony of his position was completely lost on him.

"No, the Arabs are different altogether. We need to get rid of them."

I said I thought Paris would have race riots in the future like we had in Detroit and Watts, and that somehow the French needed to learn to integrate those Muslim youths, most of whom were born in France and are French citizens, with French passports—as French as Jules is.

That didn't go over well, and the rest of the evening was stilted and way too long, and I don't have to go there again. Ever.

November 20, 2000
JOURNAL ENTRY

The first day of the conference/exhibition, I walked into the long, vaulted cave-turned-dining-room at the Abbeye de Sylvanès for the introductory lunch later than the others. I had been waiting in my car, listening to the breaking news of the presidential election in the United States, hoping to hear some final tally. I was still slightly in shock, trying to absorb what the indecision meant. There were about fifty people already seated in the room, and as I stood in line for my box lunch without seeing any other artists, I wondered if I should even be there. I sat down with my tray, smiled, and started to introduce myself to those near me. In France, art criticism is part of the philosophy curriculum at their universities, and most of the critics at this event, with the exception of those from the big newspapers, were professors who sidelined in art criticism. There were two, a man from Limoges and a woman from Lyon, already seated at my chosen table. The man asked me where I was from, and when I told him I was American, he turned beet red and began a tirade that started with my obvious political corruption and vote tampering, went on through my literary ignorance and finished with my inhumanity, because I *obviously*, his word, supported the death penalty. I felt he had been waiting a long time to deliver this diatribe to a real American. I was stunned by what felt like a personal attack, with absolutely no questions asked. I found my face getting redder and redder as my own anger mounted.

I finally interrupted his rant in my best French, voice shaking, "*Avez-vous fini, monsieur? Sinon, je m'en vais.*" I had every intention of getting up and leaving if he wasn't finished with his tirade. I then asked him calmly how many years he'd lived in the United States to be so knowledgeable about our weaknesses.

"I have never and never would live there," he replied haughtily.

"Well, how many months did you spend there, and where did you travel?" I asked.

"I've never spent months there," he said in a quieter voice.

"Weeks?" I asked. "Have you ever been there, monsieur?" the *monsieur* an insult, as I knew he was a *professeur* and should be addressed as "*Docteur Machin.*"

When he said he'd never been there, it was in an even quieter voice, which evoked sly grins from the others around us, who were obviously embarrassed by his fulmination. The woman from Lyon asked me kindly how many years I've been in France. When I told her seven, she asked me what conclusions I had come to, based on my experience.

"I only know that the more I learn the more I realize I can't generalize about sixty million Frenchmen. I can't imagine how someone can dare generalize about three hundred million Americans," I said slowly, staring at the jerk across from me. One of the other professors at the end of the table, smiled broadly, applauded softly and began to ask me about myself. I must say it felt good to keep my composure, and have enough language to put him down with perfect grammar. I've come a long way.

The lectures were held in a smaller vaulted cave: it was dark, but the blond stone shone warmly in the low light. I sat with the other Aveyronnais artists through four hours of droning lectures, bored and angry that I had traveled over five thousand miles to watch a dozen art critics perform that special mental masturbation known as art speak, performing for fifty government officials who hung on their every word. They never mentioned the artists in the room, never encouraged the officials to go to the three exhibition sites, just droned on and on about the philosophical ramifications of the introduction of contemporary art into a uneducated community setting. Even the officials weren't sure whether they were being insulted or not!

That evening, after the last lecture, the organizers announced that there were buses to take everyone to the various exhibition sites. None of the critics went to any of the sites. They excused themselves to go do whatever philosophers do in the evening, leaving in the lurch the twenty Aveyronnais artists who had worked so hard, some of them producing site-specific work that would never be seen by anyone but their fellow artists. I drove home that night in tears, frustrated more for my colleagues than myself, since I hadn't spent months preparing. I had refused an invitation to go to dinner at Michel Juillard's, one of the artists, since I knew it would deteriorate into too late a night for my jet lag.

The next morning, I walked into the conference room to a silent demonstration organized by my colleagues. The night before they had agreed to come early and occupy the speakers' table, refusing to let the critics/philosophers sit in their places. They sat silently, expressionless, not speaking one word. I sat down quietly with the other artists, taking my lead from them. After what seemed like an hour, the monsieur/*professeur* from Limoges stood up and shouted, "What do you want? We can't do anything if you don't tell us what's the problem." Stephen Got, one of the most accomplished artists in the group, a shy and sensitive man, stood up, reached over, and picked up the crystal water pitcher intended for the speakers. He reached beyond the edge of the table toward the audience, who had slowly, in confusion, filled the seats, and slowly turned the pitcher upside down, spilling and splashing the water onto the time-worn stones of the abbey. He set the pitcher down, and all the artists, including me, filed out of the room without saying a single word.

FAREWELL, BERNARD PIERRE

November 24, 2000
JOURNAL ENTRY

I'm huddled in the mill, which is cold and dark, a drenching rain pounding outside on the rocks, watching as the flowers of my illusions are depetaled, one at a time. Now it's Bernard *pierre*, our faithful friend and stonemason. In the past seven years, he has eaten tens of dozens of meals and consumed gallons of pastis at the mill, and has touched almost every one of its stones. He knows our children, has built guard rails for Linda, driven me five hours to the Barcelona airport in the middle of the night when my son was very ill in New York and the damn French airlines were on strike. He was a constant bearer of gifts: the fixture from his grandfather's hotel restaurant hangs over our dining room table; a zinc tube in which his father used to store blueprints now houses Mike's drawings; we have stacks of his home repair magazines; his notes from the Beaux Arts on lintel repair line my studio shelves; wines from his father's *cave* are in one of the chimney tiles in our *cave*, his contribution to our lunches.

But for me, his most important gift was the confidence he gave me to dare to attempt the large-scale installations I've been doing the last seven years. He's taught me how to make do, to build the tool if I don't have it, and to make impossible structures in silence and with joy. He has helped me build, hang, and take down every show, treating me as patiently as his apprentice, Patrick. Our relationship had transformed, that cursed word again, from employer/employee to teacher/student to friend/friends.

This summer, we noticed he was often late and obviously hungover, but he always managed to plow through, a Gauloise hanging from his lip. Then one day when he was to help Mike put up an exhibition, he just didn't show. The next day, he came to tell us he and his wife had finally separated after fifteen tortuous years. We'd seen him through several suicide attempts on her part and at least a dozen grand schemes that had cost him his entire inheritance and his home. At fifty, he was having to start over again, a stonemason with worn and calloused hands, knees swollen from carrying tons of cement and rock from the age of fourteen.

Then earlier this month, he helped me install my work at the château. But when he arrived he was grouchy and angry as he helped me carry the piece up to the *grande salle*, smelling slightly of alcohol even at nine in the morning. Over the obligatory, perhaps enabling, evening pastis, his eyes filled with tears: "*Je n'en peux plus.*" "I can't take it any more." His wife was in another manic phase of her disease, and even though they were separated, she'd run up an insurmountable bill at a local store and Bernard had had to ask his boss for a loan to bail him out. He was humiliated and exhausted. I offered to help, but he refused, then left, shoulders dropped, without so much as a *bisou*.

I have tried to reach him several times in the past three weeks, but his phone has been disconnected. He was supposed to come this morning to help take down the show, but he didn't come and he didn't call. Fortunately, the *châtelain*, still under some illusion that I could help him, told me I could leave the banners hanging all winter and he'd show them as part of his normal castle tour.

At three o'clock, Bernard showed up at the mill, still quite inebriated, haggard, his face that red that you see only on drunks on the streets. I fed him coffee and a square meal, which he hadn't had in some time. I asked him what I could do to help him. He shook his head and slurred, "*J'sais pas.*" A friend had lent him a place to stay, but he didn't have any furniture. I told him to back the truck up to the house, and we loaded a bed, a chair, a small table, dishes and silverware, a coffeepot, and enough pans for a small kitchen. I piled some sheets, a pillow, and towels on top and packed a picnic basket full of food. When he was ready to leave, he held his thumb and forefinger in the universal sign for "just a little one for the road."

I took his rough mason's hand in mine and told him, "*Je n'en peux plus.*" He needed to know that I couldn't tolerate his alcohol abuse any longer, and that "When you're ready to stop drinking, we will be there for you." For a long time, he sat in his truck loaded with his new life, sobbing and slamming the steering wheel, until he finally pulled out over the bridge, leaving La Pilande Basse behind.

November 26, 2000
Dear Linda,

One last one before I hit the road. Last letter, that is. I'm leaving the mill, the long shadows and short days of winter to go back to California where all the girls are blond, the men are all buffed, and the children pious and obedient. I have a poignant sense of guilt and relief at the wonderful life I have, here and there.

I said goodbye yesterday to Bernard *pierre*, that sweet man you flirted with and he flirted back, my friend whom I've written countless pages about, I'm afraid for the last time. He's fallen head first into the pastis, and until he hits bottom I don't think he'll be back. I hope he remembers that I told him we'd be there when he was ready.

Christelle and I wrestled the shutters in place, laughing at our lack of upper-body strength and our good fortune at having loving husbands. Yes, it's a miracle: Christelle is actually happy with Maran; after seven years of training, he takes baths regularly and is even looking forward to going to Madagascar with her for the winter.

Remember Sir Julien, the fake *châtelain* at the château in Coupiac? It turns out he is the distant cousin of the real *châtelain* of the Château de Fayet, where I exhibited this month. In fact, Julien had listed him as a reference. All the artists who had to work with Julien this summer know exactly how arrogant, sleazy, and incompetent he is, but somehow he fooled the board of directors of the château, led by Madame Creste, who always seems a little too friendly with him.

In July, we had a tense board meeting with our art commission group, all eleven of us in attendance. Sir Julien had recommended that the château drop its support of contemporary art in favor of pushing the theme of a medieval fortress. Even in front of Madame Creste, we offered our frank opinion of Julien and what he was doing to the château, but as usual, commerce won over art. So everyone on the art commission, the tight-knit group of artists we'd carefully assembled over the last seven years, decided to take a year's sabbatical. In other words, we quit, we disbanded, we caved. All the artists, after years of working to build the reputation of the château as a quality contemporary art center, filed out of the room without saying a word. We didn't even pour a pitcher of water over Madame Creste's tapestry rug.

At the conference this week, one of the artists on our old commission group told me that he learned that after the *ministre de la culture* had asked that we submit a request for funding for the château for our contemporary art exhibitions, Julien had taken it on himself to write that grant without speaking with any of the artists about what had been done in the past or how we might spend the money. He asked for a ridiculous amount of money, with no explanation as to how it would be spent, and the request had been quickly turned down, with a note saying not to bother asking in the future. It was then that Julien recommended to the board of the château that they abandon contemporary art and get on the medieval château circuit.

As I was leaving my banners behind at the Château de Fayet, I asked the *châtelain* about Julien. He confirmed that he was a distant cousin and that he had even asked Julien to help him at Fayet with a conference last winter. When I asked him how that had gone, he turned beet red, complaining that while Julien had been hired to serve refreshments, he refused to do so, tried to take over the conference, and had the nerve to write a six-page letter telling the *châtelain* everything he was doing wrong in his own home. When I asked him why he didn't tell the board at Coupiac this when they checked Julien's references, he replied, "They never asked me! I would have given them an earful." Don't ask, don't be told?

—*Hugs, Judy*

CHARTREUSE ON THE HILLS

February 27, 2001

JOURNAL ENTRY

There's already chartreuse on the hills, checker-boarding with patches of winter-wheat stubbles and gray/purple bare plowed ground. The cold, clear air makes the slopes pop out, foreshortened against the sky like a poorly painted screen set. The sheep still move in swarms, like bees in the distance, cutting honey-colored patterns in the yellow/green pastures. The days are still short, and the sun, still low in the sky, fills the mill room near the river with a warm, bright light. Only the angle of the sun and the quilted colors of the hills change with the seasons. A few people die, a few are born, a rock may fall from the cliff into the river, but nothing much changes at La Pilande Basse.

I've been levitating, looking down at myself, wondering why I'm here, why I think I can make something called art. The why? I realized that it is this atmosphere of silence/peace that I'm looking for in what I do or at least in what I've done so far: the reassuring presence of a kind, quiet, benign acceptance of the enormity and banality of our existence. The lanterns almost had it, as did the house-of-cards banners, bleached-out relics of formerly regal events. The "pages turning" part of the manifesto worked pretty well, as did the "light well" in the *oubliette*.

Richard Berger said everything we do is a self-portrait, and if that's true, then I'm calm and peaceful, as well as bleached out and left behind. Maybe what we do is what we want our self-portrait to be? Or what we're searching for and can't find?

I'm back to prepare for a show at Cordes-sur-Ciel north of Albi, showing with a painter, Jean-Claude Leroux, who will use the walls, me, the air. The exhibition space is in a covered courtyard in a thirteenth-century three-story limestone building. The roof is a canopy of glass, which lets in a soft light that warms the pale stones. Everyone who enters the space looks around, senses the presence of the sky, and slowly looks upward searching for the light. The glass roof, sixty feet above, has thirteen trapezoid-shaped panels that lead one's eyes to the center and out to the clouds above. I want to float thirteen translucent kites that mirror those glass panels far above the heads of the spectators, exaggerating their lower side to increase the sense of perspective. But I can't block that light. Should they bob in some unseen current of air?

March 1, 2001
Dear Linda,

We're back and nothing has changed. I still miss Francis when I drive by Les Magnolias, still under reconstruction. For some reason, I'm speaking in chopped sentences. Is this e-mail language, or my disposition? Chop, chop.

Christelle has been by and looks quite rested after spending the winter in Madagascar with Maran and her family. It seems her family treated him like royalty, fanning him, bathing his feet. When I gave her a look that said, "Did they need it?" she laughed and said, "When it's hot there, it's hot."

Germain is having problems with his back, and Martou is just having problems, real and imagined, but none too serious. Her hypochondria has driven even her children away, and their Sunday dinners are more and more rare. Germain seems angry with her all the time, and his used-to-be *boff*ing at her few remarks has become more of a sneer. We, too, go up to Le Bousquet less and less often.

And I haven't had one word from Bernard *pierre*. He hates the telephone so I doubt he will call, and I have no way of reaching him, so we must wait to see if he shows up. I can still see him through tears, his and mine, driving off, slamming his hands on the wheel as he climbed up the road toward Trébas. And I still don't know if my tough love was right or wrong, but I know I couldn't keep enabling him. I'm still hopeful.

This morning we had a visit from Jean-Claude, making good on this year's deal. Two years ago Mike did a trade with him: a painting for a pile of manure for our garden. When we arrived that spring we found a ten-foot-high pile of sheep shit, plopped somewhat unceremoniously beside the steps going up to Mike's studio and the guest house, directly on our driveway and just above our front terrace where we eat breakfast, lunch, and dinner when we don't have flotillas of flies wafting in the breeze above a huge pile of shit. The only way to get it to the garden, which is on the terrace above the barn, was to carry it, bucket by bucket. I don't know how many buckets of manure are in a ten-foot pile, but I know it took Mike most of the spring and well into the summer to remove it. So this year, same deal, except Jean-Claude promised to deliver it up on the terrace. He explained how, but his *r*-rolling patois accent makes him hard to understand sometimes, and neither Mike nor I could figure out the unfolding arm gesture he kept using to show us how.

This morning we heard him coming down the road from Coupiac, his new tractor whining in the lowest gear as he came down the hill with the front bucket loaded with sheep manure. I ran down the stairs, terrified he would dump it again in front of the house. He saw me running up the drive, smiled broadly, and waved, then repeated the weird arm gesture. He then stopped at the edge of the cliff by the road (the same spot where Bernard and the other artisans used to pee against the cliff each morning.) The cliff is the end of the upper terrace, where, ideally, we need the manure. Without the usual *bisou*, Jean-Claude dropped the huge shovel with its payload low to the ground, pulled some other levers on the tractor dashboard, and smiled broadly as a twelve-foot stabilizing arm slid out beside the load. More levers were adjusted and then, slowly, a hydraulic arm previously folded behind the shovel started to move forward, the shiny shaft of metal growing ever longer and moving ever higher against the bright yellow of the tractor car. Then, after three suspenseful minutes of lifting and erecting, the fully loaded bucket at the end of that phallus turned, tilted, and then *ploof*, it disgorged a ton of steamy fresh sheep manure high up on the terrace. Jean-Claude jumped out, slapped the somewhat astonished Mike on the back, gave an unshaven cheek peck-peck *bisou*, jumped back in the cab of the tractor, lifted the bucket off the terrace, slid his you-know-what back into the shaft, turned and puffed back up the hill, dragging his testosterone behind him. Who was that masked man?

Mike and I stared at each other, first with glee, then with now-whats? Great, but now what do we do with the construction crane that Bernard *bois* left on our bridge? Over the winter. his crew was redoing the roof on our bread oven and the *porcherie* using the crane to lift the heavy stone roofers over the house. He knew that Jean-Claude would bring another load of manure this spring, so he left the crane there so we could lift the steamy stuff to the upper terrace. We can always say we didn't know when Jean-Claude was coming! My dear, we don't have these problems in San Francisco. That's why I love it here!

Frankly, I think Bernard *bois* doesn't want the crane back at his workshop, one hundred feet up the road. They're not quite done with the roof jobs because we are short of *lauzes*, the stone shingles of our region, and besides, Bernard can't decide what to put between the roof and the oven bricks. In the old days, it was clay dug from the hillside up the road next to the old creamery. But that has been bulldozed to make a road going up to Le Carassier, so they're talking maybe sand or fiberglass. Sand has to be hauled through the house and up the terrace steps, bucket by bucket, or hoisted over the house with the famous crane. The crew is voting for fiberglass, and I'm having hissy fits about toxic materials around my bread. The bigger question is will we ever again use the damn bread oven? It takes two weeks to dry out another three days to warm it up using a cord of wood and continual attention, and it smokes and heats up the barn terribly. (There is a reason that Germain's father bricked it up.)

But back to the crane: the center shaft is about fifty feet long and the small arm at the top about fifteen feet on the perpendicular. It swings so easily in the wind that sometimes it looks like a slow-moving top. After staring at the metal monster in the middle of our lovely old bridge for more than three weeks, I finally couldn't control myself. I went into the barn/studio, where I should be carefully constructing my kite structures, and hauled out a huge sheet of thin gardening cloth about ten feet wide and fifty feet long. Armed with a wide brush, I painted a twenty-foot black arrow in the middle of the cloth. I staple-gunned the two ends to wooden battens, screwed in some hook-eyes on one end, and called Mike, our designated knot-maker guy, and handed him some cord from my Cordes show. He enthusiastically tied up the top of the flag, arrow pointing down, bull's-eyed a loop over the top of the arm, hauled up the "Look at Me, Bernard, I'm Still Here" poster. Stunning. It blows lightly in the wind, turning the arm so it points down on one side of the bridge, then the other. Neighbors, of course, stop and ask us what's up, and we point out that it's down. Strangers pull over to the side of the road, approach the edge of the cliff and lean over to look down into the creek bed below, one eyebrow raised. Confused, they walk away, sometimes to come back to see if they missed something. If Bernard doesn't show up soon, we'll switch the arrow so it points up!

—*Hugs, Judy*

CORDES-SUR-CIEL AND
THE MEANING OF LA PILANDE BASSE

March 21, 2001
Dear Linda,

Time seems to move so fast/slow here. The days slide together while we work on our projects. I'm building kite structures, Mike's working on a big show called *Arteology* where he's depicting skeletal remains of Joseph Beuys, Duchamp, and others in long thin formats which he'll "hang" flat on the floor, surrounded by large monotypes of wonderfully mysterious *parure*, or frivolous objects. It's an important show in Rodez, supported by the government, in a large space, so Mike's canvasses are getting bigger and bigger. I've been invited to have a show there next year. I guess it's age before beauty?

It seems every time we come back, we have to go through a relearning curve: How does the answering machine, the remote, the alarm system work? For example, one would think that grinding flour would be relatively simple: open the sluice gate and let the water hit the turbine, which turns the twenty-five-foot axis that connects to the top stone, dump twenty pounds of grain in the grain dumper, *knock, knock* as the wooden shaft hits the dumper, *swish, swish* as the stones grind the grain, and it comes out here. But no, *le meunier*, Mike, can't make the flour to suit the *boulangère*, *moi*. I'm convinced the grain is being ground so fine that the excess bran can't be sifted out, and that's why the bread comes out heavy and dense. Either that, or the wheat is the wrong kind, or the stones are too close together, or the humidity is off. It can't be *my* fault.

Even though we've been back three weeks, I'm just getting into a normal rhythm. We've made two trips to Rodez, four to Cordes-sur-Ciel, where my show is next month, and several to the Château de Taurines, where I hope to have a show next year; held four from-scratch dinner parties; opened the studio; and kissed lots of cheeks, and today I've been flat on my back trying to get my jet lag behind me and get started on the show I must hang in less than a month.

In Cordes, the space where my show will be bears no resemblance to the place I remember, the pictures I took, or the maquette that I built in my studio at the beach house. I have no idea how I'm going to hang thirteen 15-foot kites sixty feet in the air, and Bernard *pierre*, who has always saved my ass in these situations, has totally disappeared, toes up in the pastis. (I joke, but I'm still terribly sad about losing him as a teacher and friend.)

But am I panicked? I should be, but instead I'm writing you, not for advice, sympathy, or even solace. I'm just not panicky *yet*. It always works out, and I've learned I can't push it too hard. I'll go to the studio and start building it and doing drawings and it will come together. So far, this calm assurance is the only good thing I can say about getting old. —*Hugs, Judy*

March 25, 2001
Dear Linda,

As usual, the project is coming together, just in time since I install it in two weeks. The kites will hang from cables stretched across the space, high up near the roof. I have to haul them 60 feet in the air, so that means I need 120 feet of cord for each kite, 60 feet up and 60 feet down to reach the cable thirteen times, or over half a mile of cord. And you know me when something gets tangled, or a zipper gets stuck? Tantrums. So I went to Albi to see a *cordier*, someone who actually makes cord, to buy some cord for Cordes. I thought I might need fine steel cable, which he pooh-poohed immediately, telling me that theatrical cord was the answer, strong, cheap, and almost tangle-proof. He even had the tiny fixtures used to attach the lines to the support structures. This installation has me terrified without Bernard's calm presence. Mike has offered to help, but he'd rather see Bernard and me nose to nose.

I've been pitching for a gig at the Château de Taurines for next year, and while building my kites, I've been building a maquette to develop an idea. The château is in a small village between the mill and Rodez and is supported by the equivalent of our National Endowment for the Arts. If they accept a proposal, they finance a catalog of the artist's work and have significant enough resources to finance original work. They had seen my portfolio and had asked me to show alone, but I would like to include some artist friends who have helped both Mike and me. So I asked Jean-Claude Leroux and Jean-Michel to work, in collaboration with me, not just with my ideas, but to, well, collaborate. Neither had ever approached this type of integrated work (nor had I—I had only observed it), so we were really winging it.

We had the final meeting yesterday with the committee that manages their exhibitions, and they sat through each picture we showed them, smiled in all the appropriate places, and enthusiastically agreed. That means I can have some fun in the studio this spring, gigs assured for two years, and a summer without too much looming overhead. I was scheduled for a show in Rodez at the government-supported gallery, Galerie de Sainte-Catherine, next year, but they said they would change my show accordingly, so I'm set for two years without any marketing.

Okay, that brings you up to date on me. Plaisance had its elections this week, and we went to the vote-counting ceremony to see if our neighbor Brigitte would be on the city council, the members of which are elected every six years by appearing on a list that is submitted to the mayor's office, who officiates over the voting. There can be one list or twenty, mixed by party, but they usually consist of friends with similar ideas. The elected city council then elects the mayor. It often gets nasty, with feuds that last for years.

Of the 267 people in our commune registered to vote, 250 showed up. Then, starting at 6 p.m., everyone stood inside and outside the mayor's office to witness the count. He called out every vote and every name on the list for every voter. The room, about two hundred square feet, got to about body temperature before we bailed out for air, until 9 p.m. when he finished. I mean, everybody stayed there, no making the *pipi*, nothing. (They are trained from infancy to stay at the table and not fidget, so a mere three-hours of ballot counting was easy.) Our preferred list won, including Brigitte, gorgeous and brilliant, who was elected along with the "young" slate. Much tooth-sucking on the older side and *beaucoup de* high-fives on the other!

We love the idea of Brigitte the hippie-turned-politician. She, Bernard *bois*, Max, their neighbor at Le Mousse Bas, and eight other people actually squatted at their hamlet when they were very young, living together in a commune, smoking dope, and carrying on. The inevitable happened and their Charlie was born, they bought the place, started repairing their own roofs, and then Bernard turned into a roofer, Brigitte went back to school in Albi to become a nurse, Bernard became a contractor, then got a diploma from the Architects of France so he could work on historic monuments. *Voilà*, respectability. But Germain and other locals still call them "ippies," even after twenty-some years.

But the real story here though is the mad-cow epidemic. The pictures coming from England, with piles of dead cattle being burned, are terrifying our local farmers. If it spreads farther south they'll see not only the price crash for beef that they are already experiencing from the mad-cow scare, but the possible wholesale destruction of their herds of Roquefort sheep. These almost goat-like sheep are an inbred race, limited to the Roquefort territory, and if they all have to be destroyed, there's no breeding stock in other places. Keep hoping for our friends.

—*Hugs, Judy*

March 26, 2001
Dear Linda,

Happy birthday, my dear. You are almost to the six-o! Soo much wiser, but soooo much older than *moi*.

It is officially spring, but still chilly when the sun goes behind the hills, so yesterday, in the late afternoon we were sitting around the fire after I had tried to get my kite structures to hang in the barn. It was cold and our tea mugs felt good on stiff fingers. I heard footsteps on the gravel, and not feeling social, I was tempted to hide, but Mike sprang up and opened the door to a handsome white-haired gentleman, nattily dressed, his beret in his hand. In a booming voice he introduced himself as Monsieur Breaux, a retired *evangeliste de Cadix*, which is just downstream from Trébas, which is where the Rance River joins the Tarn, which is just down river from where the Mousse joins the Rance, and on the Mousse is where one finds La Pilande Basse and Monsieur Breaux. (If he fell into Le Mousse, he would soon find himself *chez lui*.)

Twisting his hat, he asked if we knew the meaning of La Pilande Basse, which we did not. He claimed he had the answer and if we had a few minutes, he'd be happy to share it with us. Mike invited him in, we offered a pastis or a tea, and he accepted the latter. We pulled up another chair, and Monsieur Breaux began to tell us his story.

His brother is the mayor of Brasc and a Roquefort cheese farmer of some repute. Our guest, being the younger brother with no claim to the farm, went into the seminary after high school. In the fifties, when the Algerian war broke out, he was sent there as a chaplain, where he served eight long years until the end of that bloody conflict. As he recounted this part of the story, his neck retreated into his shoulders, his eyes avoiding contact. Then, suddenly, he switched subjects and, his neck extended, his head held high, running his hand through his thick white hair, he told us about his research in linguistics since his retirement a few years back.

He said he'd been patiently putting the names of local villages and farms into a computer and researching the roots of the regional patois, Occitan, the basis for most of those names. He went on to say that long ago, instead of writing horizontally, men of letters often wrote vertically. So for La Pilande Basse, the *L* would have stood for some word, the *A* another, the *P* for something else. We had never heard of this curious writing system, but were intrigued. I ran for a piece of paper and another cup of tea. Writing vertically, he explained that often "la" referred to a *chemin*, or a path, and *p* was short for a verb meaning "to join," the *i* probably stood for the Occitan word for *ruisseau*, or river, the *l* meaning *vers*, or "toward," and the *ande* probably was a *gué*, or a ford in the river. In other words, "a path toward the ford in the river." This seemed entirely plausible, since we did know that at one time there was a ford in our little river, right in front of the mill.

We were quite enthusiastic about his explanations, even though he seemed puzzled by La Pilande Haute, a cluster of buildings high above us on the hill, nowhere near the river, so we asked him to show us the meaning of Ambialet, a beautiful village with a monastery high on a cliff overlooking a U-turn on the Tarn, downstream from his village, Cadix, which is downstream from Trébas, where the Rance joins the Tarn, just below where La Pilande Basse sits with its feet in Le Mousse.

As he wrote the letters vertically, he left out the *b*, saying it wasn't used much in Occitan. But the *a* certainly referred to another *chemin*, the *m* meaning "toward," the *i* for "river" and the *l* and *et* short for *gué*. In other words, "a path toward the ford in the river." When I mentioned that this name seemed remarkably similar to the one for La Pilande Basse, he commented that most villages were on rivers and usually had some sort of bridge or at least a ford. Mike gave me an eyebrow-raised side glance as I asked Monsieur Breaux to do Mialet, a land-locked hamlet up the road with no river and no ford. When the *m* proved to mean *chemin*, he reminded us that all places were connected by paths. But when the *l* and the *et* came out as going toward a river and a *gué*, it became obvious that this handsome man was more a wounded soldier than a linguistic expert.

After he left, I called Germain and asked him if he knew Monsieur Breaux. He practically shouted, "*Mince, tu ne l'as pas laissé passer dans la maison, non?*" When I told him we had indeed invited him into the house, he hurriedly gave me the full story: when Monsieur Breaux came back from Algeria, he was in a traumatized state. His brother vouched for him and the diocese decided to give him the church in Réquista, the village high above us where we go for the real farmers' market. Everything went quite well for a time, until one day he set fire to the church and stood and watched it burn down. After that, they put him in a home at Cadix, near Trébas, where the Rance River joins the Tarn.

—*Hugs, Judy*

April 1, 2001
JOURNAL ENTRY

Antoine Taillon, our young *paysagiste*, or landscape architect, came to the door this morning. His large red motorcycle was parked at the end of the bridge, leaning into the gravel as though it were still moving without him. His red curly hair was slicked back, his eyes wild, red, and runny. He almost spat "*Bonjour*," but nothing else; he just stood there, weighed down by something more than the bright red helmet in his hands.

"*Rentre, rentre*," I insisted. He stepped through the door, still silent, unexpressive, his *bisou* perfunctory. He kept his red leather jacket on but accepted a coffee, which he didn't touch. When I started to tell him how pleased we were with the plantings he'd done last year, his eyes filled with tears.

"Antoine, what's the matter?"

"*Mon père s'est suicidé cet hiver.*" He staggered as he told us his father had committed suicide this past winter. No wonder he was in such a state.

We had never met his father, but knew from friends that he was about our age, a *bon vivant*, an unpredictable character prone to grand gestures and a mean temper. Suzie, who knew the father from her time in Provence, always put her finger against her temple and rotated her wrist in the French equivalent of our finger-circling-an-ear gesture. He owned a stern château in Esplas, a dour thirteenth-century building that he ran as a *table d'hôte,* a restaurant where one sits at the table with the host—a way to run a restaurant without all the encumbering government regulations. He apparently was a good chef but a difficult employer. His wife had left him years before.

"Oh, my God, I'm so sorry, Antoine. Had he been depressed?"

"Non. On se disputait et il a pris un pistolet et s'est tire une balle dans la tête devant moi."

I couldn't believe my translation of his French. How could a father possibly shoot himself in the head in front of his son, even if they were arguing? Stunned, I said nothing. We sat in total silence, my thoughts racing. What is there to say to someone who has witnessed such a violent, vicious act? How could one's own father be so cruel as to leave that legacy? I couldn't help but think of my suspicions about Antoine's homosexuality and that perhaps his father had discovered his secret life. Or maybe that Antoine had been trying to tell him? I dared not ask the only real question: why?

"He must have been crazy," I offered lamely.

"Oui, mais maintenant, c'est moi qui suis fou." "Yes, but now it's me who's gone mad."

He got up to leave, zipping up his red leather jacket, covering most of his suffering face with the bright red helmet, his words echoing inside, assuring us that he was getting professional help, that friends and family have closed around him, and that he knew he would survive. Watching his reckless exit from the end of the bridge on his huge red motorcycle, I could only hope.

April 8, 2001
Dear Linda,

I've been remiss in not writing sooner, but I had to finish and hang my show at Cordes-sur-Ciel. It went up yesterday, and I'm basking in total relief. Mike played Bernard *pierre*, without the customary nose-to-nose argument. He thought it would take at least two days, and I didn't want it to take that long so I carefully planned the installation, measuring every cord and cable, making detailed drawings of the order of the installation. I won't tell you about the long poles I taped to the ends of hand clamps so we could reach unreachable places in the middle of the room. I won't tell you how quickly Mike got the cables in place and the lines fed through the fixtures, or how gracefully the kites lifted off the floor as Mike pulled from the third-floor balcony while I maneuvered them from below so they could fit sideways between the low-tension lines and delicate lights stretched between them.

"Pull, pull. Stop. Now, pull." And *poof*, they emerged into the free space, climbing ever higher until they floated with their pointy ends gesturing toward the center of the

glass ceiling. (The theatrical cord, which I had wound compulsively around spools so it wouldn't tangle, didn't, tumbling down just like the *cordier* promised.) I definitely will not tell you how the end of the eleventh kite caught on one of the sets of thirty-foot low-tension electrical lines and pulled them and their lights down to the stone floor with a loud crash. (The mayor's maintenance guys assured us that they fall regularly and that it wasn't our/my fault.)

But I will tell you we finished in only six hours, and the kites are truly spectacular floating in their space. The sunlight shone through the thin handmade paper, with the slightest hint of the cast arches. The points of all thirteen came together, forming an open circle with the long ends squaring off with the sides of the room, as planned. A slight breeze from some ventilation holes in the roof makes them rock gently against the backdrop of the sky through the glass ceiling. I call the piece *Les cintres volants*, or *Flying Coat Hangers*, since the weight of the paper made the kite structures arch and the paper bow, like hanging starched fabric. The curator of the show said that when people enter the space they always look up to see the source of the soft light. He said I had sculpted that gesture. That felt good.

—*Hugs, Judy*

April 15, 2001

JOURNAL ENTRY

Yesterday, a bright blue van pulled into the little hamlet of Mialet, with lights on the top and "Gendarmes" in white letters on the side. With their round, billed black hats down tight on their heads, they knocked on the door and asked Natalie Signet to step outside. They then began to question Natalie, our housekeeper for over eight years, telling her she had been denounced by someone about working *au noir*, or while not paying taxes.

She walked over to the mill last night at 9 p.m. to tell us, wringing her hands, visibly shaken. She said that Christelle's husband, Maran, had been denounced, too, but not Christelle, who also works *au noir chez nous*, so she doesn't think it's about us, but about her. Apparently, she had one other client like us, seasonal, whom she didn't report. She had told the gendarmes that we were just friends and that she just comes over to help out when we arrive each year, to clean up the winter mess. She was more distressed to think there was someone who hated her enough to denounce her than that she was actually doing something wrong. We got our stories straight and we're to start paying her according to the formal Employee Service System.

There's always been the threat of denunciation in France, from the Revolution through the shameful reporting and deportation of Jews and others during WWII. There are those who believe that much of the rural French Resistance was made up of people who had been denounced by the Vichy mayors in their villages for one reason or another. When Odette's ex-husband, Jacques, the doctor-turned-pig-farmer, was denounced by husband of his new girlfriend it was almost understandable, but the case of Natalie seemed truly petty.

Maran, who has been cutting brush for us for eight years, was more amused than upset. He, too, thought he'd been denounced not because of us, but because he worked for a lot of people *au noir* after his day job in the local charcuterie. He absolutely refuses to be paid by check and said, basically, that anyone who was that low could just *"Aller se faire foutre!"*, or go copulate with himself. He started up the weed-whacker and headed off on the *chemin qui va vers le gué.*

April 20, 2001
Dear Linda,

They want to buy my kites at Cordes. The city thinks they belong in that space. Frankly, I was completely unprepared for that! My manifesto says that I won't sell my art. I can trade with others, but that's all. To be continued.

This morning as I was trying yet again to make a decent loaf of bread, Mike came running in the front door, dripping wet, with mud and something else all over his overalls. "Hurry up, come and see what I found."

I ran out the door and followed him down the stone steps toward the lower terrace, below the arch of our stone bridge and the *porcherie* to the left, with the entrance to the *chambre d'eau* on the right and straight ahead the path to the river. On the opposite side of the river is a steep rocky cliff covered with blackberries, and the riverbed itself is a smooth stone bowl with huge flat boulders that sometimes bounce against the house in our many flash floods. *Et voilà*, up against the cliff side of the river, on top of a flat rock, was the shivering form of a black-faced sheep, her woolly coat matted with mud from the river and her head adorned with a crown of blackberries, but she was definitely not wagging her tail behind her.

We were stumped as to how she could have found himself there in the middle of the old ford. Our twenty-foot waterfall was behind her, with another ten-foot fall below the bridge, and vertical stone walls on either side. She must have either fallen down from the sky, or walked up the road and then down into the riverbed. Neither seemed likely. The only way out of her stone pen was a precarious staircase up our stone wall, the steps being flat rocks sticking out every ten inches or so. Mike tried to get her to climb up the steps, but she wasn't interested. I say "she," since had she been a he, Mike wouldn't have been able to even get near the beast without serious injury, much less engage it in mud-wrestling.

Most of the sheep around us are long-legged goat-like creatures that give milk for Roquefort cheese. This was obviously a sheep raised for its meat, with short muscular legs and a sweet black face surrounded by a normally full blond coat, not like the scrubby little mat on the backs of the *brebis de Roquefort*. Our neighbor Max, who drives a delivery truck for our local charcuterie, keeps black-face sheep to clean his multiple terraces and then cooks them for tasty winter meals. Every once and a while they escape, and you can see him chasing them up the steep road toward Plaisance. I called him, but he said he was sure it wasn't his since they hadn't arrived yet this year.

While most of our neighbors are Roquefort farmers with a few hundred of the long-legged variety for their milk, many of them raise a few black-face ones, selling their meat at the Réquista market. We decided she must have come downstream, since going up would have been impossible. We called Christophe Berlan, the bachelor at La Creste, which is the first farm upstream. He didn't think he was missing anybody but said he'd call Monsieur Alibert, Jr., the son of the adulterous woman in Réquista and whose father had died of a broken heart (and lots of booze), and Monsieur Something-or-other. I should have understood him, but Christophe rolls his *r*'s even tighter than Jean-Claude, so Mike and I just smile and nod when he talks.

Ten minutes later they all showed up, one after another, in assorted farm vehicles, berets cocked backwards, Gauloises being rolled, as they descended the *chemin qui va vers le gué*. There was much tooth sucking and lifting of berets with thumb and forefinger to scratch balding heads with the three fingers that remained. *"Non, non, elle n'est pas à moi."* Repeated three times. Seems she didn't belong to anybody.

"We can't just leave her there," Mike said.

So Christophe jumped down into the riverbed, deftly grabbed the startled animal by one back leg and the corresponding front leg, upended the eighty-pound sheep as though she weighed nothing, hauled her up the stairs ,and unceremoniously deposited her in the *porcherie*. "There, that's that," he said, and slapped his hands on his work pants.

Although it was four in the afternoon, three pastis were gratefully accepted, and the real reason the men had come became evident. They just wanted to see the mill and what those Americans were doing there, anyway. It was obvious they knew none of their sheep were missing when Christophe called, probably to say, "Now's your chance to see *le moulin*." The mill having been visited, the pastis thrown back, they all started up the drive to go home, when I startled even myself by saying, "Stop! What are we going to do with the sheep?"

"Well, you can keep her until someone shows up," Christophe offered.

"But we have no grain, no straw, we can't even catch her! Let's draw straws," I announced.

I didn't even know if that concept existed in rural France, but I ran and got some matchsticks anyway. They didn't question me, they all drew one, and Christophe got stuck. I told him we'd call as soon as we found the owner and if we didn't, well, "If we can't find the owner we'll have a barbecue in August!" That seemed to satisfy everyone, and off they went, sheep and all.

–Hugs, Judy

INTERVIEWING GERMAIN

May 1, 2001

JOURNAL ENTRY

Mike and I have talked about taping an interview with Germain since we bought La Pilande Basse eight years ago, but were waiting until our French was adequate enough. So I finally went up last week, tape recorder in hand, in the interest of preserving the history of the mill. As I drove through the narrow path between some Parisians' summer house on the right and the small house where Martou was born on the left, I thought to myself: *Another coat of* crepi *on either wall and even the Twingo won't pass.* Her birthright house was abandoned when Martou's parents traded some land for the sturdy stone house, separated by a narrow driveway, where Martou and Germain now live. Her eyes always fill with tears when she talks about her father being wounded in World War I, one of the few of his generation to survive. (She has brass shells from the war, in various sizes, lined up on her sideboard, souvenirs, origins unknown, brought back from the first war by Marthe's father.)

The house is connected to the old pig-scalding shed, which also shelters the bread oven, now filled with pieces of metal: everything from empty paint cans to nails and broken tractor axles too valuable to throw out. (The feud between Germain and M. Parnat, the only local *brocanteur*, ensures they'll stay hidden behind the metal door until after Germain's death since Germain would rather die than have Parnat profit from them.) The roof of the house is wavy, with sunken beams weighed down with *lauzes* sliding down as their nails rust through the rotten wood. The front porch, the scalder, and the oven are protected with a corrugated plastic roof installed by one of their sons. Rough cement stairs lead up to the front porch and into the kitchen/living area. There's a stone sink in the back corner, covered in old mason jars and canning equipment in need of repair. The center wooden table, legs disintegrating from powder-post beetles, is piled high with zinc washing tubs, grape baskets, a plastic baby bathtub, and old tools, all covered with a thick layer of gray dust. A creaky stairway, with missing steps, leads to the two small bedrooms above, both equally filled with rusty bedsprings, more zinc pails, and ladder-back chairs too small for today's generation. A two-by-ten-inch piece of wood, one end studded with over fifty long, rusty hand-crafted nails, lies points up on an old *chevet*, or bedside table; it's a device Martou's mother used to card wool before she spun it on her distaff.

Germain has long since transformed the front porch of the crumbling house into a small workshop with his hand tools carefully arrayed on nails, all joined together by impressively intricate spider webs. The gauzy light shining through the translucent plastic warms the scene, romanticizing the obvious austerity of the existence in the house. Germain is always embarrassed when I ask if a friend can see his workshop. He doesn't understand its charm at all.

Germain was waiting impatiently for me, a stack of genealogic evidence beside him. I was armed with a questionnaire that had been given to me by a professor at one of our mill conferences. The list was quite pedantic: "How do you know the mill? Who lived there? What was your relationship? How long did the mill function? What did they make? Who came as clients? Describe how the mill worked. What was the daily life like there? How many sets of millstones were there?" As I glanced through the list, it was clear I already knew the answers to most of my questions and was hesitating as to where to start, fiddling with the tape recorder, explaining what I was going to do. As I clicked Record, Germain began, no questions asked.

In his telephone-answering-machine voice, each word clipped short and grunted with equal emphasis, he started: "The earliest traces we have are of a Marianne Vallat, born in 1780, in the little house on the hill, then called Le Foulon, built before the long mill house below. She married a Pommier, and their daughter, Marianne, was born in 1807."

From there I tried to follow a family tree that folded out four pages wide and two down, with lines from Monsieur Antoine Tournié, who was born sometime before 1749, down to the seven children of Martou and Germain. Another Monsieur Tournié climbed down the hill, across the Rance River, and up Le Mousse from Le Truel in 1824 to marry the young Marianne. With their seven children, they started a legacy of Tourniés who would own the mill until Émilie Tournié, Germain's mother, married Louis Blanc, just before World War I.

Up to this point, Germain was quite didactic, ruffling through papers to be sure his dates were right. But when his thick finger tapped on the family tree where his mother's name was written in a careful French scroll—*Tournié, Émilie, née le 23 janvier, 1888 à la Pilande, décédée le 20 septembre, 1935 à la Pilande*—a tear dropped on the plastic tablecloth. He pushed up his glasses and squeezed his eyes with his other hand. He drew a deep breath and continued. *"J'avais sept ans."* "I was seven years old."

There was a long pause while, at seventy-three, Germain composed himself enough to continue his mother's story. She lived in the little house on the hill with her mother and her father, Joseph Pierre Tournié, while her grandfather lived below in the big mill, where they made thread, walnut oil, flour, and cornmeal. (Her uncle had built another mill, down below the waterfall, after the bridge, and Germain's mother would sneak down there to get flour, since her uncle's was whiter than that of her father's, ground in the big mill. That infuriated her father.)

Then, one day—the dates were fuzzy, but probably around 1900—*les hommes en noir*, the men in black, came and repossessed the mill, throwing them out of their home. Germain's grandfather had made a bad investment, enlarging the mill too fast, and he couldn't keep up the payments. They were forced to go live in Curvalle, just across the Rance River from Plaisance, and run a mill for someone else to make up the payments on La Pilande Basse. While they lived near Plaisance, Germain's mother, Émilie, went to school there with her younger brother, Joseph Émile. She eventually went on to graduate from a private school with the highest advanced degree and started teaching school in Clermont-Ferrand d'Hérault.

In the meantime, her father paid his debts and moved back to La Pilande Basse, which had been empty during their absence. Germain pushed the papers away, placed his hand under his thighs, and rocked gently as he continued his mother's story. It was always assumed that Émilie's brother would take over the mill from their father, so she stayed in the Hérault, where she met and fell in love with a young man, also a schoolteacher. "She was smart, you know. She had the highest diploma!" Germain repeated.

They were engaged to be married, and had even bought rings, when she brought him back to the mill to meet her parents. In that same year, her brother died unexpectedly, and her parents refused to let her marry her own choice. They needed someone to take over the mill, and the fiancé wasn't suited for, or perhaps didn't want to do, such work. So her young man returned to the Hérault, alone. Her parents, in a compensatory non sequitur, bought her a sewing machine, a rare commodity in 1911 when everyone still made their own clothes by hand. Martou, who had been sitting quietly in the corner while Germain spoke, sat up straight and said: "*Je l'ai encore.*" "I still have it."

Germain *boff, boff, boff*ed at her comment. He stared up at the wagon-wheel-turned-chandelier over his head, the energy-saving twisted neon bulbs with a slight layer of dust throwing a flickering yellow light on his face. "*C'était l'époque,*" or "It was another era," he said, apologizing for his grandparents.

Germain was much less emotional when giving the facts on his father, Louis Blanc, *né le 15 avril, 1887, décédé le 23 juillet, 1966 à La Pilande Basse.* Born at La Claparié near Coupiac, he had been a menial worker for a lamb vendor in Montclar, but had a strong back and an aptitude for work. He was presented as a candidate in an arranged marriage to the parents of Émilie, Germain's mother. "They had never met. They would never love each other."

Germain looked up at a photo of his father hanging high on the wall. Mike had Photoshopped a scanned image of Louis Blanc into a picture of Germain with one of his sons, Yves, and Sébastian, a grandson. Germain's eyes darted and he squinted slightly. No other expression on his leathered face. He rubbed his balding head, shiny and brown from working every day for over sixty years in the sun. Whatever emotion he felt, he held it in while he continued the story.

Louis and Émilie married in 1913, and Germain's sister, Maria, was born a year later. Louis Blanc left for World War I and was in the army in Tunisia until 1918, while his wife, Émilie, stayed at the mill with her parents. She made everyone's clothes, did all of the laundry and cooking, took care of the pigs and the sheep. When Louis returned, he worked for his father-in-law, carrying sacks of grain, tending the garden, and doing odd jobs for neighbors, until Joseph Pierre Tournié died in 1925 and Louis Blanc took over as the *meunier.*

Germain was born ten years after his father returned from the war, when his mother was forty years old. He remembers his mother as being *douce et accueillante,* or "sweet and friendly," and his father as *dur,* which means "tough" or "harsh." *"Il ne m'a jamais pris dans ses bras."* He doesn't ever remember his father taking him in his arms. Part of the man's comportment was the era, Germain thinks, but also it was his personality. (His consumption of six liters of wine a day is legend in the area. Germain *bof*s and says there wasn't much alcohol in his father's wine.) Louis Blanc's family doesn't appear at all on Germain's family tree, and Germain knows almost nothing about his father's earlier life.

When Germain was five years old, his mother became ill and couldn't take care of him, so he went to live with his much older sister at her sheep farm La Vernière, two miles up the hill toward Solage, coming down only occasionally to see his parents. (His sister had a son only a few years younger than Germain, which made Germain his uncle!) It was many years after his mother's death that Germain was told that his mother had had cancer, and at that time, the disease was thought to be contagious and shameful. So he saw little of her near the end, and only at a distance when he visited.

We took another long pause while Germain struggled to control his trembling chest and I pretended to fiddle with the tape recorder. He started again slowly, picking up after his mother's death.

At the time of their mother's death in September 1935, Germain's sister had two small children, so he was sent to live up above Plaisance with a sister of his father, a demanding woman whom he detested. He begged his father to bring him home, which he did, but not until the end of July 1936. Germain lived alone with his father at the mill, and his mother's aunt, who was a little *dingue,* or crazy, would come to do the laundry and clean house.

Germain learned the stories about his mother and her family from this spinster great-aunt, and I don't know if the bitterness in his voice was the result of her twisted memories or his own, marked by the trauma of his childhood. Germain folded his arms, avoiding my eyes as he rushed through the rest of his grade school and high school years.

In 1937, his father remarried, a widow with a son of her own. In 1943, at fifteen, Germain wanted to go to work in a *minoterie*, or a steel-rolling mill, in the Gard, but his father refused to let him go, asking Germain who would take care of him when he was old. So Germain refused the position. He later had a chance to take over a mill near Gaillac that would have provided a better living for all of them than La Pilande Basse, but his father refused to leave. So he spent the next nine years working for his father and living with him and his stepmother, a woman he disliked. (A normal term for a mother-in-law or a stepmother is *belle mere*, or "pretty mother." But Germain used only the more pejorative *tante de papi*, or "grandpa's aunt," when he spoke of her. When I asked him why, he remarked curtly, "She wasn't my pretty mother.")

The older people in our village all remember taking grain to the mill, mostly in wagons drawn by cows, although Germain said that Madame Mejean, the tiny mother of the baker in Plaisance, walked two miles to the mill every day by a path up above the present road, with thirty pounds of grain on her back. She walked back with her freshly ground flour and a small sack of bran in her hand to give to her chickens. He had already told me how during the war, there were severe limits on how much grain was allowed, so people would climb high above the mill and hide sacks of grain, and Germain or his father would cross the dam in the dark and bring the grain back to the mill, grind it, walk back over the dam, and put the flour in its hiding place.

Stories from others paint Louis Blanc as a *bon vivant*, always smiling, sharing a meal or a glass of wine with customers of the mill. Sometimes, people came by wagon from as far away as Balaguier-d'Olt, with hundreds of pounds of grain. They would often spend the night and enjoy a leisurely meal while Germain ground their grain.

Germain had other miscellaneous things he wanted to be sure we knew about, such as the washing rock, a large, flat piece of slate still leaning against the wall of the chute that brings water to the reservoir behind the mill house. Germain's stepmother would scrub their sheets on that washing stone using rough soap made from the cinders from the stone basin next to the chimney.

In 1952, when he was twenty-four, Germain climbed up the hill to Le Bousquet and married Marthe Pommier and began working for her father, continuing until his death. They had six cows, a few sheep, and a large garden where they grew, and still grow, all of their own vegetables and meat. Their pastures were five hundred feet up a steep hill, which they both climbed twice a day. Martou in her daily milk-carrying excursions went over the bridge of La Pilande Basse twice a day. She never stopped at the mill. Not once.

She produced seven children, one after another, all living in close quarters in their small three-bedroom house. Martou's parents stayed in what is now the unused dining room, until the father died and the mother moved into a tiny storage space off of Martou and Germain's bedroom, while the four girls shared one bedroom and the three boys the other. (The toilet and shower were downstairs in the wine *cave* until this past winter, when the now-married children chipped in to install a bathroom upstairs.)

Meanwhile, back down the hill, directly below Le Bousquet, Germain's father continued to run the mill. Newer steel-roller mills made flour faster and more consistently than his solid flint millstones, but there were those who believed stone-ground flour was better so they continued to come and throw their grain sacks over the wall of the bridge to the terrace below.

From there, Germain's father would carry the grain into the mill and weigh it in round wooden boxes before either cleaning it or pouring it directly into the grain box, or *trémie.* From the back door of the mill, Germain's father could pull on a rope that ran the full hundred feet to the top of the dam where the sluice gates were, and open the *vanne*, or small door, to let the water run down the chute to fill the reservoir behind the house. Another waterfall would form from the water rushing over the side wall of the reservoir back into the river. A two-foot hole through the lower wall of the mill allowed the water to burst through and turn the six-foot horizontal metal turbine in the *chambre d'eau*, or water chamber, directly under the millstones above on the main floor.

Just like Mike does today, from in front of the millstones on the main floor Louis Blanc would pull on a twenty-five-foot metal rod that went through a small hole in the floor down to the *vanne* on the inside of the hole in the base of the house. As the door opened, the water, backed up in the reservoir, would rush through and crash into the curved paddles of the turbine, which would slowly start moving, turning the long, perpendicular shaft connected to the half-ton millstone above. The top *meule*, groaning awake, turned as the grain entered from the *trémie*, sitting on top of the sturdy six-sided box that protected the millstones and contained the flour as it dribbled out to the sides from between the *meules*. The shaft would turn a spindle close enough to the *trémie* to knock gently against the wooden slide that fed the grain slowly in between the stones below. Connected to that wooden chute was a small bell that chimed sweetly each time the wooden spindle turned and knocked. Even if Louis Blanc were at the other end of the long mill room, he could tell the speed of the stones by the chiming of the bell. If it changed, he would run and adjust either the flow of the water to the turbine or the height of the top stone, add more grain, or stop the stones from turning by clanking shut the *vanne* below. (If the stones, made of flint, turned without any grain and they touched, sparks could fly and start fires in the wooden boxes.)

The voices of the big waterfall, the water pounding from the chute behind the house, the stones churning, and the bell clanging made a distinct song that echoed up the road in both directions and up the steep path that Martou took twice every day to Le Bousquet, where Germain hoed his garden. (An elderly lady stopped by recently, telling us she'd heard that the millstones were turning again and she wanted to hear "*la musique du moulin.*")

When the grain was ground, the bran was still in the flour, so Louis Blanc would carry it upstairs to the room above the stones and drop it through a hole in the floor into the 16-foot flour sifter, or *bluterie*. He would attach a 1-foot-wide canvas loop to an 18-inch pulley run by a large gear coming out of one of the sets of millstones and force the other end of loop over another large pulley that turned the axis of the long frame inside the wooden doors of the *bluterie*. Stretched over that structure were different grades of silk, from fine to coarse, letting the finest flour tumble out at the beginning and the hunks of bran at the other. He would open the *vanne* to let the water hit the turbine again, but this time it was the canvas belt that began to turn, driving the giant flour sifter inside its wooden box. Metal weights would clack down as the axis turned, shaking the flour against the cloth and knocking it through. Slats at the bottom of the V-shaped doors allowed the various grades of flour to be dumped into sacks underneath as well as the bran, all to be weighed in separate sacks. A client expected to leave with almost the same weight of flour and bran as he had brought in grain, with perhaps a 3 percent loss to the stones and silk. Some millers were thought to spill flour under the stones to keep for themselves, but Louis Blanc was considered an honest *meunier*.

For fifty-three years, Louis Blanc hauled sacks of grain, adjusted the millstones, ground the grain, hauled and sifted and sacked the flour. He hoisted the stones off their bases to be cleaned and dressed, repaired the dam, hoed the garden, slaughtered the sheep and pigs, tended his vineyard, made his wine. For twenty-nine years, Germain's stepmother worked by his side.

Then one day in 1966, his father sent for Germain. He had been suffering with what he thought was an infected tooth, but it turned out to be cancer.

To that point, Germain had been rushing through his father's years with hand gestures and little expression. But now, he switched to days, and his hands dropped to his lap. It was a Sunday when they took his father to Saint-Affrique to the hospital, though he didn't want to go. He didn't think he would return, but they brought him home the next Sunday, when it was obvious he was dying. Germain slumped forward, looking at his entwined fingers in his lap, his eyes filling with tears. The unexpected emotion surprised even him. "He died a few months later," he sputtered. "He was seventy-nine."

With his father's passing, the mill reverted to Germain and his sister, according to Napoleonic law. They offered to let their stepmother stay at the mill and even brought her up to live with them, their seven children, and Marthe's parents at Le Bousquet for a few weeks, but it was too crowded, so she went back to the mill. There was no electricity, no plumbing, no water in the house, and she was almost eighty years old. She stayed for about a month and then left to live with relatives at Saint-Pierre at the mouth of the Rance River. From that point on, she had no rights to anything from La Pilande Basse other than one-fourth of the profits from the time she worked there with her husband, a meager sum at best.

There was a long silence while Germain contemplated the justice of the departure of his stepmother. "It's the law," he finally said. In the past, he had told me that she had been mean to him, but he didn't repeat that accusation. I wondered if he, at seventy-three, was more sympathetic to her, a woman of seventy-eight years of age when his father died.

Again, Germain was silent. I waited to see which direction he would take. He finally changed the subject to the eventual sale of the mill three years later to the people from whom we bought it. "I didn't want to sell it. But I'd promised my mother that nothing would come between my sister and me." He didn't have any means to pay his sister her fair share of the mill, so even though her husband told Germain he'd sign off on anything that Germain could offer, he decided to put it on the market. He just didn't have the means to take care of the abandoned buildings.

A couple, the Roziers from Graulhet, about sixty kilometers toward Toulouse, bought La Pilande Basse in 1970 as a second home. They tried to transform the main mill room into a living space, emptying out the stable and pouring a foot of concrete over the stone pavers. They whitewashed the stone walls, painted the chestnut ceiling white, put beanbag cushions on the millstone boxes. They made a back terrace over the reservoir and put wallpaper with bright peacocks all over the walls and ceilings upstairs in the old kitchen-turned-bedrooms. The outhouse was still there, and one circuit of electricity ran into the mill room. Then one day, they took down the six large wooden doors of the *bluterie*, the handsome flour sifter, and put them out by the road as garbage. Germain recounted again, with a faraway look in his eyes, how he had driven by and saw the doors, stopped, and surreptitiously jammed them into the back of his car (it took three trips), took them up to Le Bousquet, and stored them in his tobacco barn for twenty-eight years, until he knew we were serious about restoring the mill. (We still keep one of the doors propped open, so you can see the twirling cage.)

I wanted to ask Germain more questions about daily life at the mill, but he was exhausted. Two hours of revisiting his mother's death, his banishment from his home, and his father's treatment of him as a child, then as a worker. He wagged his finger. *"Je peux plus."* "No more."

May 31, 2001

JOURNAL ENTRY

I've got too many proposals, I'm starting to panic. The Taurines project is huge, and we artists, Jean-Michel, Jean-Claude, and I, have suggested that we replace the château walls with visual hints of what was there, which requires thousands of feet of bright red tubing. When Mike thinks I'm crazy, I am. And I've been asked to do an installation in Barcelona, too far, too complicated. My kites, flying high in the still-hot air at Cordes are starting to come unglued. I've replaced two, hauling them up and down through those damn low-voltage lights. Next week, I'm taking them all down and sewing the ends. No more talk of buying them now!

NATIONAL MILL DAY AT LA PILANDE BASSE

June 15, 2001
Dear Linda,

Every June there's a Journée du Moulin, or a National Mill Day, in France, and we've said every year we're going to open the mill to the public and then we can't: Mike gets a new stent in his heart, the river floods, the river has no water, we are hiking in the Alps. But this year there's no impediment in sight. We made up a modest little poster with a transparent overlay of Germain's father standing in front of the mill, and we posted it in five villages: Plaisance, Trébas, Coupiac, Saint-Sernin, and Martrin. Given we would be open from 2 to 6 p.m., we thought we might get ten people an hour, which would give us a nice turnout and would allow us to grind some grain and give a little flour to each person who came. Germain agreed to hold court at the end of the mill near the stones, grinding some flour and answering questions, while Nadou agreed to keep me company between visitors. Martou, unexpectedly, came with Germain, saying she wanted to keep watch over the little house. She climbed up the uneven path, sat down in a comfortable chair, and settled in for a long, dull afternoon.

We were totally unprepared for what followed. Promptly at 2 p.m., about ten cars pulled up and parked along the road, four people per car. Timidly, they walked down the drive, through the one open gate, out onto the bridge, looking down at the mill. They were quiet. Some of the women were covering their mouths with their hands, as if to control their emotions. There they stood, and stood, all forty of them, nodding and whispering to each other.

I had been waiting, smiling, just outside the front door, expecting they would come down off the bridge and into the mill. But, no, they just stood there. I finally went out under the grape trellis and motioned, "*Venez, venez, rentrez.*" Somewhat reluctantly, they came down the path, and then stopped to individually shake my hand and introduce themselves to me. Madame Rousell d'Aspire, Monsieur Sureau d'Aspire, Monsieur/Dame de Fayet du Caylar, de Frayssines, de Balaguier-d'Olt, de Trébas, de Gaycre. They pointed at the terrace, switching to patois, then back to French. One woman said: "I remember bringing grain by wagon, drawn by our strongest cow, with my father. He'd throw fifty-kilo sacks of it over the bridge wall onto the terrace there. Monsieur Blanc would call him in to *boire un coup*. They drank wine while the grain was ground. Then Papa would load the grain back on the wagon and we'd start home." Her eyes filled with tears; her hand went back to her mouth.

Another woman said, "We came all the way from Balaguier, the wagon loaded. It was too far to go home, our cow too exhausted, so we'd bring our own sheets and spend the night, up in the *grenier*. Monsieur Blanc would stay up late grinding the grain, and in the morning Madame Blanc would take our sheets and scrub them in the water chute behind the house, the one that dumped water into the reservoir, and we would dry them in the sun on our way home."

From Le Caylar, Frayssines, Solage, Le Truel, La Fon del Mas, they came. Monsieur Bonnefé, Madame Trouniet, Madame Mejean from Les Peyrette, Cougasse, where Marthe was born. The crowd included Martou's relatives, Germain's cousins, friends, three mayors, and one priest. They stood on the bridge, hands to their mouths. I finally went out again and motioned, "*Venez, venez, rentrez.*" They, too, came down the path, stopped, shook my hand with one hand, berets in the other, all talking at once about when, how, and mostly with whom they had come to the mill. Then they timidly entered the house with the others.

I turned and there were thirty more on the bridge. They had come from Saint-Sernin-sur-Rance, La Borie-Haute, La Borie-Basse, La Capelle, Le Sommet, Cadix, Monestier. The same play, different characters, all touched, curious, but somewhat reluctant to go inside in case the Americans had destroyed the mill. But they did.

Now, Mike and Germain, at the end of the mill near the river, were surrounded by over one hundred people, with more on the bridge. These had come from Souyrol, Rieucros, Trancacas, and Lapaloup and were waiting to be pulled into the mill. Mike ran from the end of the room with the millworks to me at the front door: "Stop! There are two-foot beams to hold up four tons of stone, but there are ten tons of people at that end of the mill! Take them down to the turbine, dance, do anything, but don't let any more in until those disperse!"

I opened the ribbon guarding the stairs up to our rooms and invited the women to go up to see the top floor, something never done in rural France. They bounded past me, two steps at a time. I told them to go up to the little house, anywhere they wanted. The men I pulled down to the lower terrace onto the platform above the turbine, reached out and tapped the twenty-five-foot metal bar to signal Mike to open the *vanne*, something, anything, to entertain them. He did; it hesitated, then splashed into motion, turning slower, then faster as amazement spread over the faces of the men, resulting in gap-toothed grins.

I ran back up to pull more men down, waving at the people from Brasc, Montclar, Martrin, Esplas, Saint-Juéry—another forty or so on the bridge, hands to their mouths. I shooed the people d'Aspire, de Fayet, du Le Caylar, de Frayssines, de Balaguier, de Trébas, de Gaycre, out the back to the waterfall terrace and a pastis. Nadou, wide-eyed, poured the pastis and cut the loaves of our bread into smaller and smaller pieces.

I then moved the Le Caylar, Frayssines, Solage, Truel, and La Fon del Mas people up to the bedrooms and down to the turbine, inviting the Souyrol, Rieucros, Trancacas, Lapaloup crowd to the end of the mill, where even Germain was starting to fade in spite of his pride at being the man of the hours and hours.

And so it went, to the millstones to the turbine, to the bedroom, to the terrace. Over three hundred people from every hamlet and village came to rediscover the mill and their past, their *patrimoine*. Some brought their grandchildren, some their creaky aunts. They all kept repeating, "*Bravo, belle rénovation. Bravo.*" They approved of our integration of the millworks into our living spaces, and were especially pleased that we had made the *meule* turn again. They eventually retreated in the same order, but not until they stayed and they talked, they teared up, and they thanked us, again, and again, and again.

—*Love to you all, Judy*

July 18, 2001

JOURNAL ENTRY

My *Flying Coat Hangers* are melting in the summer sun. They were to be there six weeks in the spring, but the village wanted to keep them all summer. High in that enclosed space, sun beating down with outside temperatures at 100 degrees, they've been exposed to over 140 degrees, and the archival glue I used is failing and condensation is dripping down from the glass ceiling on the highest kites. And pigeons get in through the ventilation holes and drop unspeakables onto the thin paper. I'm taking them down next week so they don't die of mockery.

I'm presently worried about a complex installation at the Château de Taurines, an exhibition space funded by the national art association. The committee that decides on artists was impressed with the presentation and the fundamental concept: to visually reconstruct two of the walls torn down one hundred years ago to rebuild the church next door, while changing their orientation to allow them to pierce the interior of the building. There will be perspective panels like I put in the holes in the *oubliette* in Coupiac, but of black tarpaper, oriented toward the cemetery where the gate into the château was installed when the stones were hauled away. While most châteaux in France were either torn down or badly damaged during the Revolution, most villages try to restore them to bring in tourist trade. I feel the same need, not for tourism, however. Is it nostalgia for what was or what could have been?

The exterior wall, starting at about twenty feet from the low wall to over sixty at the top of the south tower, will be a cable strung tightly with several hundred bright red plastic tubes, normally used underground to protect electrical wires, hanging to form a curtain. There are many technical problems: weight, the curve of the conduits from being coiled, the strength of the bolts high on the château wall. Oh, Bernard, where are you?

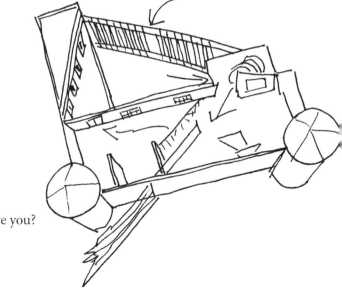

SUMMER NIGHTS AND THE POTATO CURE

August 10, 2001

Dear Linda,

We went to an unusual art event last weekend, which I'll try to describe though I'm not sure I can do it justice. A French couple we met recently, Geneviève and Emmanuel, own most of the remains of a château and chapel on a sliver of a rock formation that juts a thousand feet straight up out of the Tarn Valley north of Millau. It's a strategic place for a château, not so logical for a summer house: no water, no electricity. They have restored, with extremely good taste, several small buildings and the chapel to create a complex that forms a home with no connecting roof: the bedroom is in one building, the kitchen in another, and the chapel is the living room. They are all on different levels of the hill, with small steps sticking out of stone walls to terraced landings connecting them. The views are breathtaking. And there is art everywhere. Stunning.

Geneviève is a prof at a local high school and a sometime poet, and Emmanuel is an artist and designer of contemporary stained-glass windows. They're an unlikely pair, she a slender, beautiful woman at least twenty years younger than he, with her hair coiled precariously on the top of her head and always slipping from one side to the other, her arms in the air reclipping and poking the nest around. (She's a grand flirt, and consequently the men love her and the women distrust her.) Emmanuel has, in the prevailing style of French artists, a ponytail and a sometimes-trimmed beard growing from every hair follicle, so that he seems to wear a generous hairy napkin tied up in the back and draped down in the front. He's very slight and soft spoken, so it's startling when his baritone-bass voice emerges from the hair cloud around his head. He's well known in France on the national level and has done many public work projects to replace broken church windows with contemporary designs. His charcoal studies for those windows adorn the walls of the chapel, like ghosts of the panes that have been inserted in their own chapel-turned-living-room.

They have been fighting for years with the mayor of the village at the foot of the cliff where their hamlet is perched. The village, which rightfully owns the road and path to the complex and several square feet in the middle of the terraced spaces, wants

347

to have public access to the property for a tourist attraction. By so doing, they believe the greater public good would be served in the spirit of equality, fraternity, and the rest of the French mantra. So Geneviève and Emmanuel formed a foundation made up of all of their artist, writer, and Parisian art-collector friends to show the village that their own use of their complex is more important, more worldly, and for higher purposes than allowing a few tourists to picnic and toss garbage from a great height down into the Tarn Valley. Art trumps tourism? (Certainly not at the château in Coupiac.)

The initial members of the group, in solidarity, invited their friends, and they invited their friends, so that their group numbers now in the hundreds, many of whom are nationally known. In order to meet the requirements of the foundation, each year they hold a by-invitation-only art conference lasting three days. Each day includes open-air picnics with musicians, art hung in trees and the chapel, lectures on the geology of the limestone cliffs, and poetry readings, sometimes with a theme, mostly not. Some people come for the full three days, camping on various terraces; others, like us, stay at friends' houses in Millau and go for one afternoon and evening. Jean-Michel and Eveline insist that we stay with them in their wonderful new/old deco home overlooking the old/new cemetery. (Eveline mistrusts Geneviève's intentions even more than I do, possibly because Jean-Michel has the same ponytail-and-beard combo as Emmanuel, only more trimmed and less all-encompassing. She probably figures Jean-Michel is Geneviève's type.)

In the late afternoon, we all drove through the adversarial village, trying to look snotty and important as we passed, then onto the steep switchback hill that climbs up on the rutted dirt road that the village refuses to maintain only for them. We parked the car with the others and pulled out our baskets containing flashlights, water bottles, wine, and artwork, in that order of importance, per instructions. The path leading to the house/ruins is about three hundred yards long and clings to the side of the cliff. We arrived in the late afternoon with the rest of the twenty or so artists, their works, and wheelbarrows full of Evian. We spent a few hours installing the work, talking together about how and why one does this and the other that. Then the other guests arrived, mostly from Paris via their summer homes in the area. Several musicians were scheduled to play, one carting in a harpsichord that took him over an hour to retune after he had waited a few hours for the instrument to settle in from the trauma of the wheelbarrow.

The sunset was a scheduled event, given that it illuminated the entire Tarn Valley at our feet. There was a solemn silence as everyone appreciated the privilege of witnessing such a sight. Candles appeared, hundreds of votive candles stuffed into steel wool pillows lighting the paths, while dancing dots of flashlights betrayed those making *pipi à la nature*. There was a poetry reading by a relatively well-known French author, whose name escapes me, but then everything does.

The sixty or so guests paid about fifty dollars a couple, and the food was prepared by some of the guests who weren't clear on the instructions, so the dinner was a bit confusing. There were nuts and small squares of quiche on tables around the buildings, but also lots of wine, and by eleven at night, dinner still not served, the notables were ravenous and slightly drunk. The melons were uncut, the salad had no dressing, the dry ham was not sliced. The sausages were too few, and the wind kept blowing out the candles on the terrace. Dinner finally arrived around 1:30 a.m., and Mike and I passed on dessert at 2:30 a.m., leaving the harpsichord concert to come, and carefully picked our way back to the car and down that vertical cliff. It was unimaginable how that place could have been built a thousand years earlier.

—*Hugs, Judy*

August 15, 2001
Dear Linda,

I keep thinking our usual August storm will cool down these old stones, but *hélas*, no. Last night it was so hot I wrapped my neck with a wet bandana and fixed dinner for friends who had been rafting on the Tarn. By the time they arrived back, the sky was dark, but it hasn't rained in so long I actually believed it couldn't/wouldn't, so I had dinner set up on the terrace in front of the mill and snuggled by the bridge. We sat down, our guests still in their wet bathing suits, with cool skin and sweaty brows. As we began to eat, several large plops of rain started to disturb the zucchini pasta smothered in basil and fresh tomatoes. No one said a word. We continued to talk as the rain began, in earnest, to massage and then pelt us with soothing, then stinging little pellets of goodness. We toasted our health and our good luck and continued throughout the second course. No one moved to open the umbrella to protect us, and it was only with the thought of peach-tart dilution that we retired to the mill.

Poor Mike has had nasty leg cramps in this heat, usually in the middle of the night. They are almost always in his hamstrings, which for him is most of his body. Jumping to his feet, stomping, and yelling helps a bit but makes sleeping difficult for she who shares his bed. (That would be me.) I get them, too, but it's usually just my feet, and I can get rid of them by standing up and walking around a bit. Mike has to eventually get into the shower and spend an hour or so trying to work the cramp out. We're not the only people who get these cramps; Bernard *bois* is tortured as well, and Brigitte says her elderly patients on outlying farms ask for her advice, but no one seems to know why. Hard water? Too much, not enough water? We have tried drinking excessive water, cocktails of vitamins and minerals, quinine, you name it. But still, almost every night one or the other of us has cramps. But all that has changed.

I've told you about Nadou, our friend from Balkis, who is a *guérisseuse*, or healer. She practices *magnetisme*, which I can't translate, but it involves putting her hands on someone who has inflammatory problems, and through some mysterious transfer of energy, she disrupts the pain. I can only tell you she has saved my back from spasms more than once. When we were telling her about our cramps, she said, "No problem. Just put a *pomme de terre* in your bed!" Now we're not as naive as we seem, so I said no potatoes under my covers, thank you very much, and promptly forgot about it. A few weeks later, she was sitting at our table drinking coffee when Mike staggered down after another sleepless night. "Goddam cramps," says he. "*Ça suffit!*" says she. She went out to her car, where she had some freshly dug potatoes (don't ask me why), went to the sink and washed and dried them, climbed the stairs, and put them in our bed!

The first night was a little odd. Dodging each other is complex enough without the foot-fiddling necessary to keep a potato where you think it should be, wherever that is. (I know where you'd like to go with this, but this is serious business.) "Is that yours or mine? Should we put it in a sock or something? Hey, gimme that back." But no cramps.

Next night, my foot was cramping so I fumbled with my toes, found the potato, and slept like a baby. Mike woke with a dent in his calf that lasted until lunch, but still no cramps. The next night, I was feeling cocky—starting to believe that the weather had cooled a bit and we wouldn't be getting cramps anymore anyway, so I left my potato on the night stand. In the middle of the night, dreaming I couldn't walk because of a foot bent backward, I awoke to a real doozy. I grabbed the potato and put it on my foot . . . the cramp stopped immediately. Next night, same thing.

Okay. What's going on? Apparently, during WWII, they used potatoes to replace burned-out tubes in radios, and apparently every kid has made a little battery out of a potato for a science experiment. And apparently the little short-circuits in our legs can be interrupted with the same little tuber—either that or the placebo effect strikes again.

I thought it was the latter until I saw Mike packing up to go off to Millau to work with Jean-Michel for a few days. He had his computer, the printer, stacks of library books, a digital camera, a ditty bag, all waiting at the front door. Oops! Forgot something, up the stairs, down, unzipped his backpack and slipped in his spud . . . just in case! Another believer is born.

—*Bises, Judy*

August 18, 2001

Dear Linda,

It's still hot and hotter. Last night we were invited by some friends who own the château in Trébas, on the Tarn right at the confluence of the Rance. They had invited friends from Paris, Rodez, and Montpellier to celebrate the engagement of their son.

The château has a lovely garden with a pool, surrounded by carefully crumbling walls. When we arrived at the event, the friends of our friends were standing in their summer pastels, fanning damp brows, sipping pastis. As we walked into the group, our host presented us as "those Americans you've all heard about." After asking us if San Francisco was on the west coast or the east, the second inevitable question was asked, "Do you come to France for the food?" The French culinary chauvinism always grates on me, but I try to remember the terrible reputation the United States has for food, wine, and culture in general in most countries. Usually, I just smile and say sweetly that their food is good and so is ours. But for some reason, probably the heat, I lost it on that hot, sticky night. I told them, "We eat better in San Francisco than in Paris, and may I be frank, in the countryside, our friends' homes being the exception, we eat very badly, mostly involving Mystery Meat. It arrives swimming in Mystery Sauce, lightly gray, tough, and of unrecognizable origin." I noticed a few nods but mostly saw just slight shock and steps back. That didn't stop me; I continued on with how the world has moved on in the past fifty years and that, for the price, we and, *hélas*, even the English, eat better than the French, and our wines are winning their gold medals.

It was a long dinner, what with no one daring to speak to me and all. I had presented some Josef Schmidt chocolates as a house gift when we arrived, telling our host, Alain, that they were among the best in the world. He was shocked that we even had chocolates in San Francisco, but some guests had to admit afterward that they were certainly among the best they had ever eaten, and I noticed that Alain closed the box and hid them behind a vase! I only do that when I want some for myself later. A small revenge for me. I'm complaining about the French again. It's time to come home!

—*Hugs, Judy*

August 22, 2001

JOURNAL ENTRY

Rain, welcomed with every window open, drops plopping into the house, hot stones cooled on the terraces, grateful gardens thirsty to catch every drop. We were at dinner at the château in Trébas, huddled under a sun tent, when the thunder and lightning started. Cheers went up, the wind bothered no one, and the splooshes of rain in the pool met with applause. After two days, the welcome, now serious, rain threatens to push Le Mousse over its banks, its formerly clear water red with soil from above Coupiac, but with its *vannes* closed, La Pilande Basse just settles lower into the stream.

The project for next summer at Taurines has me frightened. I'm not sure I can really build the promised red walls, and I wish the project would just go away. I need to go home.

10

THE SWALLOWS RETURN

April 1, 2002
La Pilande Basse
Dear Linda,

I'm having trouble typing, with my shoulder still giving me fits. I thought when I broke it in January that it would be healed by now, but it still hurts to put on my bra, and gardening is impossible. Those stairs at the beach house have always scared me since there's no handrail. If I hadn't tried to stop myself by reaching out for the wall, if I'd just fallen, tuck and roll, I'd probably be out in my studio now. (The paramedic told me a shoulder dislocation seems to be the most painful injury he sees. But he knew it was broken, too, by the way I was instinctively holding it. But his little morphine cocktail made me not care at all.)

Nadou is the only person who asked me *why* it happened, not "How did it happen?" I really do believe that things happen for a reason, but other than getting me out of the Taurines project, the reason for this injury isn't clear. In retrospect, I'm glad I decided to cancel the show right away after I fell so they could arrange for something else, but I thought I'd be back in my studio by now. We're much more physically active here at the mill than at home, and I'm frustrated by my lack of strength and mobility, especially since Mike won't be here for a few weeks. His new pacemaker, the latest addition to his heart paraphernalia, needs one more checkup before he leaves San Francisco.

I sometimes feel like a fair-weather friend in France. We leave just as the cold of winter starts to settle in and come back with the first blush of green potential on the trees. *"Les hirondelles sont arrivées."* Monsieur Bertrand calls us swallows arriving for the good weather, and when our car is parked out by the road, it's a sure sign that the *hirondelles* are here. It also means I need to call Suzie and François, Bernard and Brigitte, Jean-Michel and Eveline, Nadou, Monique and Jean-Claude *tout de suite*. Germain and Martou, of course, already know. The second circle I reach within a few days, and the rest I give a broad excuse like "We got here a few weeks ago but we went straight to Paris [or the Alps or somewhere else] for a few weeks." With Antoine (the young landscape architect who has been taking care of the house and garden since we lost all our radiators in a big freeze a few years back) opening the house well in advance, people think we're already here well before we are and are slightly offended when I call. Frankly, I'm looking forward to a few days of hiding to do my nesting. I can use the jet-lag excuse only so long.

—*Grosses bises (big, sloppy French kisses on both cheeks), Judy*

April 2, 2002

JOURNAL ENTRY

The smells. When you open the door to your house, *bam*—the smells jump at you, all of them mixed in an olfactory casserole, anxious to get your attention, to share their day. When the house has been closed, it's the strongest that get to you first. Dark, green, musky, mildewy odors remind you of neglect, and smoky charcoal vapors are right behind, wafting down from the chimney caked with fall fires. Without pausing to shut the door to the mill I went straight for my incense drawer—a whole drawer devoted to shut-up-house smells, including sage from last year's crop, green tea incense, lavender oils. If I had had some onions I could have sautéed them and filled the house with the warm smells of home. *"Si j'avais eu des oignons, j'aurais pu les faire sauter pour parfumer la maison."* Good French lesson.

April 5, 2002
Dear Linda,

I couldn't avoid it: the first meal with *les Blanc*. I talked it down to *dejeuner*, hoping it would be lighter, faster. I think it was when Mike had his heart problems that it began to dawn on me that Martou was really not a very good cook, and that our meals together were more about the romance of our friendship than enjoying food. She doesn't like spices of any kind (basil makes her blood pressure spike), and thinks that *light* means "easy." Or maybe she's just getting old and doesn't or can't put out the effort. My memories are conflicting—in the past the food seemed much better. But now it's a stuffed tomato, frozen for forever, to be reheated/burned for the first course, followed by dry sausage packed in oil followed by cold duck . . . not the breast, not a leg, but the neck, *les gesiers*, or gizzards, and the wings, sticky with duck fat. Cold, dry, and bad. I poked at a gizzard and sucked on a couple of neck joints and pleaded jet lag. A nasty *fouace*, a dry pound-cake-like round loaf with a yucky aftertaste of too much orange extract that keeps for years, this one from Easter, was dessert. If I could have folded it in my napkin I would have. Not a green thing to be seen, not a bean or a leaf of lettuce. My beautiful box of Schmidt's chocolates from San Francisco was put away and not even offered. (Okay, I do the same thing with a good gift.) But I got the meal out of the way, and maybe we can pass when Mike comes. "His heart and all. One never knows." (It makes me think of you and your trick of exaggerating your hand injury with your fist to your forehead, "I've been sick, you know," to get us out of that dreadful family reunion last year.)

I really shouldn't complain, since I once again tumbled down the hill with a huge bag of spinach, some eggs, and another big ole hunk of *fouace* for dinner. I did make a béchamel for the spinach, along with a small chicken with mushrooms, and put the *fouace* in the *poubelle* where it belongs.

Yesterday, I decided I needed to empty all the cupboards so I'd know what was there when I went shopping. But in my jet-lagged state of unconsciousness, I find myself surrounded by canned goods on every surface and not enough energy or concentration to decide where to put them. Can't put dry goods in that cupboard because the *bêtes* can get to them . . . don't want the canned goods over there because . . . you know the syndrome . . . and, yikes, things get old, and what dumb things I've brought from the States. Just how many fermented black beans have I ever used, anywhere? Zero. But I've got three cans. Got any recipes?

Then I had to run off to Coupiac to face Madame Bertrand, who runs the local little grocery store, or *épicerie*, which has most of the things I need. (She is the only Frenchperson who is taller than I am, and she and her equally huge husband have created two of the largest children in rural France. It's hard not to stare.) I don't know why I'm so shy about going there. Probably because I'll have to explain again why Mike isn't here and talk about the weather and try to pronounce *œufs* correctly while I'm jet-lagged. Monsieur Bertrand corrects me every time I try to pronounce *eggs*. I sometimes go all the way to Albi to avoid facing Monsieur *Oeufs*. Seems I try to put an *r* sound at the end of *monsieur, œufs, peu, deux, feu*, etc. *Tant pis*, Fluffy. There *is* an *r* at the end of *monsieur*, so why don't they pronounce it? They pronounce the *r* in *peur, heure, leur,* why not *monsieur*? Besides, he knows what I mean. Madame Bertrand was there, imposing as ever, announcing that her son, Géant, Jr., was taking over the store so she can retire. Oh great, now every time I come back I can look forward to someone even bigger to make me pronounce *œufs* correctly.

Mike not being here seems to have already primed the rumor mill. A couple of fishermen left one of their cars in our parking area all night, and Natalie, my housekeeper and world-class gossip, sucking her teeth, asked me if I had had any company. She had seen the man leaving first thing in the morning! The more I protested the worse it sounded! Then, a stonemason from Réquista had a breakdown right in front of the house and left his enormous stone-raiser thing in the parking area. Naturally. Germain thinks that we're having work done and didn't ask his son to do it! Again, no way to protest. Only time will tell. Hmmm, you taught me: If you have the reputation, why not have the fun?

—*Bises, Judy*

April 30, 2002
JOURNAL ENTRY

I feel like I never left. Nothing really changes—the water sounds, the primulas in cracks on the path, the roses in bud. Small things change: Suzie's François found more mushrooms than usual in the first rains, France at the *boulangerie* has lost one of her front teeth, Madame Parnat has closed her pathetic little grocery store in Plaisance, but the village built a new building in the old parking lot next to Madame Touzet's now-closed café and is underwriting a bar/café and *épicerie*. Monsieur Parnat has also retired, and he and his wife sit together on the paved terrace across the street from their house and watch the cars go by. She still has her frozen smile, and while his shoulders are more stooped, his *brocanteur* eyes still dart about. The *source* hose popped and water is running down the cliff; there's evidence of a recent small flood on the banks of the Mousse. Germain is older and walks more slowly, but his brown eyes still fill with tears when he walks into the mill to see if we're up to something he should know about, like that cement truck.

But I think I'm witnessing the end of the end of rural France. In past years, when we came back in the spring, there used to be more deaths than births, more houses closed up. But in both Coupiac and Plaisance there are new stores and new houses being built. Even Le Bousquet has a new villa being framed in up the hill from Germain's garden. So there is change. There will be more.

May 1, 2002

Dear Linda,

Today is Mom's birthday. She would be eighty-five today. She's been dead almost as long as she lived. But I still talk to her, do you? I take her along on my travels, as if she couldn't go where she wants!

Yesterday's peak experience (if you don't count vacuuming behind the furniture, which was very scary) was going up to see Martou and Germain. Mike has arrived, and while we usually eat dinner with them the very first night, Martou had a cold and Germain has been coughing for weeks, then it was us, etc. We agreed that the *bisous* would be from a distance since I have an airplane bug coming on. We brought them our lame gifts (bamboo cutting board for her and a "Got Shrimp?" T-shirt from Bubba Gump's for Germain—we had eaten there in California) and pulled up to the kitchen table for the ritual *apéritif*.

We glanced around the room that never changes. In the far corner is a grandfather clock, which touches the ceiling. When we were leaving in the fall, Martou whispered that her kids were going to take it to Réquista to be repaired, and when we arrived, the brass face was polished and the pendulum was swinging for the first time in fifteen years. Martou was so proud, and Germain *boff, boff, boff*'d, saying it was a waste of time, no pun intended. But next to the *horloge* is a new small, wall-mounted clock that served to announce the hour during the grandfather's winter absence and still hollers out in hourly competition with the grand master. On the hour and the half hour, the newcomer clock strikes up a tinny rendition of "Whistle While You Work" or "She'll Be Comin' 'Round the Mountain," or one of twelve different tunes, all equally anachronistic in that setting. On the hour, the grandfather clock bongs, and the other clanks "There's No Business Like Show Business" or something else, not at all in unison. They bought the clock on one of their senior citizen trips to Andorra, a country where one must buy.

Against the two longer walls are two stuffed chairs and a couch facing each other and covered carefully with chenille throws. I've never seen what's underneath. And a brand-new radiator now sits where the wood-burning stove used to be. They are enjoying their first winter without hauling wood every morning, thanks to their children's gift of their first furnace. A television is tucked under the staircase that leads to the second floor, and an armoire with all of Martou's treasures fills up the other short wall. The Formica kitchen table sits squarely in the middle of the space, keeping the couch sitter from seeing the comfortable-chair sitter. We've never sat anywhere except at that table, or at the table in the barn that's permanently set up for thirty-one (used to be twenty-eight, but there are serious boy/girlfriends who are being initiated into La Famille Blanc). I've twice been in the parlor where Martou's mother lived before she died thirty-five years ago: once to install the answering machine we brought for them, and once last year to measure for new lampshades to cover up the longer energy-efficient light bulbs that are mounted on a wagon wheel over the wooden dining table, which has hardly been used since her mother died. I think the priest used to dine there, but he died, too.

Martou pulled the pastis bottle and a sweet wine from the belly of the wine barrel that one of their children converted into a dry bar, which sits proudly next to the grandfather clock. Germain turned the pastis bottle upside down, watching the little measuring bulb, spotted with clubs and diamonds, at the end of the bottle fill with the amber liquid, then poured the dose into the large glasses with yellow flowers on the sides. Martou pulled the cold water from the refrigerator, and we served ourselves, judging the amount by the color change as the amber liquor turned foggy white with the water. As always, Martou hesitated, then shrugged her shoulders, reached to serve herself a small ration in a small glass with etched leaves and, as always, looked first to judge the amount, then poured a bit more. She often finishes her *apéro* before we've downed the pastis, but she never takes more. As always, I feel slightly guilty that I don't join her in her sweet Muscat, a proper lady's drink.

We caught up on all the children, the garden, the births, weddings, deaths. Politics were discussed, but briefly. They know we hate Bush and they feel the same, but are more conservative in general than we are. Our friend Claude is running against the long-term mayor of Coupiac, and they don't trust him. He's a stranger. (He was born in Coupiac, has been mayor of Martrin for ten years, and the football field is named after his father, but he moved to Germany to work and came back fifteen years ago. So he's still a stranger.) We don't get involved in those discussions. No point.

When it was time to go, Germain asked his usual question: "*Pas de salade?*" I think he was relieved when I said I'd just bought some in Coupiac so I'd have to come back up tomorrow. His arthritis is so bad he didn't even get up to say goodbye, much less go out to pick lettuce in the dark on a cold night. But the *oeufs* I accepted— *merde* and all!
—*Good night, Judy*

LINDA

May 15, 2002
Dear Linda,

I'm so sorry you took a tumble down the stairs. I'm sure you've already found a snazzy outfit to match the bruises—teal blue with a chartreuse scarf might work as you go from black to blue to green to yellow. This must be the year for the Ketels girls to go down the steps. I think I fell because subconsciously I didn't want to do my show. So why did you fall?

You asked about "your garden." (I'm glad you feel possessive about my little *potager*.) It looks beautiful already, full of pansies, arugula, baby radishes, snow peas. Our huge, frilly red cabbages aren't planted yet though, and the corn can't go in before the soil is warm.

Not much news except for Germain's resolution of his lawsuit around his garden spring. For four hundred years the *source* that came out of the side of the steep hill above Germain's big garden supplied water to everyone at Le Bousquet. The surplus formed two big ponds, one for frogs (yes, they really do eat them) and the other for trout. Monsieur Rouquette, who is building the new house in the hamlet, decided that since the water comes out on his land it was his, ignoring centuries of legal easements. But he lost quickly in court and has to pay for the lawyers, though not the anguish caused to the old people he tried to sue, Germain and Monsieur Sureau.

In the meantime, another neighbor's son is building a house next to Germain's hothouse, on land he doesn't own! It belongs to his mother, and apparently they haven't spoken in years. A real soap opera. Then Madame Bertrand told me that the *boulanger* was in the hospital suffering from nervous exhaustion caused by the trauma of coming out of the closet and announcing that he's gay. Consequently, the *boulangerie* is temporarily closed, and we get to eat only the Coupaigaise, the bread made in the factory on the flat part of the Mousse River upstream from La Pilande Basse, since I can't knead any dough with this useless appendage hanging by my side.

But the big gossip is the mayor of Coupiac: his father was the mayor for years, and Monsieur Spenard followed him, not out of merit but inertia. He's often so depressed he can't function at all, so everyone just operates around him. But this past winter, after a couple of decades of marriage, his wife finally left him, for another woman. The happy couple are living next door to M. Spenard, whether to torture him or comfort him, I don't know. But the whole affair has sent him into a French tailspin. He's running against Claude, the mayor of Martrin, for reelection as mayor of Coupiac. His main persuasive argument is, "If I'm not reelected, I'll kill myself!" Behind his back, almost everyone jokingly does the shoulder-shrug, lifted-eyebrow gesture that says, "Hmmm, is that so bad?"

Over the weekend, we went to Martou and Germain's fiftieth wedding anniversary party at their daughter Geneviève's house. Fifty-five people were smashed together in their garage as the "happy couple" sat stiffly at the head of the table. There were poems, a huge cake, and fifty-five digital cameras flashing at the only kiss, a slight peck on the lips, the only *bisou* I've ever seen between them. In fact, I've never seen Germain actually touch Martou, take her arm, or help her down/up the stairs, ever.

I'm starting to do the "why, I remember" thing when I think back to when we first showed them our digital camera, only six years ago. When Germain found out we could manipulate photos, he asked us to cut the head off his aunt and put his mother's on her body so he could have a picture of his mother and father together. He still shows it proudly, but always explains, "It's not real, you know."

We're wandering into Provence for a few days with some friends. Our rule is to never cross the Rhône River after June 1 because of traffic and tourists, so we'll see if we are right!

—*Hugs, Judy*

June 10, 2002
Dear Linda,

American friends always say, "Oh, are you in Provence?" Explaining regions and departments in France is complicated, but the real Provence has the mistral, the wind that started the minute we crossed the Rhône River and didn't stop until we climbed back into the gentle hills of the Aveyron. Twenty-four hours a day, sixty miles an hour, sometimes for weeks, this wind blows. After only four days, I had Pagnolian visions of murders in the making. Remembering why we were in the Aveyron, we zipped through Saint-Tropez and Cassis for a look-see. We couldn't find a place to park, at all, in Cassis, so it was a drive by. Oddly, San Tropez was less crowded, and frankly, I was pleasantly surprised. The main town isn't all "done," and the crowds were lively and there was lots of good, chic window-shopping.

As you know, I like to use unusual things as purses, and my latest is a wicker fishing creel that I bought from Jean-Paul at the hardware store in Coupiac. It has a nice shape, is sturdy, and hangs well in front or in back. While I was walking through narrow streets with the smart shops in Saint-Tropez, a stylish woman, well coiffed and wearing Italian shoes, grabbed my arm and exclaimed, "Your purse is marvelous. Where did you find it?" Without batting an eye I told her, "Chez Jean-Paul." She asked me where that was, poised to rush down the correct street. When I told her "*C'est la quincaillerie à Coupiac dans l'Aveyron,*" she backed up in horror. Seems neither a hardware store nor the Aveyron is *très chic* in Provence.

Now we're back, with no serious visitors or projects, and a relatively clear agenda, which scares me a bit, but I've devised several smaller art projects to keep me off the streets. My shoulder is much better, but still weak. I am thoroughly enjoying the break (no pun intended), however, and wonder if something was trying to tell me something. I was asked to have a show in the same gallery as Mike for next summer, but I told them I am taking a sabbatical. I realized that I have had a major show every year for five years and have three more scheduled with no time to think or experiment. Stuff is starting to percolate. Maybe I should write. Any feedback?

I'm also taking cooking seriously. I keep a kitchen journal here, have for years, and I'm going to try to get it organized and continue experimenting with breads and fish dishes that I started and never perfected. We have a fishmonger, Monsieur Choron, who pulls into our driveway each Tuesday honking his horn; then he throws open his refrigerator truck and proudly shows off his array of delicious fish, so we do eat well from the sea, even in the mountains. He picks his wares up in Toulouse at 4 a.m., where seafood from both the Atlantic and Mediterranean are delivered in the night to be shipped to all the major cities of France. Government-subsidized merchants, like Monsieur Choron, trundle the seafood to all the small villages between here and there. When he passes by *chez nous,* if he sees our car, he stops, and I run out to score some fresh sardines or cod, and to taste the oysters, to be sure. I have some monkfish for tonight.

Well, dear, Jean-Luc, our new gardener (Mike agreed after his heart stuff that he needed some help) is at the door, Natalie is removing the wax that she so carefully put down on the oak and chestnut floors over the last eight years, Mike is digging potatoes, and I'm procrastinating. So far, I'm having a Clean Day, and I'm looking for excuses to stay so. Can you tell I desperately need a good project here or I'll be truly out of control?

—*Hugs, Judy*

June 15, 2002

JOURNAL ENTRY

Gary just called. Acute leukemia. Linda has acute leukemia. Her bruises weren't from her tumble down the stairs. They were there before. She tried to tell her doctor about them by phone, but he thought they were just another of her increasingly long list of problems. After she fell, Gary took her in and the doctor finally saw them, realized they were serious, and sent her to the hospital for tests. She's in Ann Arbor at the cancer clinic. I'm leaving tomorrow.

July 27, 2002
JOURNAL ENTRY
Ann Arbor, Michigan

My sister, Linda, died quietly in her sleep last night with her husband curled against her . . . the way she wanted it. She was brave and beautiful to the end. Her adult children, Steph and Matt, are broken dolls, and my brother-in-law keeps a towel around his neck to wipe away his tears. I'm draped in blinking lights and sobbing.

Since she was in a distant university hospital her last five weeks, her friends couldn't all come to see her. So we asked them to send her "light" in whatever form they wished. Her room slowly filled with strings of tiny patio lights, feather boas, cotton balls strung together, tiny flashlights, and wonderful blinking necklaces, pins, and rings. She would dress her hospital gown with the most outrageous jewelry and, dragging her IV pole beside her, troll the halls of the cancer ward, collecting smiles. She gave some of her blinking rings to frightened patients, some alone in their rooms, telling them to keep fighting.

The nursing staff at the University of Michigan cancer ward was extraordinary. Not only did they tolerate our lights and toe rings, but they even contributed to the growing collection of dragonflies and other symbols of transition. They embraced us when we couldn't take it anymore, they laughed with us, and they talked to Linda when we thought she was nowhere to be found. And near the end, when the dignity of departure seemed far away, they counseled us on how to contact hospice to make her exit as graceful as possible for her, as kind as possible for her children, and as private as possible for her husband.

September 13, 2002
JOURNAL ENTRY
La Pilande Basse

In the dark, droopy limbs of willows and hazelnuts swallowed our car as we rolled across the gravel drive down to the mill. And this morning the wisteria is pressed against the bedroom window, anxious to get in. We're back at the mill, still, always, *toujours* trying to beat back the vegetation that threatens to swallow our pile of stones.

The flight, on the first anniversary of September 11, which we thought would be empty, was full, the seats ratcheted even closer, Mike's knees folded on my lap. We got to the mill well after midnight on Friday morning, thereby totally losing Thursday to the sun racing west. I feel as if my heart and body were left behind with that day somewhere. We are sleeping in random four-hour shifts, and I'm struggling to not cry every waking moment. And they are everywhere: the long shadows across the face of fall.

Yet there's the reassuring beauty of the mill, and the late-garden bounty promises something. The weather has become nice after a rainy August, and a surplus of tomatoes, corn, and lettuce is threatening in its abundance. This year the basil has won the "What in the World Can I Do with All That?" title. Rows of it . . . big, lush leaves, pure and green, daring me to toss them on the compost pile. The corn waited for us, perfect ears, white and sweet. We have a ritual: water boiling first, then we go up and pick it, shucking as we go, then fresh into the pot while it's still wiggling. (By phone, Germain told us to hurry back to the mill since the crows had found it.)

For a moment I forget, and I feel a spurt of energy; then I try to act, but can't. Then I remember: Linda died on the 27th of July, Derek had another baby on the 5th of August, and Hayden got married on the 10th. For two weeks the circle of life spun crazily out of control.

Even writing this seems such drivel. I want to write to Linda, to get her tapped-out messages back, her plain talk, her encouragement.

September 28, 2002

JOURNAL ENTRY

Bernard *pierre* came to see us today. He pulled into the drive with his newest old truck loaded with tools and riding low with extra bags of cement. He brought a friend, Olivier, who wanted to see the mill, the excuse he used to show up after a two-year absence. Somehow he knew Linda had died. He knew how sad I am. I don't know how.

I saw the truck pull in, but I thought it was Pierre, the *forgeron*, so when I answered the door, I don't know who was more shocked. I'd been in the garden all morning, covering the empty basil beds, snapping stripped cornstalks, my bandana tied around my head, my eyes red from my last good cry. His teeth are mostly gone, his curly hair was matted and gray, and he's obviously still drinking heavily. But his eyes widened to see me in such a state. I wanted to ask him about his life, his children, and now, grandchildren, but I just teared up and nodded as he talked. I can't remember what he said. I suggested he show his friend the mill, and I tagged along.

We walked to the end to see the millstones, and he explained the *bluterie*, then went below to see the *chambre d'eau* and the turbine. We laughed about digging out the tunnels, the mud, the fun. He pulled Olivier and me through the mill to the back terrace where he had built the temporary handrails for Linda's visit. He looked up to see Dan's stone sculpture, now securely installed on the upper terrace, and smiled and tapped his leg where the falling stone had broken it.

We toured the garden paths he'd built, the terraces, now patinated with moss, wild strawberries growing in the cracks. He patted the fallen oak tree, lying on its side. We had insisted on saving it even though we had to step over it on the path going to the waterfall terrace. At the time he had carefully roughed up the bark and piled dirt around it, creating a new environment for roots, then laid the stones of the path. Nine years later, the tree was dwarfed, bonsaied by Bernard, but healthy. He ran his rough hands over the cement counters we'd made in the little house, explaining in detail to Olivier how fussy I was about the colors, how we had "fought" about most things, including my art projects. We laughed about the wall he'd broken down during our first flood, and contemplated the swirling thumbprints he'd laid down for Richard Berger.

Then, as quickly as he'd come, he left. After four long *bisous*, he held my shoulders with his rough hands: "*Courage, Judite.*"

October 15, 2002
JOURNAL ENTRY

I still can't believe it. When I see someone and they ask me how I am, I don't dare tell them. The tears are too close. If I say I'm fine, I can't bear the rest of the conversation. Linda's daughter, Stephanie, is coming next week for her first healing peek at rural France. She's a photographer, so there'll be lots of old stones to shoot. She needs to grieve in a safe place, and she'll be looking for wisdom.

I've decided that Linda arranged her own exit. Given her sense of humor and her cardiovascular problems, she probably feared an indecorous cardiac-induced end with her head in the laundry basket. She somehow "arranged" for her family to be available:

her angel pushed me down the stairs to bust up my shoulder just enough to make me cancel two summer shows, her son was laid off for six weeks, her daughter was forced to move from her apartment temporarily—uncannily similar events that left us available to say our thank-yous, regrets, and goodbyes.

She was not only my best friend, but the guardian of the treasures of my past. Our parents died when we were young, and she surreptitiously took care of me and cheered me on while others shook their collective heads. She was a safety net when I tumbled and a magic mirror when I tried to fool myself. I'm not sure I'm up to the challenge of being "the last Ketels standing" as one of my Michigan friends said at her funeral.

I promised myself, as soon as we returned, I would sit at the end of the mill near the river with the water sounds beneath and face my grief ritualistically, with music, incense, writing, crying. I had my journal, my tea, my music player. I put my two-thousand-plus songs on shuffle, closed my eyes and waited. Then, without even remembering I had the song, I heard Jerry Vale singing: "When I go to sleep, I never count sheep, I count all the charms about Linda . . . but miracles still happen, and when my lucky star begins to shine . . ."

November 2, 2002

JOURNAL ENTRY

I love/hate the French. Just when I think they may be okay, their hyperbureaucratic nature pops up. They refuse to renew my *carte de séjour*, which would have been good for ten years after this year, because I missed the July 1 deadline. Our mayor, his secretary, our neighbors have petitioned the government explaining my family emergency. But no. I, after ten years of the same translation of my birth certificate, my medical card, my marriage license, and my financial statement, have to start all over again. Mike has his, but I can't have mine.

And our neighbor upstream refuses to let us cut the dead trees on a cliff above the dam so they don't fall into the river and form a blockage that could back up and flood not just us, but other places upstream. Our mayor sent him a letter stating that if there were any flooding he would be responsible. I hate/love them.

THE BIRTHING OF THE LAMBS

November 14, 2002
JOURNAL ENTRY

Les Fabre de Moussac invited us to come, witness, and photograph the birthing of the lambs, an essential event for the milking season and for refilling of the caves of Roquefort with salty, blue-green-flecked cheese. Mike loaded up his huge banquet camera and off we went, forewarned to wear our boots and dirty-day clothes.

All 800,000 qualified ewes in the ninety-mile radius from Roquefort (plus one tiny region in the Pyrenees) are inseminated within a two-week period in September, and the lambs are born eight weeks later, approximately 1,600,000 of them, all within another two weeks. The 2,300 or so farmers must be present so the lambs can be quickly bonded to their mothers, tagged for quality control, and often, pulled from the womb.

Hence, either Monique, Jean-Claude, or their daughter Flo, now officially the head of the farm, are awake for a month, birthing, tagging, teasing the ewes to accept their twin young—a total of four hundred sheep and eight hundred lambs.

Monique took us into the *bergerie*, the large metal pole-barn behind the milking building where we had already watched several times the organized chaos of feeding/milking four hundred sheep in forty-five minutes flat. Roquefort farmers keep their sheep indoors in the heat of summer, so the sheep barn must be large enough to house all four hundred, this one at least eighty by one hundred feet. In the cool air of November, the side doors were wide open and the sun was streaming in, throwing long shadows against the walls.

Most of the herd was out in the fields; only the ewes who either were close to delivery, in process, or had just birthed their lambs were in the barn. Down the middle of the long barn was a narrow feeding trough with two hundred cutouts on top of it so the sheep could feed without interruption or competition from their neighbors. Raphael, the Basque hired hand, was walking down the middle of the empty trough, tossing fresh straw into the pens on each side. He raised his head in greeting.

On the right side were two large pens with about twenty sheep in each. Flo, a practiced eye scanning the scene, explained that in the farthest pen the ewes were all still in labor. Some had delivered their first lamb, while others were still staggering with the girth of anticipated twins.

Before Flo could explain the rest, she said, "*Oh, merde, venez.*" The dark-haired beauty vaulted over the low wall between the two pens and put her arm around a ewe obviously in full parturition. Speaking softly, she expertly inserted her fist, then her arm, deep into the ewe's vaginal cavity. "*Merde*, a hoof is stuck!" She gently flipped the ewe on her side, talking quietly to her, like a friend, "Don't push yet. *Doucement.*" ("Slow down.")

Whether the ewe understood or not, she did relax while Flo, now on her knees, reached even farther inside her. "Okay, *pousse.*" One little hoof and a slippery nose appeared at the end of the fully dilated birth canal. But the rest refused to come. Quickly, and no longer so gently, Flo reached in and pulled out another hoof, and with one boot against the ewe's rump, pulled until she plopped on the straw with the lamb, a slippery newborn twice the size of the first. Flo laughed, grabbed the lamb, checked his heart, and clipped the umbilical cord, never letting the lamb leave the nose of the ewe, so the olfactory bond would not be disturbed. (If the ewe loses the scent, she'll reject the lamb entirely.) There was no afterbirth, making Flo think there was probably a third lamb to come, but she didn't want to examine the ewe so soon after such a rough passage.

Jean-Claude was in the other pen, straddling a disinterested ewe, his huge hands cradling two minuscule lambs close to the teats of their mother, restraining her until they "took." Groaning as he stood up, one hand pushing against the small of his large back, he offered Mike his other wrist to shake, as his hands had been in strange places all morning, and me his scruffy cheeks to peck three times. With a contagious enthusiasm and his tightly rolled *r*'s, he explained what was happening on the other side of the trough.

There were several smaller stalls, each specializing in some troubled part of birthing. The one in front contained ten lambs that had been rejected by their moms, either because they were the weakest of triplets (ewes have only two teats), or because the ewe got distracted during the second birth and she no longer recognized her firstborn. (In moving the sheep from one stall into a nursery stall, Flo or Jean-Claude would drag the lambs upside down by their front legs with the shortened umbilical cord close to the ewe's nose to maintain the bond.)

In another pen were a few lambs dressed in overalls made from the skins of lambs who had been born dead, a trick to fool their foster ewe mothers into accepting them as their own. When a lamb is stillborn, they quickly skin it, cut off the pelt just above the navel, slip it over the back feet of a rejected lamb, tie it on with cord suspenders, and push the still-attached umbilical cord under the nose of the unsuspecting mother, still staggering and unknowing from her failed labor. These particular lambs were waiting for their step-siblings to be born so they could be both presented to the easily fooled ewe. Over a few days, as the ewe establishes a visual connection, the smell apparently is less important, and the grafted wool overalls can be removed.

Another large pen held the lambs from last week, those who had successfully appeared, been accepted, and then separated from their mother while she went out into the cool, thick grass of November to recover. They would be reunited when the herd returned and had had their ration of grain from the large trough. (If left to wander with four hundred head of sheep, the little ones could be injured in the stampede to be fed.)

After the explanations, Jean-Claude vaulted over to the other side of the pen to rescue a lamb pinned down under the flank of its own exhausted mother. Then Flo's seven-year-old daughter, Agace, pulled on my hand to bring me to the smallest pen, where the orphan lambs were fed by hand. She climbed into their soft straw bed and tugged long, thin artificial nipples over two Heineken bottles full of milk while the lambs crowded around her. Agace sat on the straw and balanced two tiny lambs while they sucked eagerly at the offering as the others licked at her face and toes, making her giggle with joy.

While Mike set up his camera, I watched Flo circulate through the emergence of life. She sometimes scooped up a newborn, checking its mouth, clipping a tag on its ear, and rubbing the umbilical cord in the nose of the ewe, then quickly noting the number on the ear tag in the book hanging from a nail between the pens. Sometimes she physically assisted another ewe with the delivery of either a stillbirth or a live, kicking lamb. She did that twenty-six times that day and the day before and before, and will continue right up to December.

We stayed and photographed until the sun went down and the herd came in from the pasture, Raphael dragging a lamb upside-down in front of its mother, exclaiming they'd missed this triplet that had arrived two days later, out in the field. He wasn't sure if the first two had survived or not. Flo checked the log, shrugged her shoulders, noted something in the book, tagged and slipped the lamb into the pen to be fed by hand, "Not enough teats for all."

The barn was closed and shut up for the evening, its heat piped in from the enormous wood-burning furnace below the two main houses. Once the doors were closed, the stench of ammonia, in spite of the fresh straw, forced us out into the cold night air.

We thought when we left, around 9:30 p.m., they'd tumble off to bed, but Flo had to finish her logs and Raphael suited up for the first part of the night shift. After the obligatory *bisou*, Monique shooed the little ones to bed and Jean-Claude herded us out, exchanging us for his cows waiting impatiently by the gate.

Judy and Linda with their mother, Reba

AFTERWORD

May 1, 2010
Dear Linda,

Happy Mom's birthday. It's been seventeen years since I wrote you the first letter about the mill and the water sounds: that smooth hush that fills the air around us. And it's been eight years since you decided you'd suffered enough. I still can't quite believe it. I find myself composing some silly anecdote about life in rural France, knowing it might tickle you, then I remember, and the joy drains out. Why it took me so long to write this letter is hard to explain. At first I didn't believe that you'd get it, and then, finally, I realized that you would help me write it, help tie up the loose ends of the tales I told you earlier.

Stephanie came to the mill in the fall after your death, for her first trip ever to Europe, and she fell in love with the garden, the stones, the waterfall, and Claude, the mayor of Martrin, with the droopiest handlebar moustache and Frenchiest hooked nose you can imagine. She promptly forgot him after she left, but I guess you know that already.

When I last wrote I was injured and had to cancel an important show I was preparing, but have since completed several big installations and some smaller ones as well, have started writing, and we've even had our first guest poet, Carolyn Miller, stay at the mill. (She has encouraged, no, pushed me to finish wrapping up these letters to you.) I won't bore you with the details of my art projects, since my previous letters explained the process I go through, and it's the process that's most important to me, more than the result. Mike continues to produce ever more complex and interesting work. As our circle of French artist friends has increased, we've decreased our visits from guest artists from the States. Charles Hobson still comes over almost every year, though. He's as romantic as ever about France in general and about our adventures in particular.

Since Francis died, Les Magnolias has been transformed into a German-run way station, putting up travelers en route to Spain and closed to anyone except hotel guests. The place was so important to us in our first years at the mill that we tried to stay neutral as the whole village turned slowly against Karl, the German owner, and his surrogate manager, Hilda, one of his scorned lovers, a nasty woman who serves as a contemporary Brunhilde presence in the heart of the village, yelling at chambermaids and alienating local merchants. I tried one last time to take Charles, who had a nostalgic urge to eat there, and Hilda was so hostile I slammed down the phone in her ear. When we first stayed there, floating in our romantic notion of the auberge, we had no idea that the village had turned against Francis because he had left his first wife for young Marie-France, and that it was probably the scorn of the locals that tore his heart apart. I somehow feel we have finally fully integrated into the community by turning our backs, somewhat belatedly, on Les Magnolias. Karl has put it up for sale, and hopefully someone fresh will return the auberge to its place as the center of the village, hosting weddings and wakes.

Christelle, who lived for years in an insufferable domestic situation, is finally actually happy. Five years ago she was offered a job at Les Magnolias as a chambermaid. When she told me, I asked her if she wanted me to help her get ready for what would be a different experience than she had had with us. I confessed to her that for years I had overlooked some inconsistency in her cleaning, reducing some of her tasks and doing them myself. I was concerned she would have a difficult time pleasing a German taskmaster. She pleaded with me to point out how she could improve, so we started with a list of things I was sure she would have to do and I followed her around correcting her ruthlessly. When I thought she couldn't stand it any longer, I asked her if she wanted me to go on. Tears in her eyes, she said, "This is for my children and my grandbabies. Please."

She worked at Les Magnolias for four years, detesting Hilda, who Christelle said treated her like a slave. But she let the insults go, taking the money, putting it into registered cash receipts, and sending it to Madagascar. Last year when Christelle needed knee surgery, Hilda fought giving her disability and would sneak over to Christelle's tiny house, hoping to catch her on her feet. She was sure Christelle was working for us (she wasn't at that time because of her knee) and would drive by the mill hoping to gather evidence. Her actions were so obviously cruel that the government's doctor finally wrote a letter stating that Christelle could collect her insurance and work anywhere else except Les Magnolias. So now she still comes once a week *chez nous* and we gossip and exchange pictures of grandchildren while she irons, her leg on a stool.

She and Maran, who is now retired from the local charcuterie, go to Madagascar every winter for a few months and stay in the modest little house she was able to build for her family. She's also campaigning to have her oldest granddaughter marry the son of her next-door neighbor in Plaisance.

I haven't seen Bernard *pierre* since his visit shortly after your death, and I have no telephone number, no way to reach him. Last winter we received an e-mail from Antoine, the accountant *chez* Pollet, Bernard's employer, who said Bernard had given him our name saying we were *sympathique* and would help him find a summer home for his son in San Francisco, which we did. I asked Antoine to have Bernard call us, but he hasn't. I still look when I see a construction truck go by when I'm near Albi. Just maybe.

The Fabres at Moussac are growing old along with us. Their daughter Flo has taken over the management of the farm, but Jean-Claude has not slowed down at all. He now has a stent in his heart, and Monique chides him for sneaking fresh milk from his cows, but he just shrugs, she smiles, and their life goes on as usual. This spring he brought another steamy pile of manure for our garden, but he had his grandson drive the tractor close to the cliff, told him how to extend the hydraulic arm, and stood by nervously as the tractor swayed with the unstable load high in the air. Monique still wipes her Dirty Day hands on her apron when I stop in to see her. She now makes her own bread, in a machine, from flour ground at Le Moulin de la Pilande Basse.

Suzie and François are never changing. She continues to add to her impressive flower garden, her excuse to escape constant mushroom preserving: drying, canning, freezing. François and Mike still go out frequently to hunt mushrooms, and Suzie is very generous about giving Mike more than his share. She continues to produce wonderful four-course meals for all her friends, sharing the bounty of François's huge vegetable garden. "The more you eat, the less I have to can."

Didier and Clémence, the jazz-loving atheists, are still restoring their hamlet, although the work has slowed down considerably in the last five years. Didier's family in Paris has been in bad health, and Clémence's drinking is totally out of control. After Didier's diatribe at dinner, we decided to only see them at lunchtime since, at least theoretically, there's less alcohol then, but the last time we saw Clémence at three in the afternoon, she could barely talk.

Nadou has continued her work as a healer, and she even came to San Francisco a couple of times to see American healers and seek their advice in building a practice. She's now working in several disciplines, having studied in Toulouse for a number of years. She's a quiet, wise presence hidden in these green hills.

Brigitte and Bernard *bois*, our closest neighbors, are watching their children turn into adults, and dealing with their own heritage of being old hippies in a new world. She's still gorgeous, he's still handsome, dying his graying hair to stay ahead of the years. Bernard came to California with his son because he wanted to rebuild our wooden deck, since he'd never done that before. We tried to explain how much more practical stone can be, but he insisted. He had come once already with Brigitte for a whirlwind tour of San Francisco and Las Vegas—a must-see for any Frenchman with a guidebook. Brigitte finally confessed to us that Germain had been extremely unkind to her when they first moved there, but she thinks he's softened since we've been here, she thinks because of us, but I think it's probably just with the years. When Jean-Michel and Eveline sold their Souyrol place and moved to Millau a few years ago, he loved his studio and house in the woods so much we thought the move would kill him, but Eveline couldn't bear the solitude of rural life. And now Jean-Michel seems to be thriving in the big/little city. He and Mike have been collaborating for several years, working in porcelain. Mike prints images and text on the wet clay, and Jean-Michel sculpts it into unexpected objects: books, torn pages, wedge-shaped words ensconced in old wooden beams.

Following his retirement, Monsieur Parnat, the local *brocanteur*, turned over the junk-collecting part of his business to his son, who has added a few refrigerator trucks to his convoy for collecting sheep milk from the local farms to take to the *crémerie* in Réquista. (I did find a new *clochette*, and paid Parnat the elder for the streetlamp base I justifiably took years ago.) The son must be doing well since he has built a large pole barn and a sparkling new stucco house high on the hill overlooking Plaisance, where it competes with the profile of the twelfth-century Romanesque church. But it is a sign of a small resurgence of rural life, albeit transformed from small agricultural businesses to large farms and the supporting services providing jobs to young people.

The Charriers—the child-slapping man and his tortured wife—moved away a few years ago, I'm sure to avoid another confrontation with the authorities over his abusive treatment of his children. The year after Christian punctured Anne's tires, he was struck by a tractor and almost died. The farmer insisted that the boy must have deliberately driven his bike in front him, since he came out of nowhere into the field he was plowing. Whenever the family comes up in conversations with friends, we all look down, ashamed of our inability to protect those children.

Shirley and Berteau still spend a few weeks each summer at their farm complex and are slowly transforming it into a contemporary art installation with huge steel windows in old barn walls and elegant parodies of classic French gardens filling their acres once grazed by sheep. Her theory that those who move to rural France are either hopeless romantics or hiding something has been proven to have merit on several occasions. I wonder if she's examined her own move to France, albeit mostly Paris, in the same light?

Odette, once Ravel, then Soulier, then Ravel again, is back. After her divorce from Jacques, the philandering doctor-turned-pig-farmer-turned-cruiser, she stayed in Montpellier for a few years, licking her wounds and consolidating her sanity. She has recently bought a hamlet near Martrin and is transforming it into a cultural center for the arts, mostly music. Last winter, Jacques was sailing off the coast of South America when his boat was boarded by pirates and he was shot twice in the stomach and almost died. He is recovering in the south of France, and I hope contemplating the irony of his fate. His young lover jumped overboard and no one knows what happened to her.

Antoine Taillon, the young landscape architect whose life was devastated by a cruel father, is living happily ever after with his lover, Fabrice, who quit his engineering job in Paris and moved to Vallèdralec to be with Antoine. Antoine's relatively tranquil life was almost upset by a classic French bureaucratic maneuver: the school where he teaches asked him to go to Paris to take a special test for an advanced diploma, which he did and passed with honors. They then told him he would have to move to a suburb of Paris to teach. When he protested, they told him he was now too qualified for his old job. When he said he didn't care, they said, okay, he could have it back, but he'd have to start over again at the lowest base pay.

For several years, Antoine and Fabrice served as caretakers for the mill while we were in the States. But when the economic crisis hit, we could no longer justify paying them plus Jean-Luc, the gardener, and we had to choose Jean-Luc since he did the actual physical work. Antoine took this very badly, and no longer speaks to us.

I see Christophe Berlan occasionally, since I park my car in his field when I go for my run/walk on the mostly deserted road that goes by his house. He is still single, still handsome, still painfully shy. He waves while passing on his green tractor, his Gauloise hanging from his lip. We always talk briefly at the village fêtes about him selling the farm and do I know any rich Americans who want to buy it. I tried, half-heartedly, to introduce him to Nadou, but they are both too timid.

When we bought the mill fifteen years ago, we imagined guest artists, visits from friends, long meals in the warm summer air. We thought we might be here five years or maybe ten, and then we would sell the mill and settle down in San Francisco, our art matured by an international experience. Somehow, we didn't imagine the real friendships we would develop with French friends, the complexity of years of shared pleasure and pain.

And we never dreamed our language skills would reach the point where we can communicate as adults, argue like children, and make up as friends. As our French improved, our illusions about a perfect society of liberty, equality, and fraternity, all with killer food, has transformed into something closer to reality: some freedom, little equality, decent food, and some very special people. I haven't told you about everyone, even some who are very close, since our rapport is quite ordinary, not the kind I thought might interest you. Our friends have struggled through our years of bad French, have invested in our cultural education, and have taught us how to cook, store wine, and sit and think about when to water the garden. They saved our house when the pipes froze in winter and keep a collective eye on the mill when we're gone. They make room for us when we reappear, and hug us when we leave. We've watched their children change into consenting adults, and now a new generation of babies is being born. Leaving these friendships behind has become too painful to contemplate.

Two years ago, Mike spent the summer organizing the rebuilding of the walnut-oil mill just outside the back door near the small waterfall. A new turbine below, built by Louis Blanc's grandson, now turns the stone, which crushes hulled walnuts into a pulp that is crushed into oil by the dark *pressoir* just inside the front door that still brings tears to Germain's eyes each time he comes to the mill.

Germain, eighty-three, and Martou, seventy-nine, are worn out and counting. Germain had back surgery a few years ago that left his left leg tingly and unpredictable so that he can barely walk, but he still struggles in his garden, standing often, his back arched and pushing out his increasing belly, his large, dirty hands supporting his backbone through the elastic truss. When I suggested he cut back on the size of his garden, he said, pointing to the earth below his feet, "*Quand je pourrai plus faire mon jardin, je serai dessous.*" And I think it's true that when he can no longer garden, he will be under the ground.

But he continues to be curious and is spending more and more time on his family tree, with much encouragement from me. He has even taken a few lessons at the Cyberbase, a government-sponsored computer center dedicated to bringing the Internet to the countryside. At first, his children weren't very supportive, but when they saw his progress, they gave him an old computer, which is ensconced in the unused dining room. He never touches it, since his real reason for going to the Cyberbase is to get away from Le Bousquet for a few hours.

For several years Martou, whose hands are bent from years of shucking corn and milking cows, retired to a hypochondriacal space that was difficult to visit. She expressed no interest in anything, not reading, cooking, sewing, nothing. Her children came to see her less and less because when they did, she would only complain about how she hurt here and here and here. Three years ago the children, for Germain's eightieth birthday, bought them an adjustable double bed with separate controls. She told them it would have to join the unused computer in the unused dining room where her mother used to sleep when she was too old to climb into the closet in their bedroom.

Their children also gave Germain a golden retriever puppy they named Dog, to keep him company, which infuriated Martou so much that she stomped out of Geneviève's garage-turned-party-room into the pouring rain. But Yves built a snug little doghouse under their front steps where we slaughtered the lambs so long ago, since for a while Martou refused to let Dog in the house. She also wouldn't come and eat anymore at the mill: "It's too chilly, it's too hot, it's too spicy." That's the house, the food, and the companionship. Then she had a small stroke, a real illness, and she seems to have snapped back to her pre-dark-time self. Smiling and trimmed down, when asked how she is, she says, "*Oof, comme tout le monde.*" And indeed, she doesn't complain any more than everyone else, even though her speech is slurred and slow in coming. And she's the one who feeds and caresses Dog, still a puppy at three years old.

Last month, I took Germain up on the Alban plateau to meet a distant relative of his who is one hundred years old and whose mind is clear, though his body is failing. The relative's grandson now manages their large Roquefort sheep farm, and as we wound down the road, which was lined with piles of manure and bales of hay wrapped in white plastic, I wondered about the fates that brought Germain to Le Bousquet with his fifteen acres and six cows, and his cousin to such a profitable spread. We sat at the Formica table as Germain went through the family tree, tracing his connection to theirs. He was looking for information on a distant relative who was born in the hamlet next to this relative and his wife. They shrugged, disinterested, glancing at their watches—there were sheep to bring in, cows to milk, hay to bale. Germain shyly explained how they all could be traced back to some obscure nobleman, his head bowed as if to say, "I don't believe it either." Watching Germain absorb their disinterest, I quickly downed a chunk of the obligatory *fouace* and warmed-over coffee so we could leave.

As we drove out I asked Germain if he had learned anything, which he hadn't, but he was pleased we'd made the effort. I took the long way home through Miolles to see if the peaches were ripe, then down the back side of the hills toward Balaguier. The golden summer colors and already lengthening shadows foreshortening the steep valleys reminded us that Mike and I would be leaving soon. Germain bemoaned our imminent departure and made practical references to how little time we had left until then. His hearing aid was broken so he couldn't really understand anything I tried to say, but it didn't matter: I was taking the time to be with him.

And I needed to be with him, since we have told him we are trying to sell the mill. I tried to explain, "We're getting older and the mill requires an enormous physical effort: the beating back of nature, who'd like to move in with us, the planting, and tending, and putting up the garden. And we miss our family and we want to watch the little ones grow, to experience the next cycle of life, hugging them along the way."

I wish I could hug you one more time, Linda, to tell you how much I miss you and how much you meant to me, but I expect you already know that, too.

—*All my love, Judy*

July 18, 2010
JOURNAL ENTRY

The inevitable has happened: We accepted an offer to buy the mill and we will be signing the final closing documents on September 17, then leaving La Pilande Basse forever on September 20, 2010. The new owners, a young English couple, found our web page several months ago and had been hoping it would still be for sale when they sold their business in England. It was, so they had a friend call us to set up a visit to see if the mill was as lovely as the pictures. We made an appointment for last Friday, an appointment I almost cancelled since we'd been overwhelmed with too many visitors, it was too damn hot, and we were negotiating with two other people: one offer too low, the other too complicated.

As they pulled into the drive and started walking slowly down the path, my eyes went directly to her shoes: sandals, which told me they were a "maybe." After months of visitors, I realized that buying a rustic mill in R.F.F. was a man's dream: turbines, waterfalls, bridges, cranes to lift huge stones, and a big oil press are just big toys, and every man who comes to see La Pilande Basse falls in love with it. But it became apparent that it would take a certain kind of woman to agree to take on a pile of old stones, with the attending creatures inside and out, the old miller's stairs, the sixty-six steps from the river to the little house. I'd begun to categorize the women by their shoes: stiletto heels, no way; sandals, a possibility; rubber river shoes, sold. One woman actually came in rubber boots. She was an artist who already had a house in the Ardèche region, so she was familiar with mills, and she desperately wanted to buy ours, but her husband said they couldn't afford it.

One of the offers was from a sweet gay Canadian man, whose partner we never saw, so my shoe theory was long and short on validation. The other offer was from a very strange couple, he Belgian, teaching marketing in the University of Moscow, she a Chinese entrepreneur who had never learned to drive a car since she'd always had a driver in Shanghai. They had paid an architect to come and visit the mill and give them an assessment on the stability of the buildings. He told us over a pastis that they intended to gut the mill and turn it into a modern, industrial living space.

Our strategy for showing the mill was to lead the visitors on a quick overview, Mike taking the man of the couple to see the millworks, and me the woman, lingering in the kitchen and gardens, and then leave them alone to wander together. We soon learned that if they left quickly, the woman would be trundling up the gravel drive, her ankles rocking in her stilettos, with the man leading, grumpy shoulders turned away from her.

In this case, we gave Spencer, Claudine, and their friend Betsy the overview and quickly retreated into the cool interior of the mill, Betsy tagging along with us to avoid the heat of high noon. It was at least ninety degrees in the shade, so we sat inside and sipped iced tea, expecting the other two to show up soon. After about half an hour, they pushed in the back door and plopped down at the table with us, sweat leaking through their clothes.

"Was it what you expected?" I asked, not knowing how to read their expressions.

"No, actually it's much better than the pictures," Spencer said, while Claudine gave him a cold stare, the good cop/bad cop routine falling apart. "It doesn't need a thing. I wouldn't change one rock of it. So what do I have to do to make all these other offers go away?"

I didn't know that Mike had innocently told him we had two offers while they were exploring the millrace. He asked, so we told him what it would take.

"Done," he said. Just like that.

We called our *notaire* to see if he could get the offer papers ready before they were due to return to England, and he agreed to tomorrow, Monday, July 19 at 11:30 a.m.

Friday afternoon, right after they left, we climbed up to Le Bousquet to tell Germain and Martou before they heard it from others. We had told them all our reasons for selling, but it never seemed real to them or us. Germain's health had deteriorated in the past few months; he has heart trouble and prostate cancer, and is on oxygen six hours a day. But his mind is there, clear and sentimental. *"On vous verra plus."* Him saying they'd never see us again cut me to the core.

"Mais, oui." But we both knew it wouldn't be the same. We also knew that this time when we left after signing the final papers, given his health, we might not ever see him again.

Martou pushed back from the table, the chair screeching on the yellow tile, and went into the kitchen, the corner of her apron covering her eyes, "I'll get some coffee," she offered.

It was hot as hell in their little antechamber, with them, us, their daughter Michelle, and her husband, Roger, crammed around the tiny table. My forearms stuck to the plastic tablecloth as I moved awkwardly from a one-sided leg-crossing to the another. Martou spilled the coffee and ran to the kitchen to get a rag, apologizing for her *saloperie*. The five-gallon pail of green beans that Roger had picked earlier stared at us from the middle of the table. We all nervously stared at a solitary fly circling over the pail. Finally. Michelle, who had been nervously taking one bean at a time and pulling off the ends with a darkened fingernail, burst into tears and ran into the kitchen to join her mother. Roger slid out the front door, mumbling something about changing the water hose.

Germain, Mike, and I sat looking at Germain's thick tanned hands as he folded and unfolded them on the table, checking his nails for garden dirt even though he hasn't been able to dig for weeks. We talked about the wedding in August of one of their grandchildren, Émilie. We waited for Martou to return and when she didn't, Germain said timidly, "When you go, could I buy the big mixer that you use to make bread?" I was surprised. He'd actually thought through our leaving, anticipating that we couldn't take European electronics to the States. I assured him that he could have it, as a gift, of course.

"*C'est trop*," he said, still staring down at his hands, his lower lip trembling.

September 23, 2010

JOURNAL ENTRY

San Francisco

The week before we signed the papers, I left early to take my last walk/run down the road that passes in front of Christophe Berlan's farm, up the hill toward the other crossroad to Coupiac. There was hardly ever any traffic on that road, though I was often stopped by Jean-Claude on his way to his other farm in Combret, twenty kilometers away toward Saint-Sernin-sur-Rance, sometimes with his animal truck swaying with a frightened calf. As I started my run, I saw their familiar white camping-car truck weaving toward me, then stop suddenly, with Jean-Claude's head sticking out the window, *coucou*-ing me to a halt. Monique was waving from the other side, shouting that they heard we had sold the mill. "Yes," I said, my eyes filling with tears. *"C'est vrai."*

I invited them to come to the reception/going away party for the new owners, but they were on their way to the Pyrenees for a month to take the cure and wouldn't be back until the day after we were to leave. *"Dommage, ça passe trop vite."* It *had* passed too fast, these seventeen years in rural France. Jean-Claude's fireplace has 1649 carved into the mantel, the year his family built the first house at Moussac. Seventeen years seemed somehow trivial.

"On se reverra, allez, ciao!" I thought we probably would see each other again, but

there in the middle of the road, the truck vanishing around the bend, I realized it would never be the same, we'd be even stranger strangers. We wouldn't have a steamy pile of manure delivered to our garden terrace, we probably wouldn't see any more lambs being born, or bring a grandchild to hold a newborn chick. We wouldn't eat in their large garden with tubs of whole roasted lambs carried by sweaty sons-in-law. Wheels of Roquefort cheese would be bought in stores, shipped from far away, their salty crusts packed in Styrofoam boxes.

"*Ciao, à bientôt,*" I shouted at the disappearing truck.

ACKNOWLEDGMENTS

My deepest thanks go to Germain and Marthe Blanc and their whole family, for their *tutorage* in language, milling, cuisine, and gardening. I am also grateful to the Fabre family, for letting us into their hearts and their barn.

Special thanks to Carolyn Miller, my editor and friend, without whose encouragement I would never have finished this book. And to Charles Hobson, artist and friend, whose romantic enthusiasm for our adventure kept us going for over seventeen years.

More thanks for the support of Anne Lemasson, my French professor and editor, and my writer friends Sheila Brady, Nora Lindahl, Alice Wingwall, and Donlyn Lyndon.

Water Paper Stone would not have been possible without my husband, Mike, who shared a fantasy of living in a foreign country and learning a new language, as well as a love of art and artists, and who not only made viable the restoration of a pile of old stones but made the millstones turn. I am forever grateful to my brother-in-law, Gary Reisig, for his help with photos and memories, and for taking such good care of my sister, Linda. And I thank our children, Eileen, Steve, Derek, Hayden, Naomi, Katie, and Jenea, who indulged us in all our escapades.

Photo of Louis Blanc in front of the mill

ABOUT THE AUTHOR

JUDY O'SHEA is an installation artist who has shown widely in France. She studied at the San Francisco Art Institute and with various artists-in-residence at La Pilande Basse, the water mill she and her husband, Mike, also an artist, restored in the Aveyron department of France. Along with her major installations, she was invited by the French government to show at a conference of contemporary artists at the Abbaye de Sylvanès, and to teach an introduction to contemporary art to schoolchildren. Her most recent installation was at the Canessa Gallery in San Francisco in 2012. Her work is currently at the SFMOMA Artists Gallery at Fort Mason, San Francisco.

Germain and Marthe Blanc and the author, making confit

Made in the USA
Monee, IL
22 August 2021

76284057R00227